結界師
KEKKAISHI

35

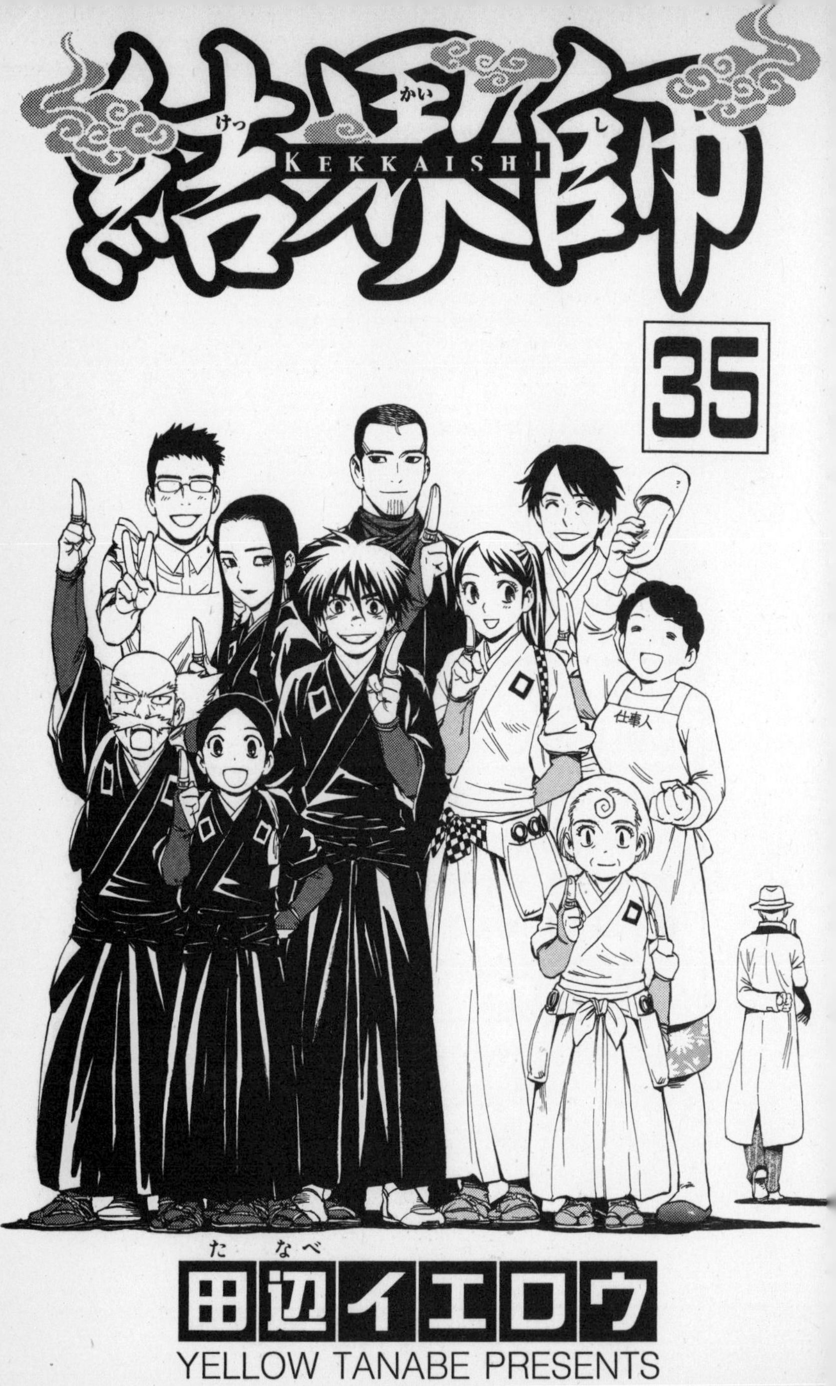

仕事人

田辺イエロウ

YELLOW TANABE PRESENTS

The Story Thus Far

The formidable leaders of the Shadow Organization rejoin forces to wrest back control of their headquarters, now in the clutches of their former Supreme Leader, Nichinaga.

While the battle rages on between Council of Twelve member Nura Kidoin's army of loyal demons and the hapless troops under Nichinaga's mind control, Masamori enters the underworld beneath to fulfill his destiny and kill Nichinaga. There, Masamori encounters a man he never expected to see...

Meanwhile, Tsukihisa manages to take over "puppet" Zero's body. Caught without his bodyguards, Nichinaga is fatally wounded. Will he take Tsukihisa down with him...? Elsewhere, it appears that the guardian deity Lord Mahora has absorbed Yoshimori's beloved Tokine...!

KEKKAISHI VOL. 35
TABLE OF CONTENTS

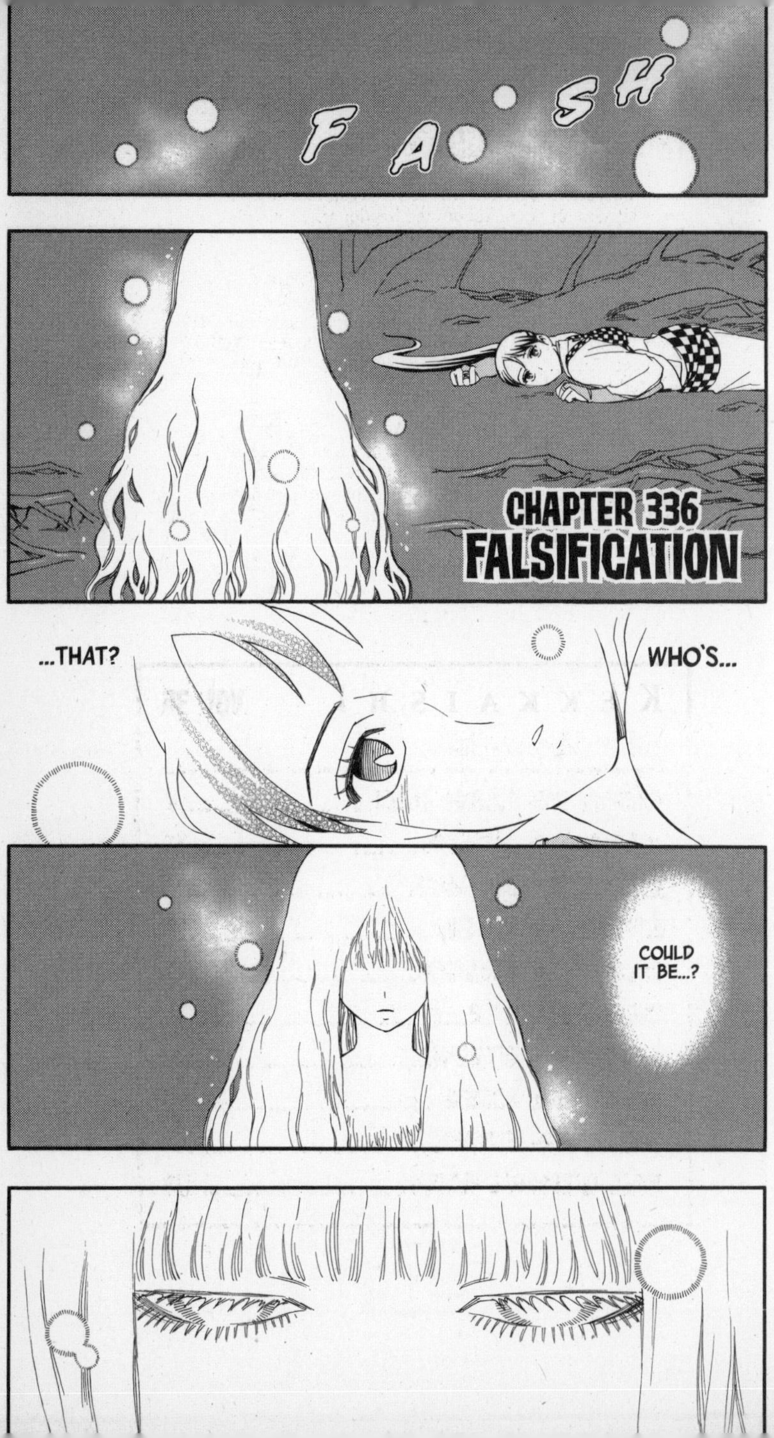
FASH
CHAPTER 336
FALSIFICATION
WHO'S...
...THAT?
COULD IT BE...?

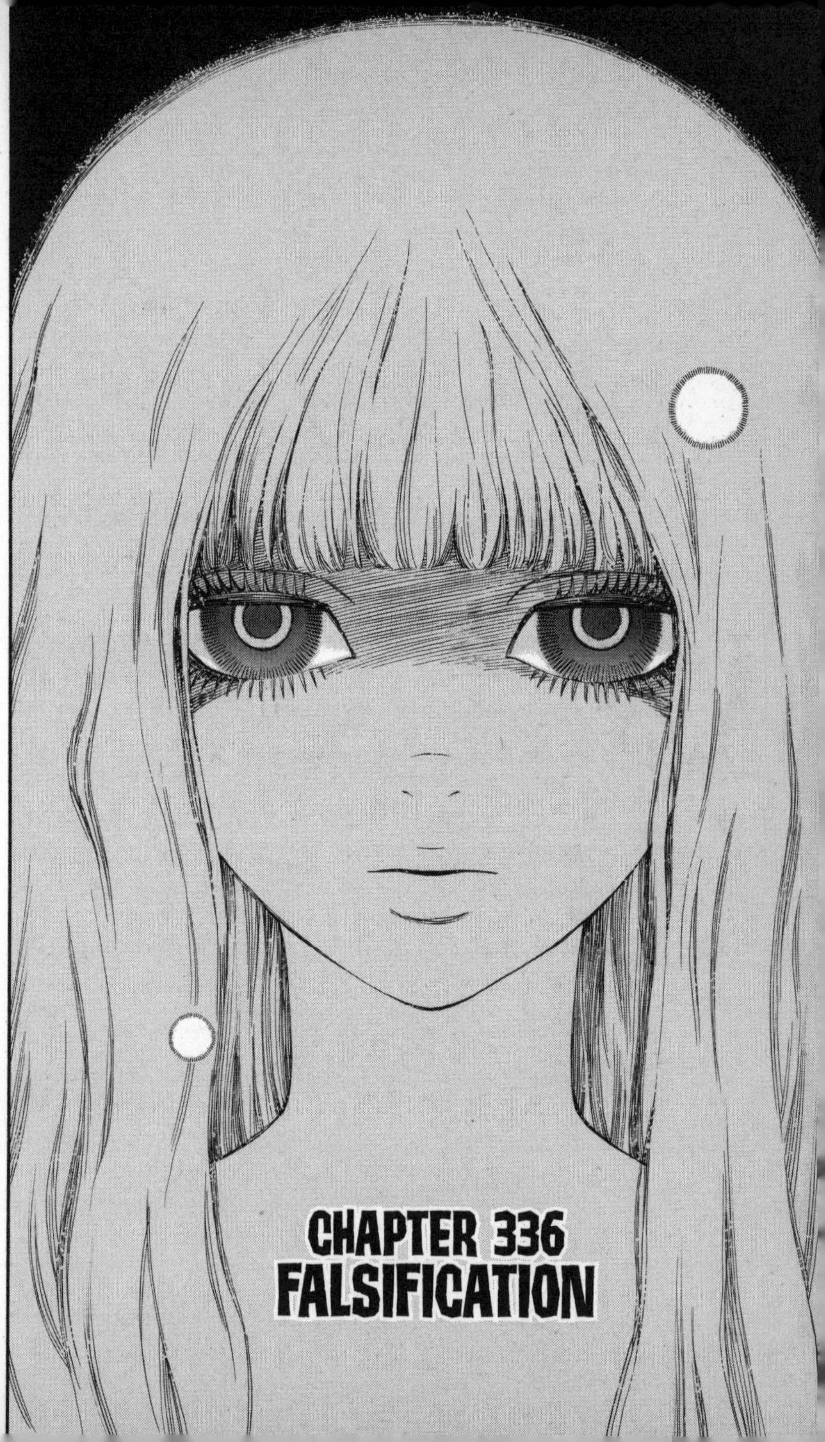
CHAPTER 336
FALSIFICATION

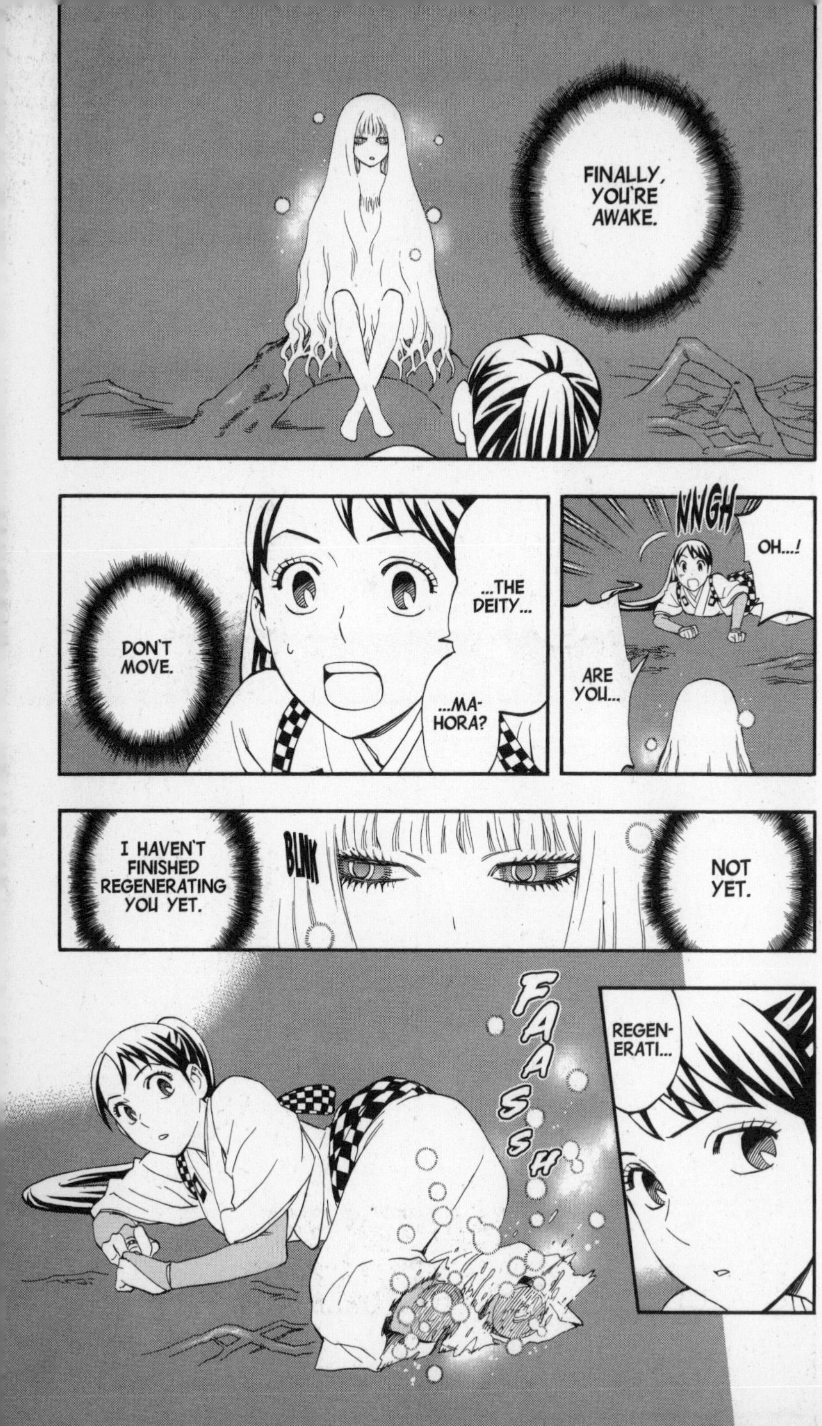
FINALLY, YOU'RE AWAKE.
NNGH
OH...!
ARE YOU...
...THE DEITY...
...MA-HORA?
DON'T MOVE.
NOT YET.
BLNK
I HAVEN'T FINISHED REGENERATING YOU YET.
REGEN-ERATI...
FAAASSH

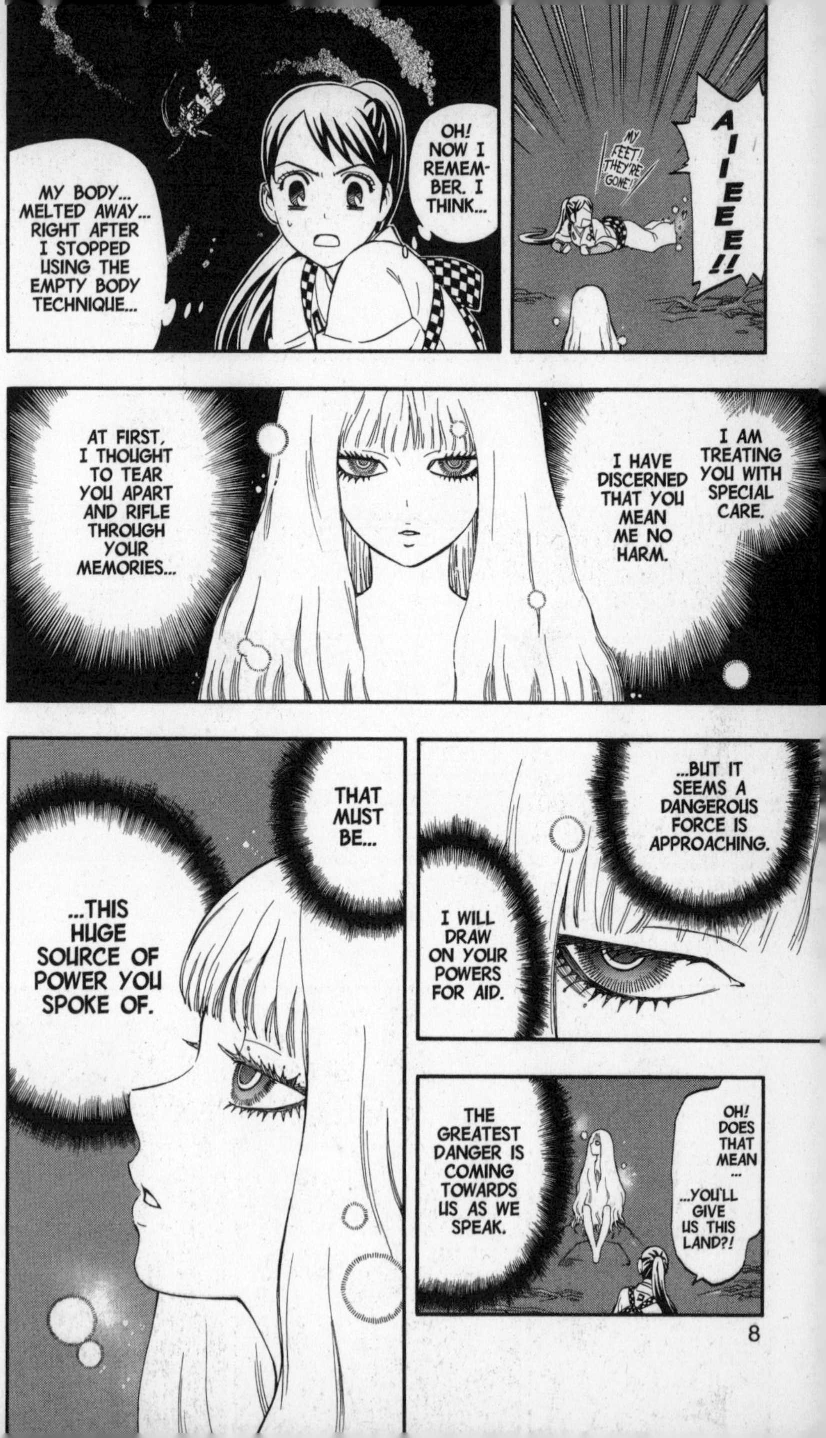
AIIEEE!!
MY FEET! THEY'RE GONE!
OH! NOW I REMEMBER. I THINK...
MY BODY... MELTED AWAY... RIGHT AFTER I STOPPED USING THE EMPTY BODY TECHNIQUE...
I AM TREATING YOU WITH SPECIAL CARE.
I HAVE DISCERNED THAT YOU MEAN ME NO HARM.
AT FIRST, I THOUGHT TO TEAR YOU APART AND RIFLE THROUGH YOUR MEMORIES...
...BUT IT SEEMS A DANGEROUS FORCE IS APPROACHING.
I WILL DRAW ON YOUR POWERS FOR AID.
OH! DOES THAT MEAN...
...YOU'LL GIVE US THIS LAND?!
THE GREATEST DANGER IS COMING TOWARDS US AS WE SPEAK.
THAT MUST BE...
...THIS HUGE SOURCE OF POWER YOU SPOKE OF.

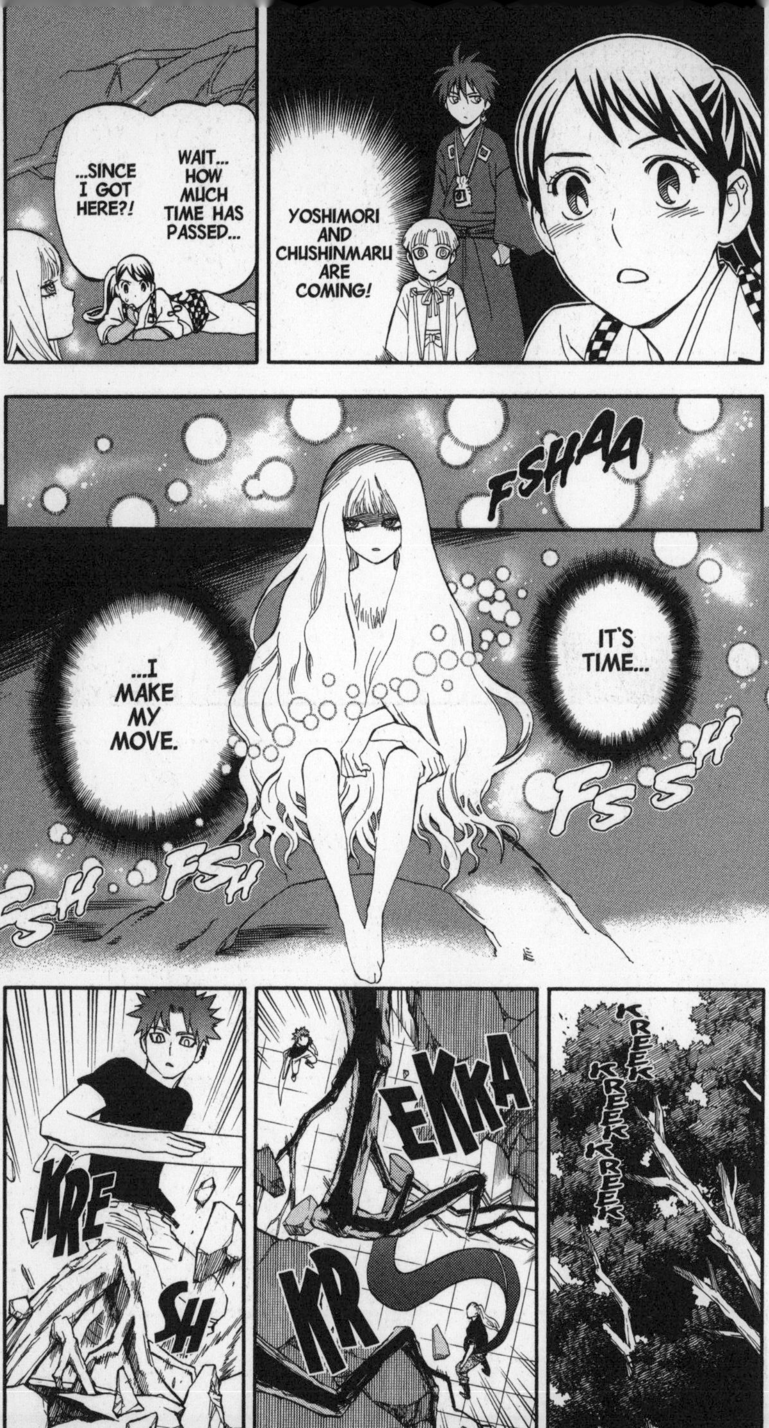
YOSHIMORI AND CHUSHINMARU ARE COMING!
WAIT... HOW MUCH TIME HAS PASSED...
...SINCE I GOT HERE?!
FSHAA
IT'S TIME...
...I MAKE MY MOVE.
FS SH
FSH
FSH
KREEK KREEK KREEK
EKKA
KR
KRE
SH

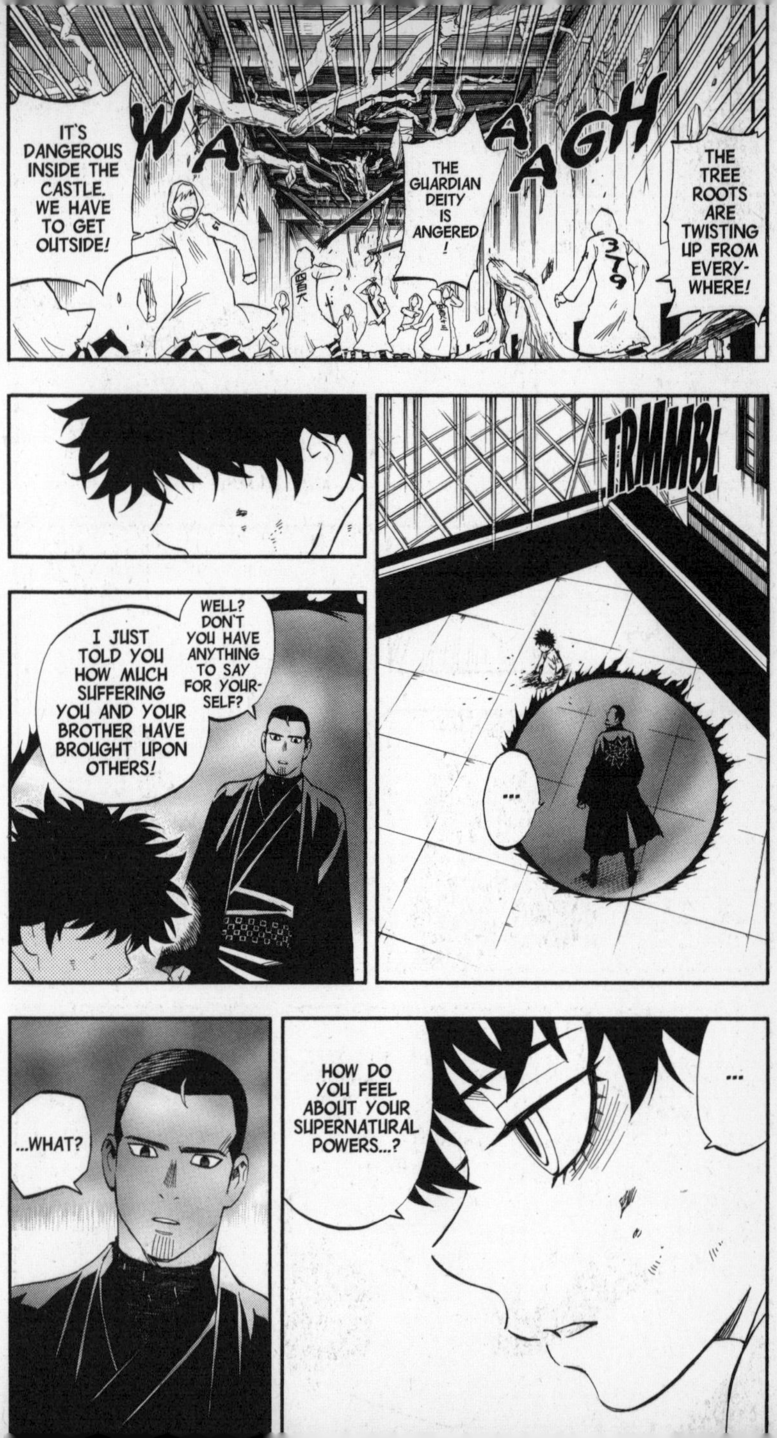
THE TREE ROOTS ARE TWISTING UP FROM EVERY-WHERE!
WAAAGH
THE GUARDIAN DEITY IS ANGERED!
IT'S DANGEROUS INSIDE THE CASTLE. WE HAVE TO GET OUTSIDE!
TRMMBL
...
WELL? DON'T YOU HAVE ANYTHING TO SAY FOR YOUR-SELF?
I JUST TOLD YOU HOW MUCH SUFFERING YOU AND YOUR BROTHER HAVE BROUGHT UPON OTHERS!
...
HOW DO YOU FEEL ABOUT YOUR SUPERNATURAL POWERS...?
...WHAT?

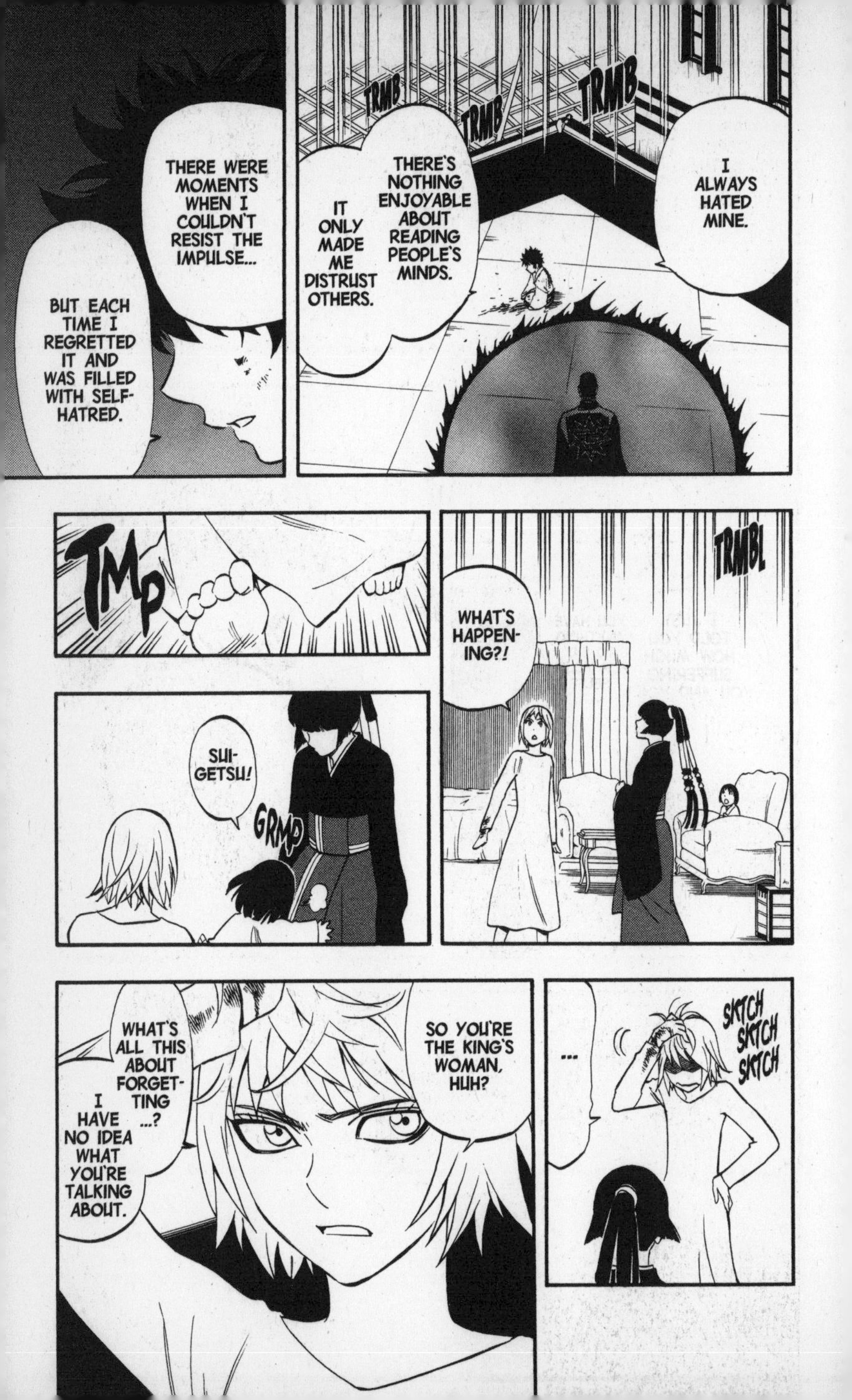

I ALWAYS HATED MINE.
TRMB
TRMB
TRMB
THERE'S NOTHING ENJOYABLE ABOUT READING PEOPLE'S MINDS.
IT ONLY MADE ME DISTRUST OTHERS.
THERE WERE MOMENTS WHEN I COULDN'T RESIST THE IMPULSE...
BUT EACH TIME I REGRETTED IT AND WAS FILLED WITH SELF-HATRED.
TRMBL
WHAT'S HAPPEN-ING?!
TMP
SUI-GETSU!
GRMP
SKTCH SKTCH SKTCH
...
SO YOU'RE THE KING'S WOMAN, HUH?
WHAT'S ALL THIS ABOUT FORGET-TING...?
I HAVE NO IDEA WHAT YOU'RE TALKING ABOUT.

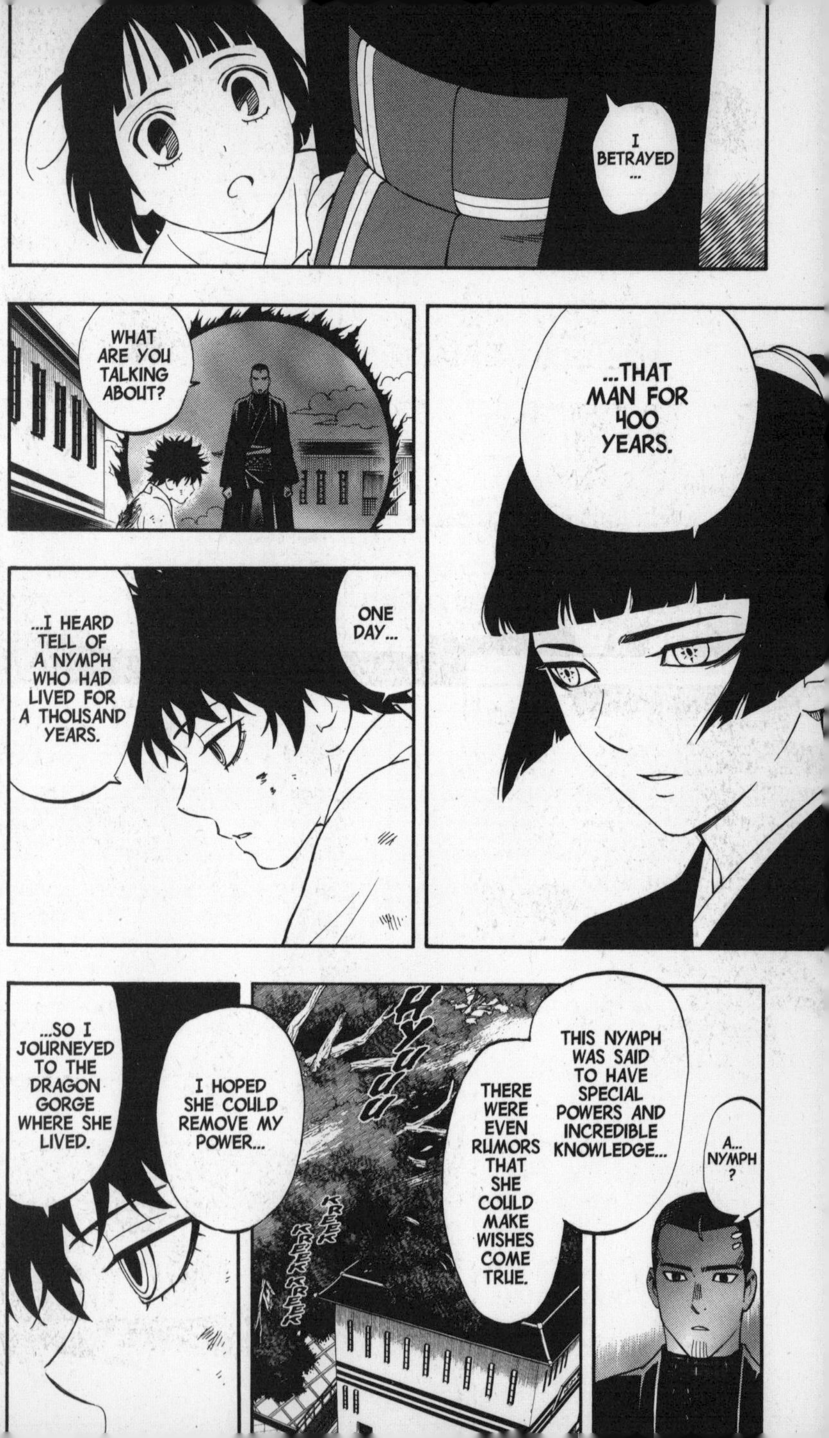
I BETRAYED ...
...THAT MAN FOR 400 YEARS.
WHAT ARE YOU TALKING ABOUT?
ONE DAY...
...I HEARD TELL OF A NYMPH WHO HAD LIVED FOR A THOUSAND YEARS.
A... NYMPH?
THIS NYMPH WAS SAID TO HAVE SPECIAL POWERS AND INCREDIBLE KNOWLEDGE...
THERE WERE EVEN RUMORS THAT SHE COULD MAKE WISHES COME TRUE.
HYUUU
KREEK KREEK KREEK
I HOPED SHE COULD REMOVE MY POWER...
...SO I JOURNEYED TO THE DRAGON GORGE WHERE SHE LIVED.

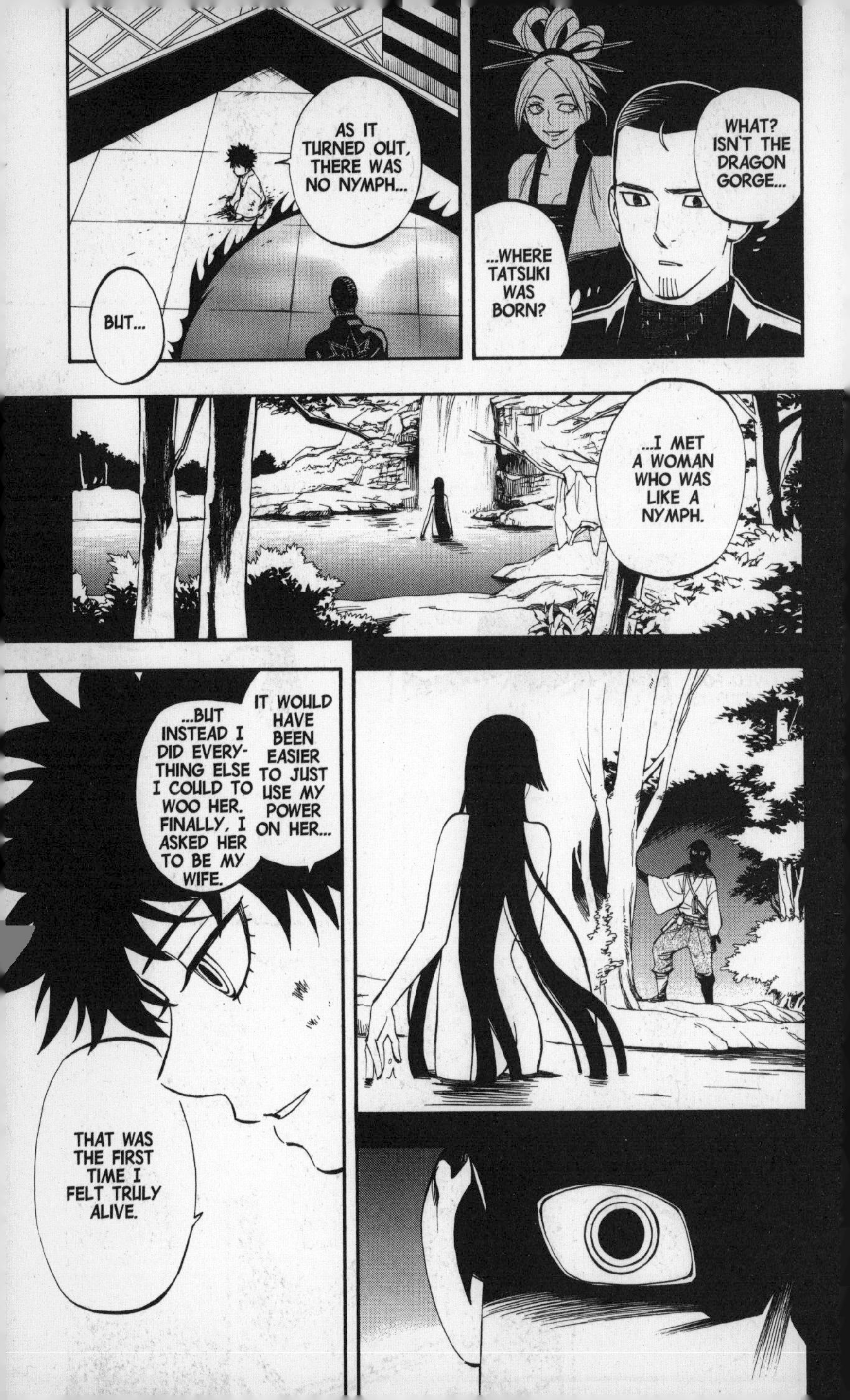
WHAT? ISN'T THE DRAGON GORGE...
...WHERE TATSUKI WAS BORN?
AS IT TURNED OUT, THERE WAS NO NYMPH...
BUT...
...I MET A WOMAN WHO WAS LIKE A NYMPH.
IT WOULD HAVE BEEN EASIER TO JUST USE MY POWER ON HER...
...BUT INSTEAD I DID EVERY-THING ELSE I COULD TO WOO HER. FINALLY, I ASKED HER TO BE MY WIFE.
THAT WAS THE FIRST TIME I FELT TRULY ALIVE.

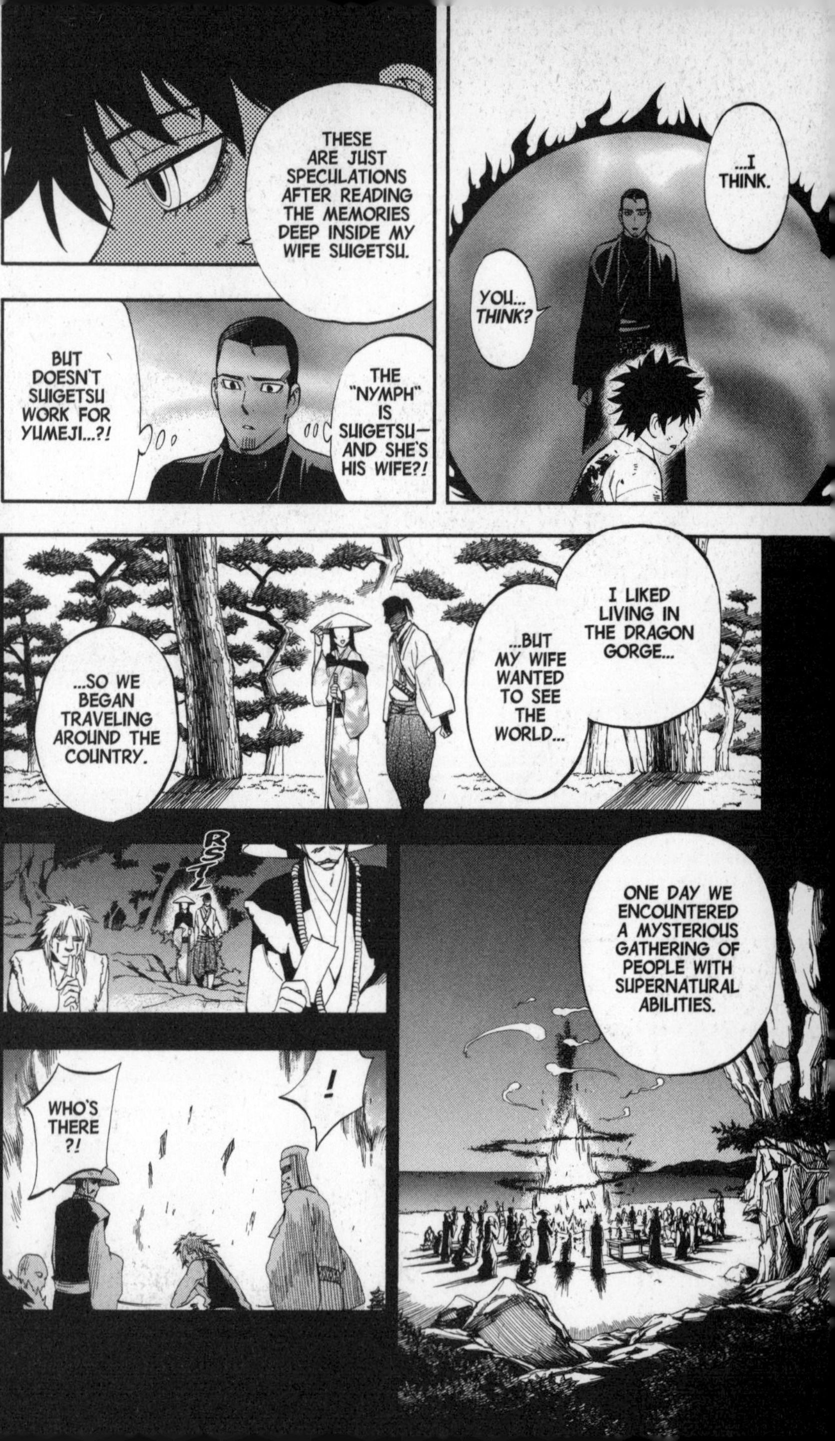
THESE ARE JUST SPECULATIONS AFTER READING THE MEMORIES DEEP INSIDE MY WIFE SUIGETSU.
THE "NYMPH" IS SUIGETSU— AND SHE'S HIS WIFE?!
BUT DOESN'T SUIGETSU WORK FOR YUMEJI...?!
...I THINK.
YOU... THINK?
I LIKED LIVING IN THE DRAGON GORGE...
...BUT MY WIFE WANTED TO SEE THE WORLD...
...SO WE BEGAN TRAVELING AROUND THE COUNTRY.
ONE DAY WE ENCOUNTERED A MYSTERIOUS GATHERING OF PEOPLE WITH SUPERNATURAL ABILITIES.
RSTL
!
WHO'S THERE ?!

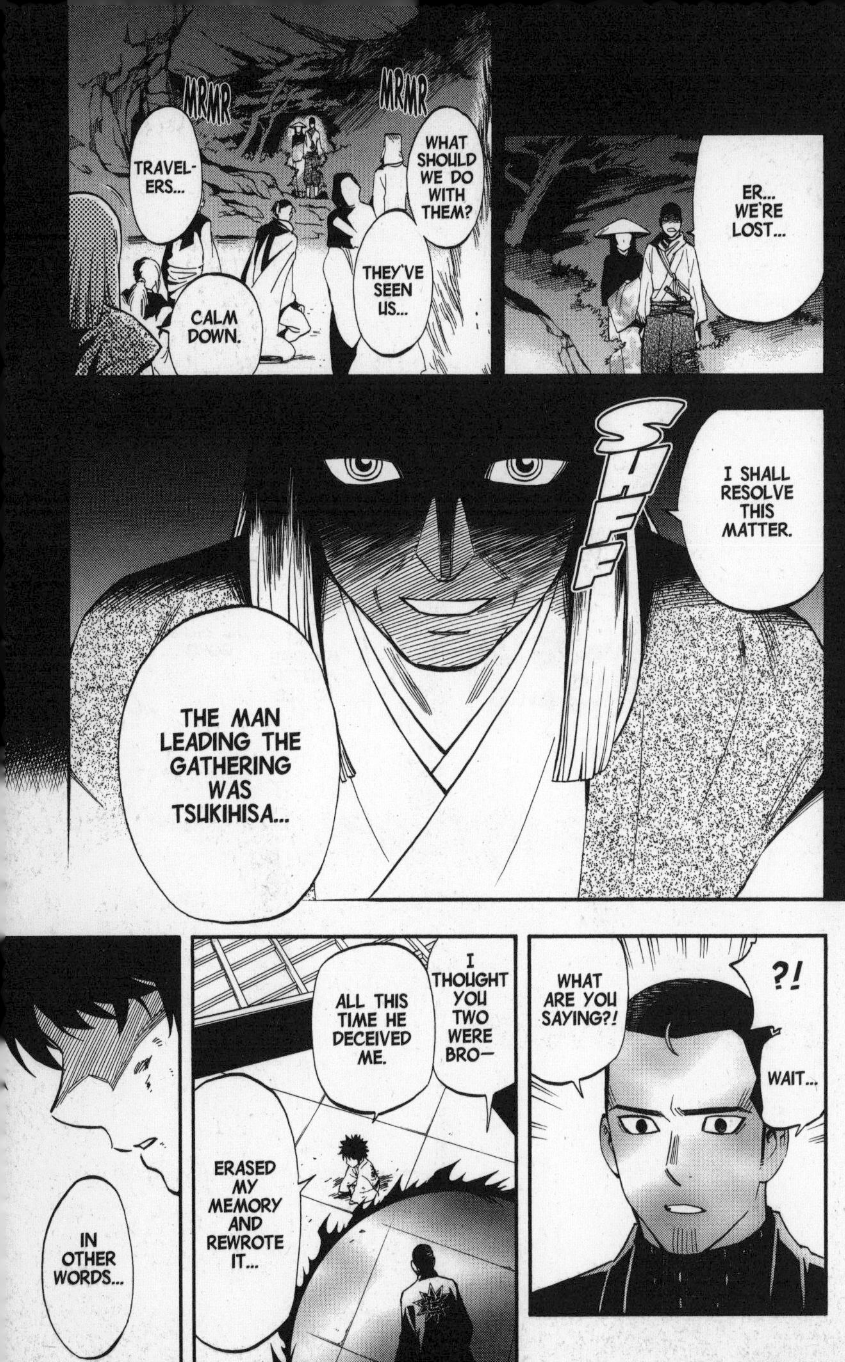
ER... WE'RE LOST...
MRMR
WHAT SHOULD WE DO WITH THEM?
MRMR
TRAVEL-ERS...
THEY'VE SEEN US...
CALM DOWN.
SHFF
I SHALL RESOLVE THIS MATTER.
THE MAN LEADING THE GATHERING WAS TSUKIHISA...
?!
WHAT ARE YOU SAYING?!
WAIT...
I THOUGHT YOU TWO WERE BRO—
ALL THIS TIME HE DECEIVED ME.
ERASED MY MEMORY AND REWROTE IT...
IN OTHER WORDS...

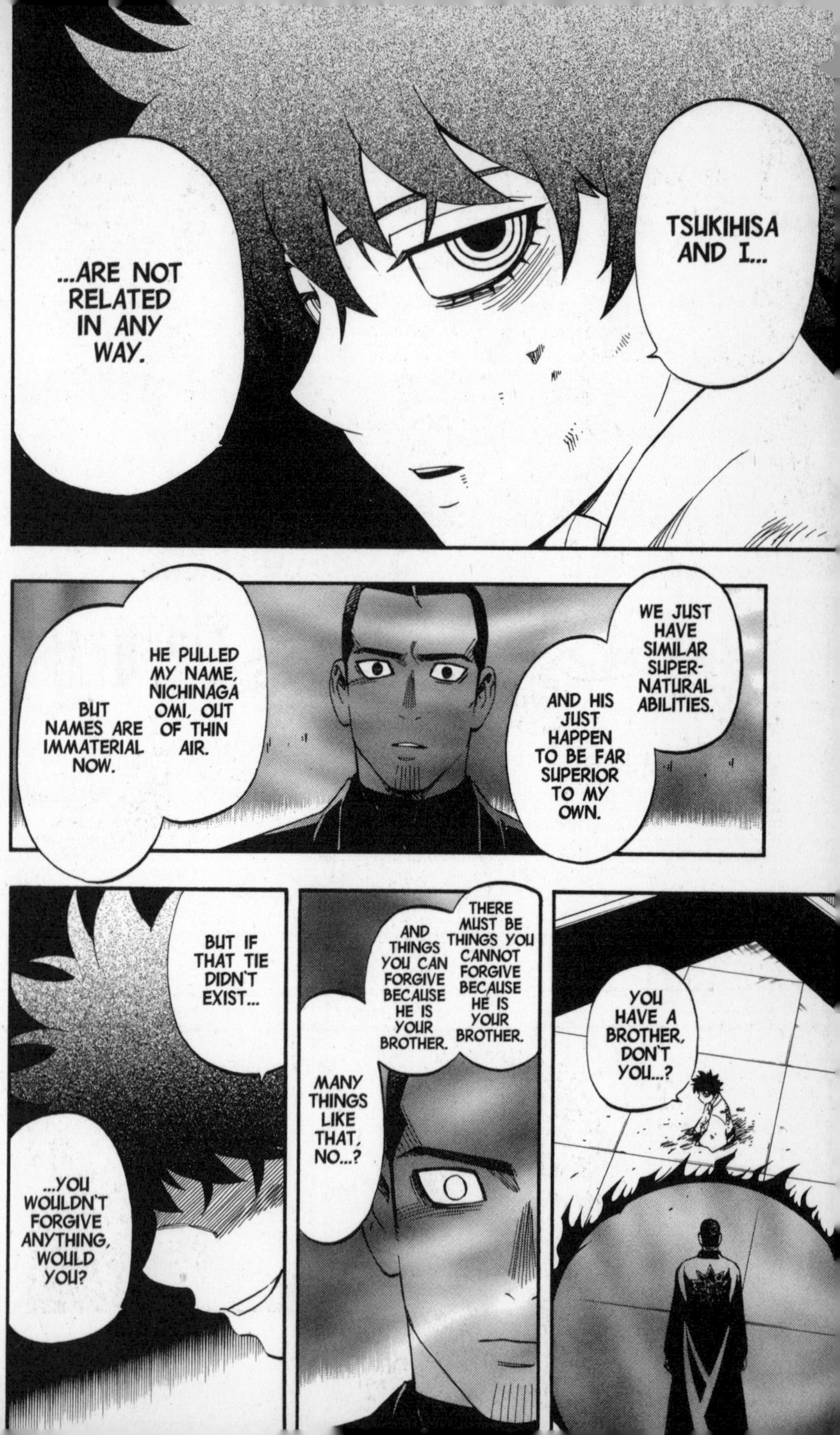
TSUKIHISA AND I...
...ARE NOT RELATED IN ANY WAY.
WE JUST HAVE SIMILAR SUPER-NATURAL ABILITIES.
AND HIS JUST HAPPEN TO BE FAR SUPERIOR TO MY OWN.
HE PULLED MY NAME, NICHINAGA OMI, OUT OF THIN AIR.
BUT NAMES ARE IMMATERIAL NOW.
YOU HAVE A BROTHER, DON'T YOU...?
THERE MUST BE THINGS YOU CANNOT FORGIVE BECAUSE HE IS YOUR BROTHER.
AND THINGS YOU CAN FORGIVE BECAUSE HE IS YOUR BROTHER.
MANY THINGS LIKE THAT, NO...?
BUT IF THAT TIE DIDN'T EXIST...
...YOU WOULDN'T FORGIVE ANYTHING, WOULD YOU?

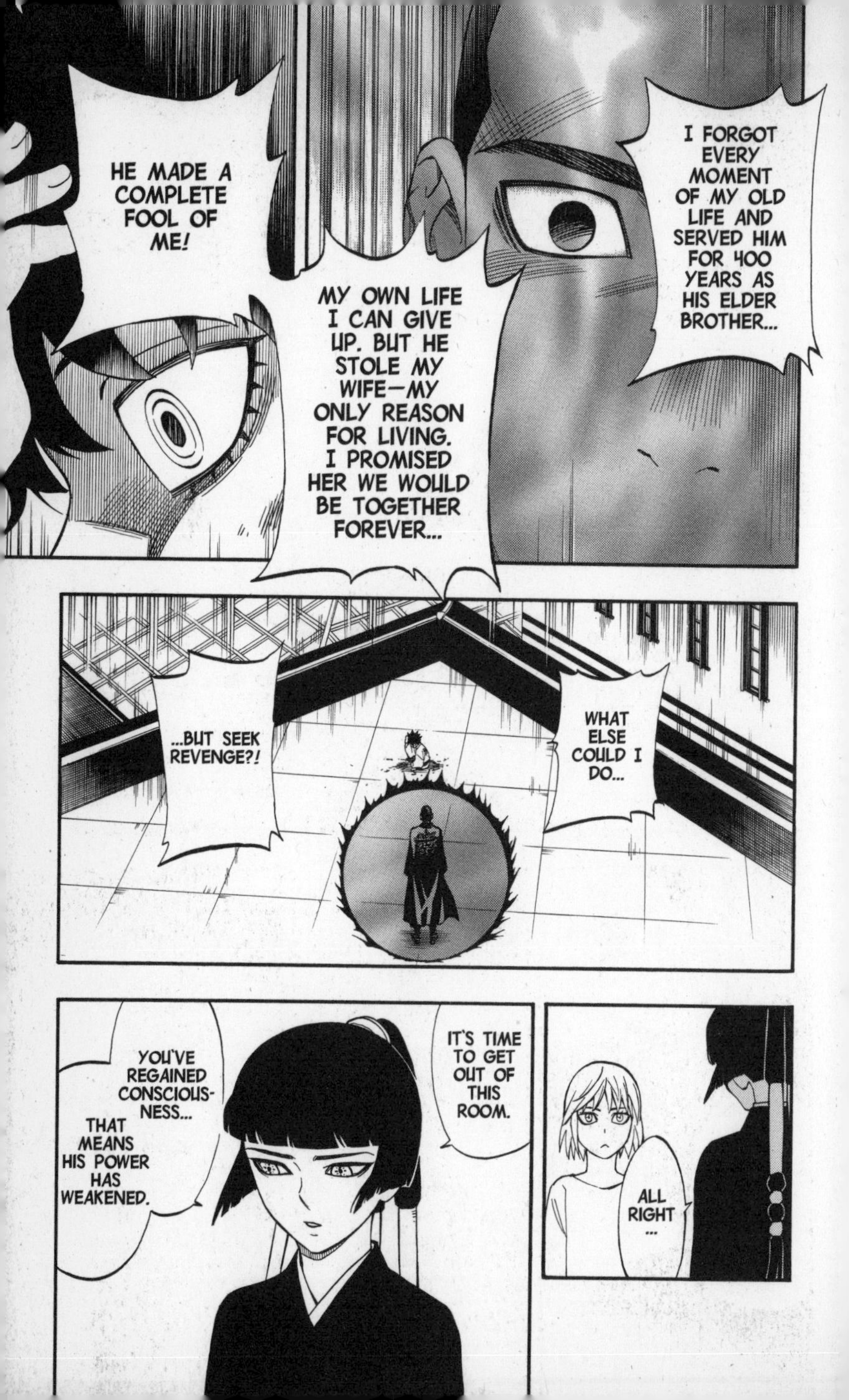
I FORGOT EVERY MOMENT OF MY OLD LIFE AND SERVED HIM FOR 400 YEARS AS HIS ELDER BROTHER...
HE MADE A COMPLETE FOOL OF ME!
MY OWN LIFE I CAN GIVE UP. BUT HE STOLE MY WIFE—MY ONLY REASON FOR LIVING. I PROMISED HER WE WOULD BE TOGETHER FOREVER...
WHAT ELSE COULD I DO...
...BUT SEEK REVENGE?!
ALL RIGHT...
IT'S TIME TO GET OUT OF THIS ROOM.
YOU'VE REGAINED CONSCIOUSNESS...
THAT MEANS HIS POWER HAS WEAKENED.

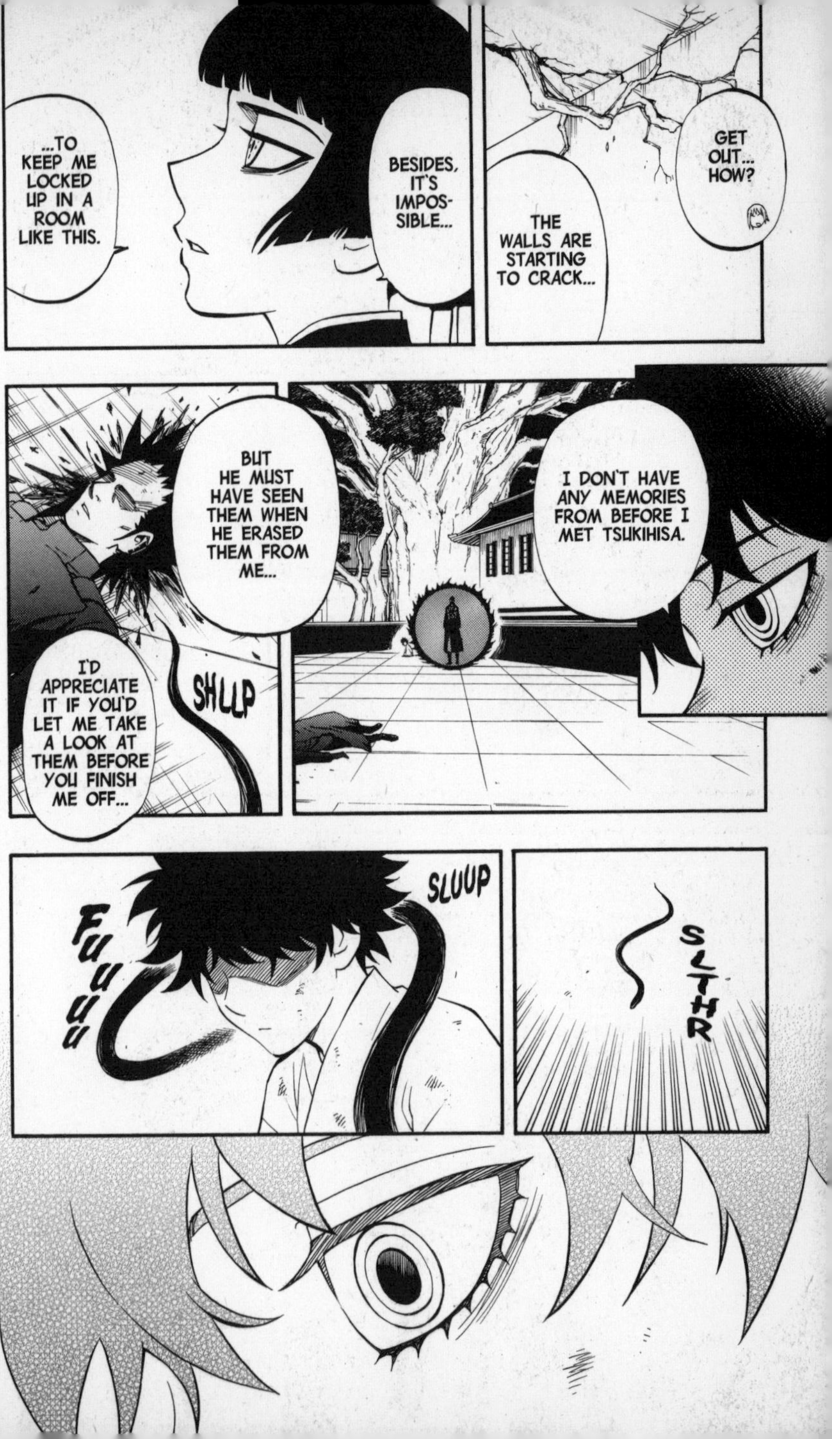
GET OUT... HOW?
THE WALLS ARE STARTING TO CRACK...
BESIDES, IT'S IMPOSSIBLE...
...TO KEEP ME LOCKED UP IN A ROOM LIKE THIS.
I DON'T HAVE ANY MEMORIES FROM BEFORE I MET TSUKIHISA.
BUT HE MUST HAVE SEEN THEM WHEN HE ERASED THEM FROM ME...
I'D APPRECIATE IT IF YOU'D LET ME TAKE A LOOK AT THEM BEFORE YOU FINISH ME OFF...
SHLLP
SLTHR
SLUUP
FUUUUU

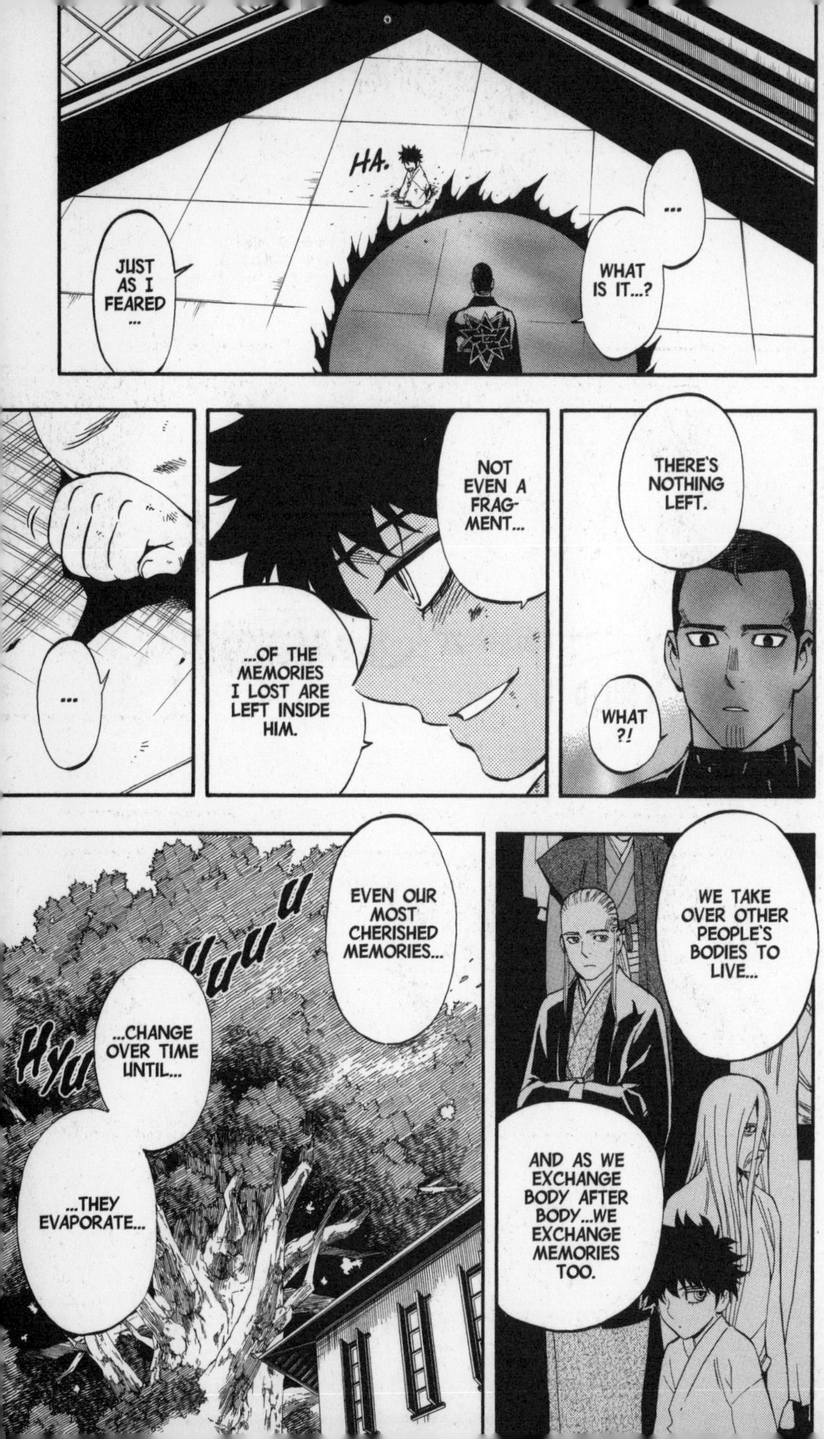
...
WHAT IS IT...?
HA.
JUST AS I FEARED ...
THERE'S NOTHING LEFT.
WHAT ?!
NOT EVEN A FRAG-MENT...
...OF THE MEMORIES I LOST ARE LEFT INSIDE HIM.
...
WE TAKE OVER OTHER PEOPLE'S BODIES TO LIVE...
AND AS WE EXCHANGE BODY AFTER BODY...WE EXCHANGE MEMORIES TOO.
EVEN OUR MOST CHERISHED MEMORIES...
HYUUUUUU
...CHANGE OVER TIME UNTIL...
...THEY EVAPORATE...

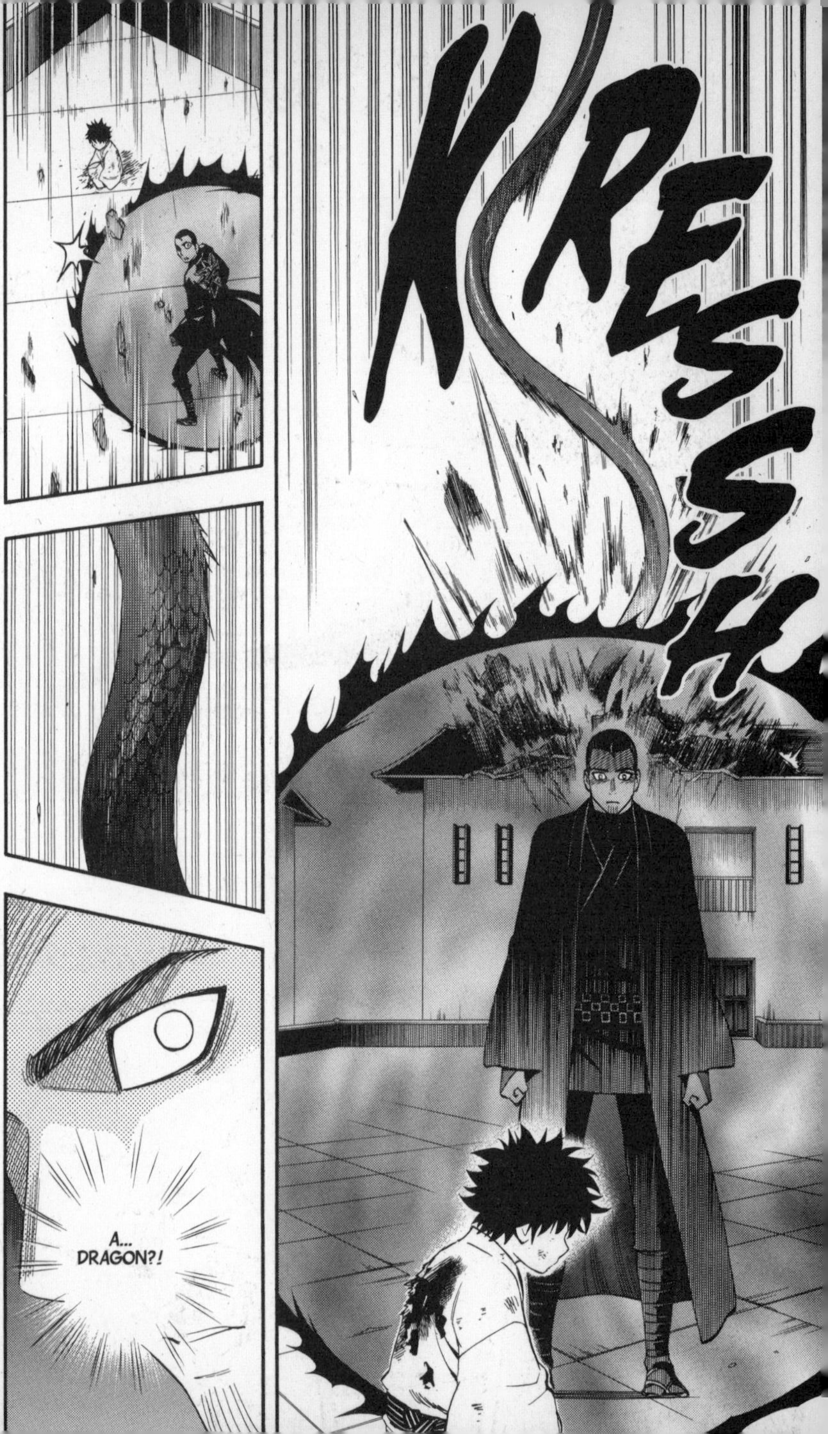
KRESSH
A... DRAGON?!

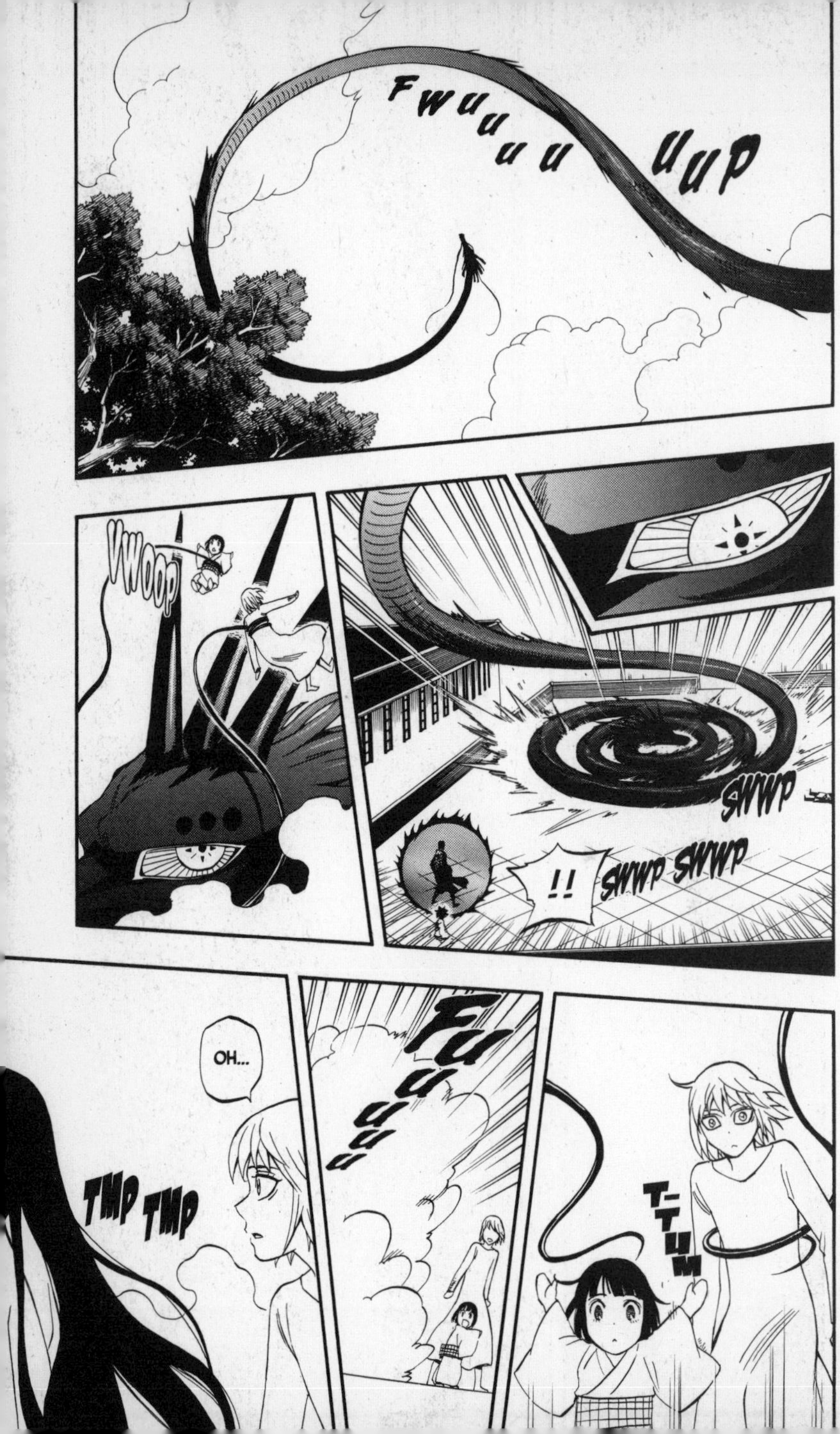

FWUUUUU UUP
SWWP
!!
SWWP SWWP
VWOOP
T-TUM
FUUUUUU
OH...
TMP TMP

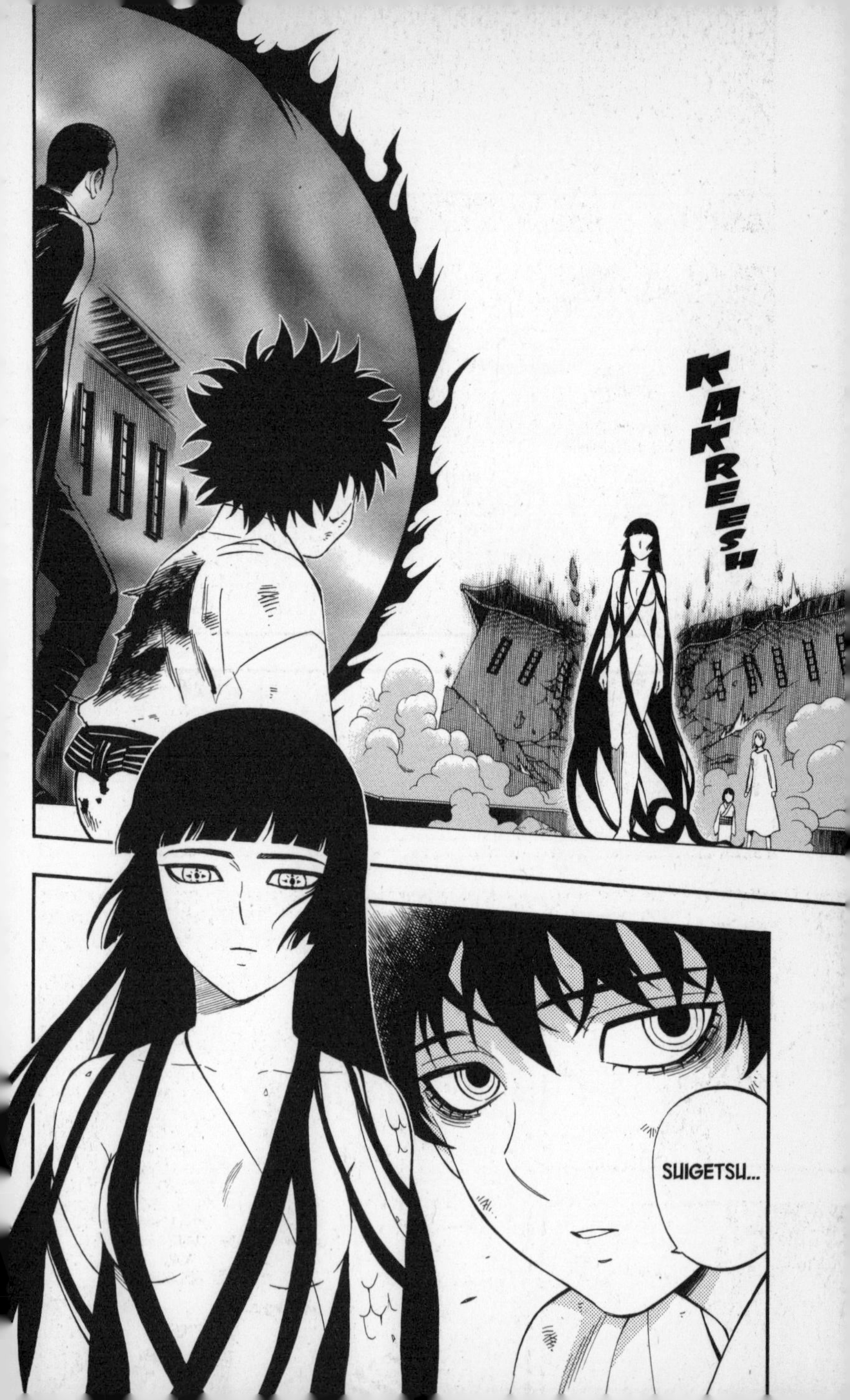
KAKREESH
SUIGETSU...

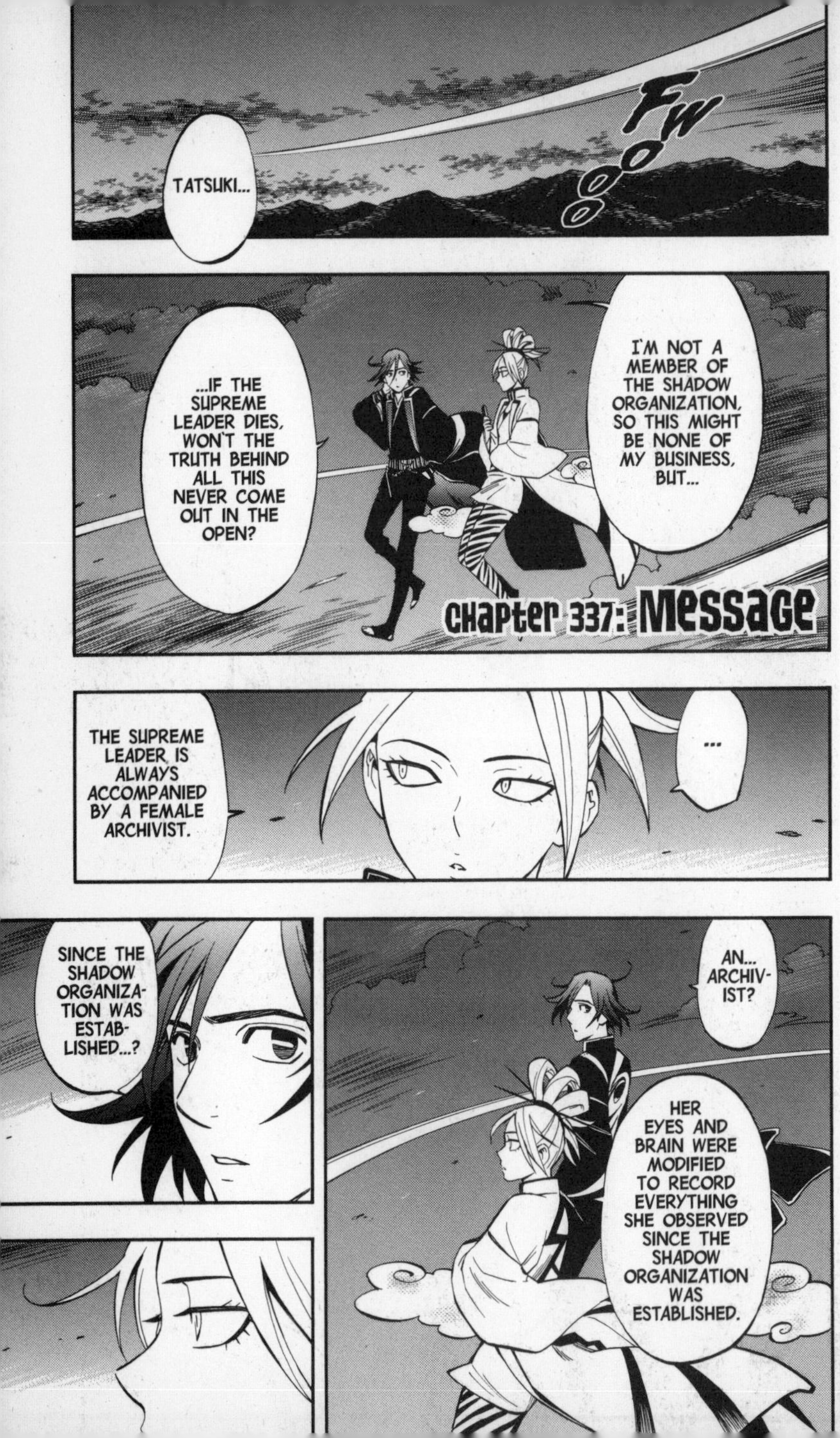
FWOOO
TATSUKI...
I'M NOT A MEMBER OF THE SHADOW ORGANIZATION, SO THIS MIGHT BE NONE OF MY BUSINESS, BUT...
...IF THE SUPREME LEADER DIES, WON'T THE TRUTH BEHIND ALL THIS NEVER COME OUT IN THE OPEN?
Chapter 337: Message
...
THE SUPREME LEADER IS ALWAYS ACCOMPANIED BY A FEMALE ARCHIVIST.
AN... ARCHIVIST?
HER EYES AND BRAIN WERE MODIFIED TO RECORD EVERYTHING SHE OBSERVED SINCE THE SHADOW ORGANIZATION WAS ESTABLISHED.
SINCE THE SHADOW ORGANIZATION WAS ESTABLISHED...?

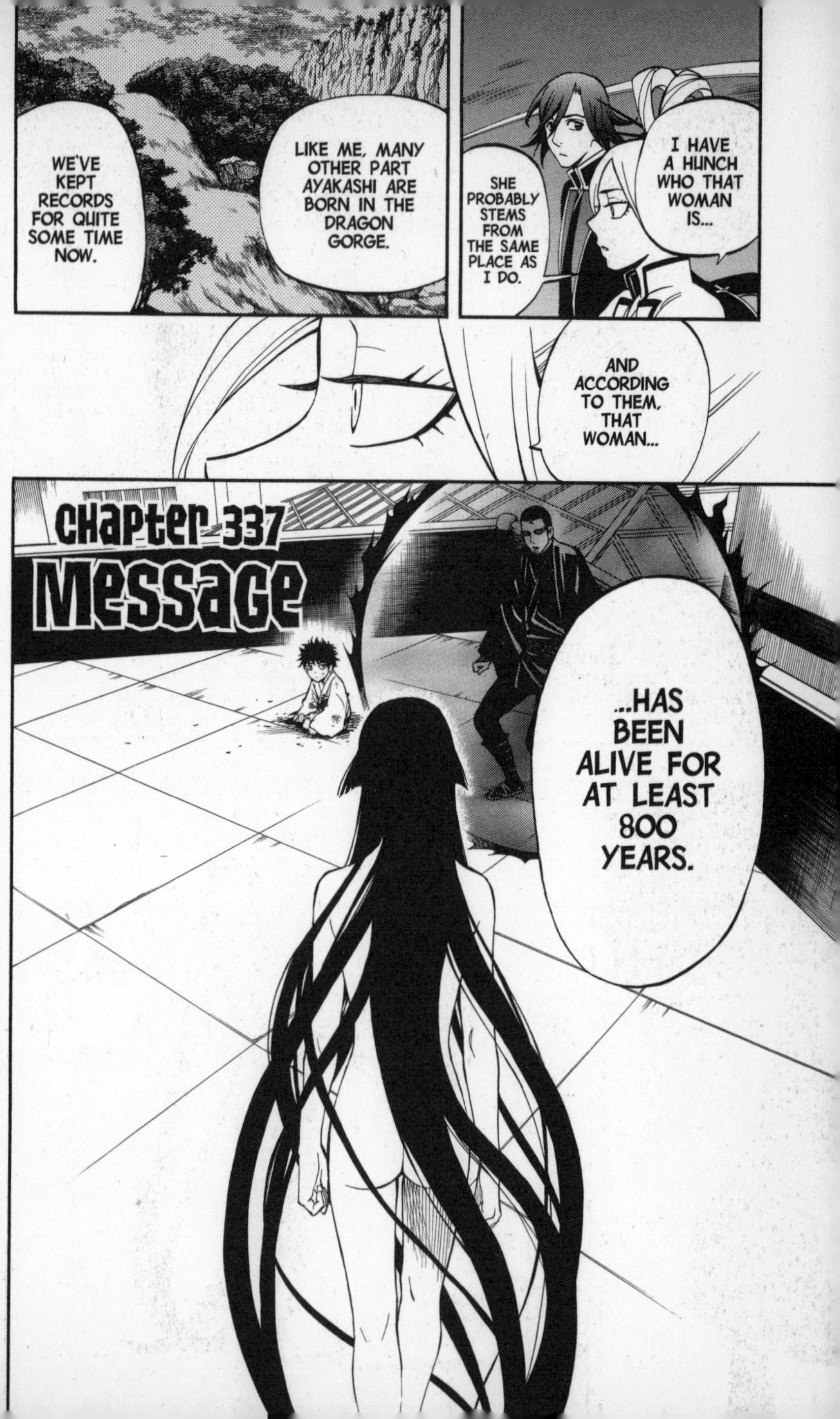
I HAVE A HUNCH WHO THAT WOMAN IS...
SHE PROBABLY STEMS FROM THE SAME PLACE AS I DO.
LIKE ME, MANY OTHER PART AYAKASHI ARE BORN IN THE DRAGON GORGE.
WE'VE KEPT RECORDS FOR QUITE SOME TIME NOW.
AND ACCORDING TO THEM, THAT WOMAN...
...HAS BEEN ALIVE FOR AT LEAST 800 YEARS.
Chapter 337
Message

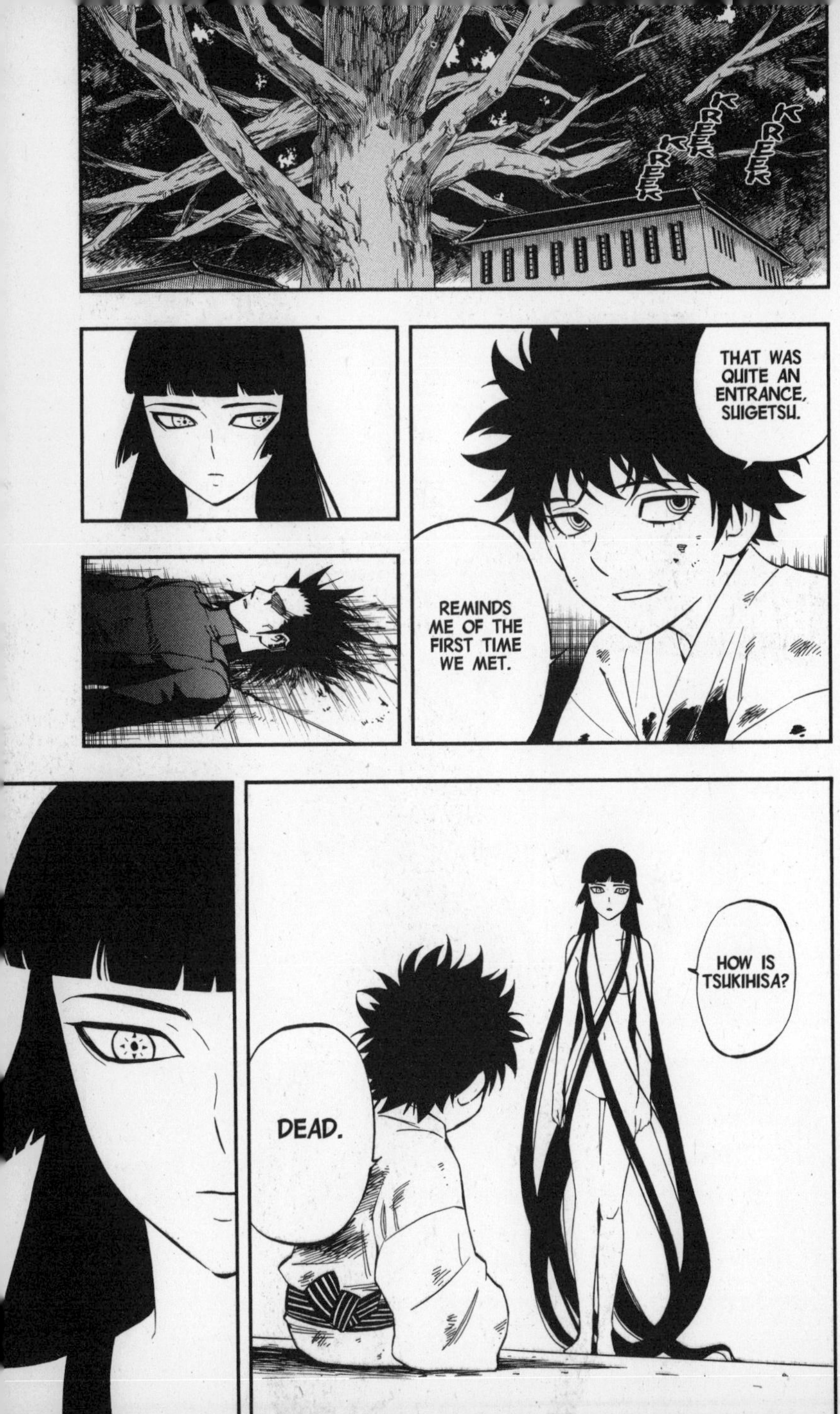
KREEK
KREEK
KREEK
THAT WAS QUITE AN ENTRANCE, SUIGETSU.
REMINDS ME OF THE FIRST TIME WE MET.
HOW IS TSUKIHISA?
DEAD.

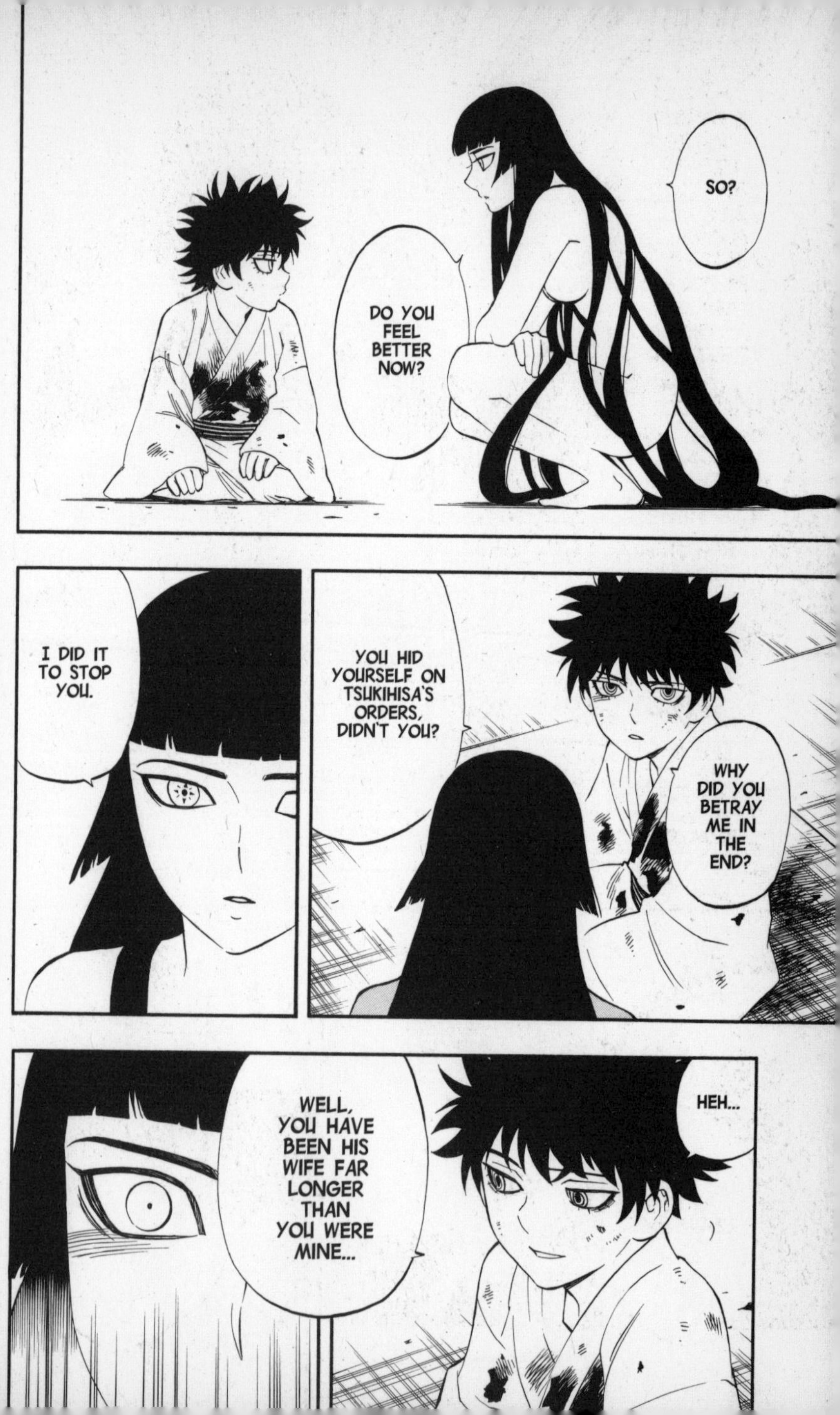
SO?
DO YOU FEEL BETTER NOW?
YOU HID YOURSELF ON TSUKIHISA'S ORDERS, DIDN'T YOU?
WHY DID YOU BETRAY ME IN THE END?
I DID IT TO STOP YOU.
HEH...
WELL, YOU HAVE BEEN HIS WIFE FAR LONGER THAN YOU WERE MINE...

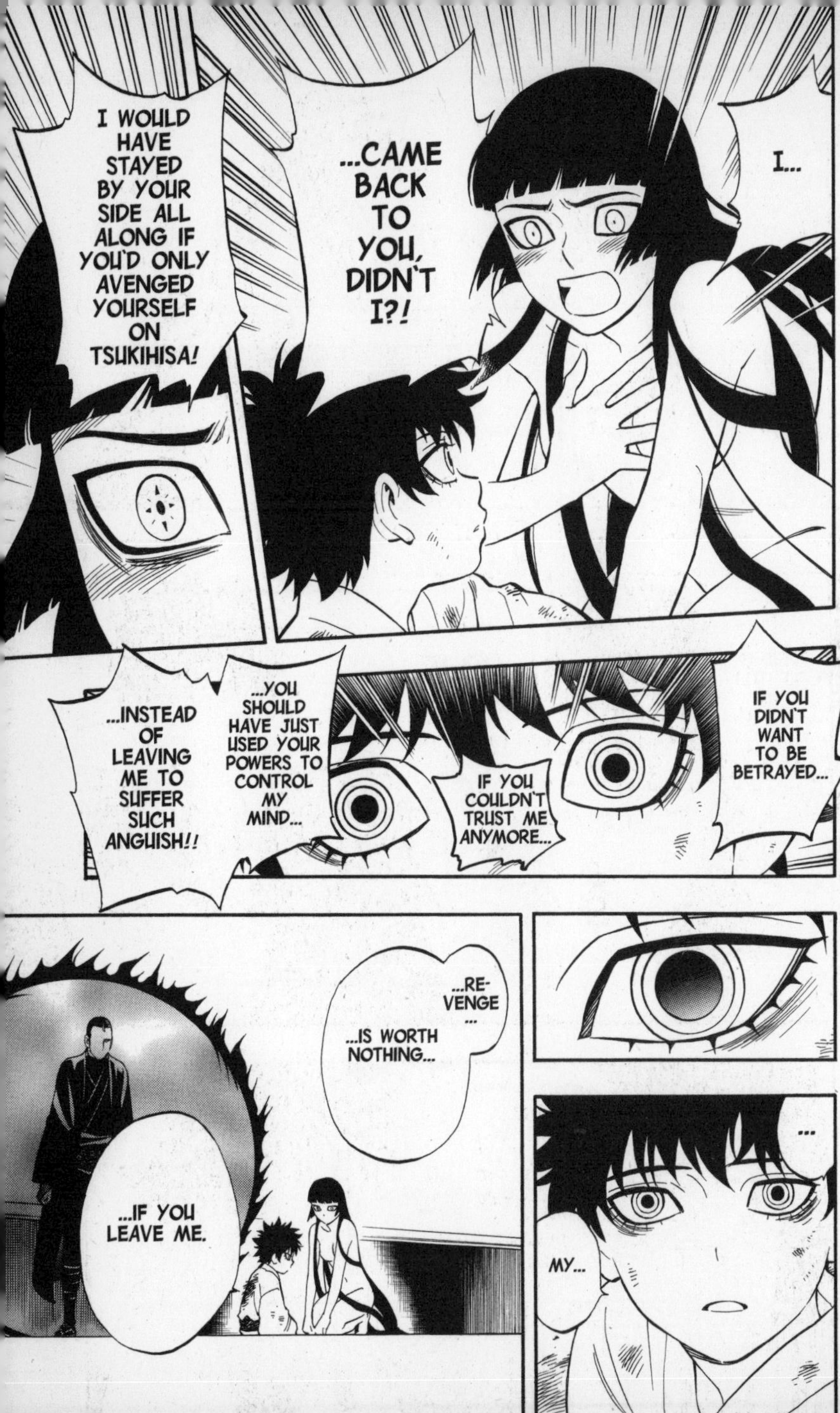
I...
...CAME BACK TO YOU, DIDN'T I?!
I WOULD HAVE STAYED BY YOUR SIDE ALL ALONG IF YOU'D ONLY AVENGED YOURSELF ON TSUKIHISA!
IF YOU DIDN'T WANT TO BE BETRAYED...
IF YOU COULDN'T TRUST ME ANYMORE...
...YOU SHOULD HAVE JUST USED YOUR POWERS TO CONTROL MY MIND...
...INSTEAD OF LEAVING ME TO SUFFER SUCH ANGUISH!!
...
MY...
...RE-VENGE...
...IS WORTH NOTHING...
...IF YOU LEAVE ME.

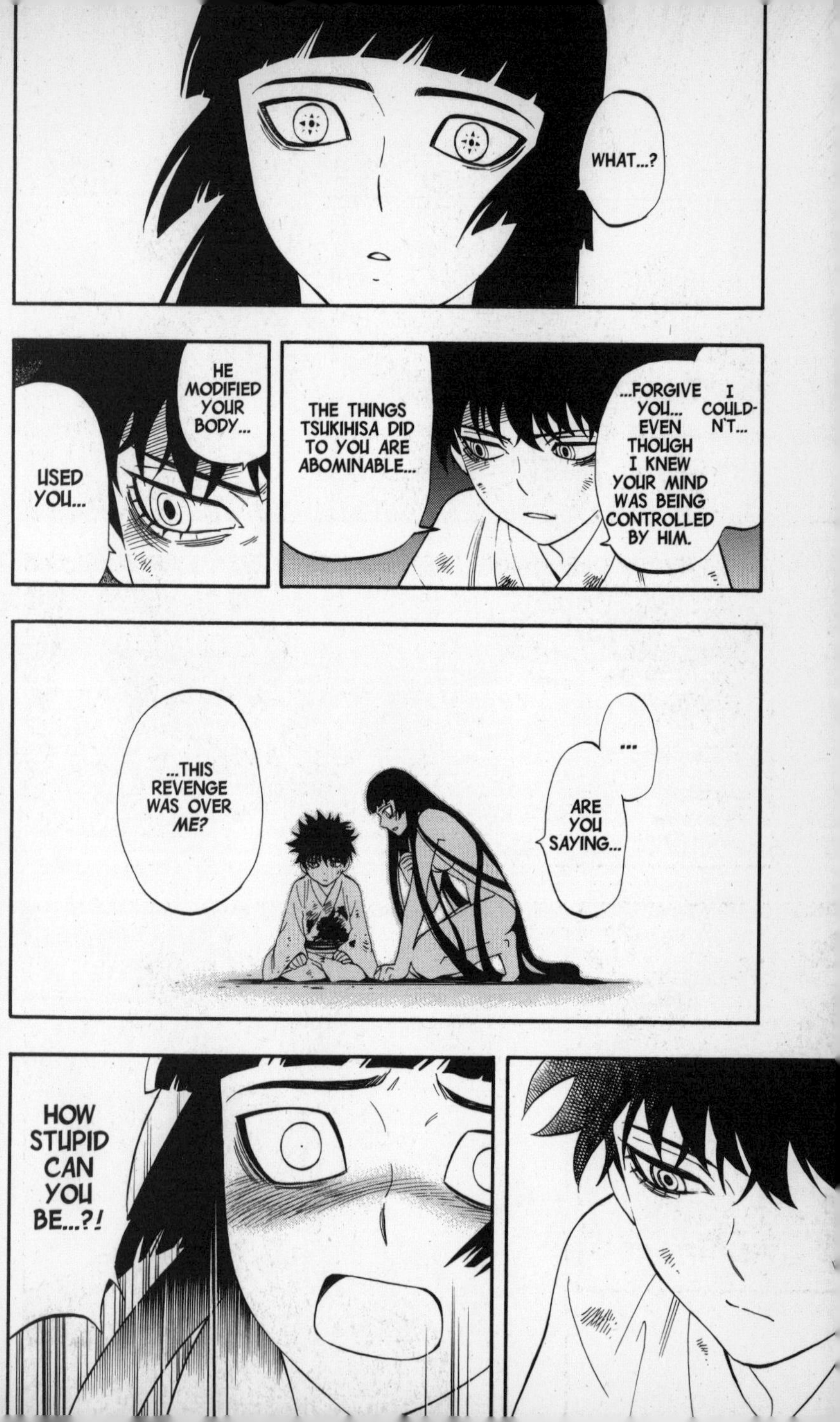
WHAT...?
I COULDN'T... ...FORGIVE YOU... EVEN THOUGH I KNEW YOUR MIND WAS BEING CONTROLLED BY HIM.
THE THINGS TSUKIHISA DID TO YOU ARE ABOMINABLE...
HE MODIFIED YOUR BODY...
USED YOU...
...
ARE YOU SAYING...
...THIS REVENGE WAS OVER *ME*?
HOW STUPID CAN YOU BE...?!

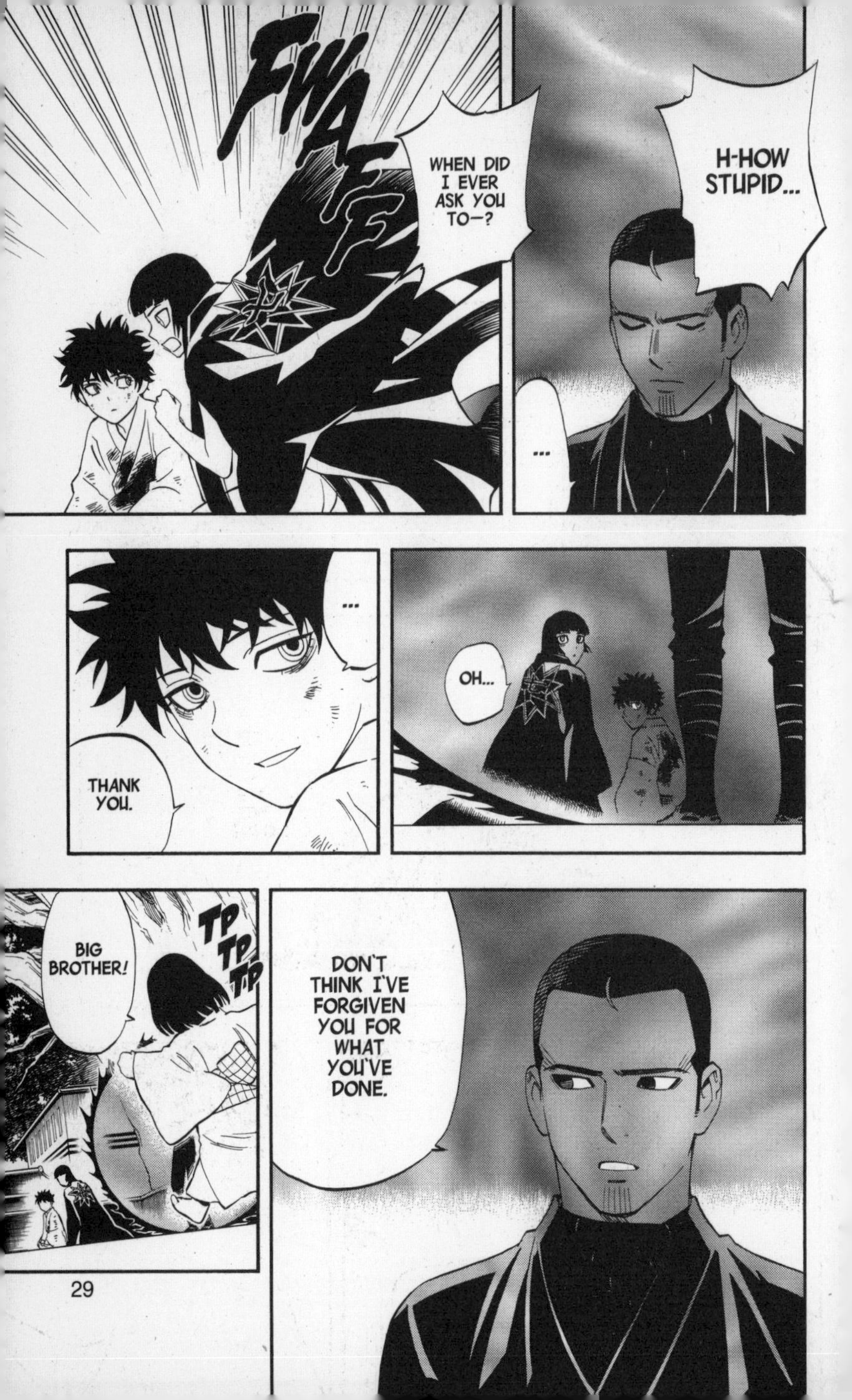
H-HOW STUPID...
...
WHEN DID I EVER ASK YOU TO—?
FWAFF
OH...
...
THANK YOU.
DON'T THINK I'VE FORGIVEN YOU FOR WHAT YOU'VE DONE.
TP TP TP
BIG BROTHER!

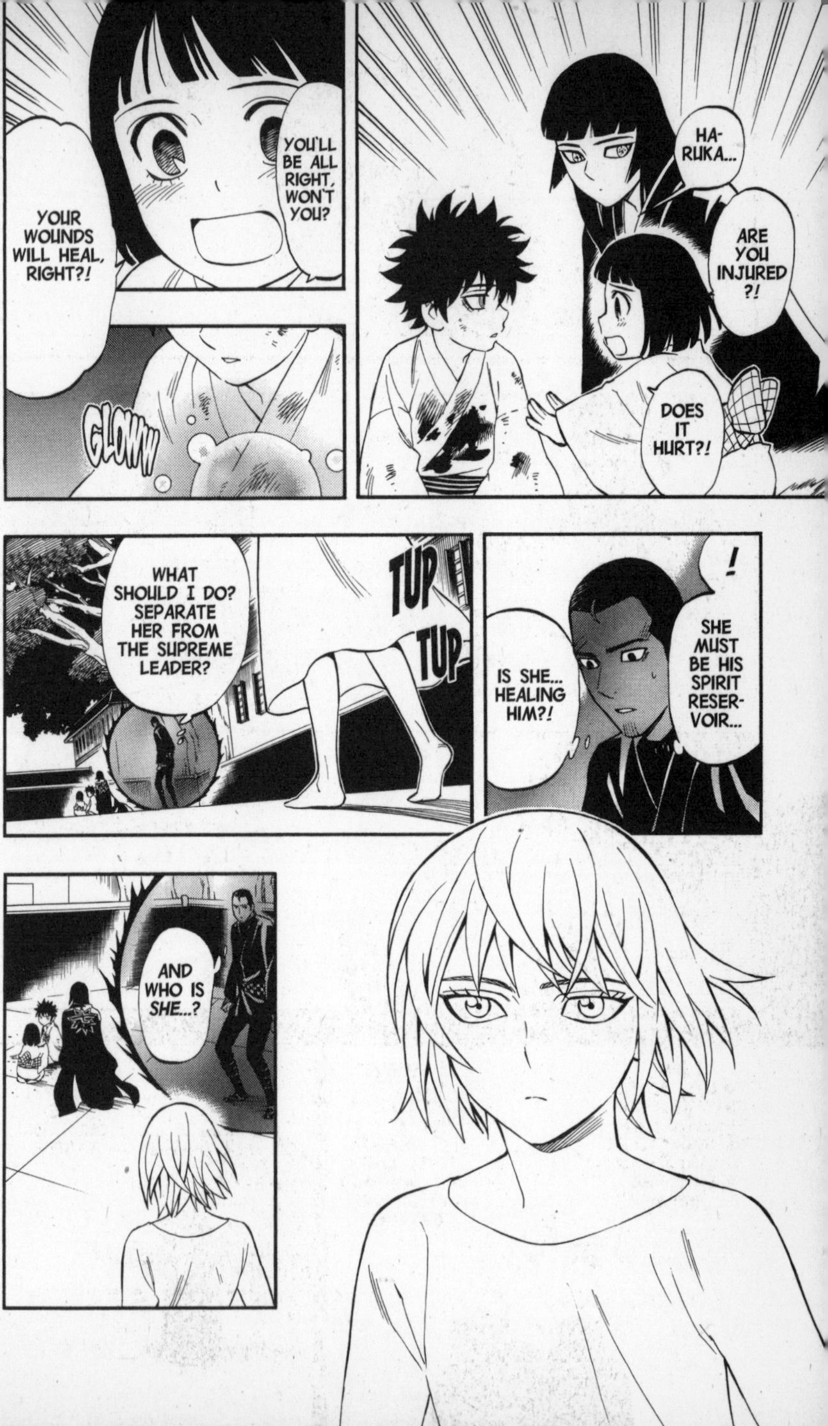
HA-RUKA...
ARE YOU INJURED?!
DOES IT HURT?!
YOU'LL BE ALL RIGHT, WON'T YOU?
YOUR WOUNDS WILL HEAL, RIGHT?!
GLOWW
!
SHE MUST BE HIS SPIRIT RESERVOIR...
IS SHE... HEALING HIM?!
TUP
TUP
WHAT SHOULD I DO? SEPARATE HER FROM THE SUPREME LEADER?
AND WHO IS *SHE*...?

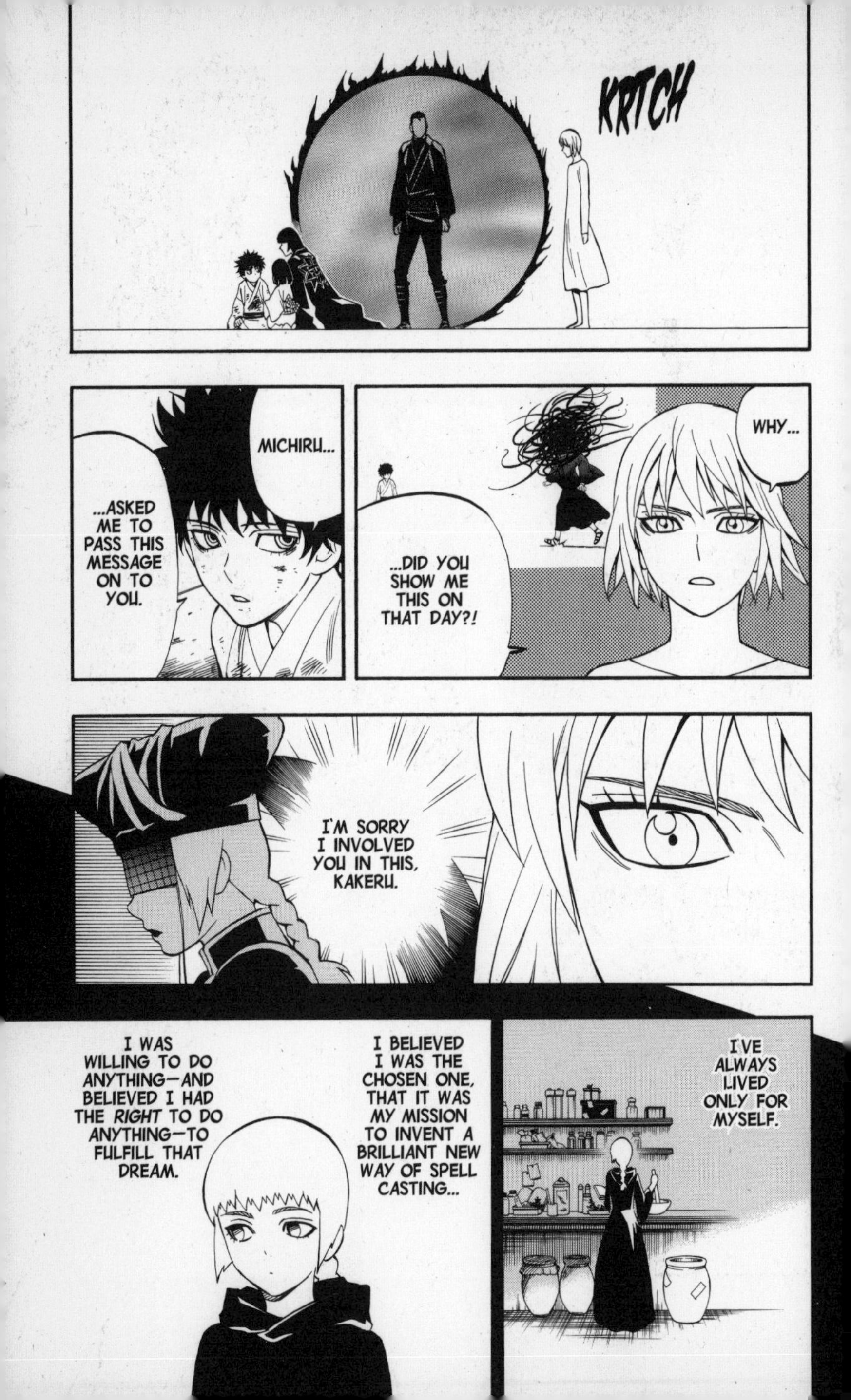
KRTCH
WHY...
...DID YOU SHOW ME THIS ON THAT DAY?!
MICHIRU...
...ASKED ME TO PASS THIS MESSAGE ON TO YOU.
I'M SORRY I INVOLVED YOU IN THIS, KAKERU.
I'VE ALWAYS LIVED ONLY FOR MYSELF.
I BELIEVED I WAS THE CHOSEN ONE, THAT IT WAS MY MISSION TO INVENT A BRILLIANT NEW WAY OF SPELL CASTING...
I WAS WILLING TO DO ANYTHING—AND BELIEVED I HAD THE *RIGHT* TO DO ANYTHING—TO FULFILL THAT DREAM.

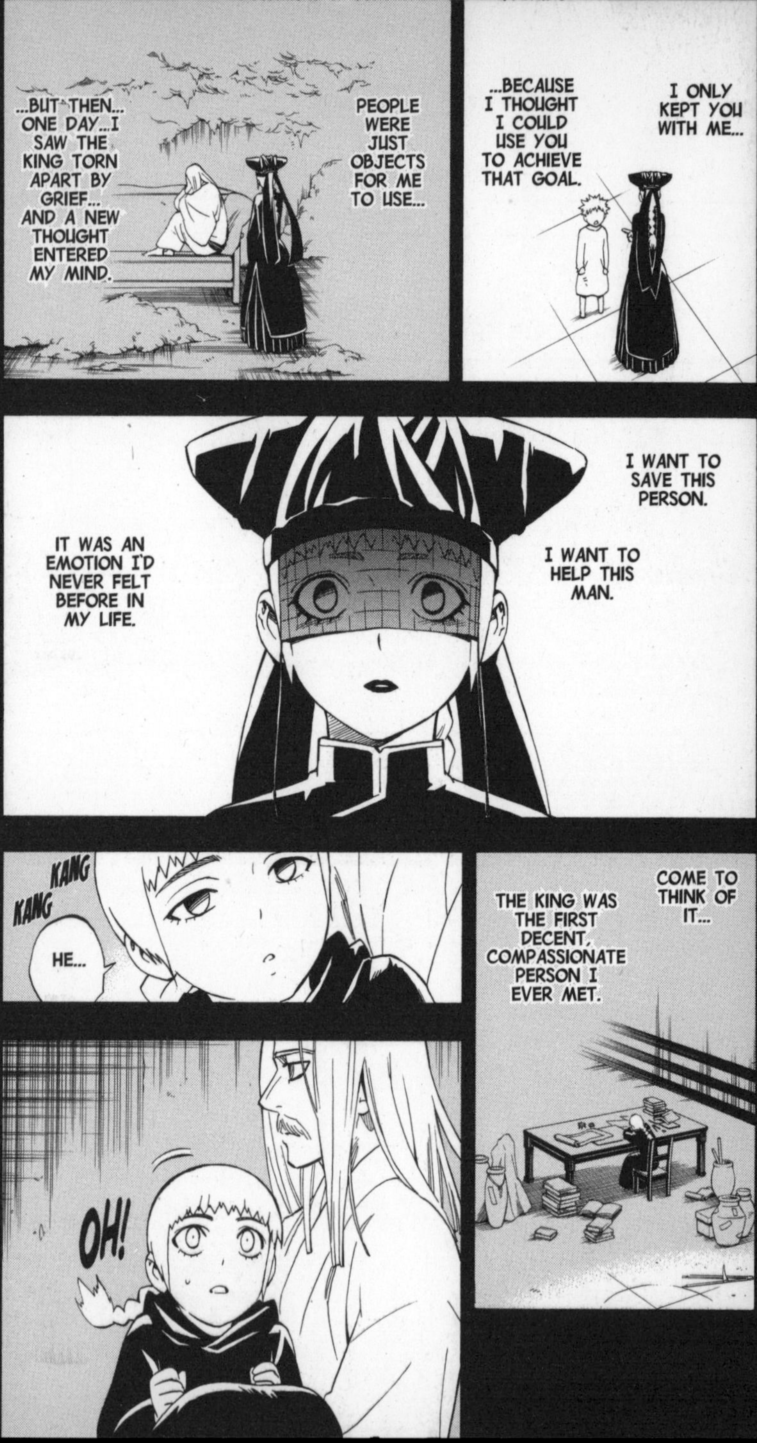
I ONLY KEPT YOU WITH ME...
...BECAUSE I THOUGHT I COULD USE YOU TO ACHIEVE THAT GOAL.
PEOPLE WERE JUST OBJECTS FOR ME TO USE...
...BUT THEN... ONE DAY...I SAW THE KING TORN APART BY GRIEF... AND A NEW THOUGHT ENTERED MY MIND.
I WANT TO SAVE THIS PERSON.
I WANT TO HELP THIS MAN.
IT WAS AN EMOTION I'D NEVER FELT BEFORE IN MY LIFE.
COME TO THINK OF IT...
THE KING WAS THE FIRST DECENT, COMPASSIONATE PERSON I EVER MET.
KANG
KANG
HE...
OH!

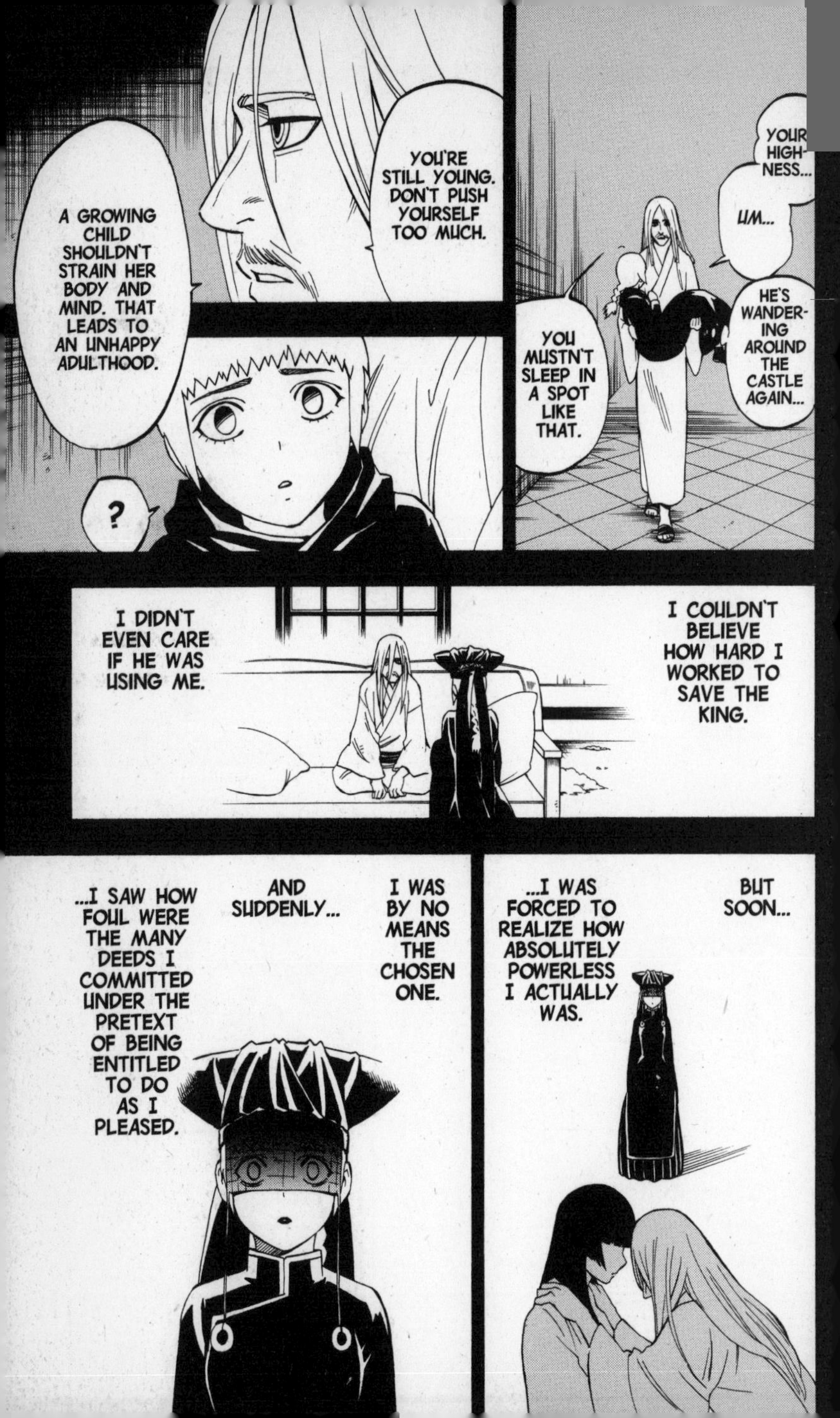
YOUR HIGHNESS...
UM...
HE'S WANDERING AROUND THE CASTLE AGAIN...
YOU MUSTN'T SLEEP IN A SPOT LIKE THAT.
YOU'RE STILL YOUNG. DON'T PUSH YOURSELF TOO MUCH.
A GROWING CHILD SHOULDN'T STRAIN HER BODY AND MIND. THAT LEADS TO AN UNHAPPY ADULTHOOD.
?
I COULDN'T BELIEVE HOW HARD I WORKED TO SAVE THE KING.
I DIDN'T EVEN CARE IF HE WAS USING ME.
BUT SOON...
...I WAS FORCED TO REALIZE HOW ABSOLUTELY POWERLESS I ACTUALLY WAS.
I WAS BY NO MEANS THE CHOSEN ONE.
AND SUDDENLY...
...I SAW HOW FOUL WERE THE MANY DEEDS I COMMITTED UNDER THE PRETEXT OF BEING ENTITLED TO DO AS I PLEASED.

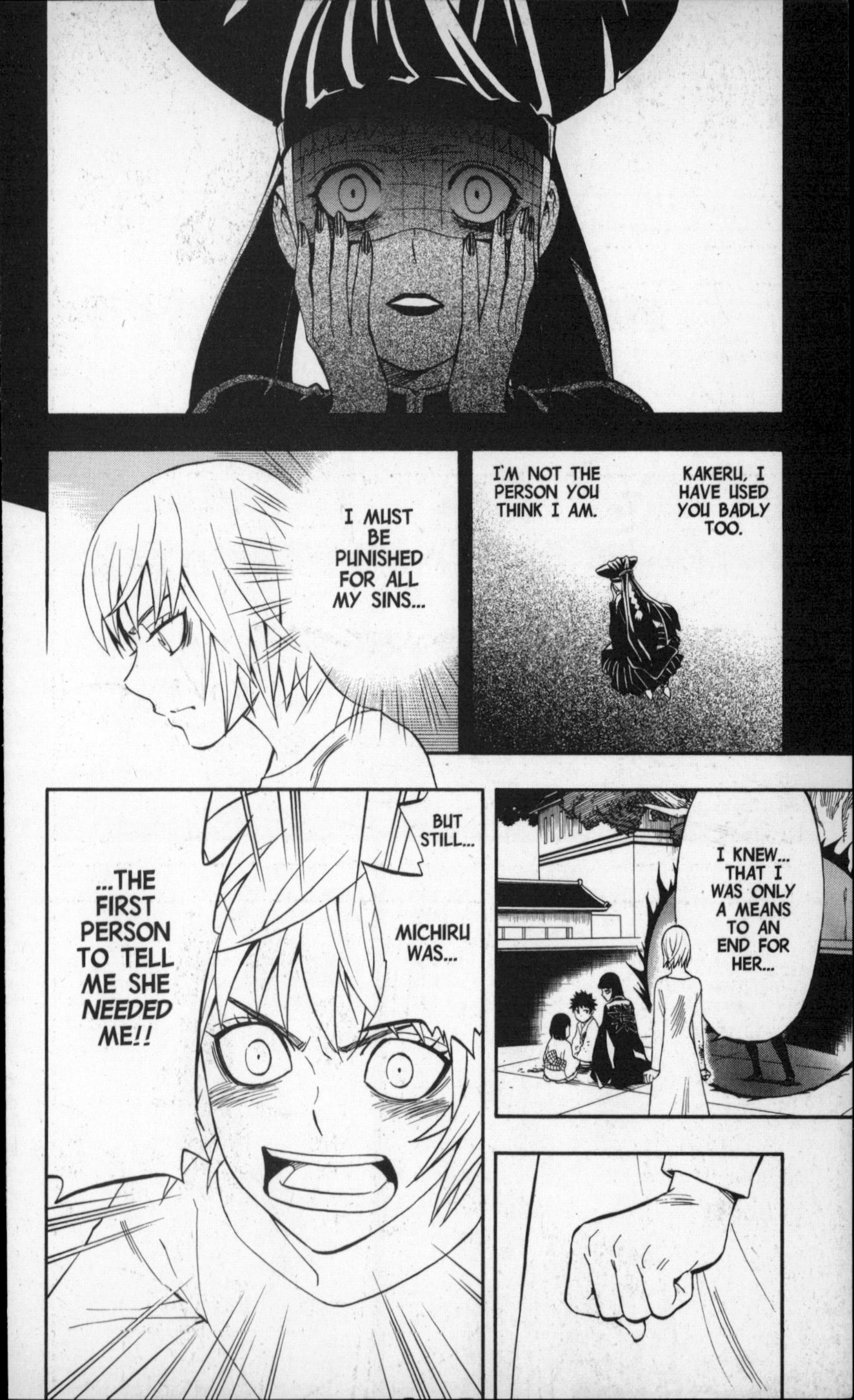
KAKERU, I HAVE USED YOU BADLY TOO.
I'M NOT THE PERSON YOU THINK I AM.
I MUST BE PUNISHED FOR ALL MY SINS...
I KNEW... THAT I WAS ONLY A MEANS TO AN END FOR HER...
BUT STILL...
MICHIRU WAS...
...THE FIRST PERSON TO TELL ME SHE *NEEDED* ME!!

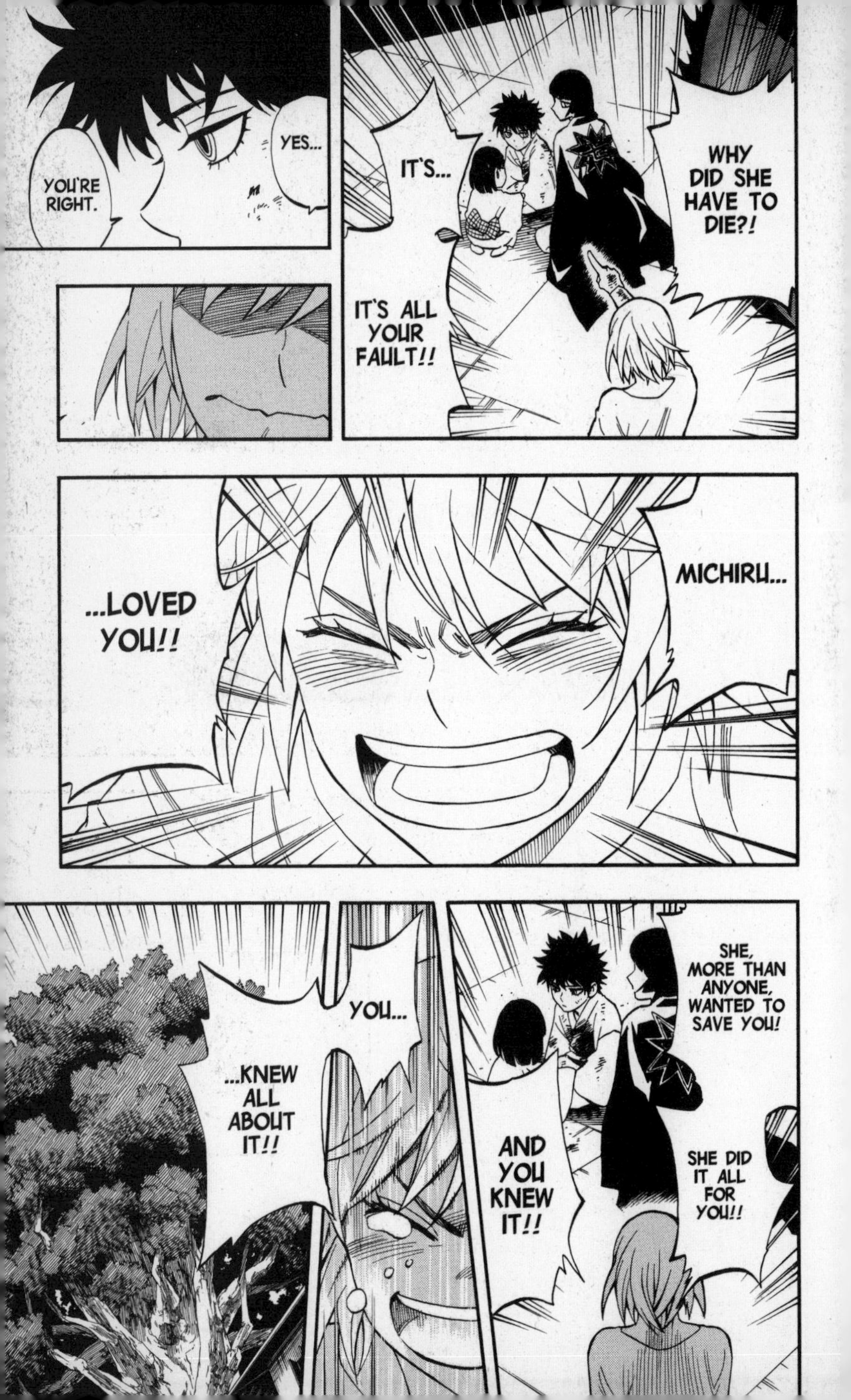
WHY DID SHE HAVE TO DIE?!
IT'S...
IT'S ALL YOUR FAULT!!
YES...
YOU'RE RIGHT.
MICHIRU...
...LOVED YOU!!
SHE, MORE THAN ANYONE, WANTED TO SAVE YOU!
SHE DID IT ALL FOR YOU!!
AND YOU KNEW IT!!
YOU...
...KNEW ALL ABOUT IT!!

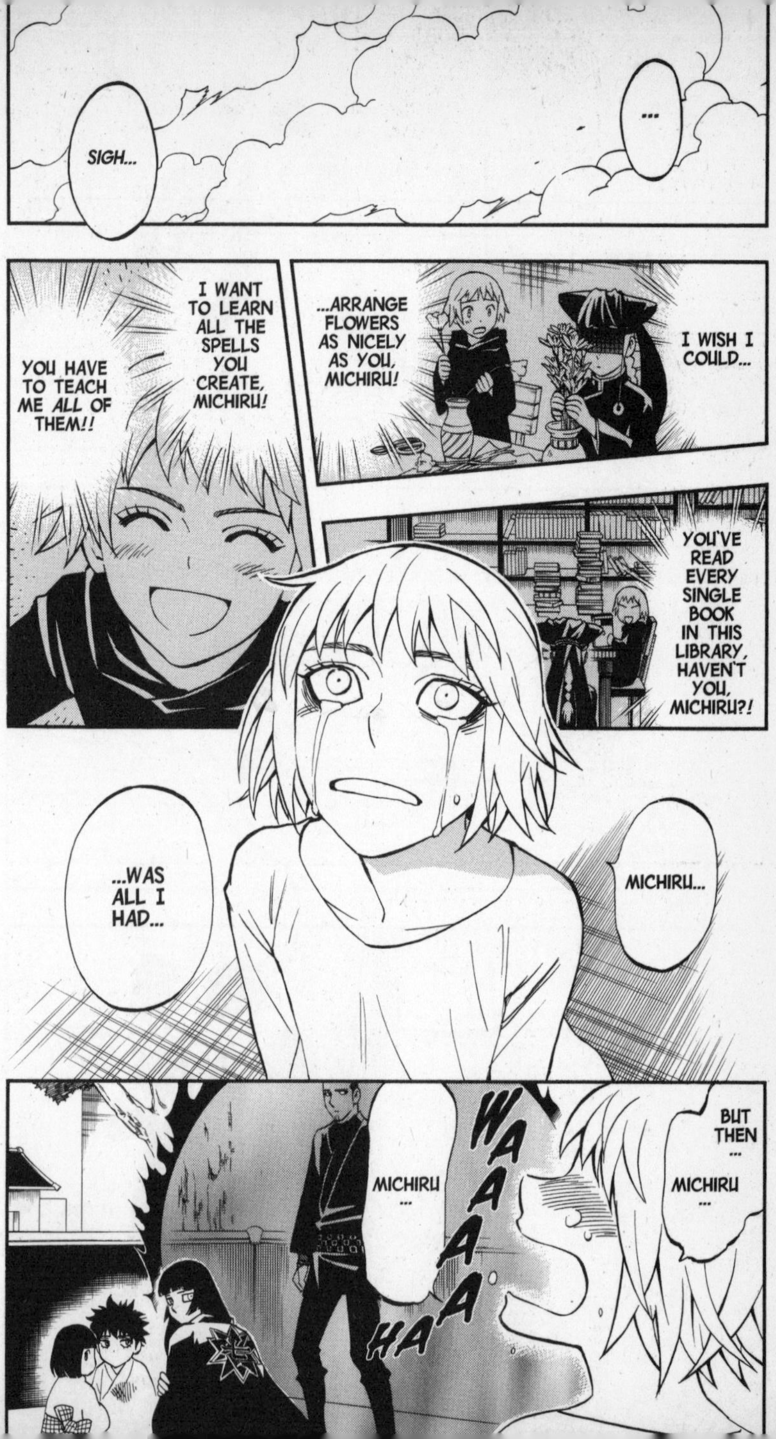
...
SIGH...
I WISH I COULD...
...ARRANGE FLOWERS AS NICELY AS YOU, MICHIRU!
YOU'VE READ EVERY SINGLE BOOK IN THIS LIBRARY, HAVEN'T YOU, MICHIRU?!
I WANT TO LEARN ALL THE SPELLS YOU CREATE, MICHIRU!
YOU HAVE TO TEACH ME *ALL* OF THEM!!
MICHIRU...
...WAS ALL I HAD...
BUT THEN...
MICHIRU...
WAAAAAHA
MICHIRU...

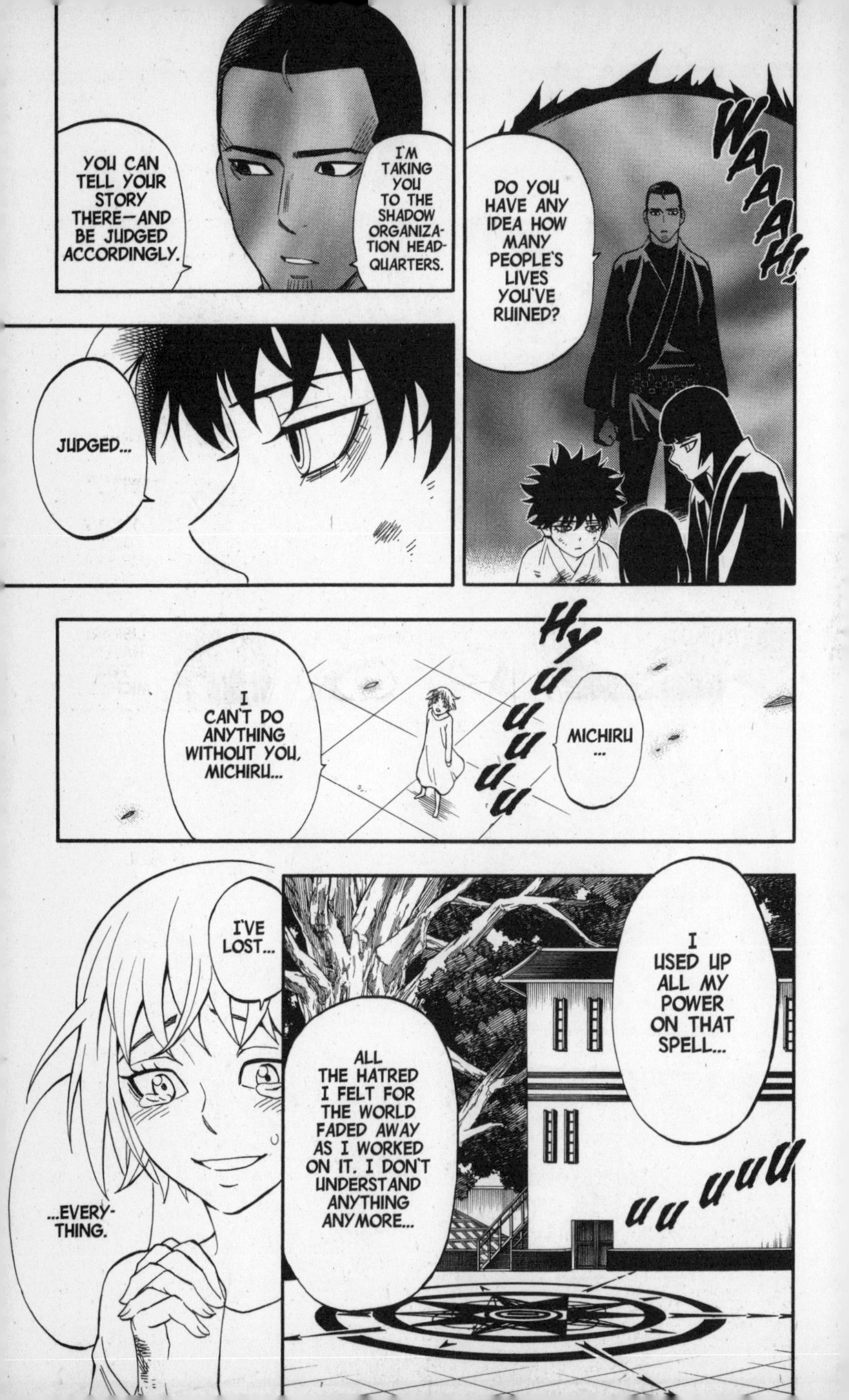
WAAAH!
DO YOU HAVE ANY IDEA HOW MANY PEOPLE'S LIVES YOU'VE RUINED?
I'M TAKING YOU TO THE SHADOW ORGANIZATION HEADQUARTERS.
YOU CAN TELL YOUR STORY THERE—AND BE JUDGED ACCORDINGLY.
JUDGED...
HYUUUUUU
MICHIRU...
I CAN'T DO ANYTHING WITHOUT YOU, MICHIRU...
I USED UP ALL MY POWER ON THAT SPELL...
UUUUU
ALL THE HATRED I FELT FOR THE WORLD FADED AWAY AS I WORKED ON IT. I DON'T UNDERSTAND ANYTHING ANYMORE...
I'VE LOST...
...EVERYTHING.

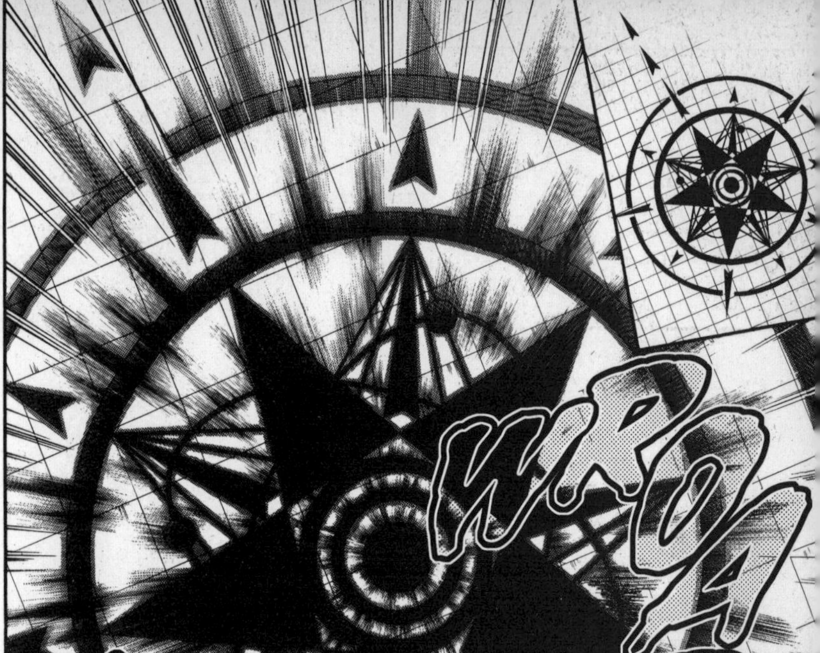
WROARR
HW

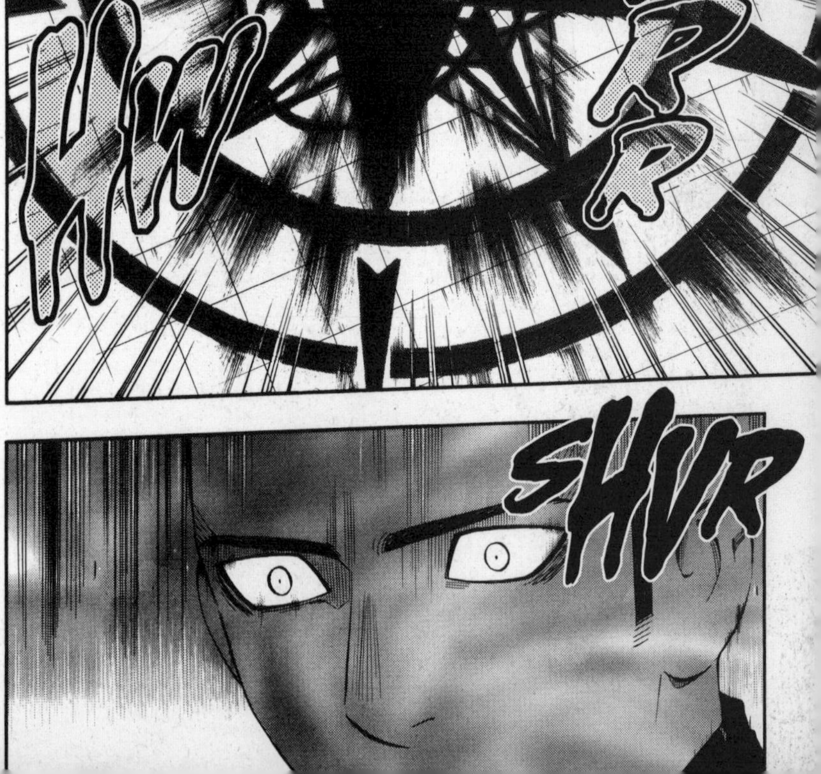
SHVR

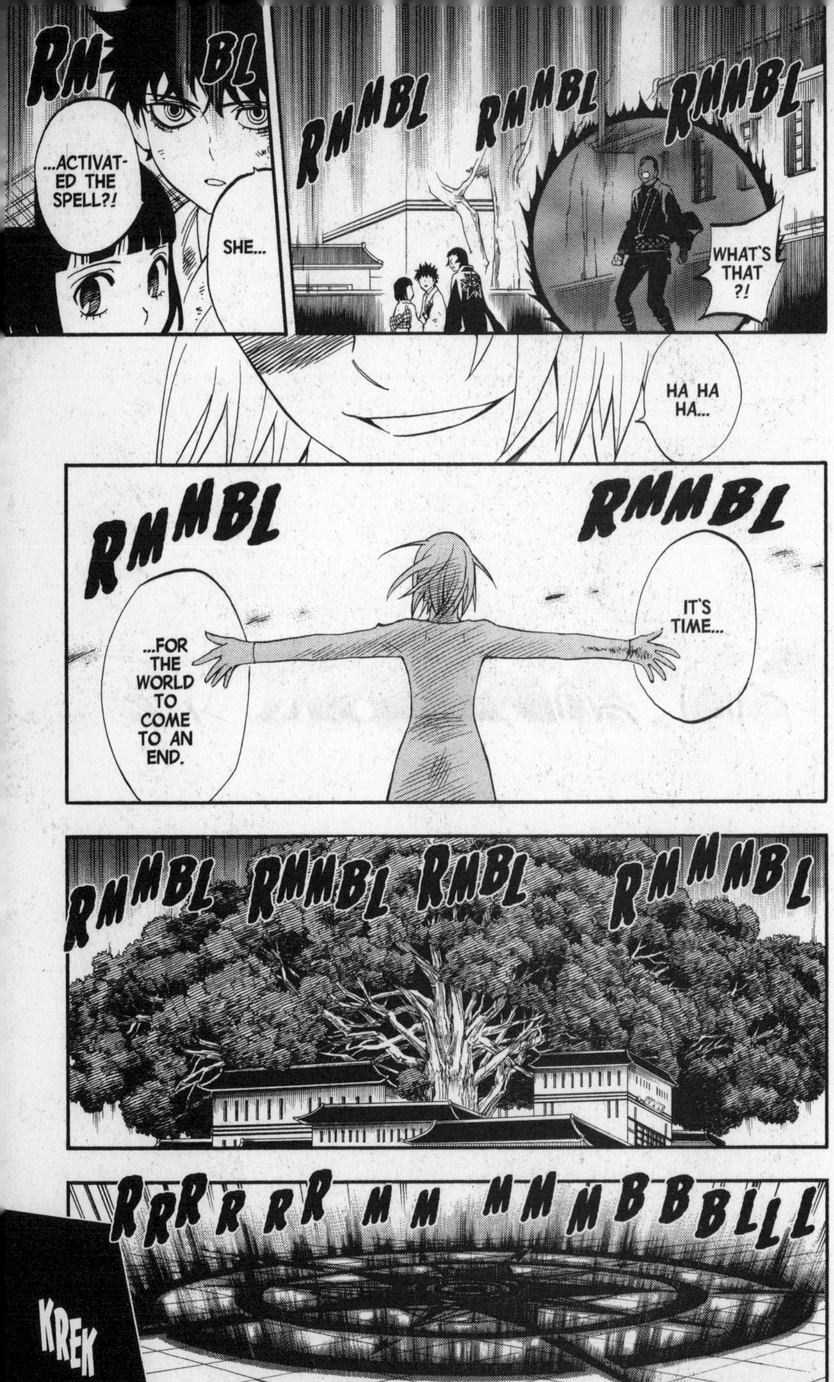
RMMBL
RMMBL
RMMBL
WHAT'S THAT?!
RM-BL
SHE...
...ACTIVATED THE SPELL?!
HA HA HA...
RMMBL
IT'S TIME...
RMMBL
...FOR THE WORLD TO COME TO AN END.
RMMMBL
RMBL
RMMBL
RMMBL
RRRRRR MM MMMBBBLLL
KREK

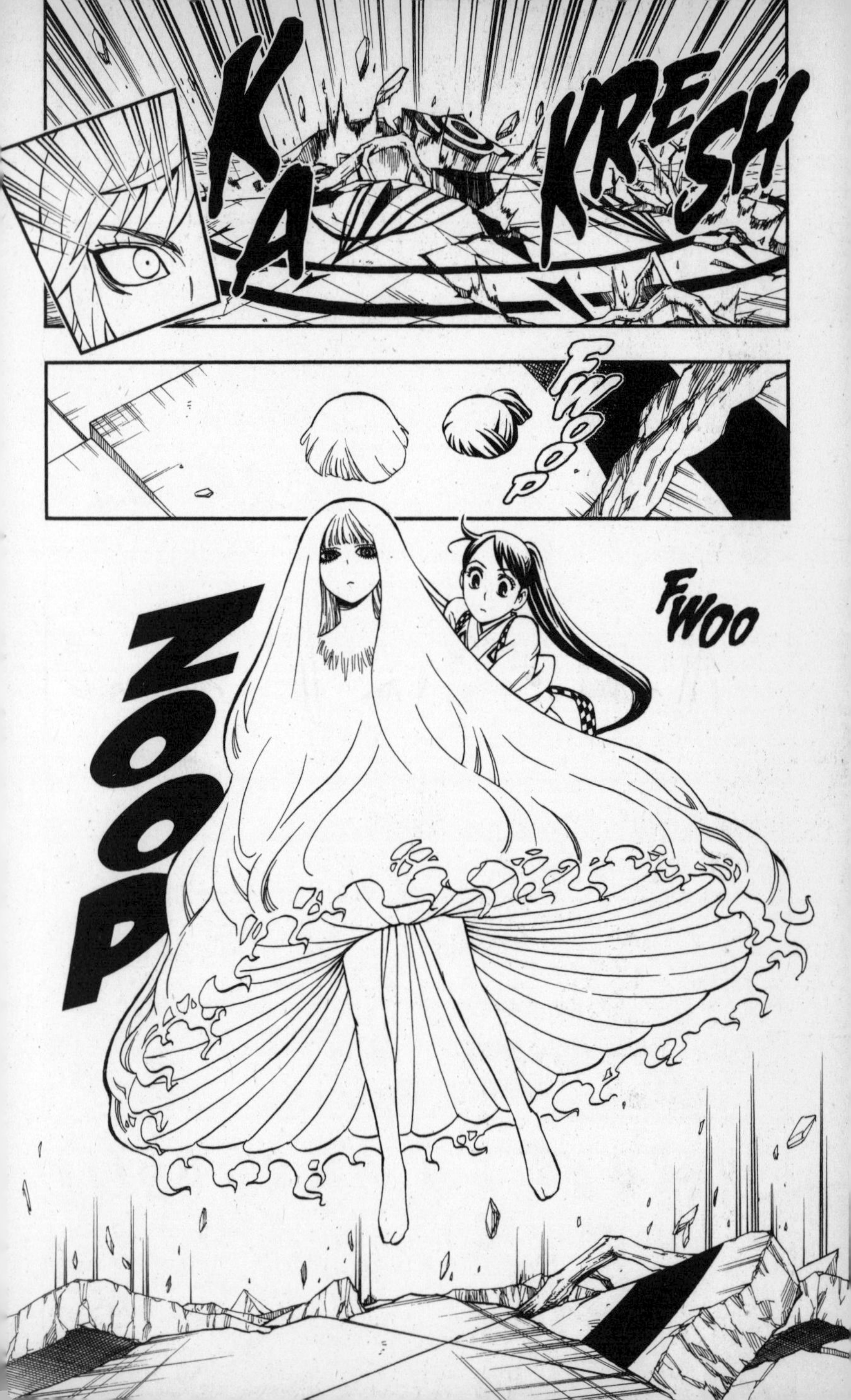
KA
KRESH
FWOOP
FWOO
FWOOP

Chapter 338: Judgment

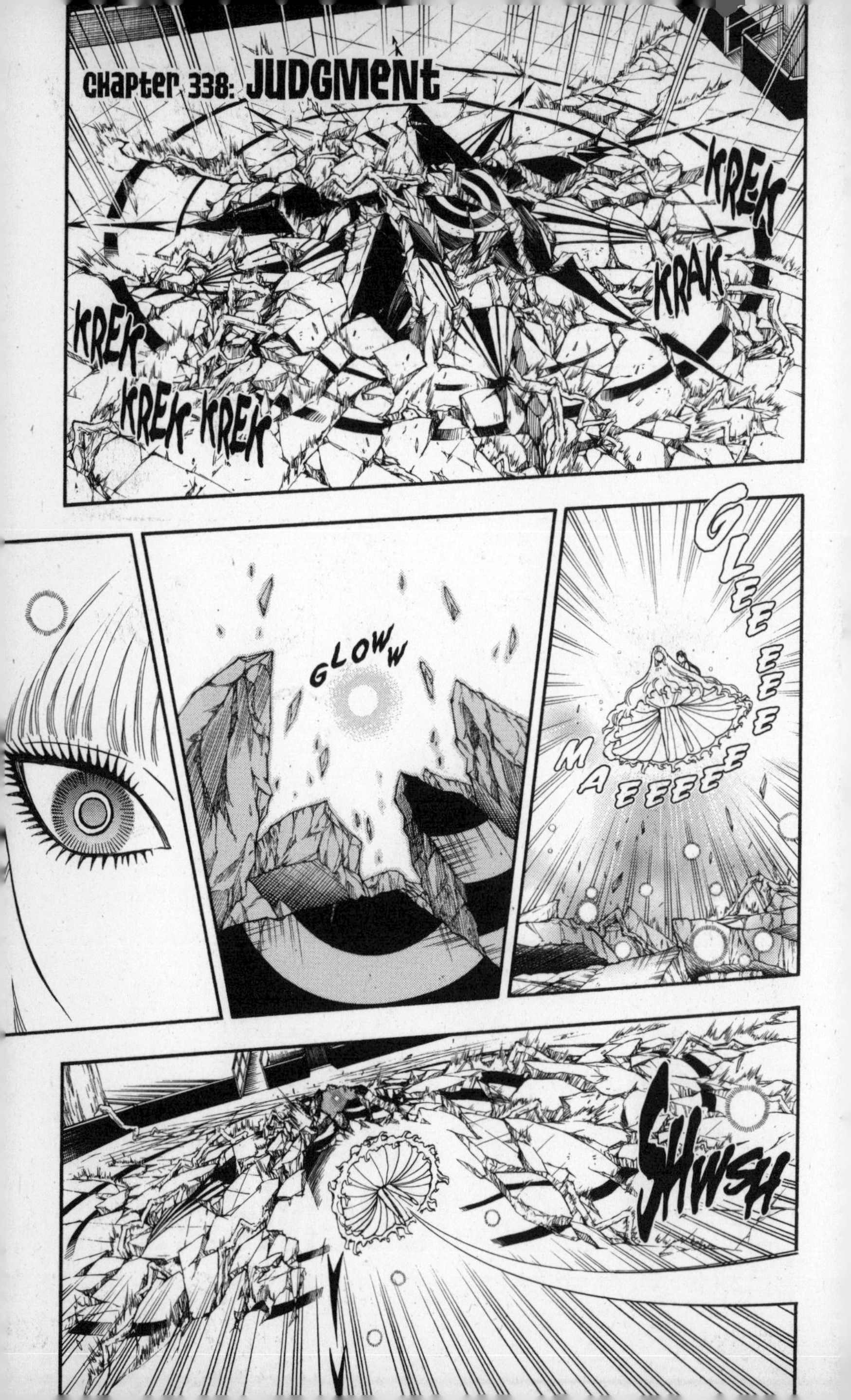
KREK
KRAK
KREK
KREK KREK
GLEEEEEEE
MAEEEE
GLOWW
SHWSH

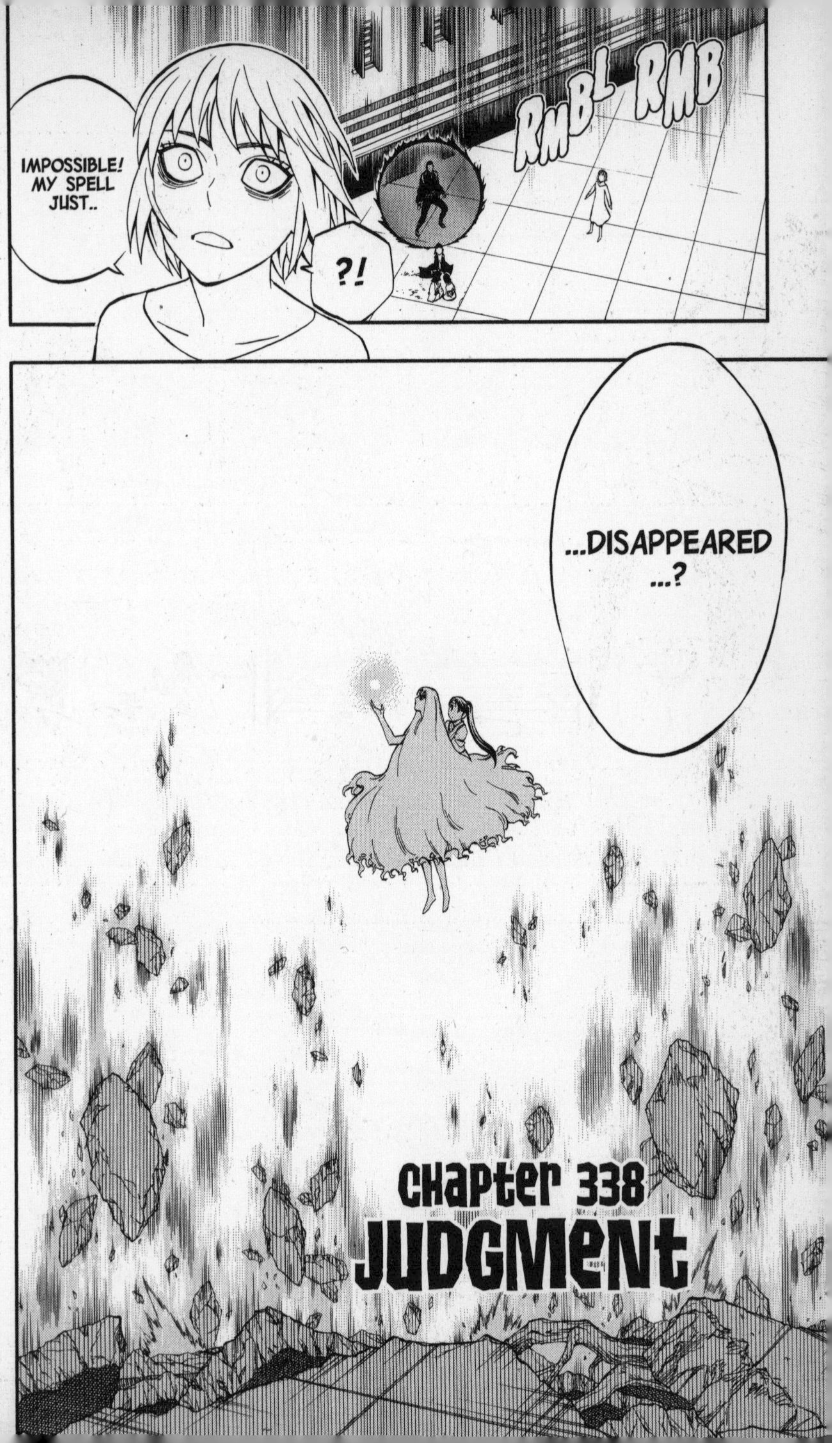
RMBL RMB
?!
IMPOSSIBLE! MY SPELL JUST..
...DISAPPEARED ...?
CHAPTER 338
JUDGMENT

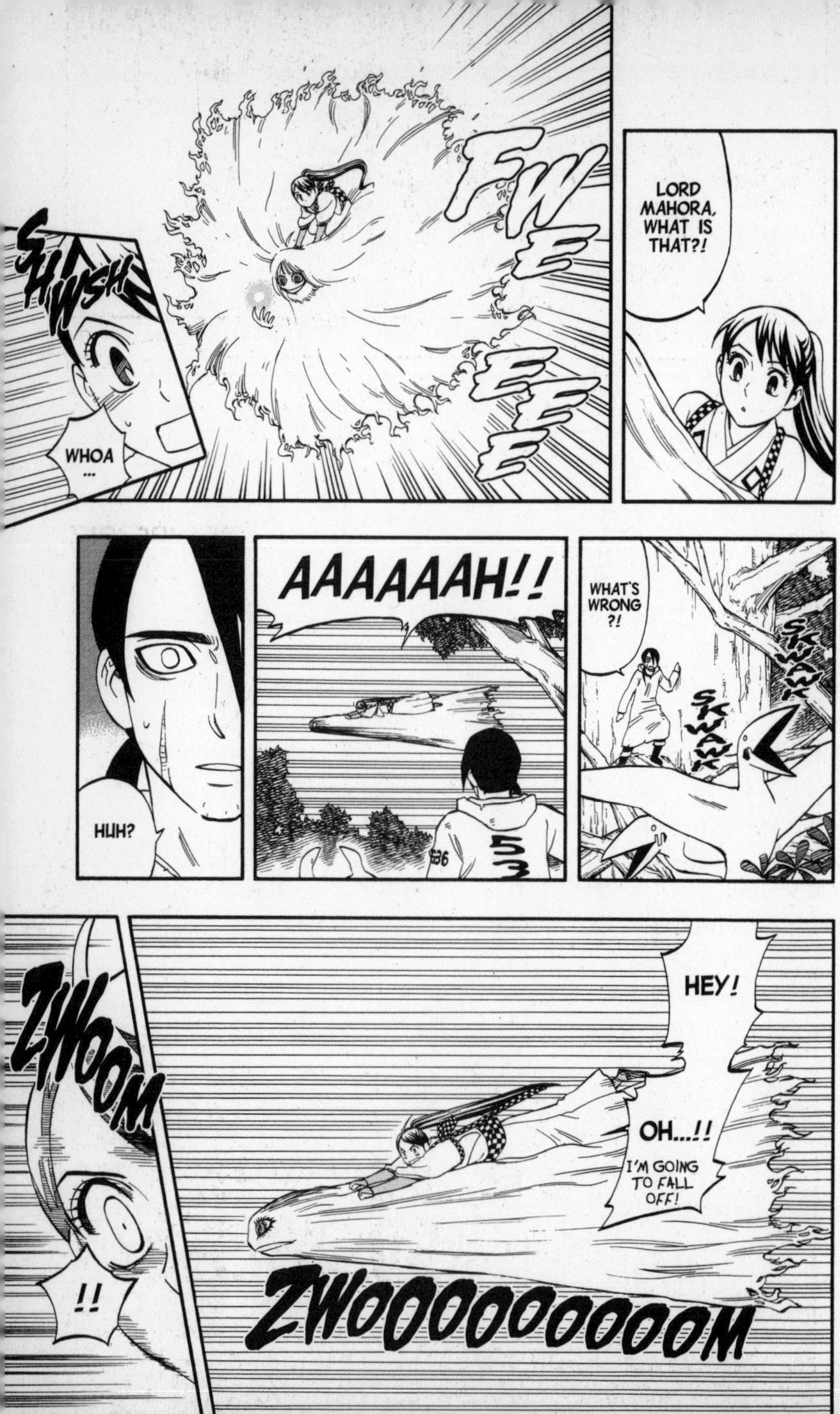
LORD MAHORA, WHAT IS THAT?!
FWEEEE
SHWSH
WHOA ...
WHAT'S WRONG ?!
SKWAWK
SKWAWK
AAAAAAH!!
HUH?
HEY!
OH...!!
I'M GOING TO FALL OFF!
ZWOOOOOOOOOM
ZWOOM
!!

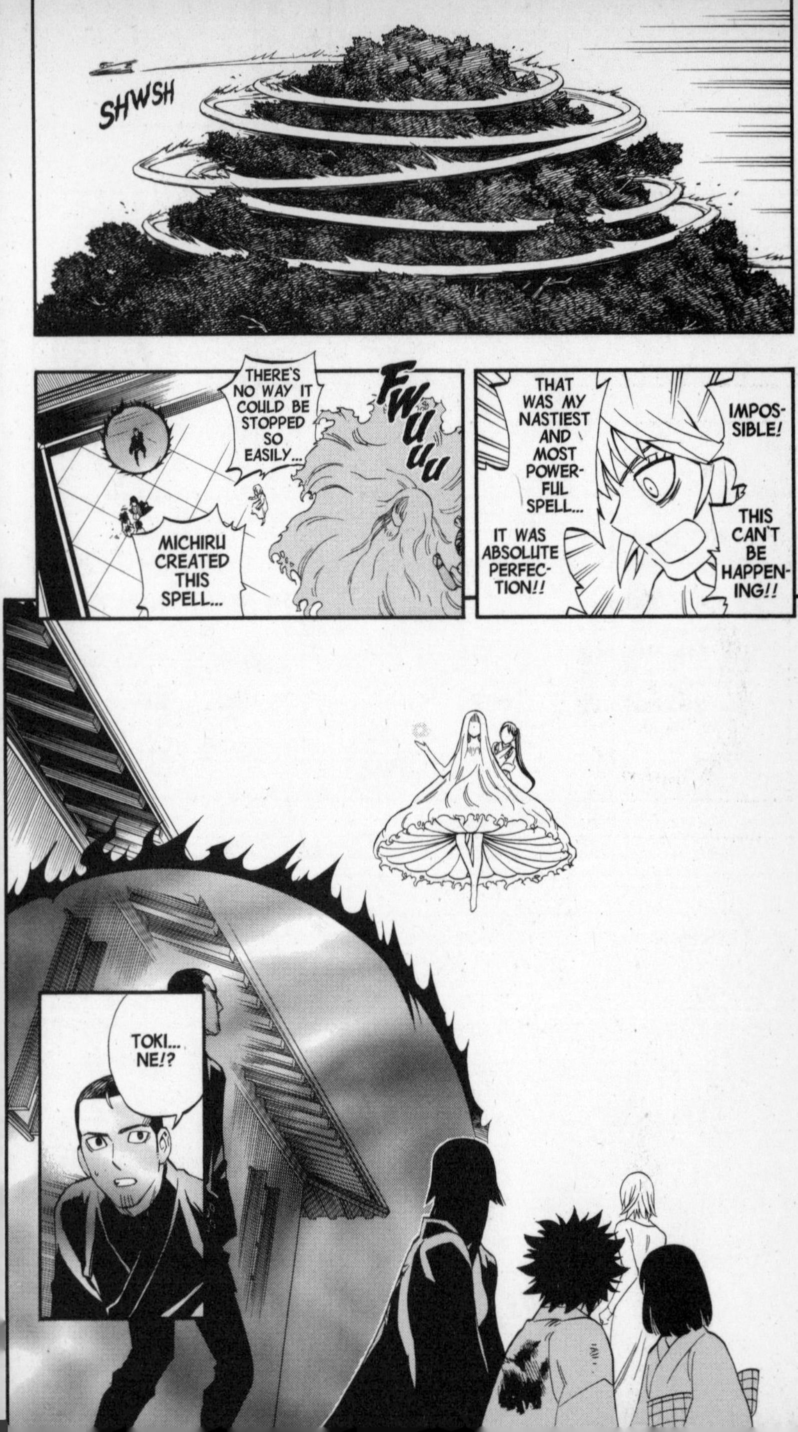
SHWSH
IMPOSSIBLE!
THAT WAS MY NASTIEST AND MOST POWERFUL SPELL...
THIS CAN'T BE HAPPENING!!
IT WAS ABSOLUTE PERFECTION!!
FWUUU
THERE'S NO WAY IT COULD BE STOPPED SO EASILY...
MICHIRU CREATED THIS SPELL...
TOKI... NE!?

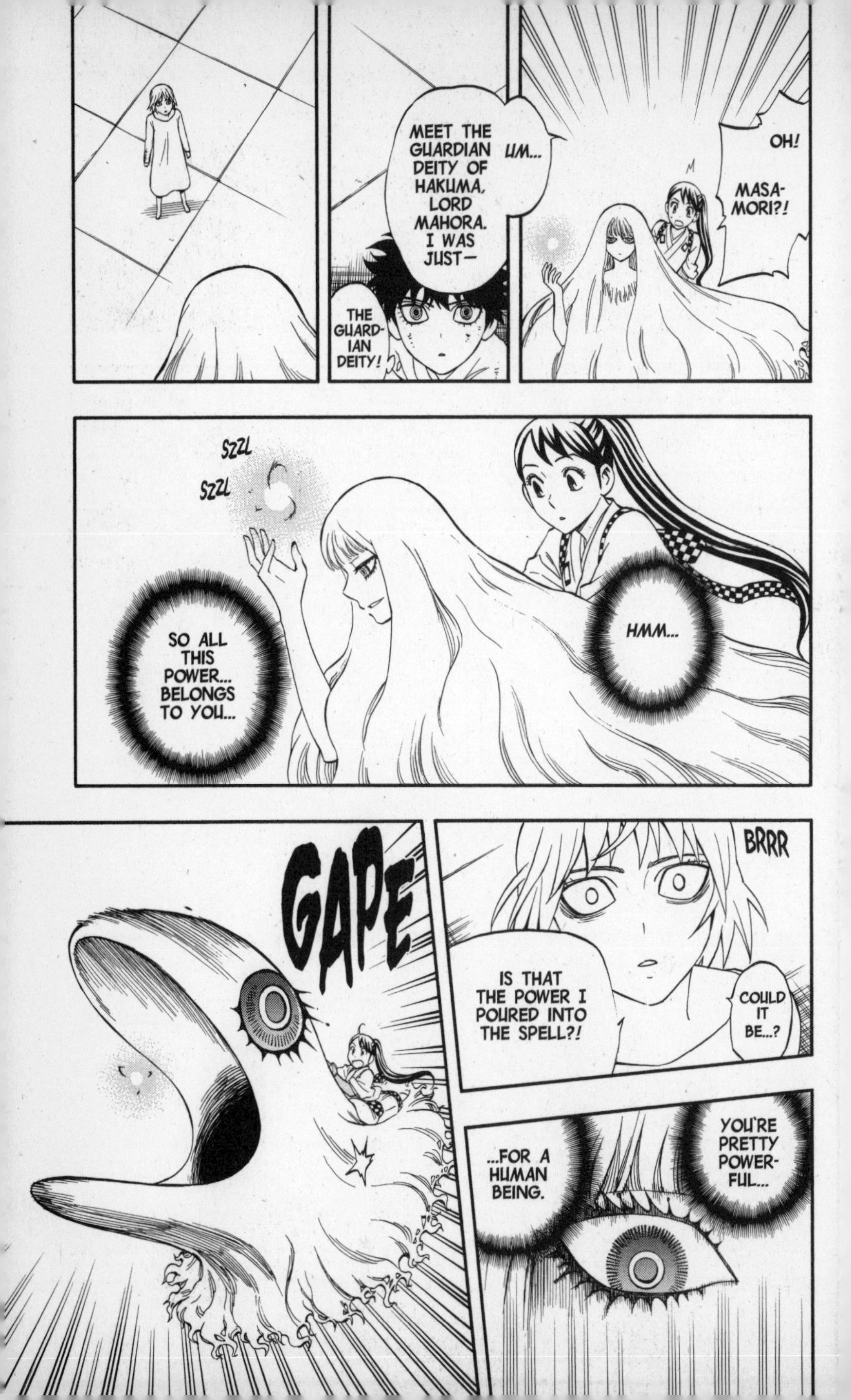
OH!
MASA-MORI?!
UM...
MEET THE GUARDIAN DEITY OF HAKUMA, LORD MAHORA. I WAS JUST—
THE GUARDIAN DEITY!
HMM...
SZZL
SZZL
SO ALL THIS POWER... BELONGS TO YOU...
BRRR
COULD IT BE...?
IS THAT THE POWER I POURED INTO THE SPELL?!
YOU'RE PRETTY POWER-FUL...
...FOR A HUMAN BEING.
GAPE

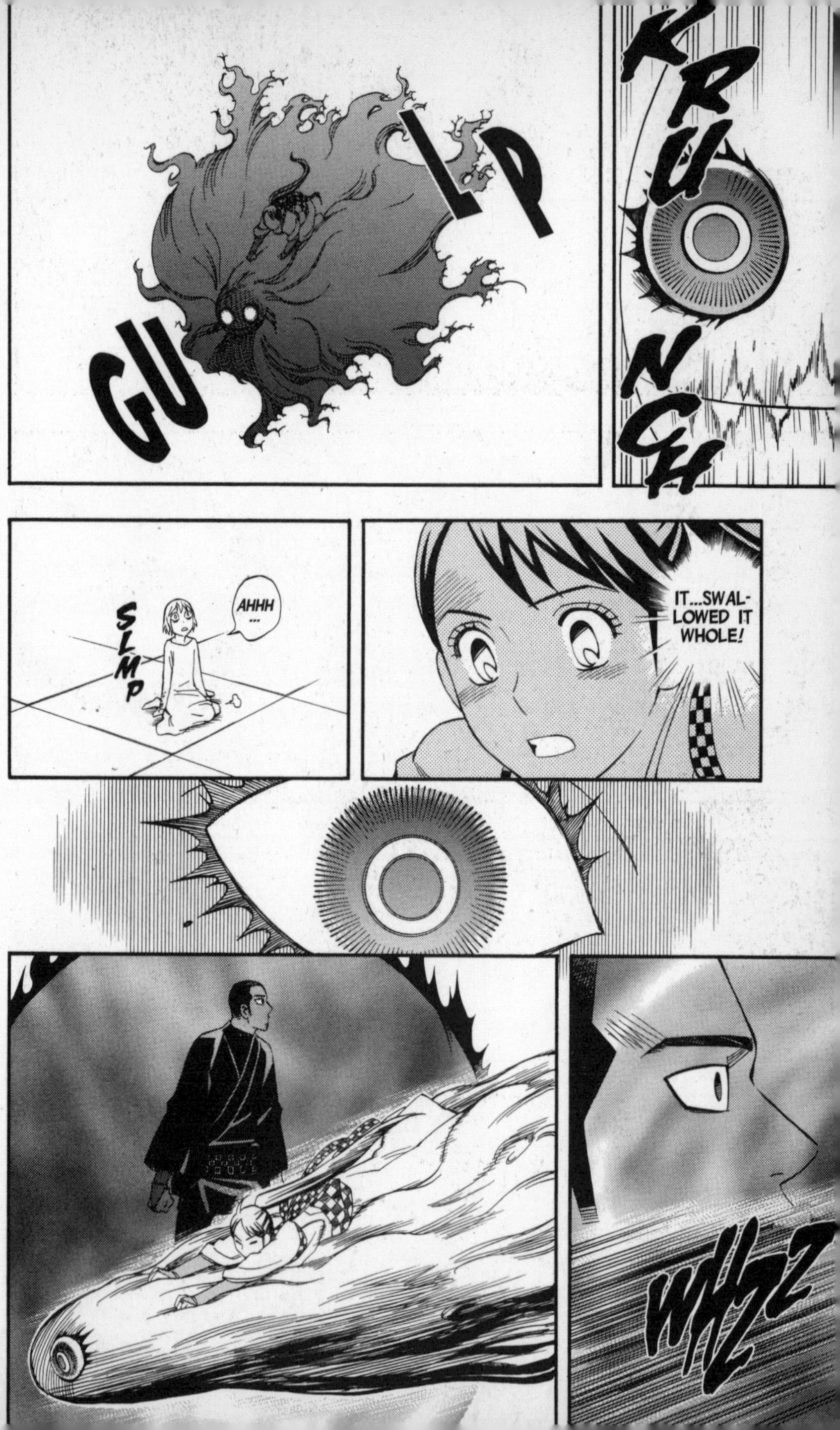
KRUNCH
GULP
IT...SWAL-
LOWED IT
WHOLE!
SLMP
AHHH
...
WHZZ

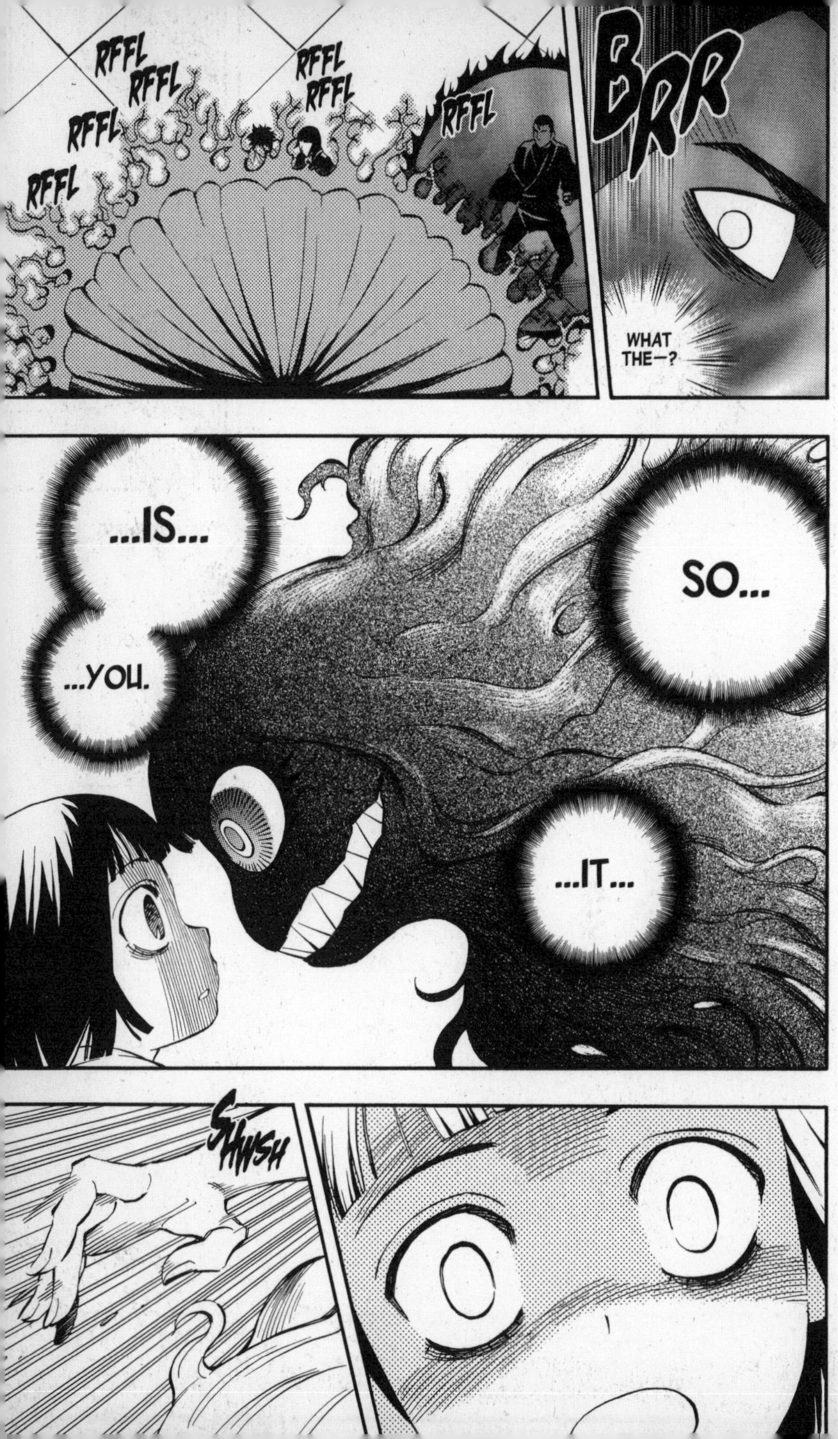
BRR
WHAT THE—?
RFFL
RFFL
RFFL
RFFL
RFFL
RFFL
SO...
...IT...
...IS...
...YOU.
SHWSH

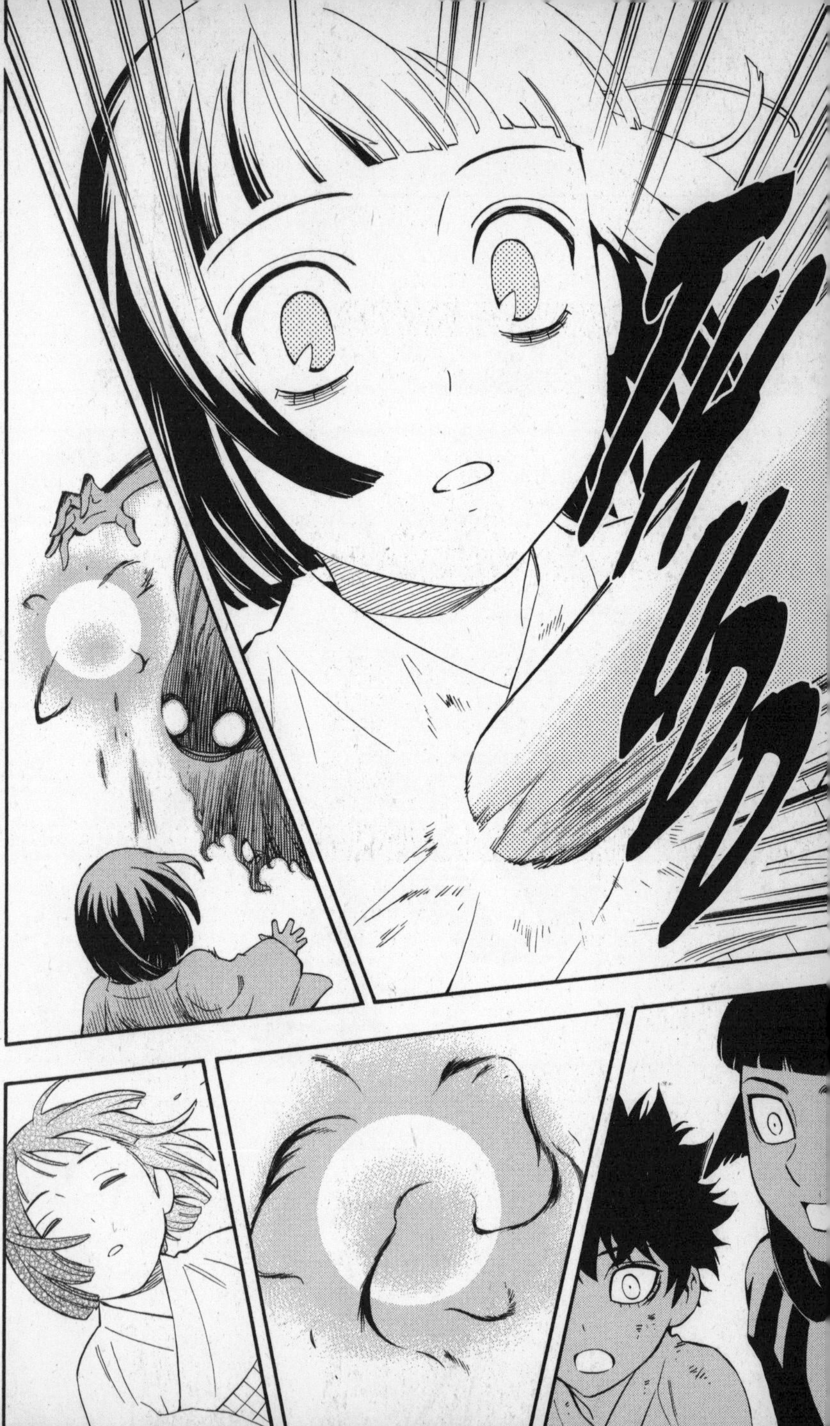

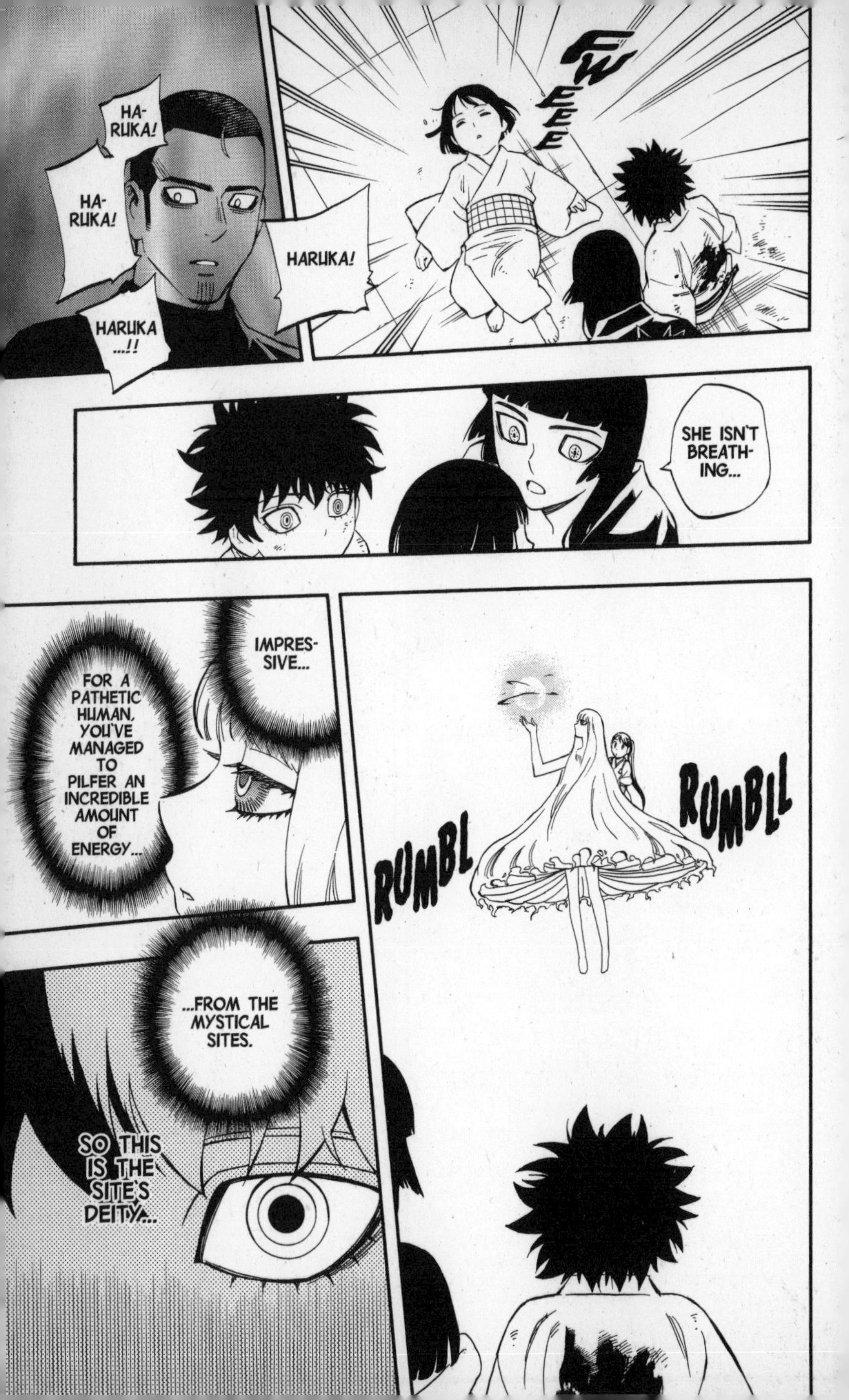
FWEEEE
HA-RUKA!
HA-RUKA!
HARUKA!
HARUKA ...!!
SHE ISN'T BREATH-ING...
RUMBLL
RUMBL
IMPRES-SIVE...
FOR A PATHETIC HUMAN, YOU'VE MANAGED TO PILFER AN INCREDIBLE AMOUNT OF ENERGY...
...FROM THE MYSTICAL SITES.
SO THIS IS THE SITE'S DEITY...

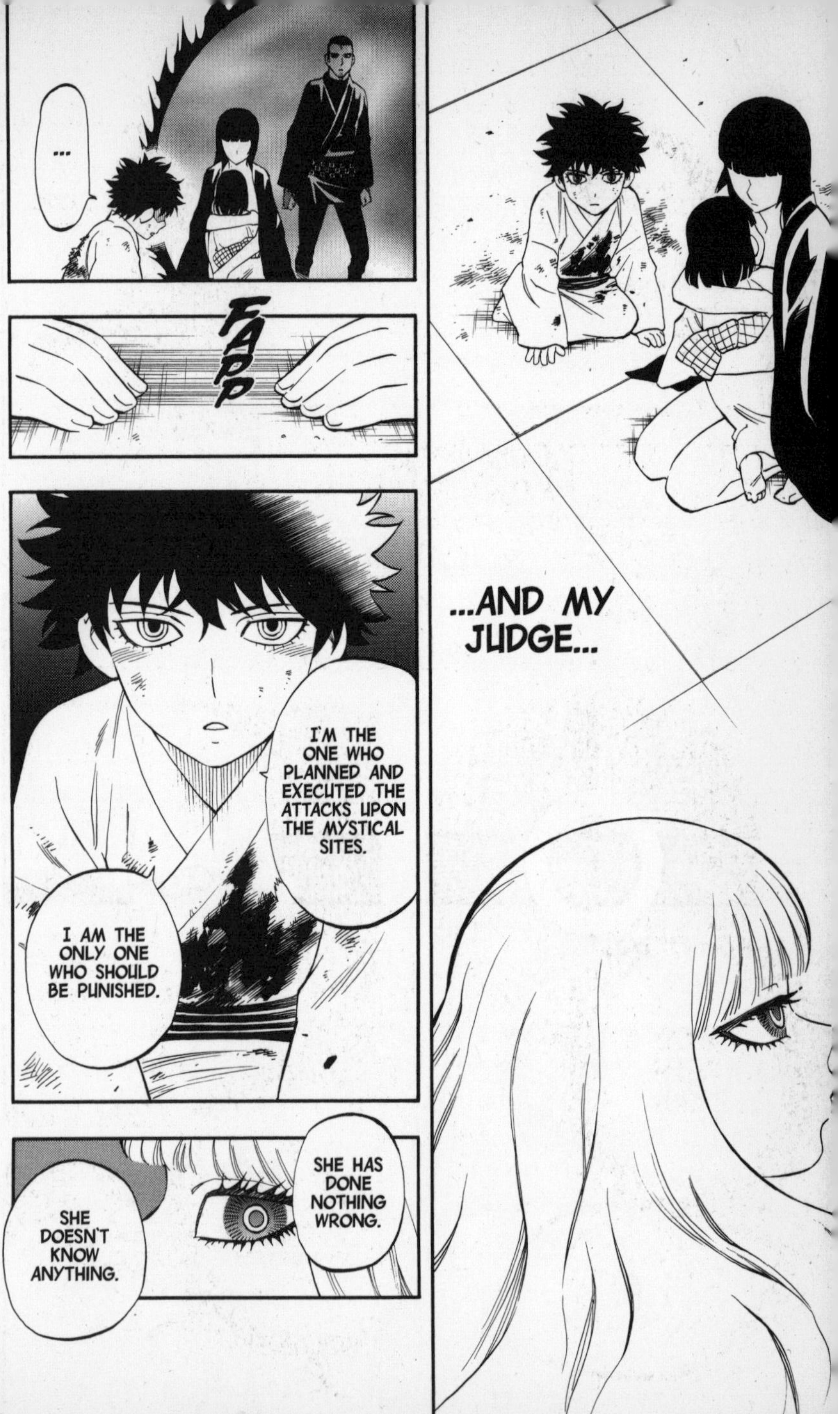
...AND MY JUDGE...
...
FAPP
I'M THE ONE WHO PLANNED AND EXECUTED THE ATTACKS UPON THE MYSTICAL SITES.
I AM THE ONLY ONE WHO SHOULD BE PUNISHED.
SHE HAS DONE NOTHING WRONG.
SHE DOESN'T KNOW ANYTHING.

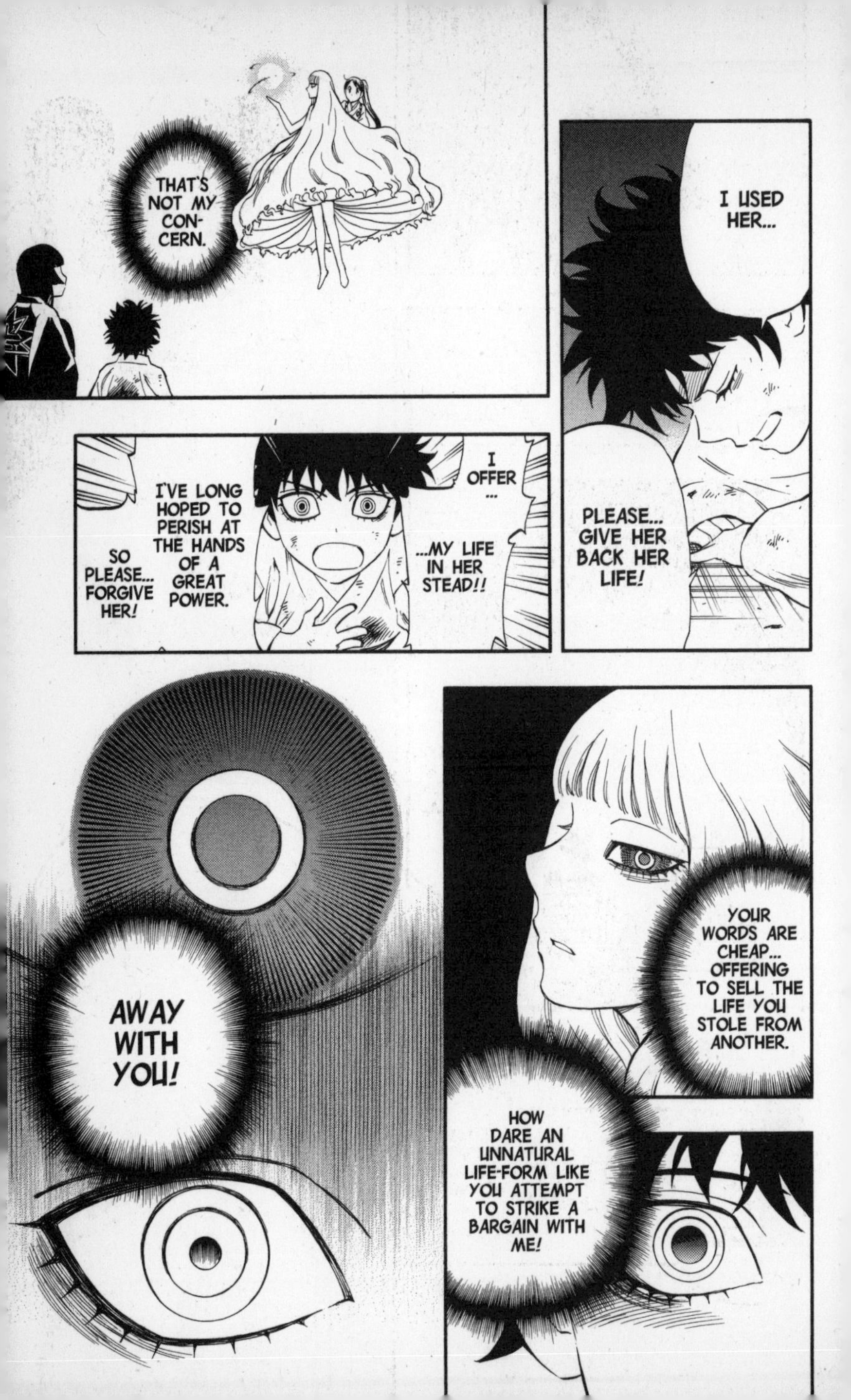
THAT'S NOT MY CON-CERN.
I USED HER...
PLEASE... GIVE HER BACK HER LIFE!
I OFFER ...
...MY LIFE IN HER STEAD!!
I'VE LONG HOPED TO PERISH AT THE HANDS OF A GREAT POWER.
SO PLEASE... FORGIVE HER!
YOUR WORDS ARE CHEAP... OFFERING TO SELL THE LIFE YOU STOLE FROM ANOTHER.
HOW DARE AN UNNATURAL LIFE-FORM LIKE YOU ATTEMPT TO STRIKE A BARGAIN WITH ME!
AWAY WITH YOU!

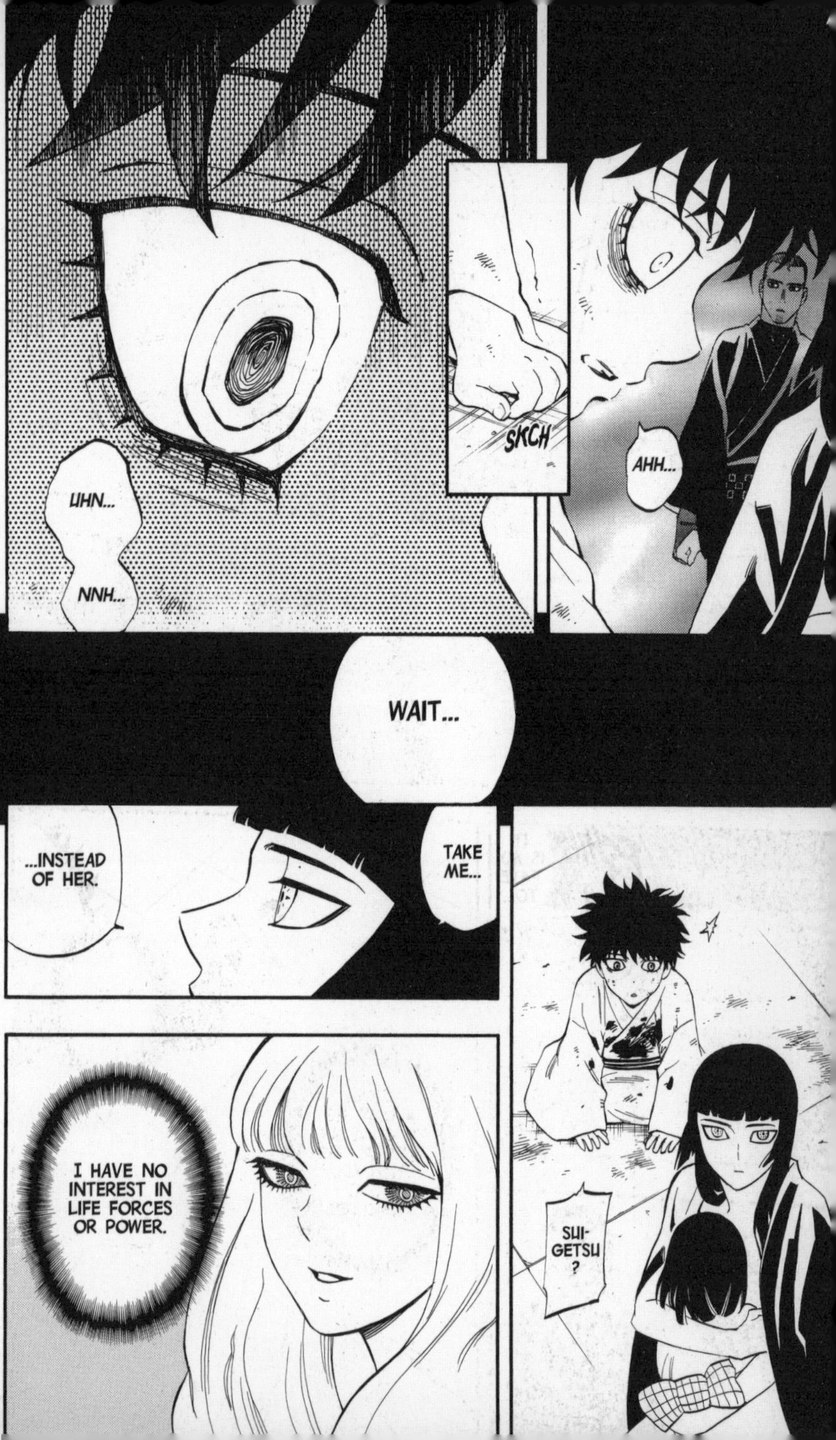
AHH...
SKCH
UHN...
NNH...
WAIT...
SUI-GETSU?
TAKE ME...
...INSTEAD OF HER.
I HAVE NO INTEREST IN LIFE FORCES OR POWER.

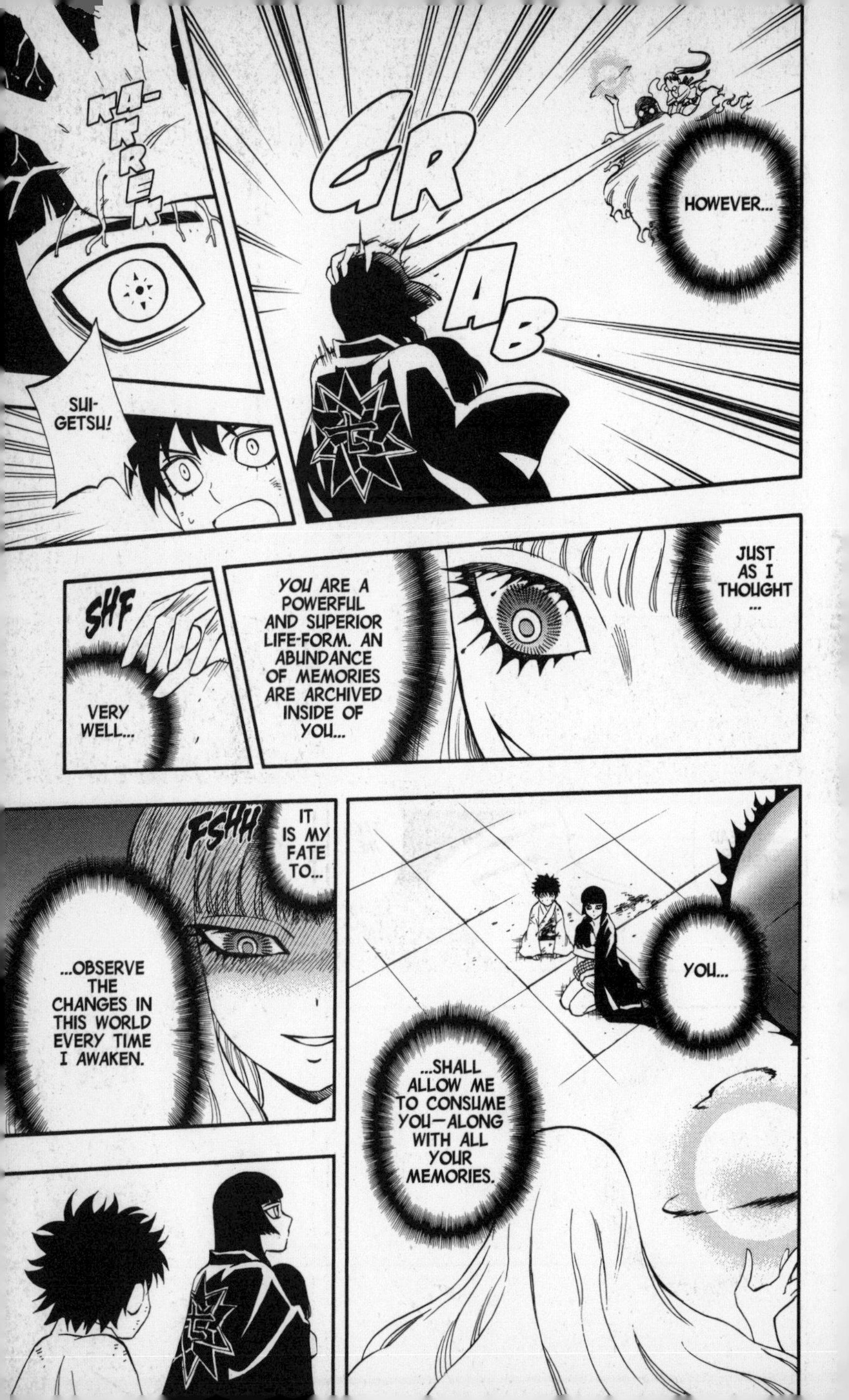
HOWEVER...
GRAB
KA-KREK
SUI-GETSU!
JUST AS I THOUGHT...
YOU ARE A POWERFUL AND SUPERIOR LIFE-FORM. AN ABUNDANCE OF MEMORIES ARE ARCHIVED INSIDE OF YOU...
SHF
VERY WELL...
YOU...
...SHALL ALLOW ME TO CONSUME YOU—ALONG WITH ALL YOUR MEMORIES.
FSHH
IT IS MY FATE TO...
...OBSERVE THE CHANGES IN THIS WORLD EVERY TIME I AWAKEN.

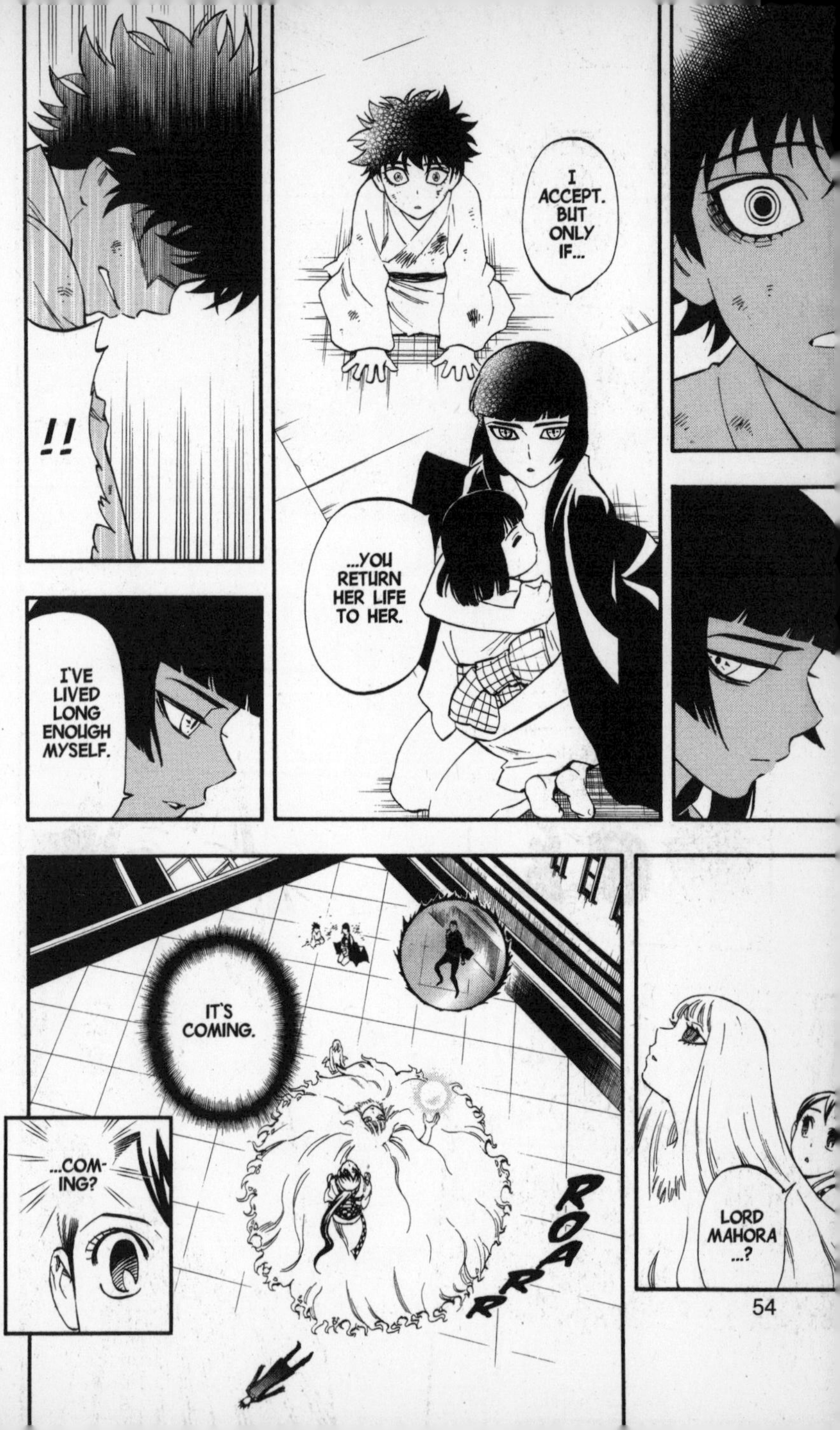
I ACCEPT. BUT ONLY IF...
...YOU RETURN HER LIFE TO HER.
!!
I'VE LIVED LONG ENOUGH MYSELF.
LORD MAHORA ...?
IT'S COMING.
ROARRR
...COM- ING?

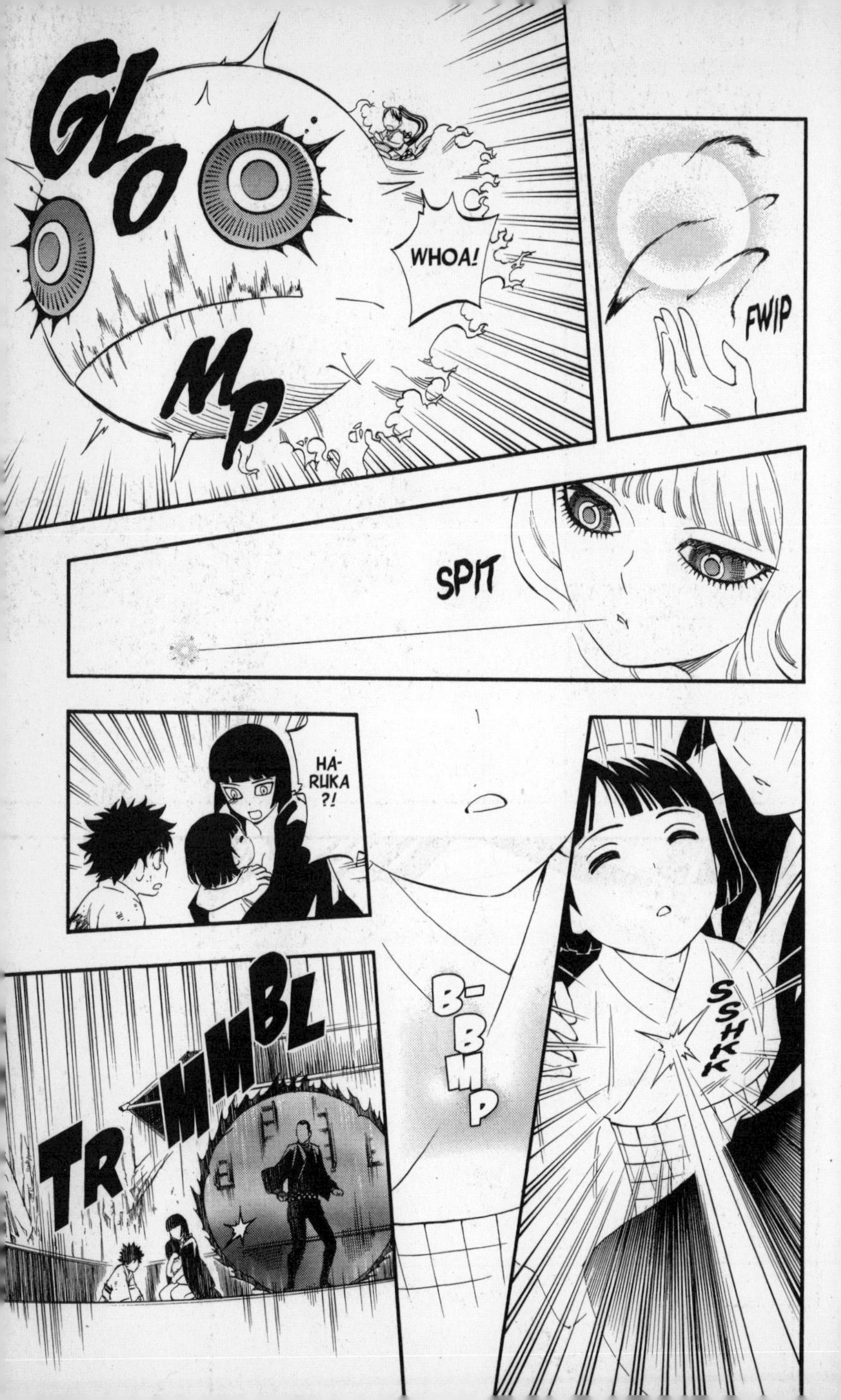
FWIP
GLOOMP
WHOA!
SPIT
SSHKK
B-BMP
HA-RUKA?!
TRMMBL

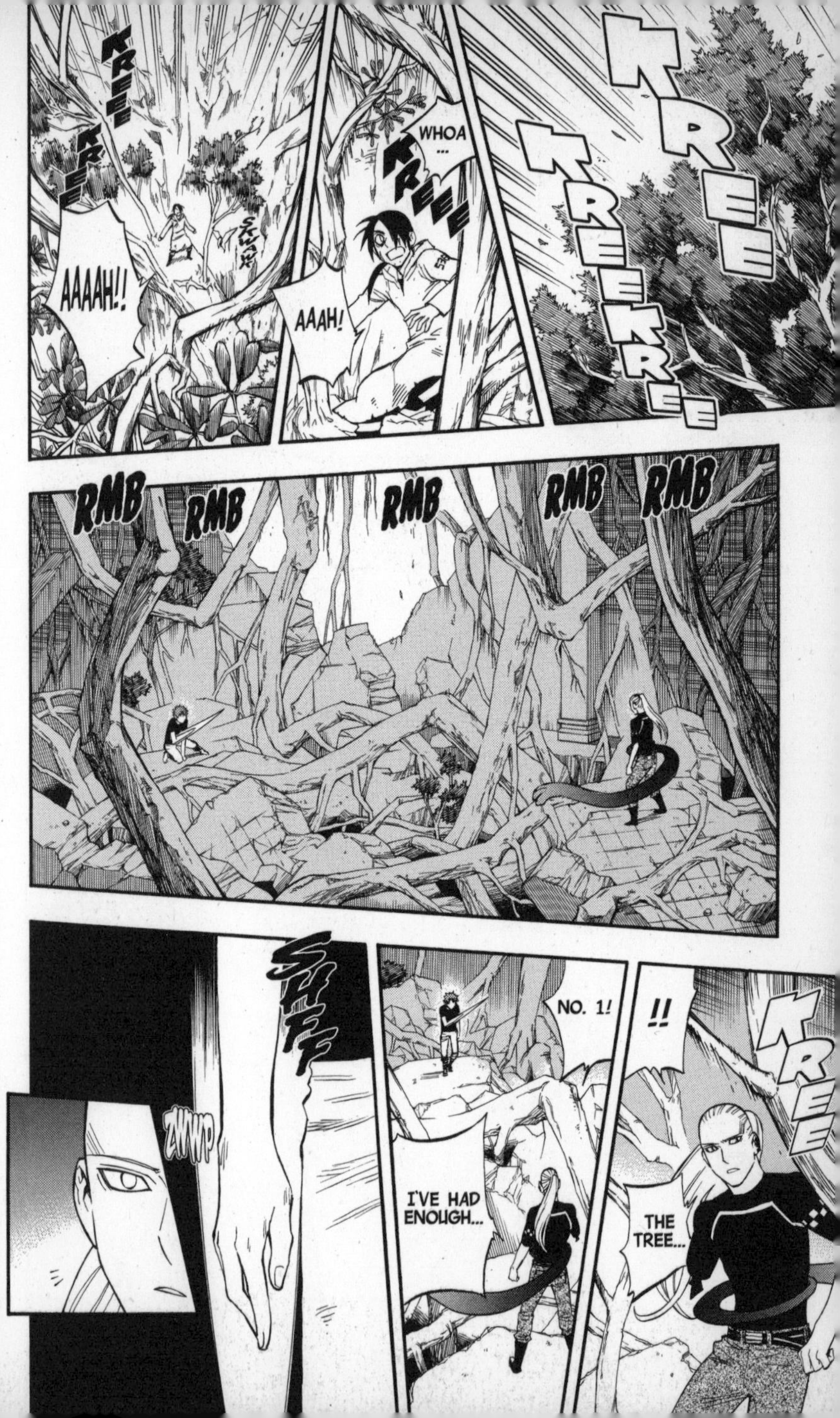

KREE
KREEKREE
WHOA...
KREEE
AAAH!
KREEE
KREE
SKWAWK
AAAAH!!
RMB
RMB
RMB
RMB
RMB
KREE
!!
THE TREE...
NO. 1!
I'VE HAD ENOUGH...
SHFF
ZWWP

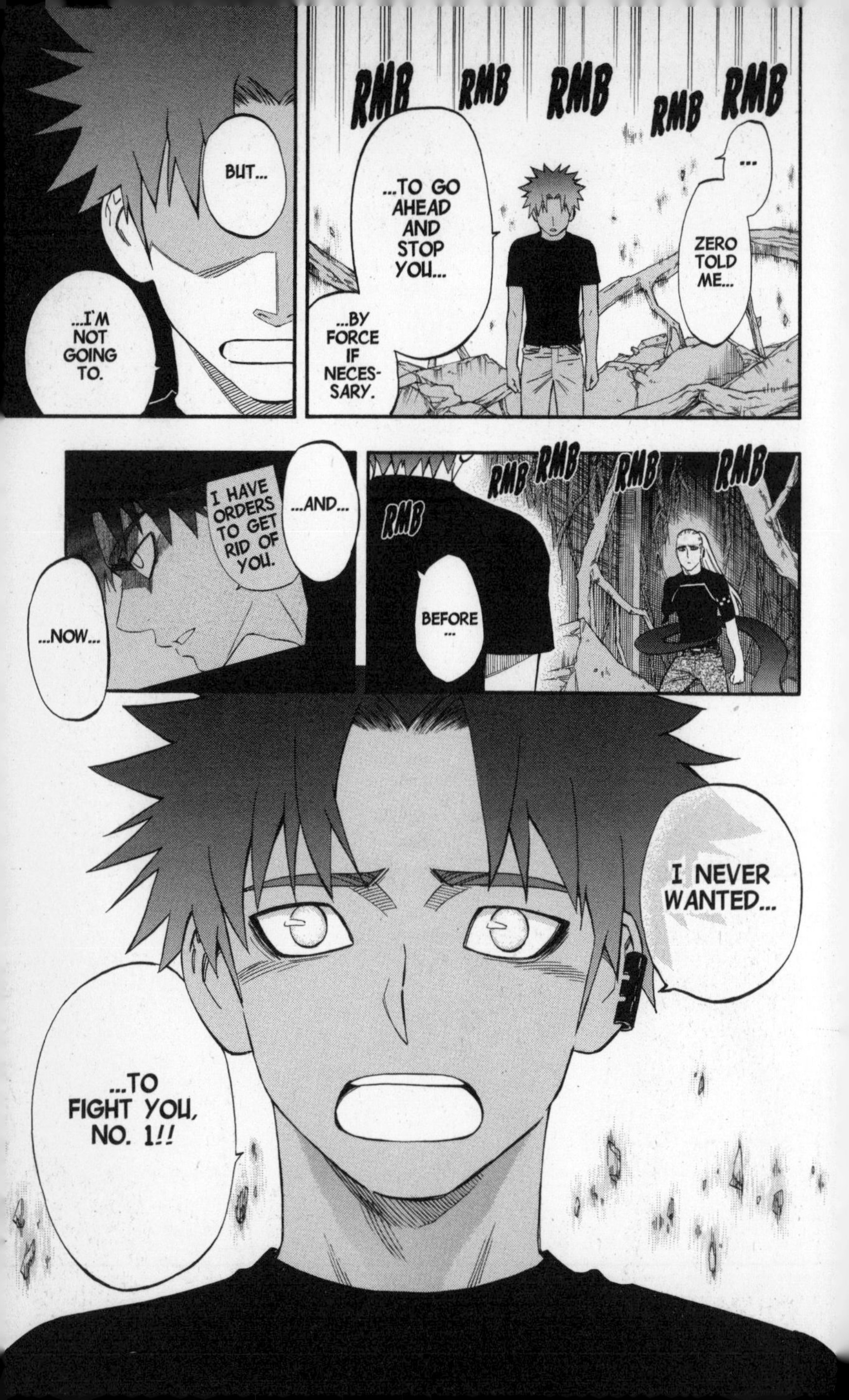
RMB RMB RMB RMB RMB
...
ZERO TOLD ME...
...TO GO AHEAD AND STOP YOU...
...BY FORCE IF NECESSARY.
BUT...
...I'M NOT GOING TO.
RMB RMB RMB RMB
RMB
BEFORE ...
...AND...
I HAVE ORDERS TO GET RID OF YOU.
...NOW...
I NEVER WANTED...
...TO FIGHT YOU, NO. 1!!

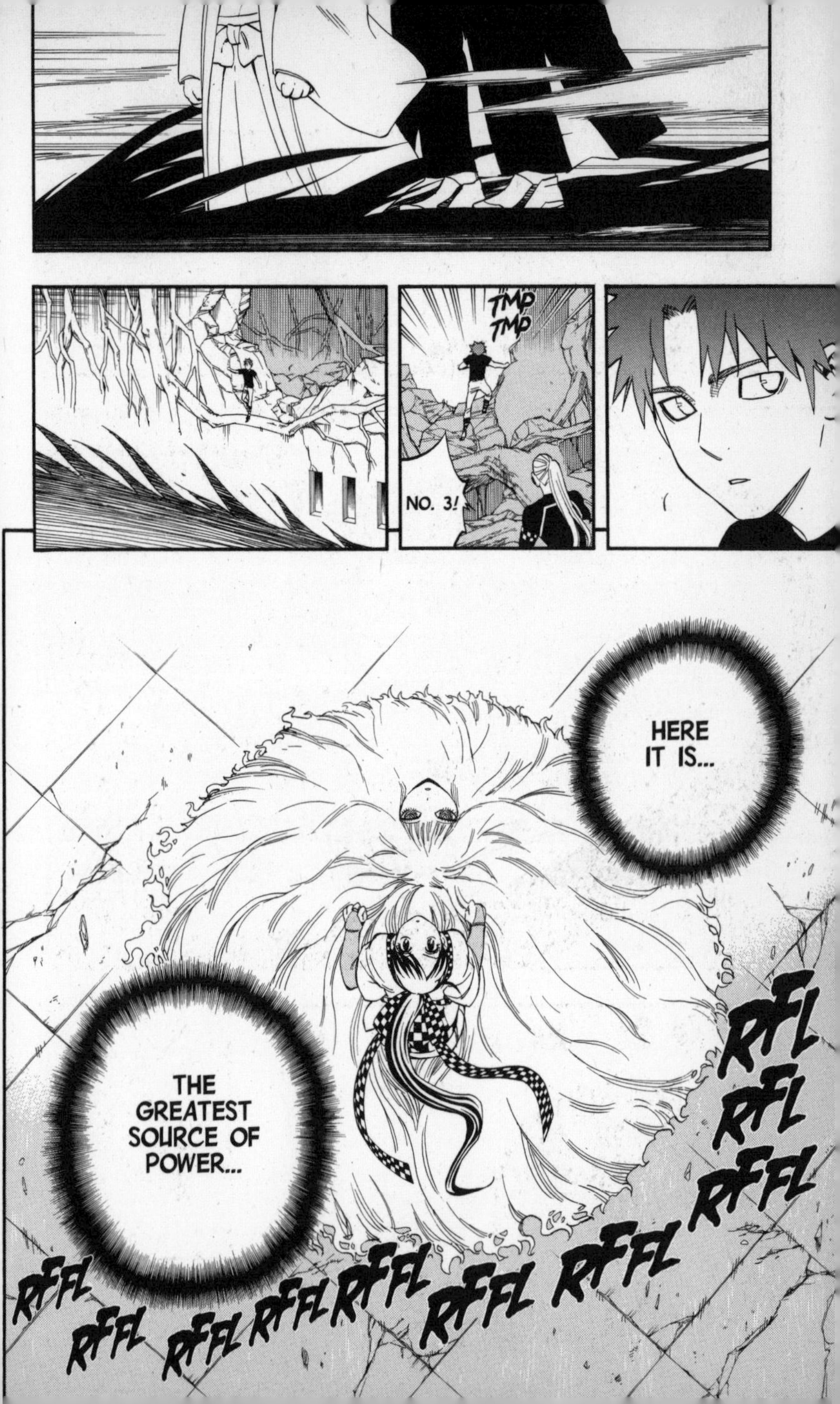
TMP TMP
NO. 3!
HERE IT IS...
THE GREATEST SOURCE OF POWER...
RFFL RFFL RFFL
RFFL RFFL RFFL
RFFL RFFL RFFL RFFL RFFL

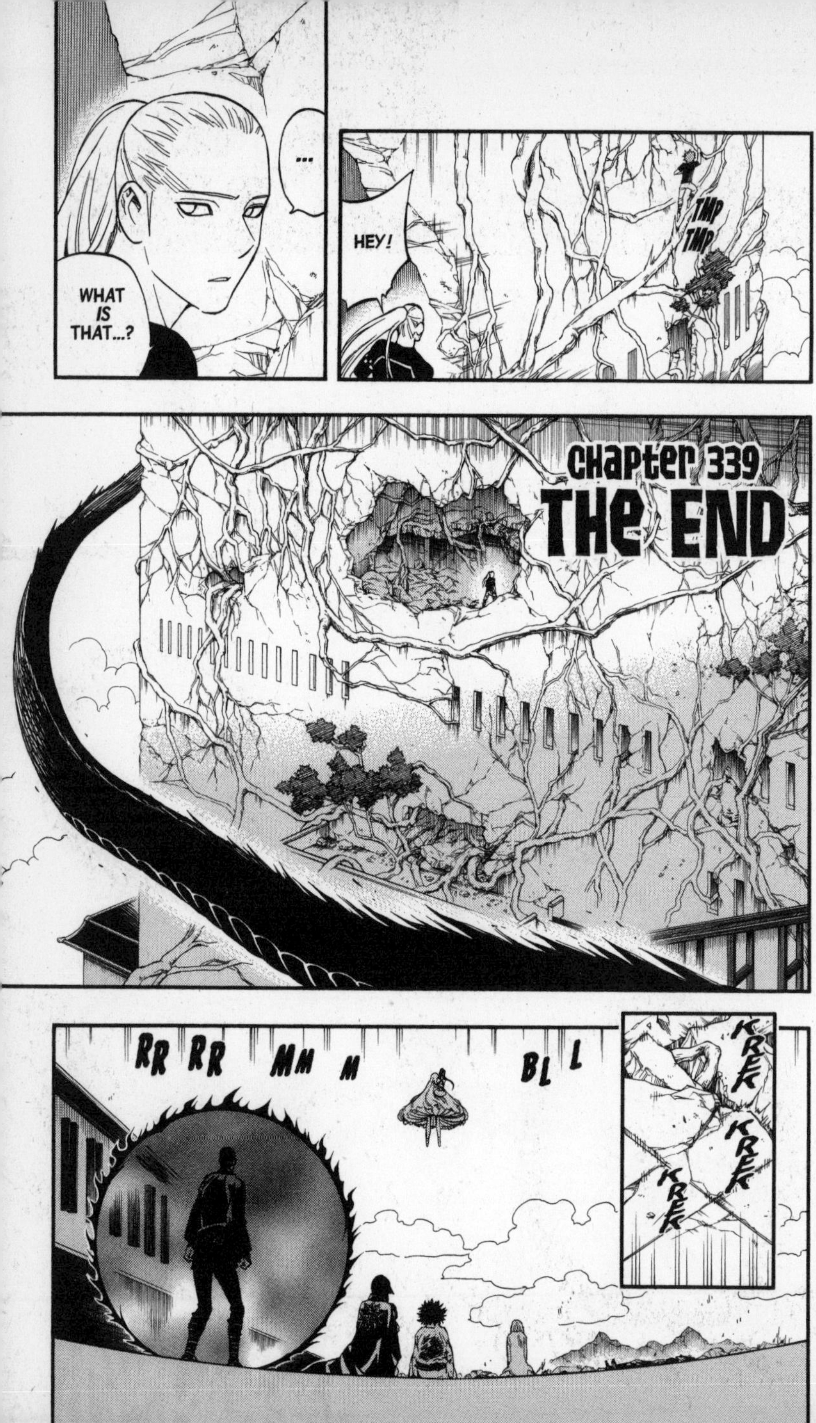
HEY!
TMP TMP
...
WHAT IS THAT...?
Chapter 339
THE END
KREK KREK KREK
RR RR MM M BL L

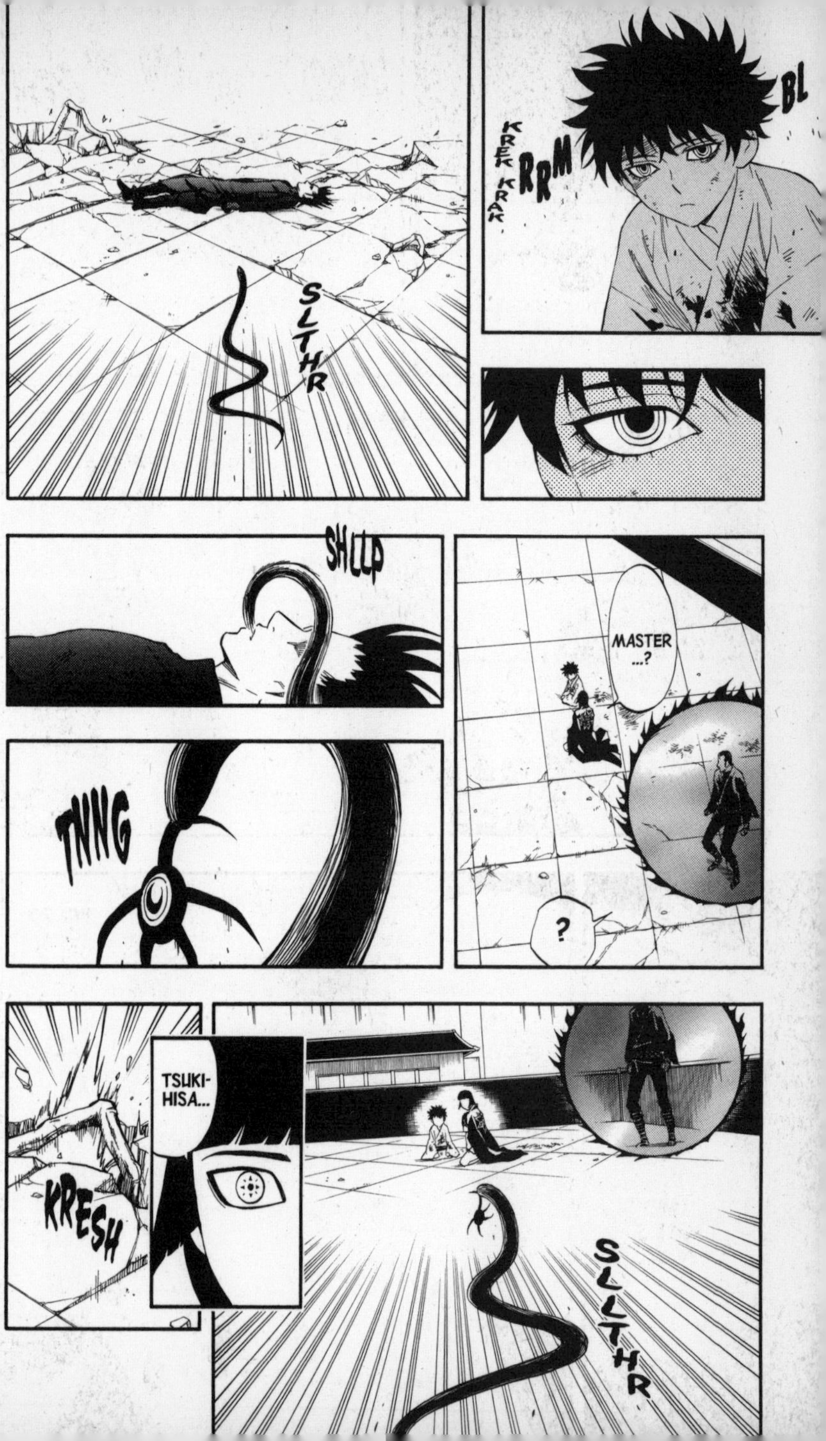
BL
RRRM
KREK KRAK
SLTHR
MASTER ...?
?
SHLLP
TNNG
SLLTHR
TSUKI-HISA...
KRESH

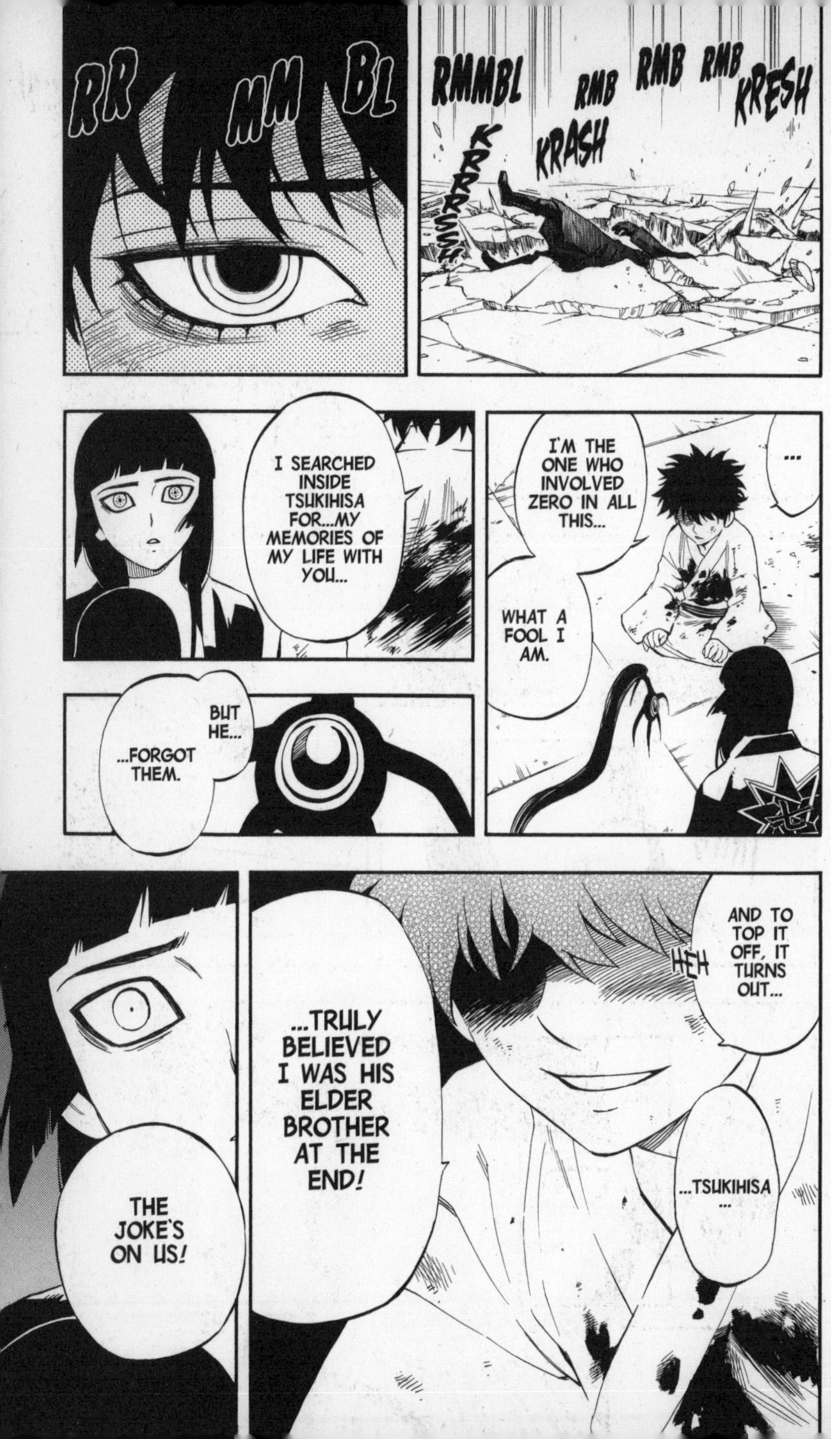
RMMBL
RMB
RMB
RMB
KRESH
KRASH
KRRRRSSH
RR MM BL
...
I'M THE ONE WHO INVOLVED ZERO IN ALL THIS...
WHAT A FOOL I AM.
I SEARCHED INSIDE TSUKIHISA FOR...MY MEMORIES OF MY LIFE WITH YOU...
BUT HE...
...FORGOT THEM.
AND TO TOP IT OFF, IT TURNS OUT...
HEH
...TRULY BELIEVED I WAS HIS ELDER BROTHER AT THE END!
...TSUKIHISA...
THE JOKE'S ON US!

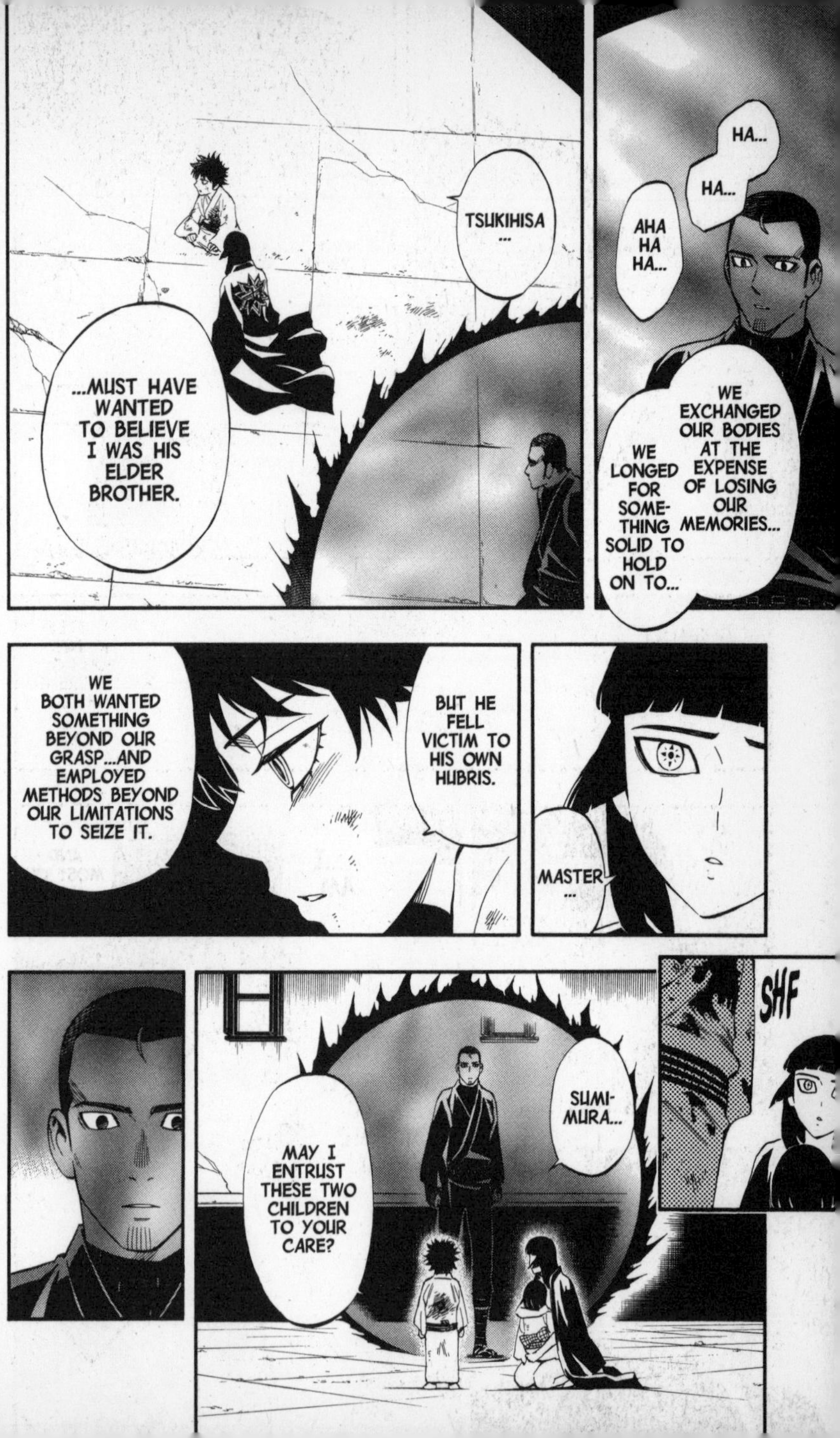
HA...
HA...
AHA HA HA...
WE EXCHANGED OUR BODIES AT THE EXPENSE OF LOSING OUR MEMORIES...
WE LONGED FOR SOMETHING SOLID TO HOLD ON TO...
TSUKIHISA...
...MUST HAVE WANTED TO BELIEVE I WAS HIS ELDER BROTHER.
MASTER...
BUT HE FELL VICTIM TO HIS OWN HUBRIS.
WE BOTH WANTED SOMETHING BEYOND OUR GRASP...AND EMPLOYED METHODS BEYOND OUR LIMITATIONS TO SEIZE IT.
SHF
SUMIMURA...
MAY I ENTRUST THESE TWO CHILDREN TO YOUR CARE?

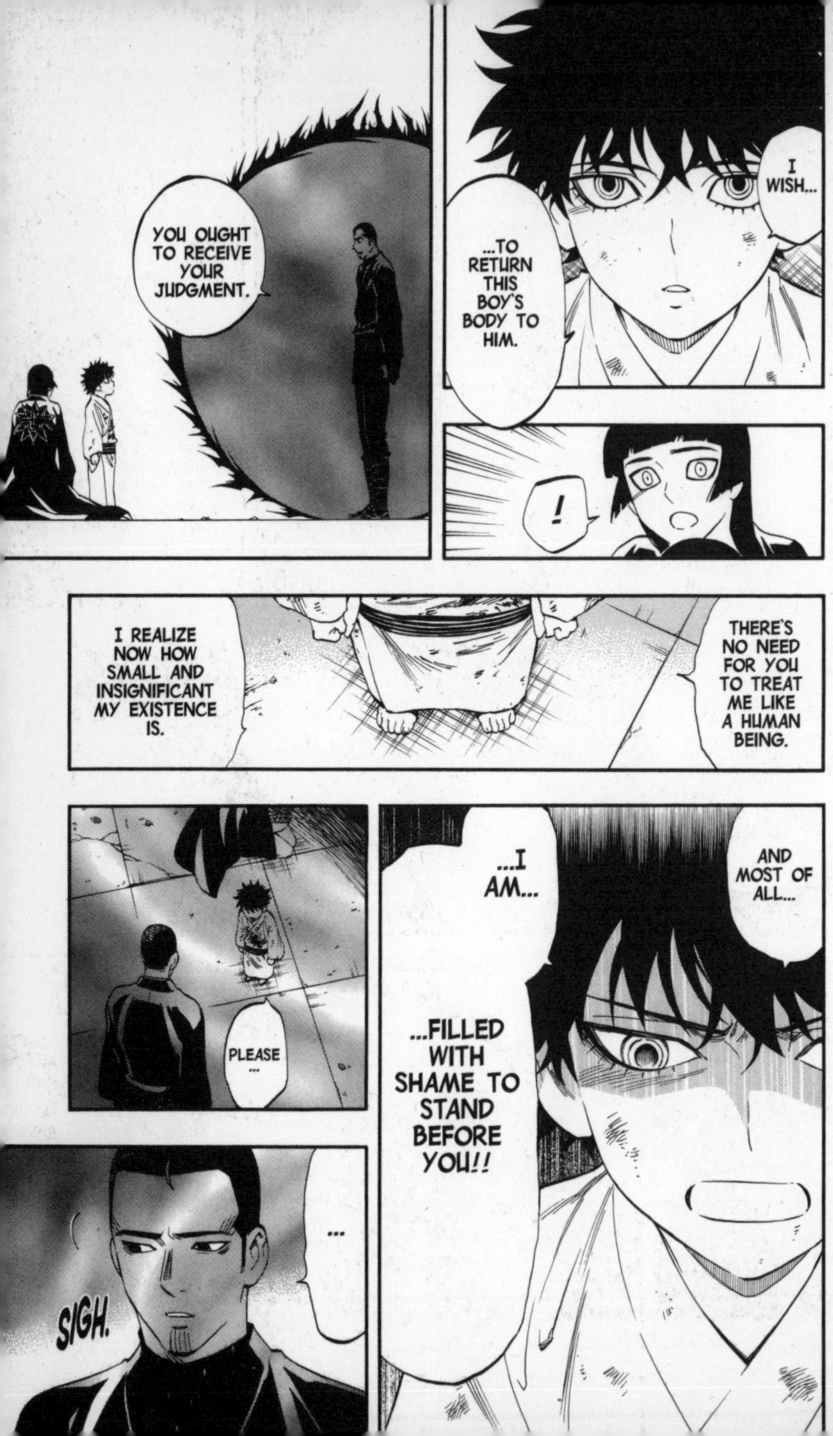
I WISH...
...TO RETURN THIS BOY'S BODY TO HIM.
!
YOU OUGHT TO RECEIVE YOUR JUDGMENT.
THERE'S NO NEED FOR YOU TO TREAT ME LIKE A HUMAN BEING.
I REALIZE NOW HOW SMALL AND INSIGNIFICANT MY EXISTENCE IS.
AND MOST OF ALL...
...I AM...
...FILLED WITH SHAME TO STAND BEFORE YOU!!
PLEASE...
...
SIGH.

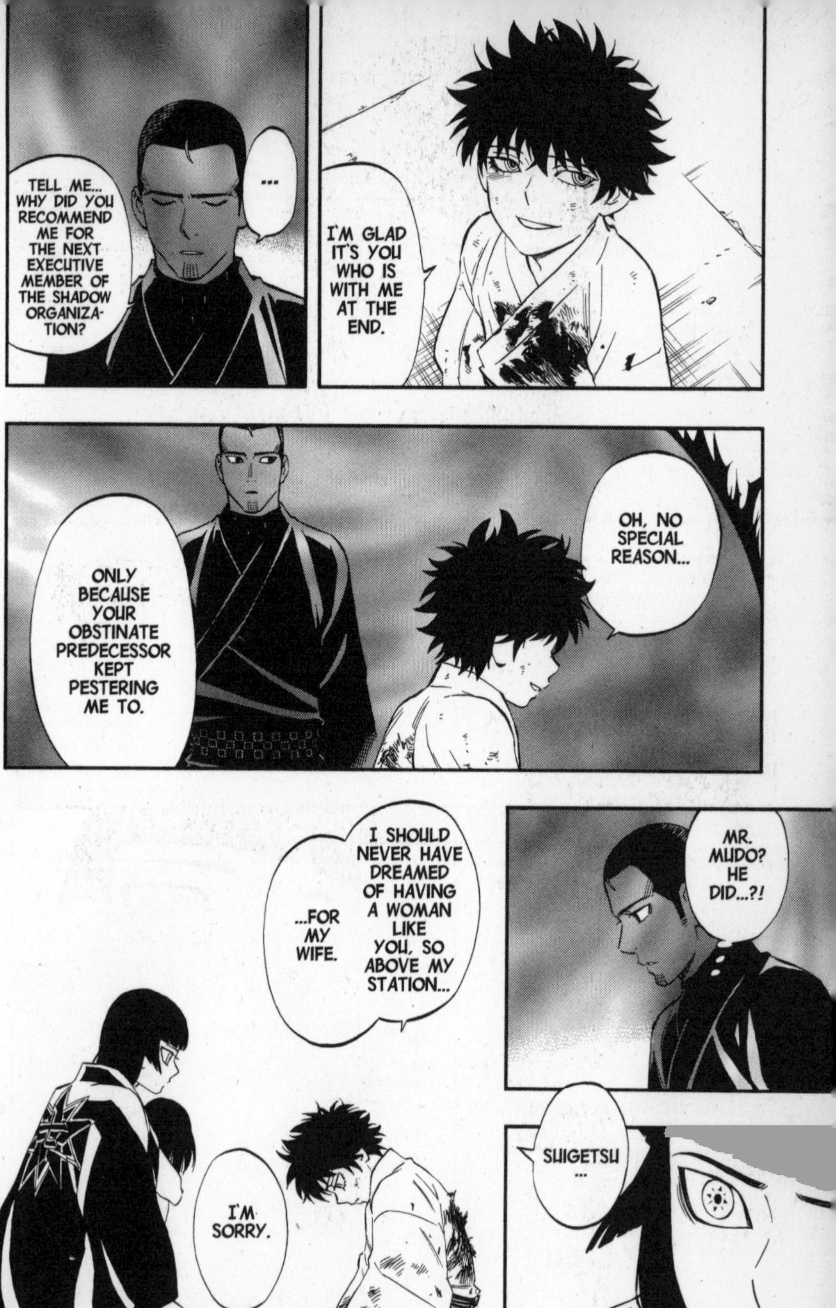
I'M GLAD IT'S YOU WHO IS WITH ME AT THE END.
...
TELL ME... WHY DID YOU RECOMMEND ME FOR THE NEXT EXECUTIVE MEMBER OF THE SHADOW ORGANIZATION?
OH, NO SPECIAL REASON...
ONLY BECAUSE YOUR OBSTINATE PREDECESSOR KEPT PESTERING ME TO.
MR. MUDO? HE DID...?!
SUIGETSU...
I SHOULD NEVER HAVE DREAMED OF HAVING A WOMAN LIKE YOU, SO ABOVE MY STATION...
...FOR MY WIFE.
I'M SORRY.

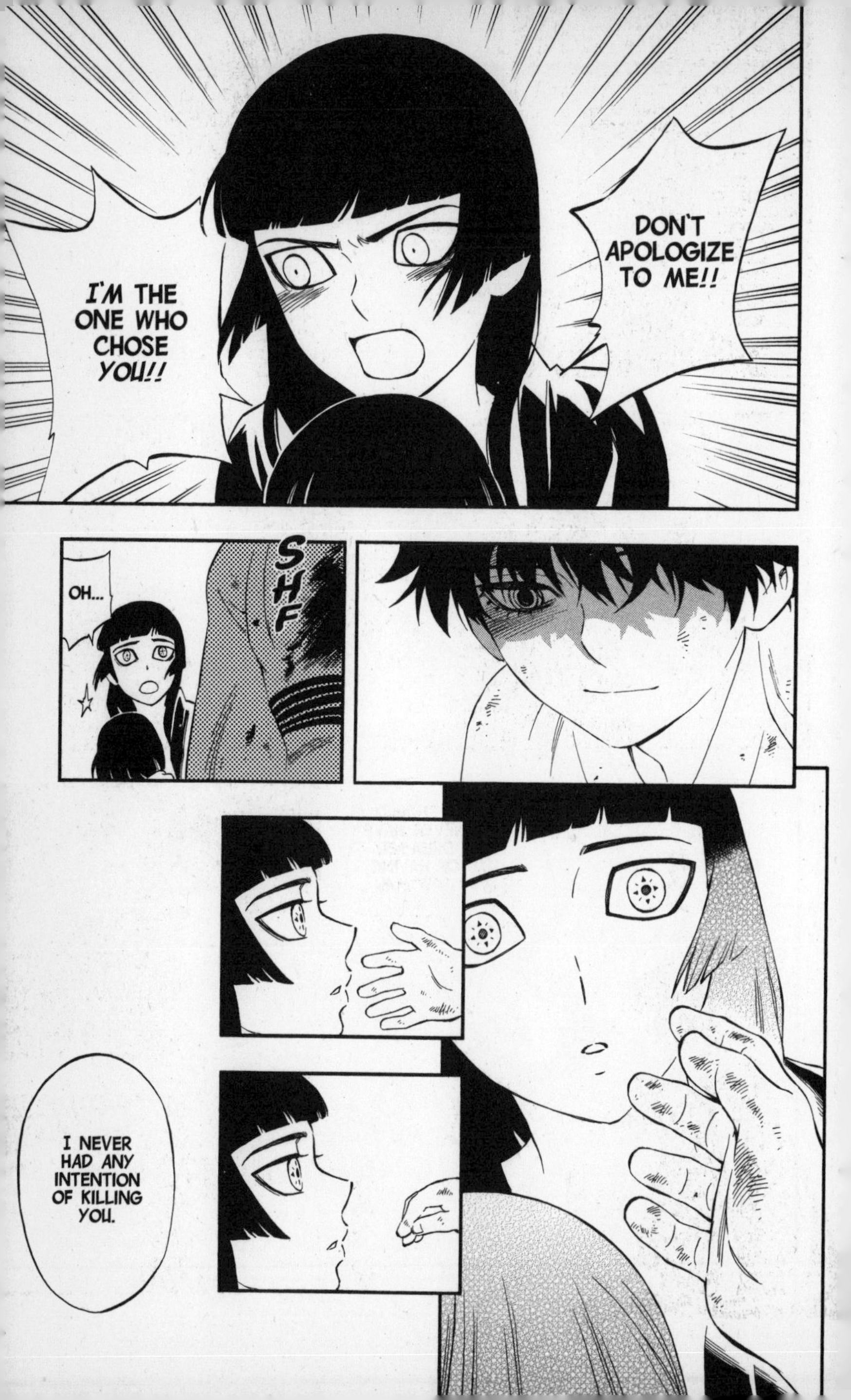
DON'T APOLOGIZE TO ME!!
I'M THE ONE WHO CHOSE YOU!!
SHF
OH...
I NEVER HAD ANY INTENTION OF KILLING YOU.

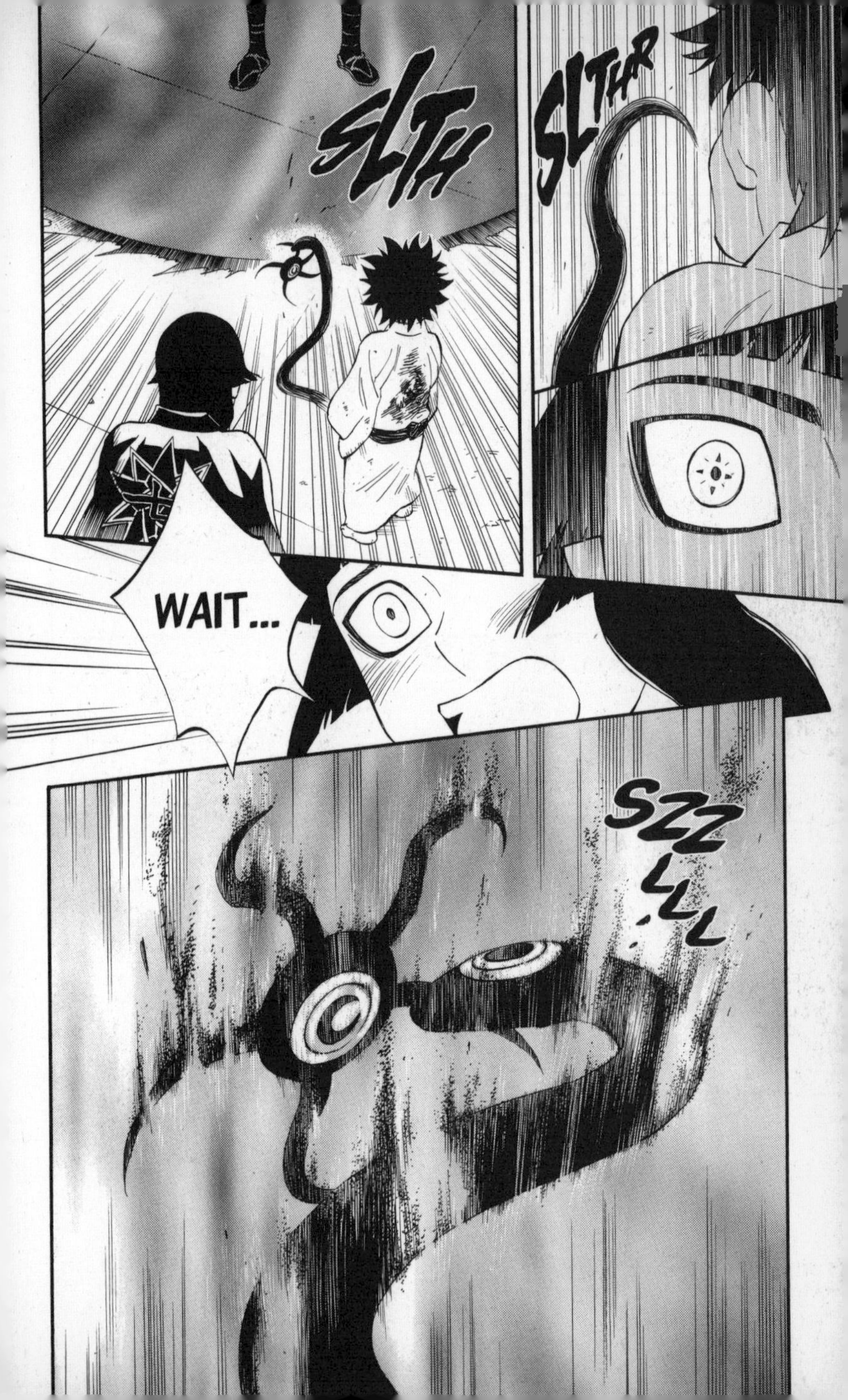
SLTHR
SLTH
WAIT...
SZZLLL

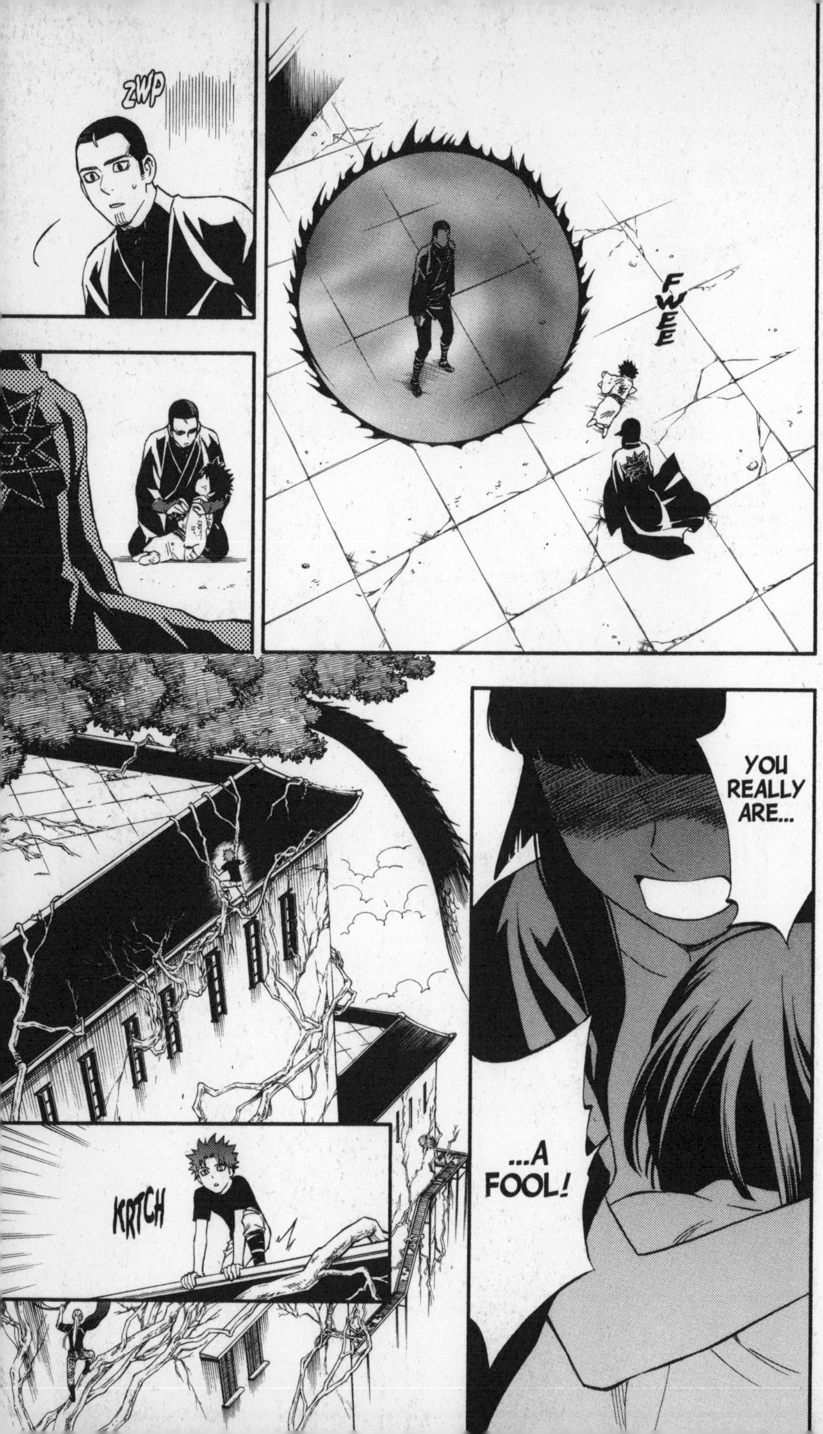
FWEE
ZWP
YOU REALLY ARE...
...A FOOL!
KRTCH

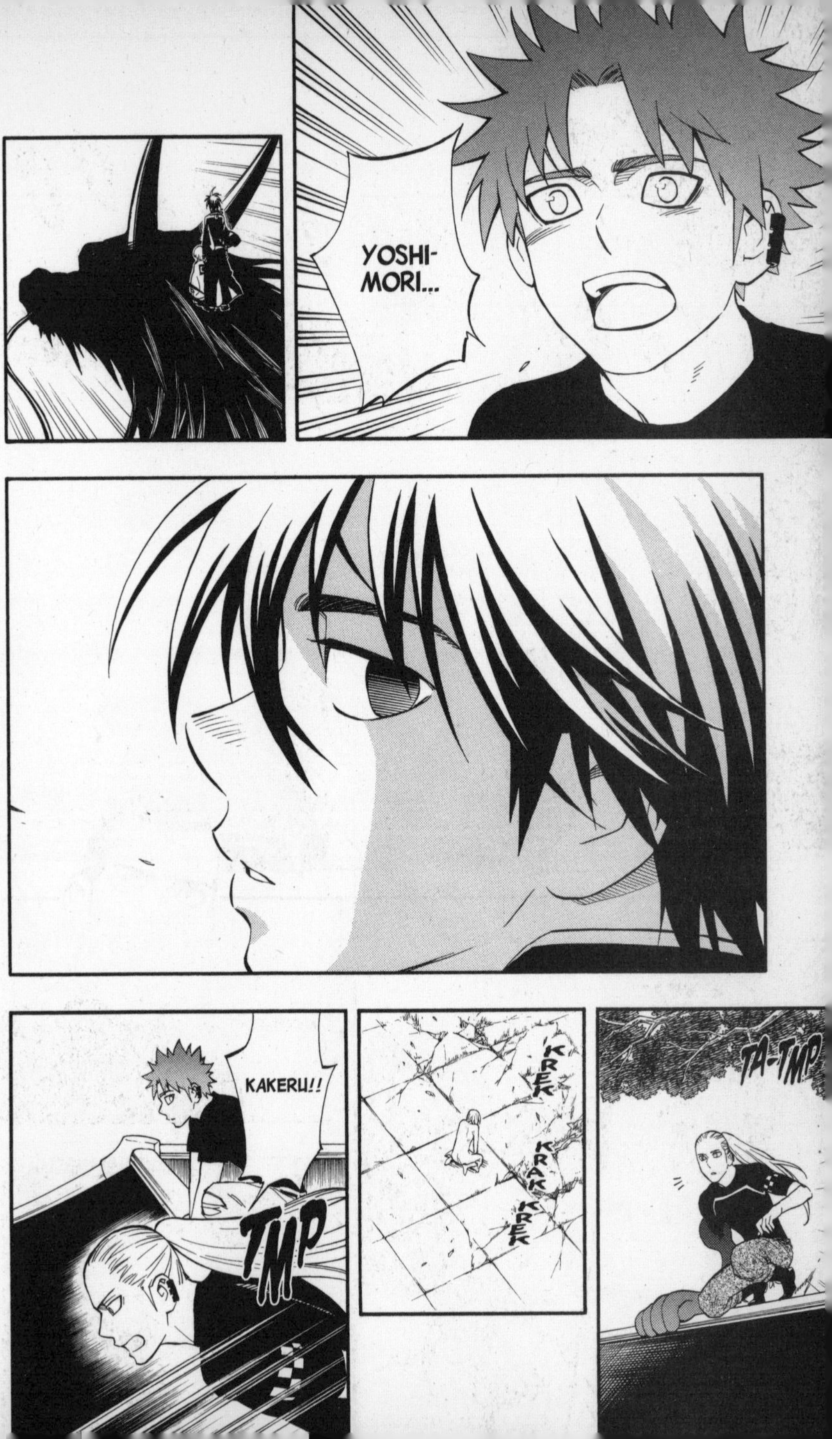
YOSHI-
MORI...
TA-TMP
KREK
KRAK
KREK
KAKERU!!
TMP

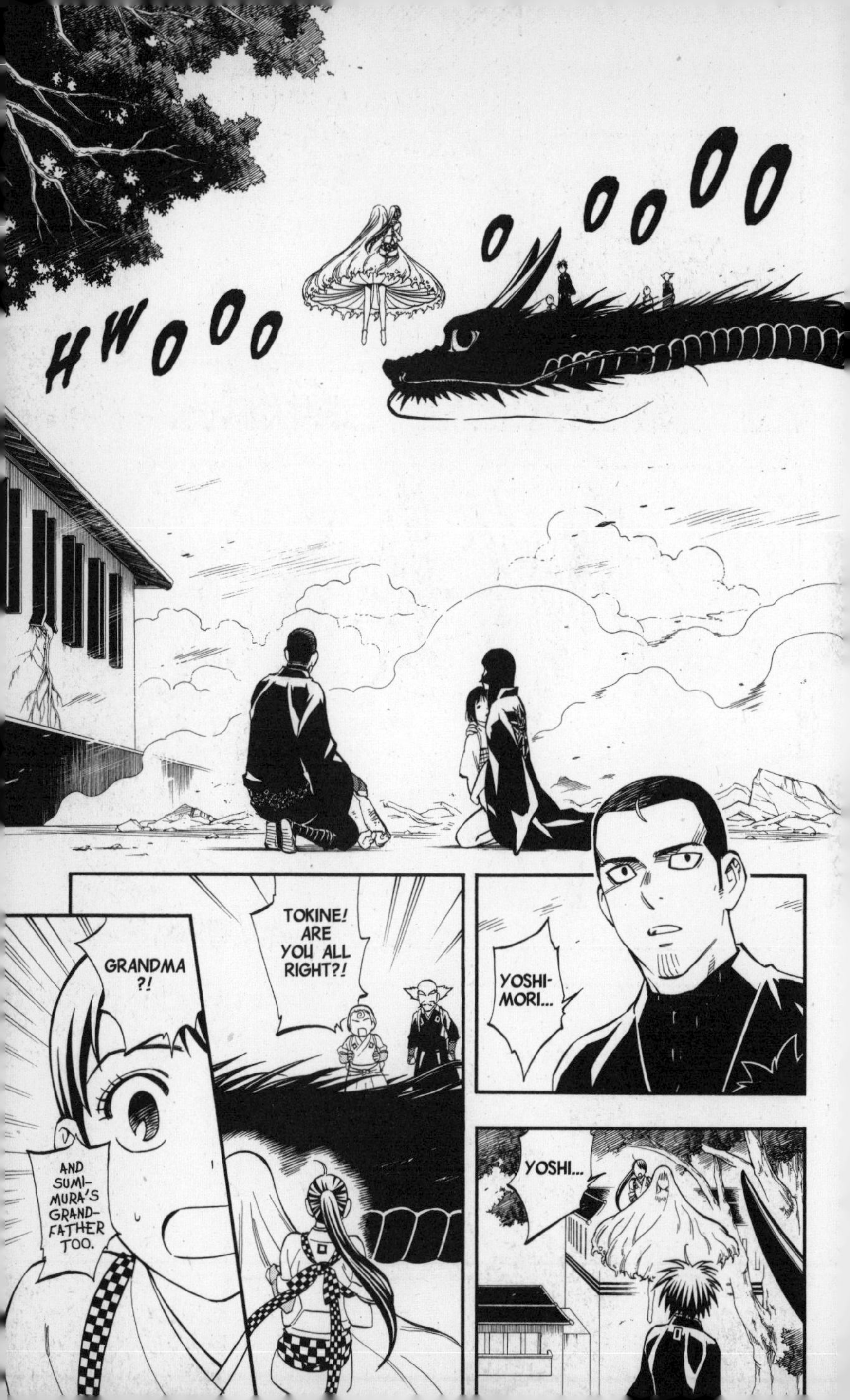
HWOOOOOOOOO
YOSHI-MORI...
YOSHI...
TOKINE! ARE YOU ALL RIGHT?!
GRANDMA?!
AND SUMI-MURA'S GRAND-FATHER TOO.

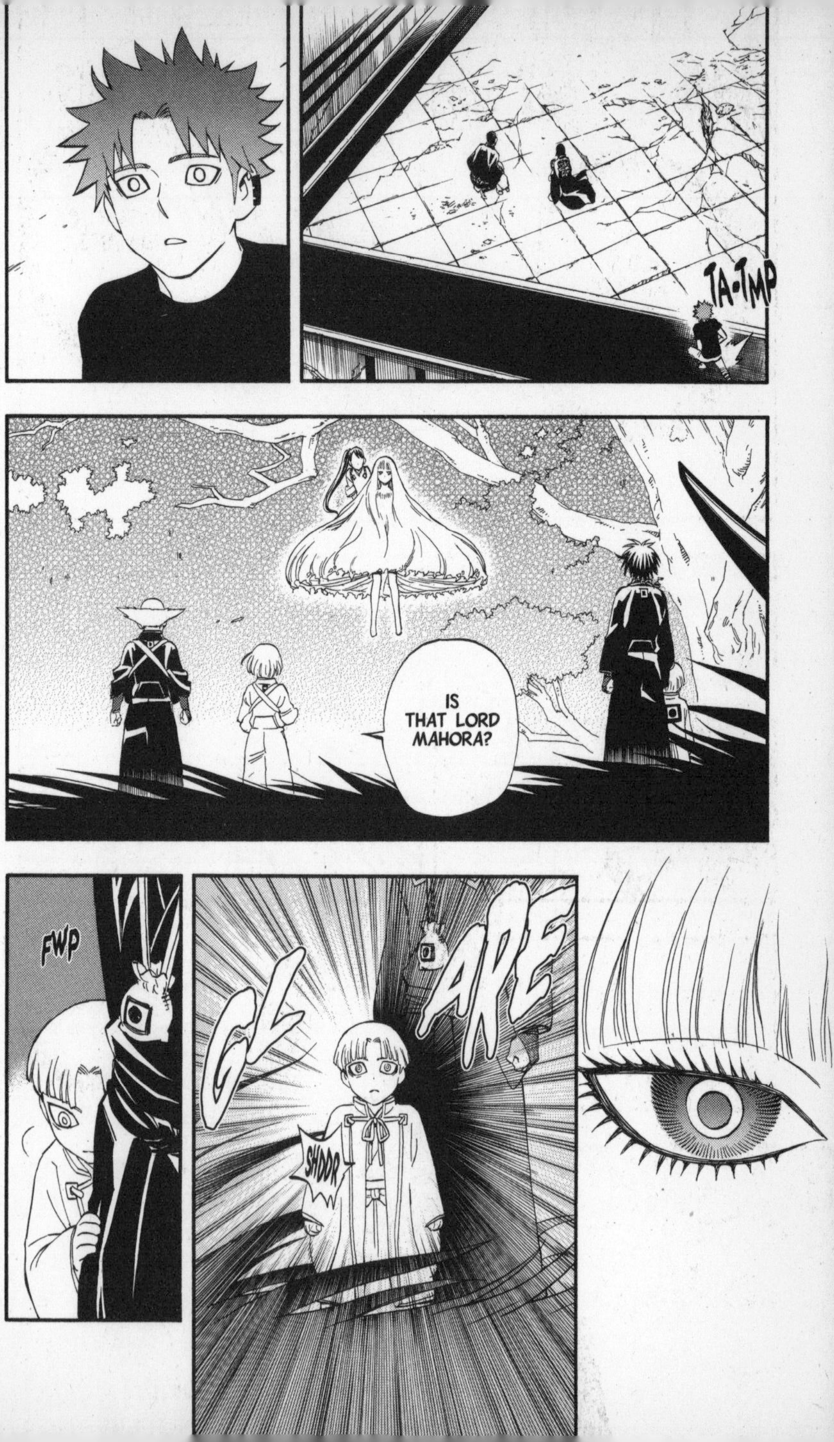
TA-TMP
IS THAT LORD MAHORA?
GL ARE
SHDDR
FWP

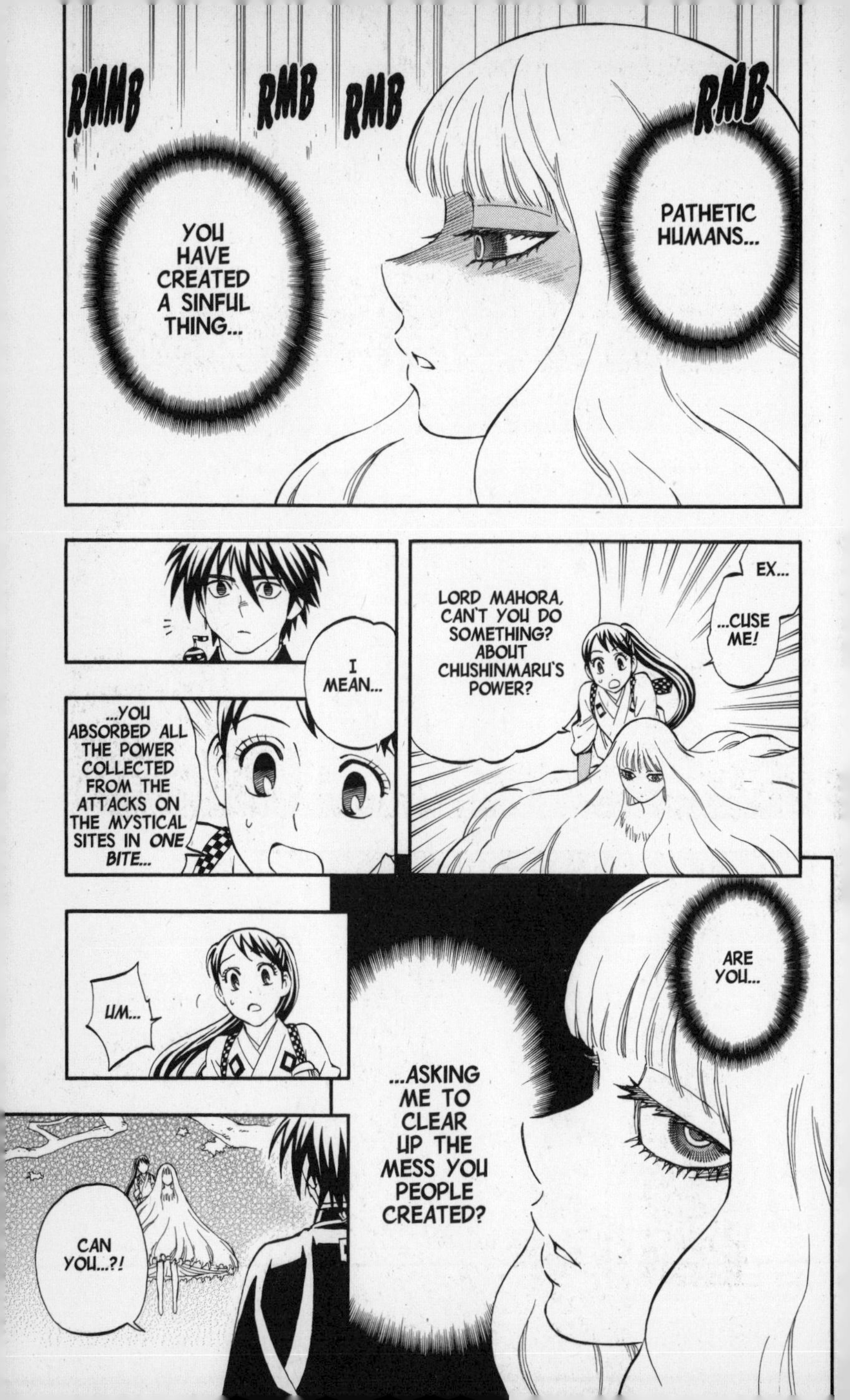
RMB
RMB
RMB
RMMB
PATHETIC HUMANS...
YOU HAVE CREATED A SINFUL THING...
EX...
...CUSE ME!
LORD MAHORA, CAN'T YOU DO SOMETHING? ABOUT CHUSHINMARU'S POWER?
I MEAN...
...YOU ABSORBED ALL THE POWER COLLECTED FROM THE ATTACKS ON THE MYSTICAL SITES IN ONE BITE...
ARE YOU...
...ASKING ME TO CLEAR UP THE MESS YOU PEOPLE CREATED?
UM...
CAN YOU...?!

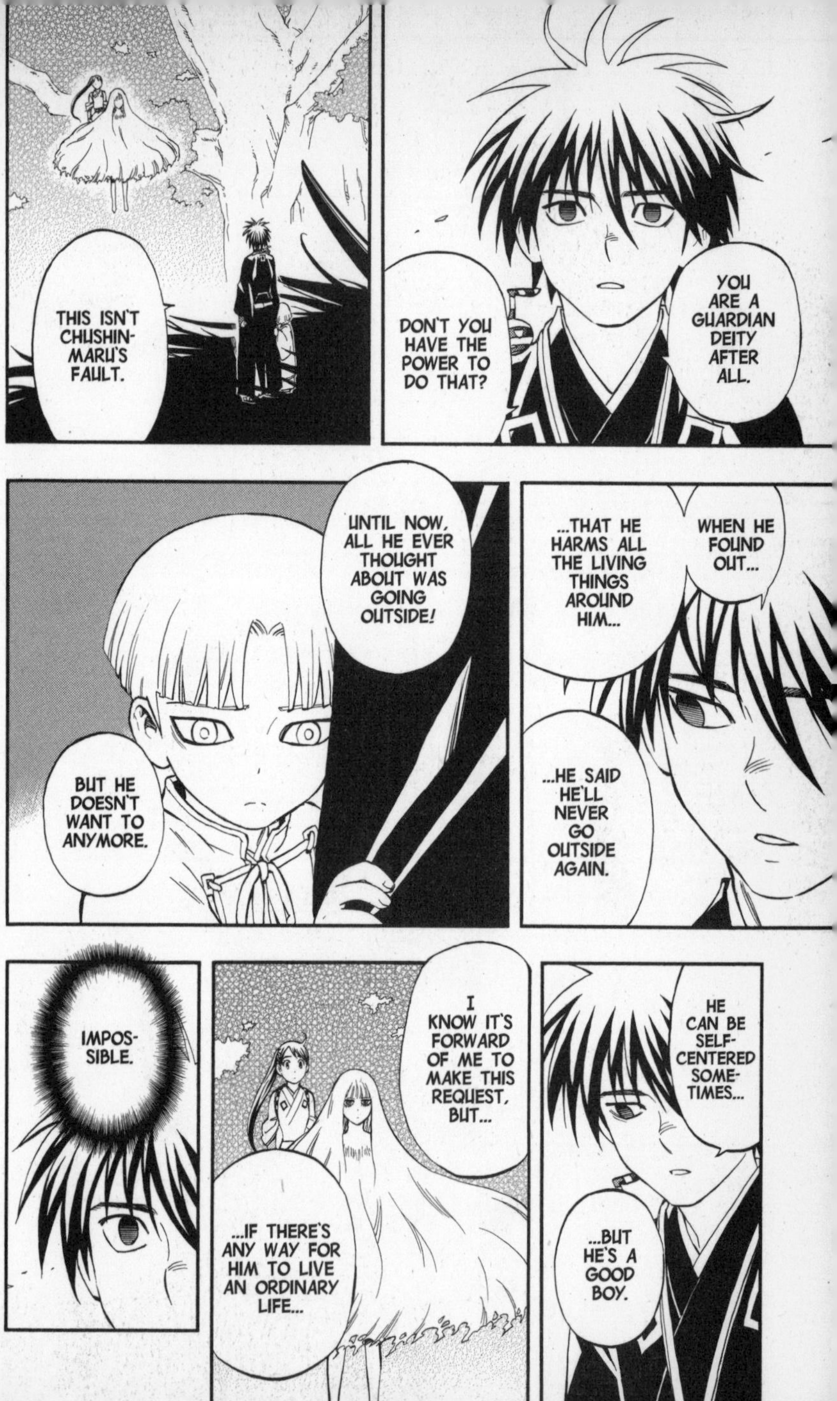
YOU ARE A GUARDIAN DEITY AFTER ALL.
DON'T YOU HAVE THE POWER TO DO THAT?
THIS ISN'T CHUSHIN-MARU'S FAULT.
WHEN HE FOUND OUT...
...THAT HE HARMS ALL THE LIVING THINGS AROUND HIM...
...HE SAID HE'LL NEVER GO OUTSIDE AGAIN.
UNTIL NOW, ALL HE EVER THOUGHT ABOUT WAS GOING OUTSIDE!
BUT HE DOESN'T WANT TO ANYMORE.
HE CAN BE SELF-CENTERED SOMETIMES...
...BUT HE'S A GOOD BOY.
I KNOW IT'S FORWARD OF ME TO MAKE THIS REQUEST, BUT...
...IF THERE'S ANY WAY FOR HIM TO LIVE AN ORDINARY LIFE...
IMPOSSIBLE.

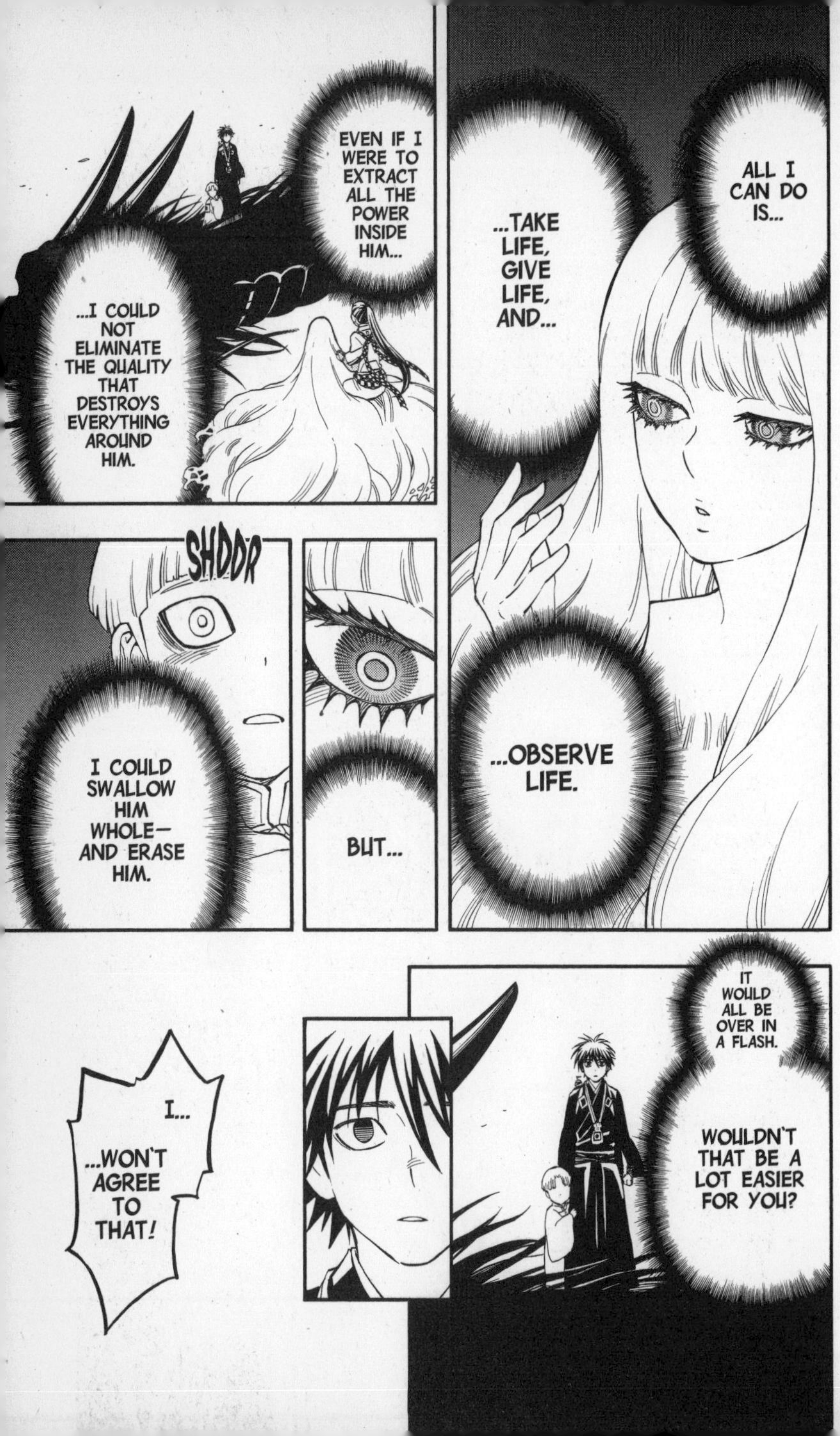
ALL I CAN DO IS...
...TAKE LIFE, GIVE LIFE, AND...
...OBSERVE LIFE.
EVEN IF I WERE TO EXTRACT ALL THE POWER INSIDE HIM...
...I COULD NOT ELIMINATE THE QUALITY THAT DESTROYS EVERYTHING AROUND HIM.
BUT...
SHDDR
I COULD SWALLOW HIM WHOLE— AND ERASE HIM.
IT WOULD ALL BE OVER IN A FLASH.
WOULDN'T THAT BE A LOT EASIER FOR YOU?
I...
...WON'T AGREE TO THAT!

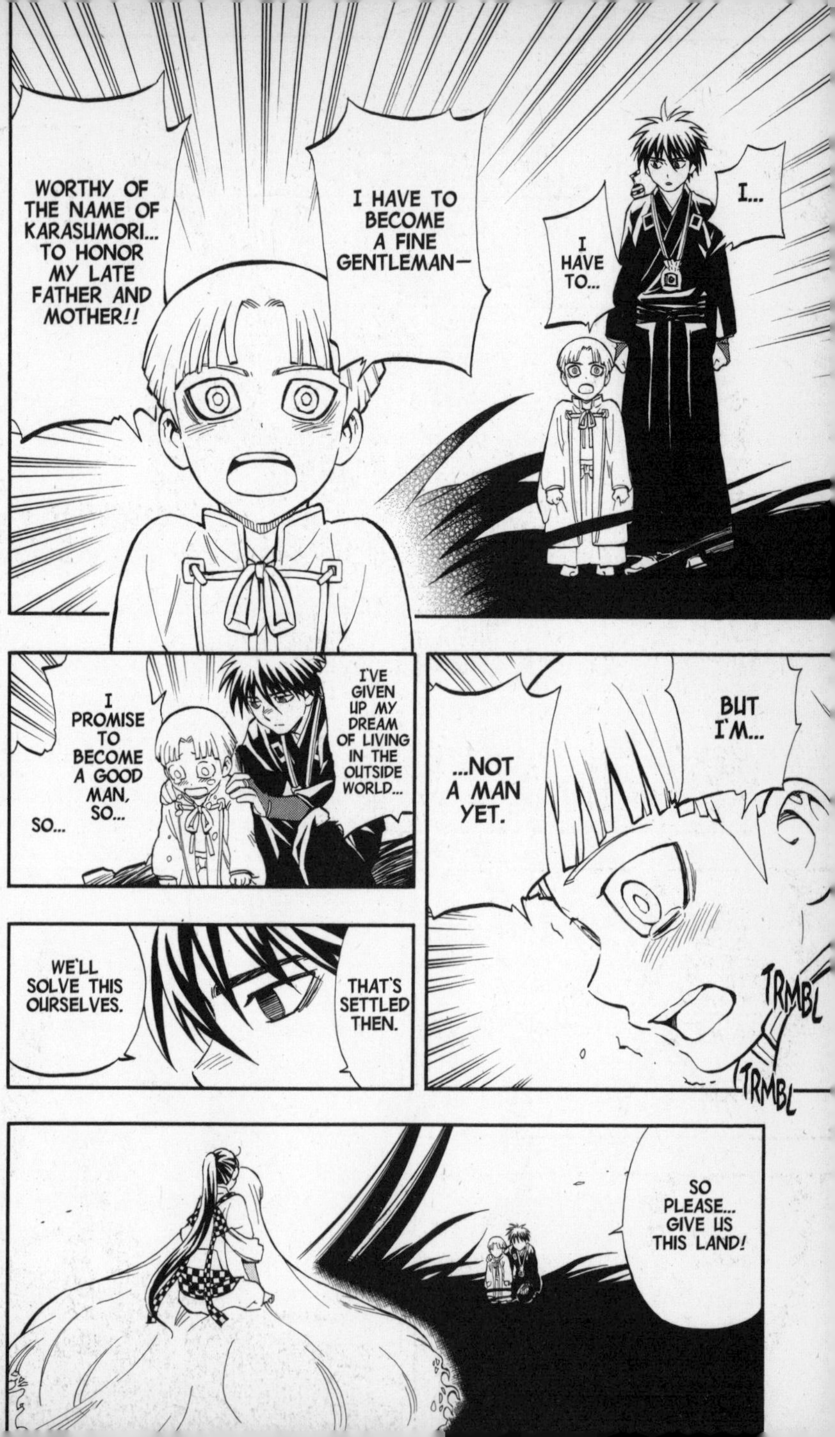
I...
I HAVE TO...
I HAVE TO BECOME A FINE GENTLEMAN—
WORTHY OF THE NAME OF KARASUMORI... TO HONOR MY LATE FATHER AND MOTHER!!
BUT I'M...
...NOT A MAN YET.
TRMBL
TRMBL
I'VE GIVEN UP MY DREAM OF LIVING IN THE OUTSIDE WORLD...
I PROMISE TO BECOME A GOOD MAN, SO...
SO...
THAT'S SETTLED THEN.
WE'LL SOLVE THIS OURSELVES.
SO PLEASE... GIVE US THIS LAND!

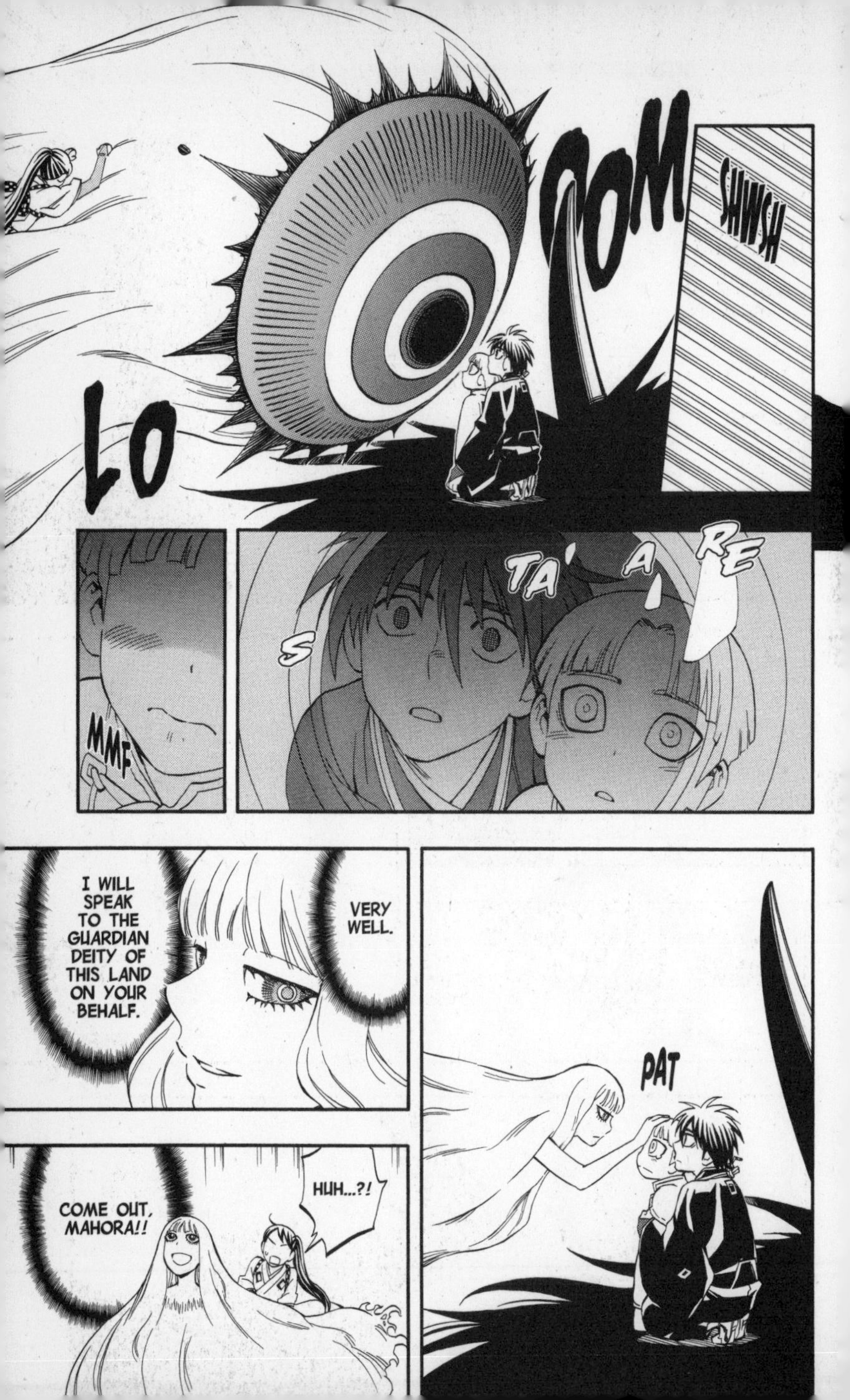
SHWSH
LO
OOM
S
TA
A
RE
MMF
PAT
VERY WELL.
I WILL SPEAK TO THE GUARDIAN DEITY OF THIS LAND ON YOUR BEHALF.
HUH...?!
COME OUT, MAHORA!!

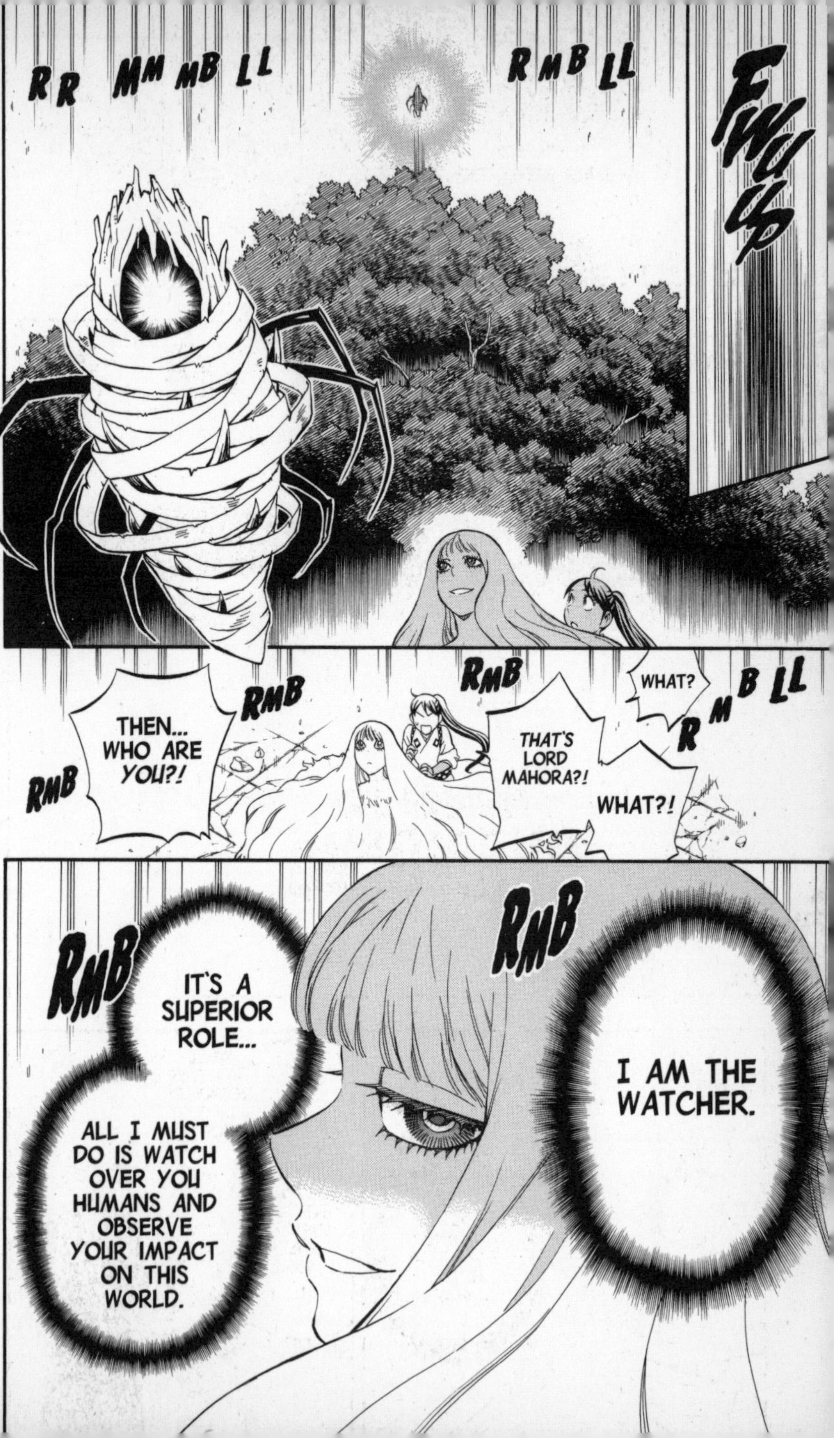
FWUSH
RMBLL
RR MMMMB LL
WHAT?
RMBLL
THAT'S LORD MAHORA?!
WHAT?!
RMB
RMB
THEN... WHO ARE YOU?!
RMB
RMB
I AM THE WATCHER.
IT'S A SUPERIOR ROLE...
ALL I MUST DO IS WATCH OVER YOU HUMANS AND OBSERVE YOUR IMPACT ON THIS WORLD.
RMB

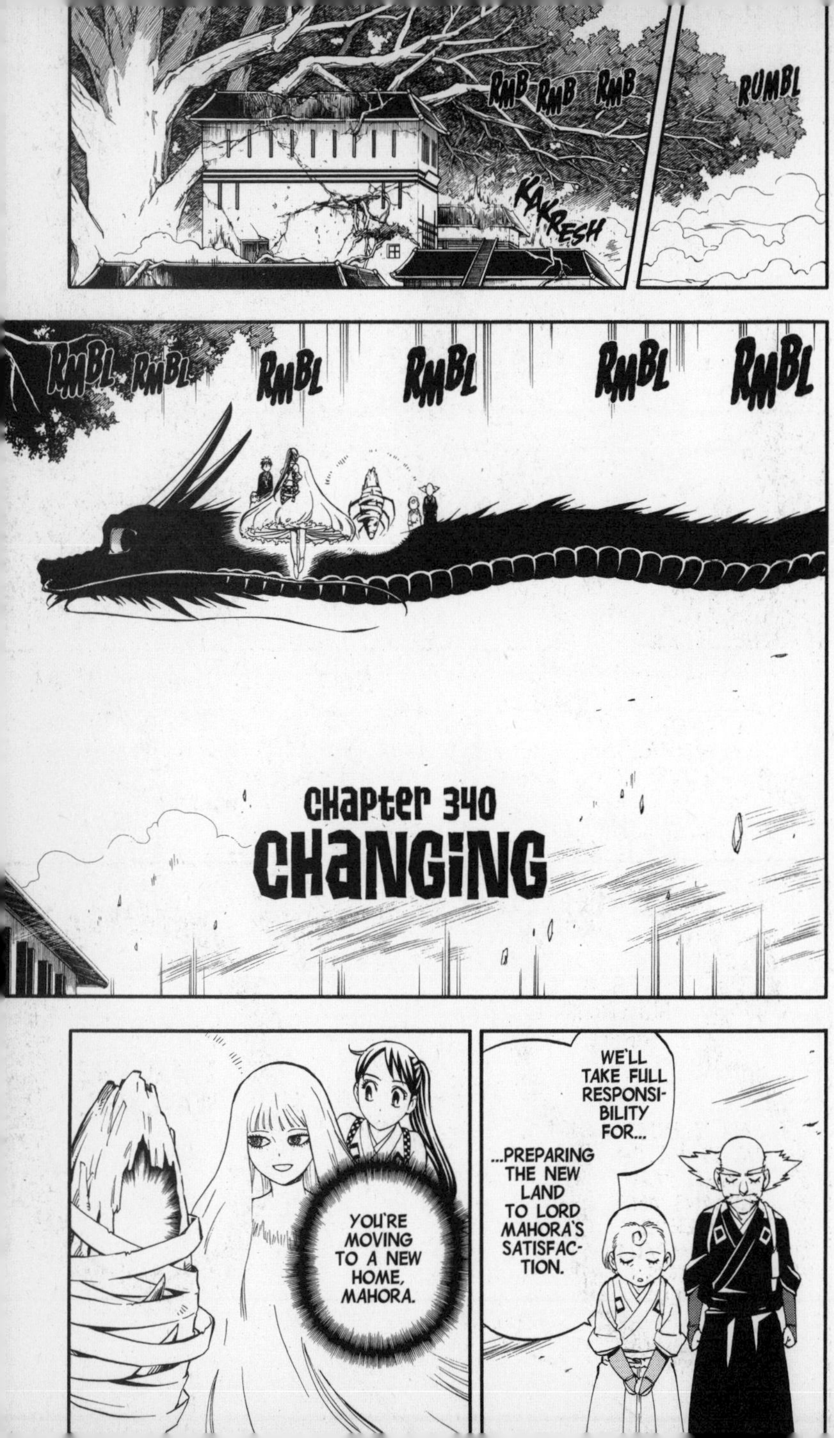
RUMBL
RMB RMB RMB
KAKRESH
RMBL RMBL RMBL RMBL RMBL RMBL
Chapter 340
CHANGING
WE'LL TAKE FULL RESPONSIBILITY FOR...
...PREPARING THE NEW LAND TO LORD MAHORA'S SATISFACTION.
YOU'RE MOVING TO A NEW HOME, MAHORA.

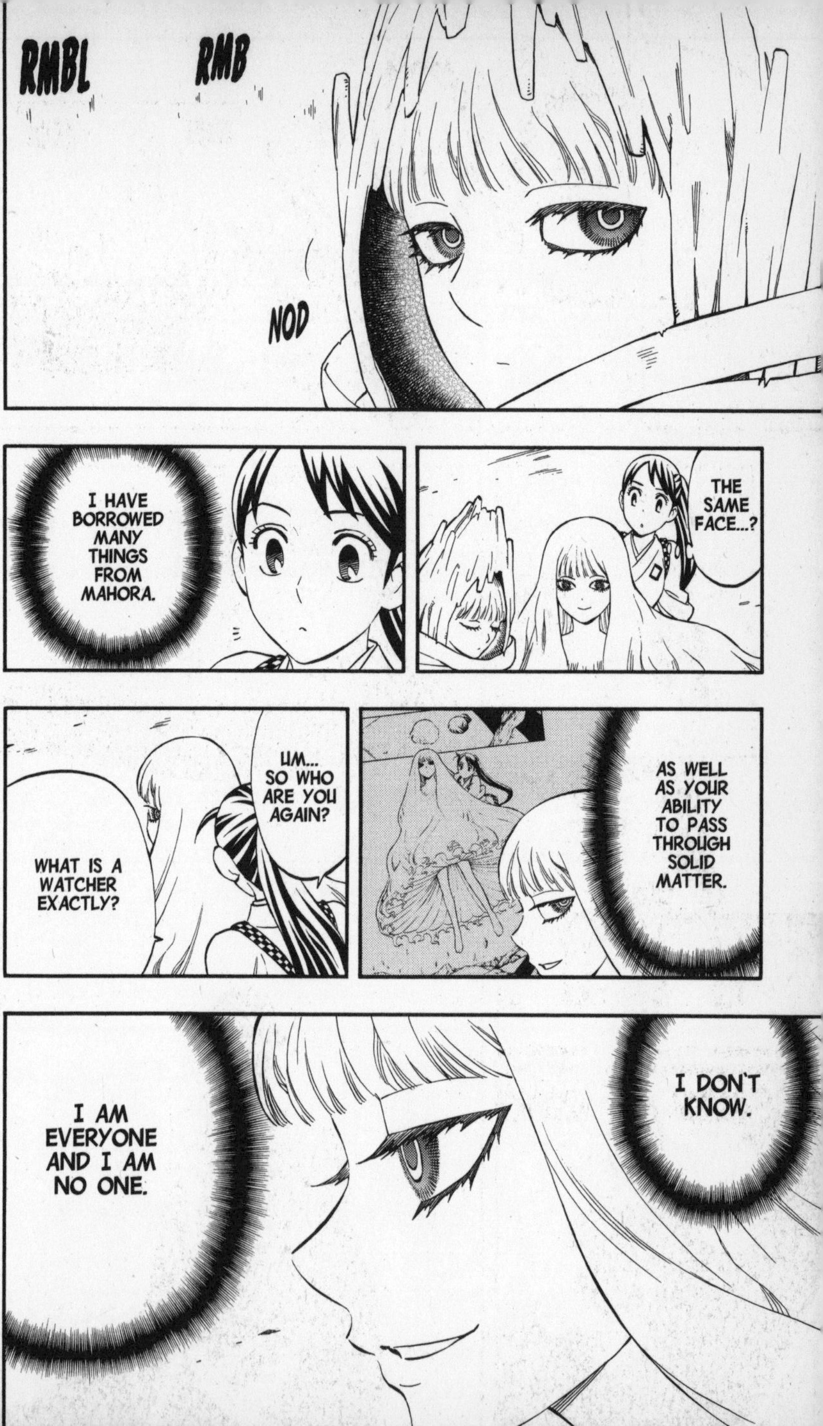
RMB
RMBL
NOD
THE SAME FACE...?
I HAVE BORROWED MANY THINGS FROM MAHORA.
AS WELL AS YOUR ABILITY TO PASS THROUGH SOLID MATTER.
UM... SO WHO ARE YOU AGAIN?
WHAT IS A WATCHER EXACTLY?
I DON'T KNOW.
I AM EVERYONE AND I AM NO ONE.

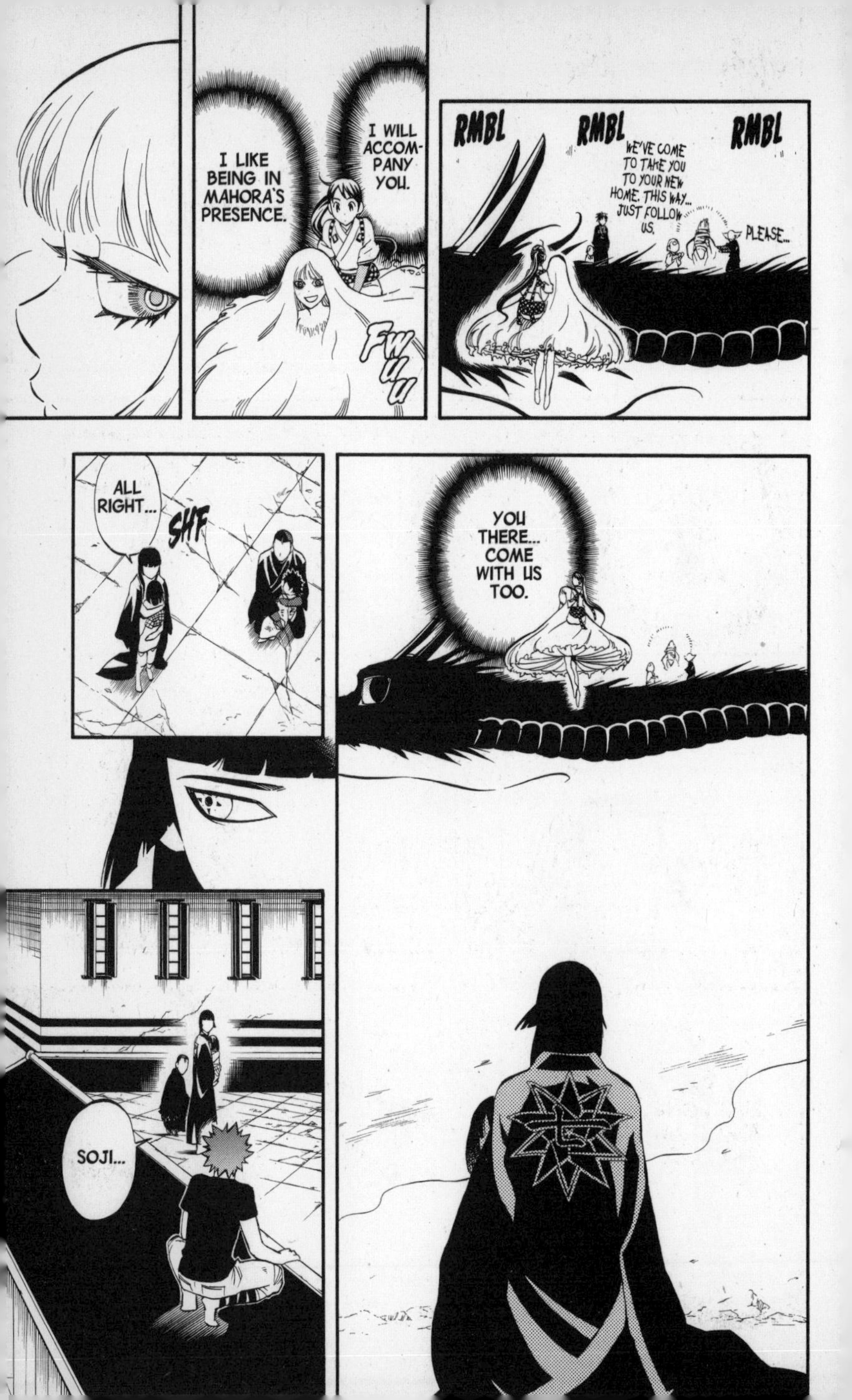
RMBL
RMBL
RMBL
WE'VE COME TO TAKE YOU TO YOUR NEW HOME. THIS WAY... JUST FOLLOW US.
PLEASE...
I WILL ACCOMPANY YOU.
I LIKE BEING IN MAHORA'S PRESENCE.
FWUU
YOU THERE... COME WITH US TOO.
ALL RIGHT...
SHF
SOJI...

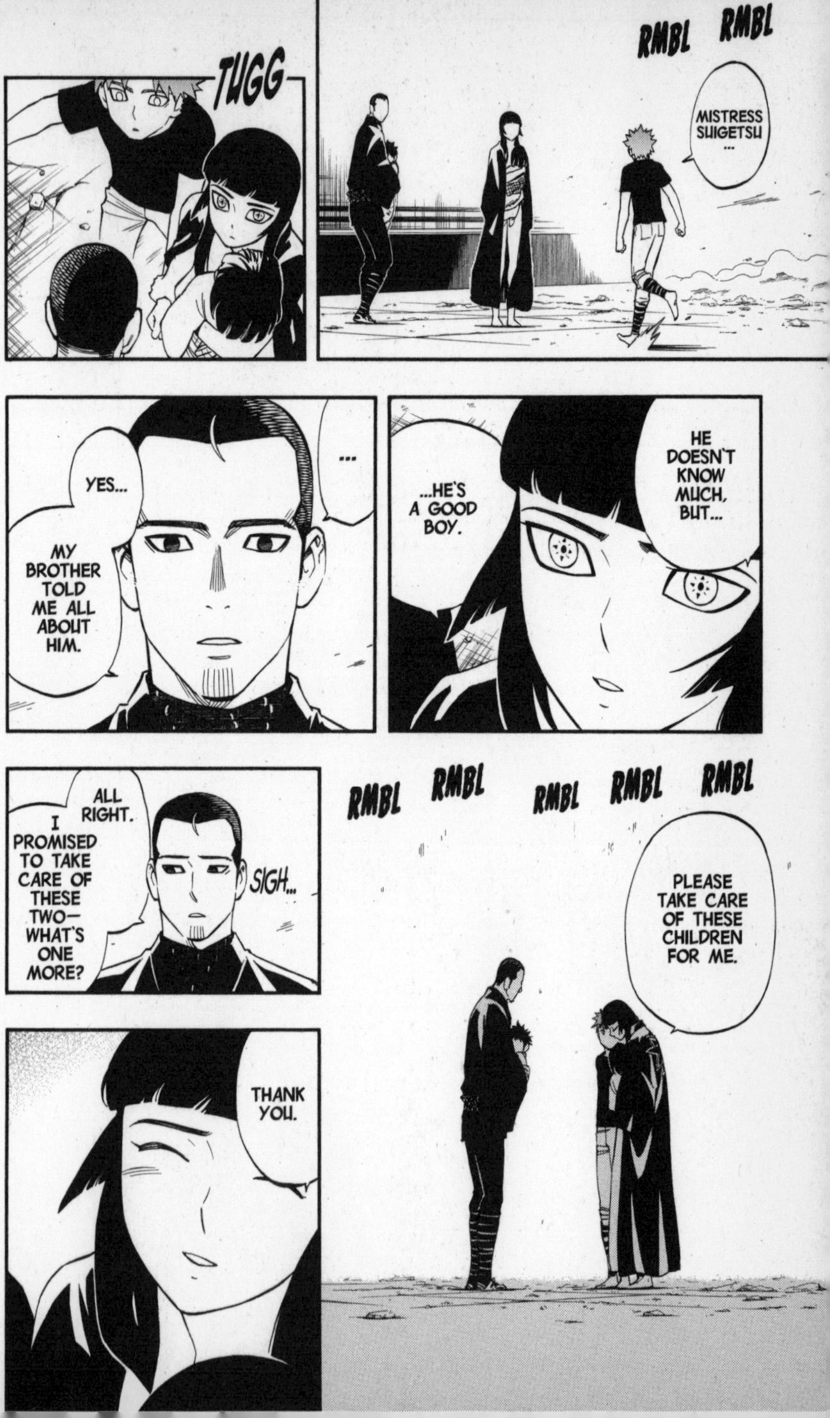
RMBL RMBL
MISTRESS SUIGETSU ...
TUGG
HE DOESN'T KNOW MUCH, BUT...
...HE'S A GOOD BOY.
...
YES...
MY BROTHER TOLD ME ALL ABOUT HIM.
RMBL RMBL RMBL RMBL RMBL
PLEASE TAKE CARE OF THESE CHILDREN FOR ME.
ALL RIGHT.
I PROMISED TO TAKE CARE OF THESE TWO—WHAT'S ONE MORE?
SIGH...
THANK YOU.

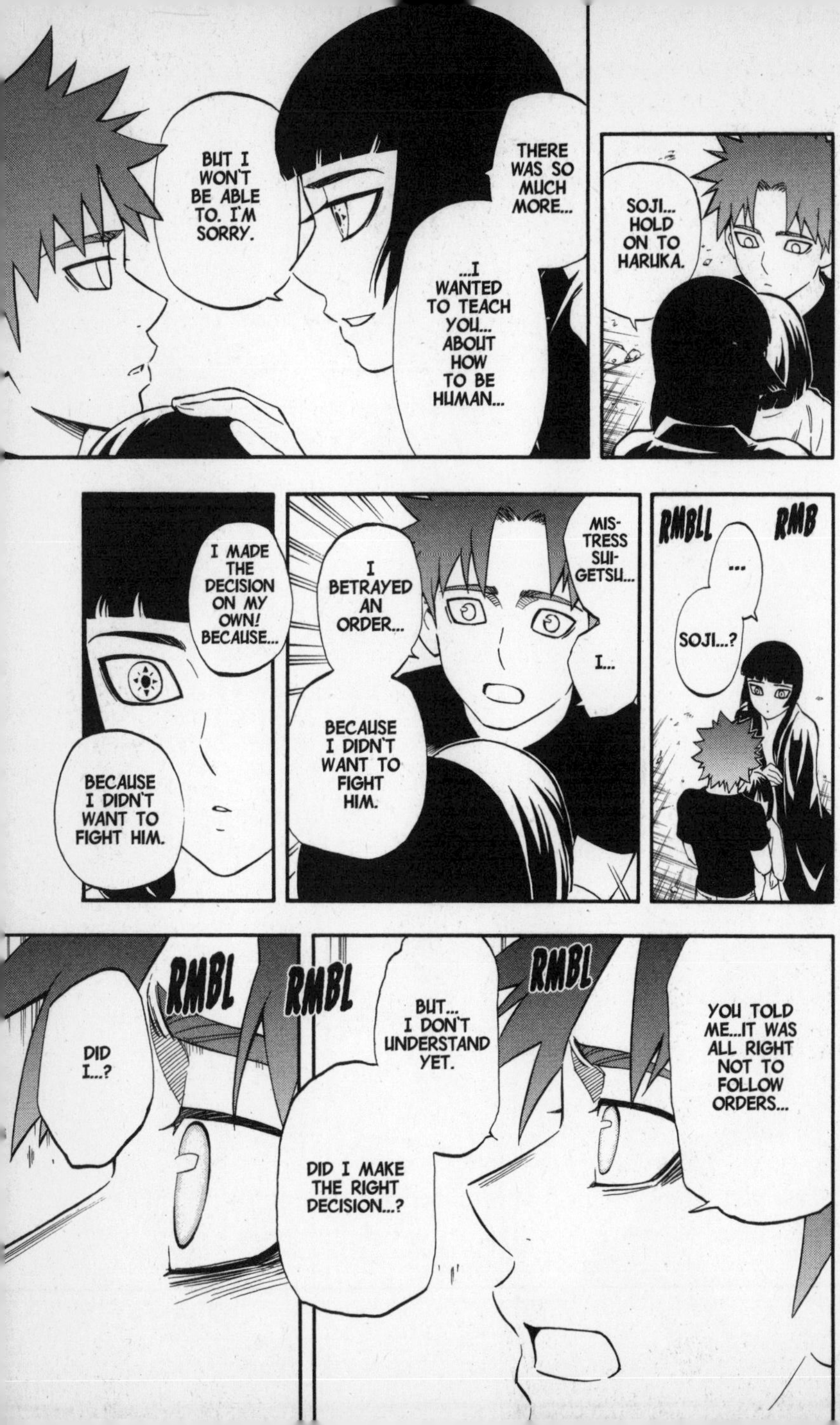
SOJI... HOLD ON TO HARUKA.
THERE WAS SO MUCH MORE...
...I WANTED TO TEACH YOU... ABOUT HOW TO BE HUMAN...
BUT I WON'T BE ABLE TO. I'M SORRY.
RMBLL
RMB
...
SOJI...?
MIS-TRESS SUI-GETSU...
I...
I BETRAYED AN ORDER...
BECAUSE I DIDN'T WANT TO FIGHT HIM.
I MADE THE DECISION ON MY OWN! BECAUSE...
BECAUSE I DIDN'T WANT TO FIGHT HIM.
RMBL
YOU TOLD ME...IT WAS ALL RIGHT NOT TO FOLLOW ORDERS...
BUT... I DON'T UNDERSTAND YET.
DID I MAKE THE RIGHT DECISION...?
RMBL
RMBL
DID I...?

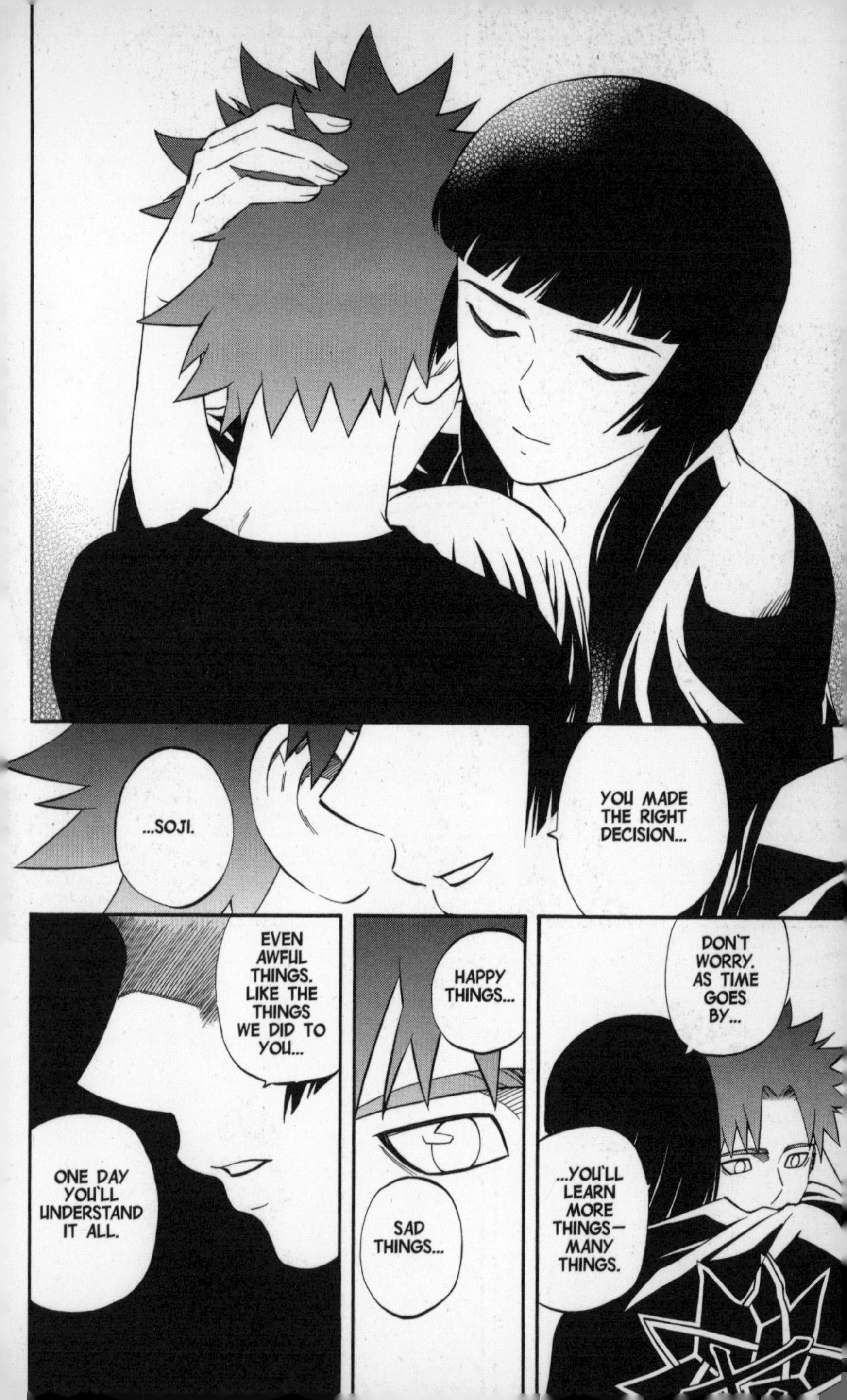
YOU MADE THE RIGHT DECISION...
...SOJI.
DON'T WORRY. AS TIME GOES BY...
...YOU'LL LEARN MORE THINGS—MANY THINGS.
HAPPY THINGS...
SAD THINGS...
EVEN AWFUL THINGS. LIKE THE THINGS WE DID TO YOU...
ONE DAY YOU'LL UNDERSTAND IT ALL.

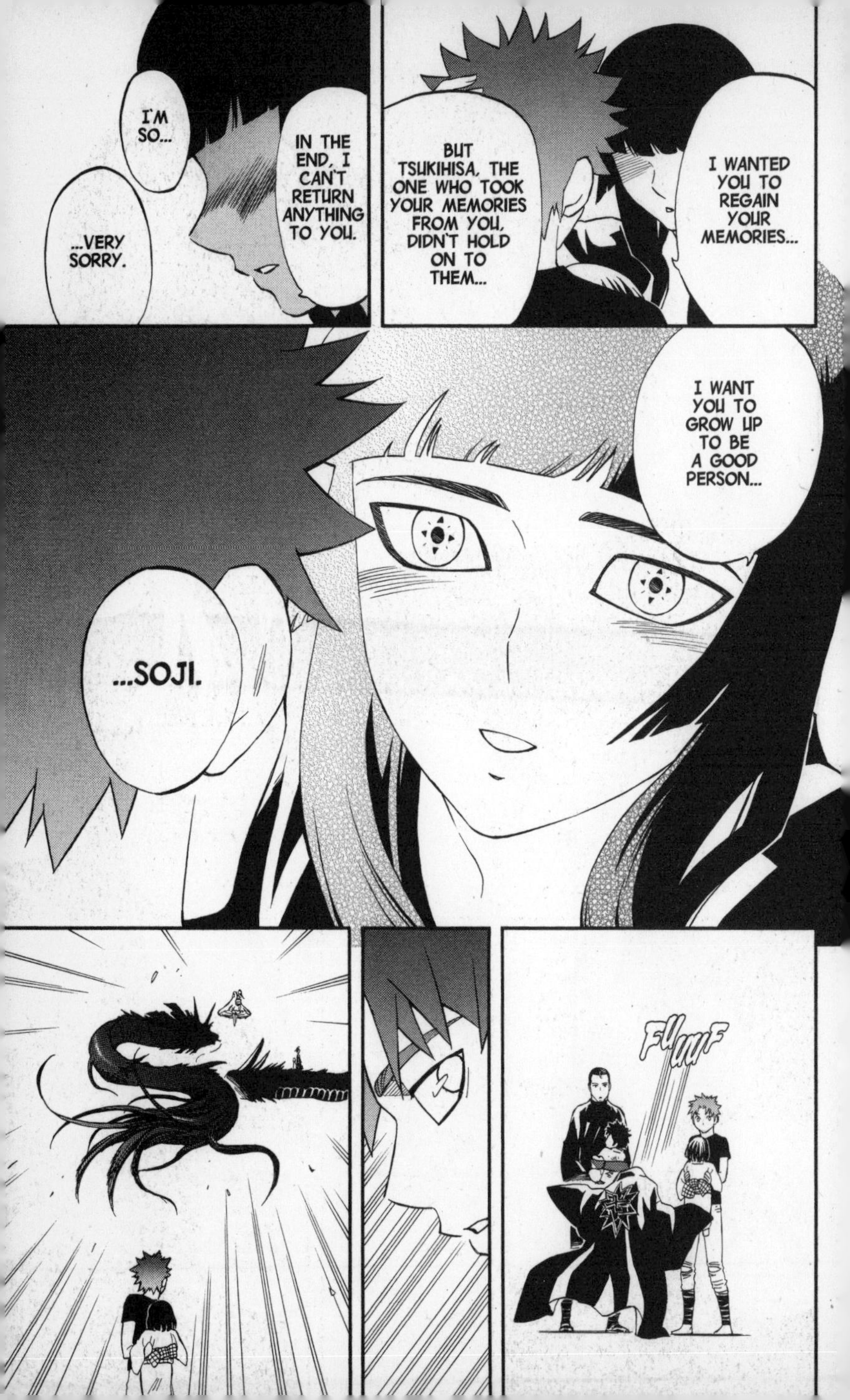
I WANTED YOU TO REGAIN YOUR MEMORIES...
BUT TSUKIHISA, THE ONE WHO TOOK YOUR MEMORIES FROM YOU, DIDN'T HOLD ON TO THEM...
IN THE END, I CAN'T RETURN ANYTHING TO YOU.
I'M SO...
...VERY SORRY.
I WANT YOU TO GROW UP TO BE A GOOD PERSON...
...SOJI.
FLUMF

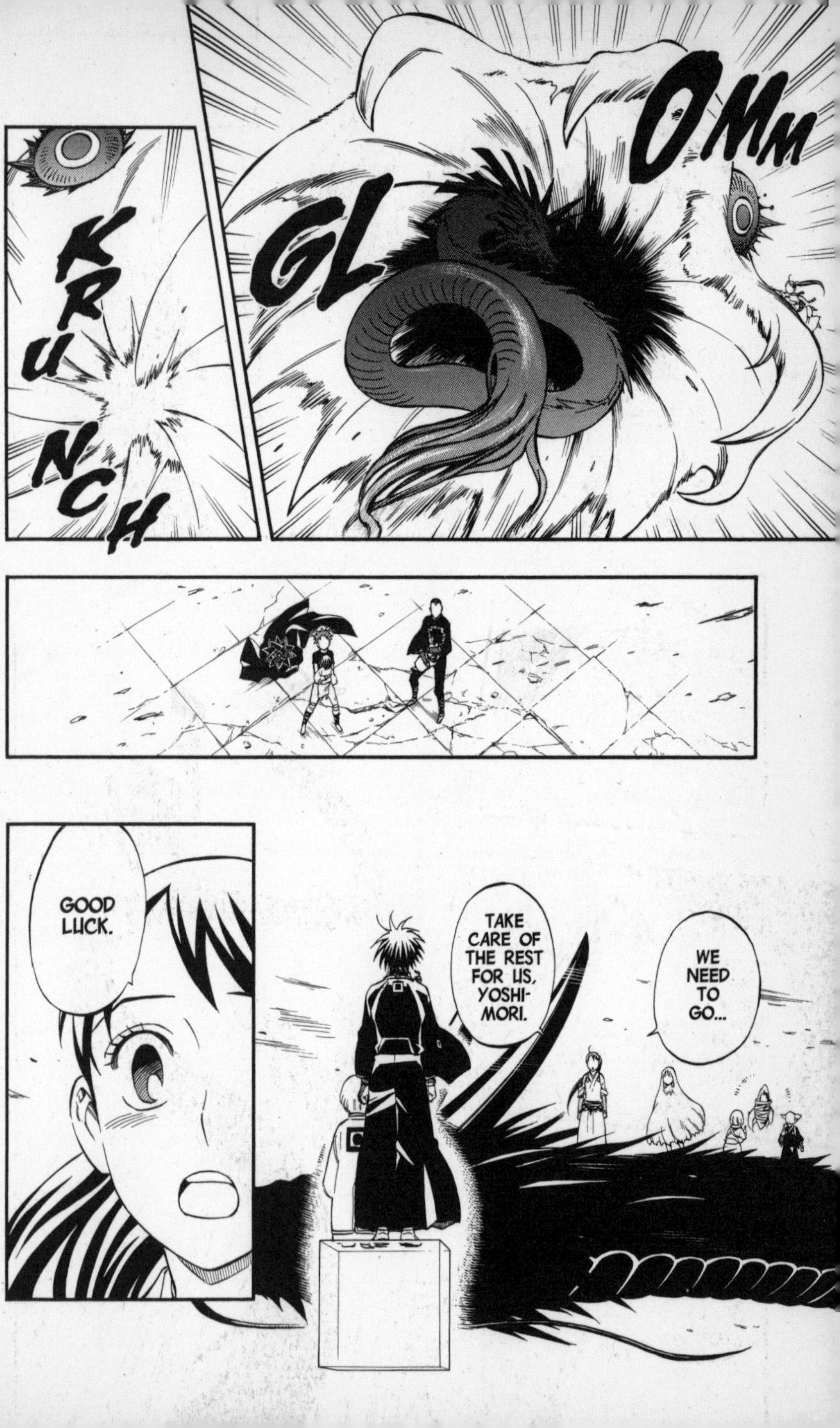
OMM
GL
KRUNCH
WE NEED TO GO...
TAKE CARE OF THE REST FOR US, YOSHIMORI.
GOOD LUCK.

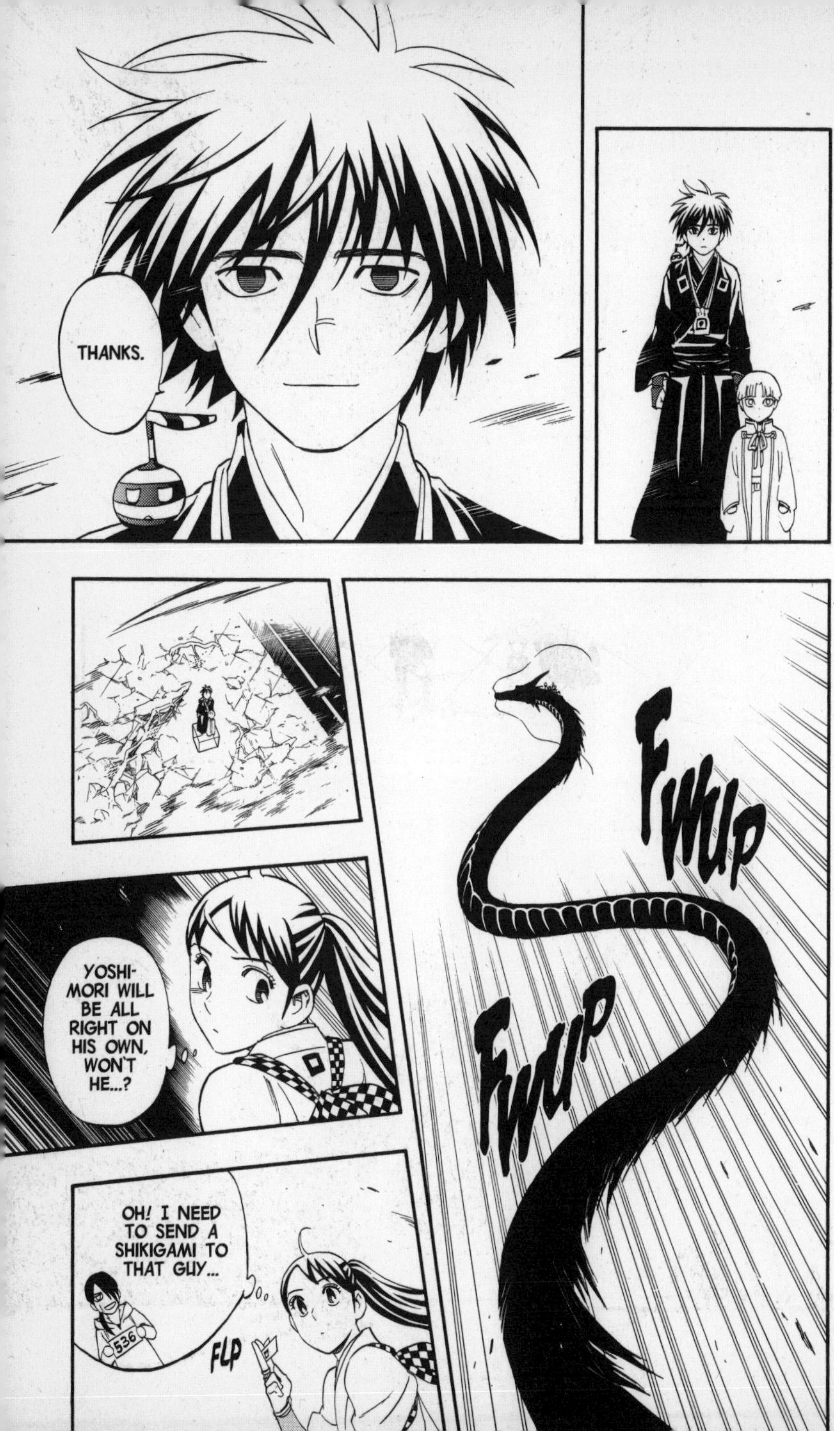
THANKS.
FWUP
FWUP
YOSHIMORI WILL BE ALL RIGHT ON HIS OWN, WON'T HE...?
OH! I NEED TO SEND A SHIKIGAMI TO THAT GUY...
FLP

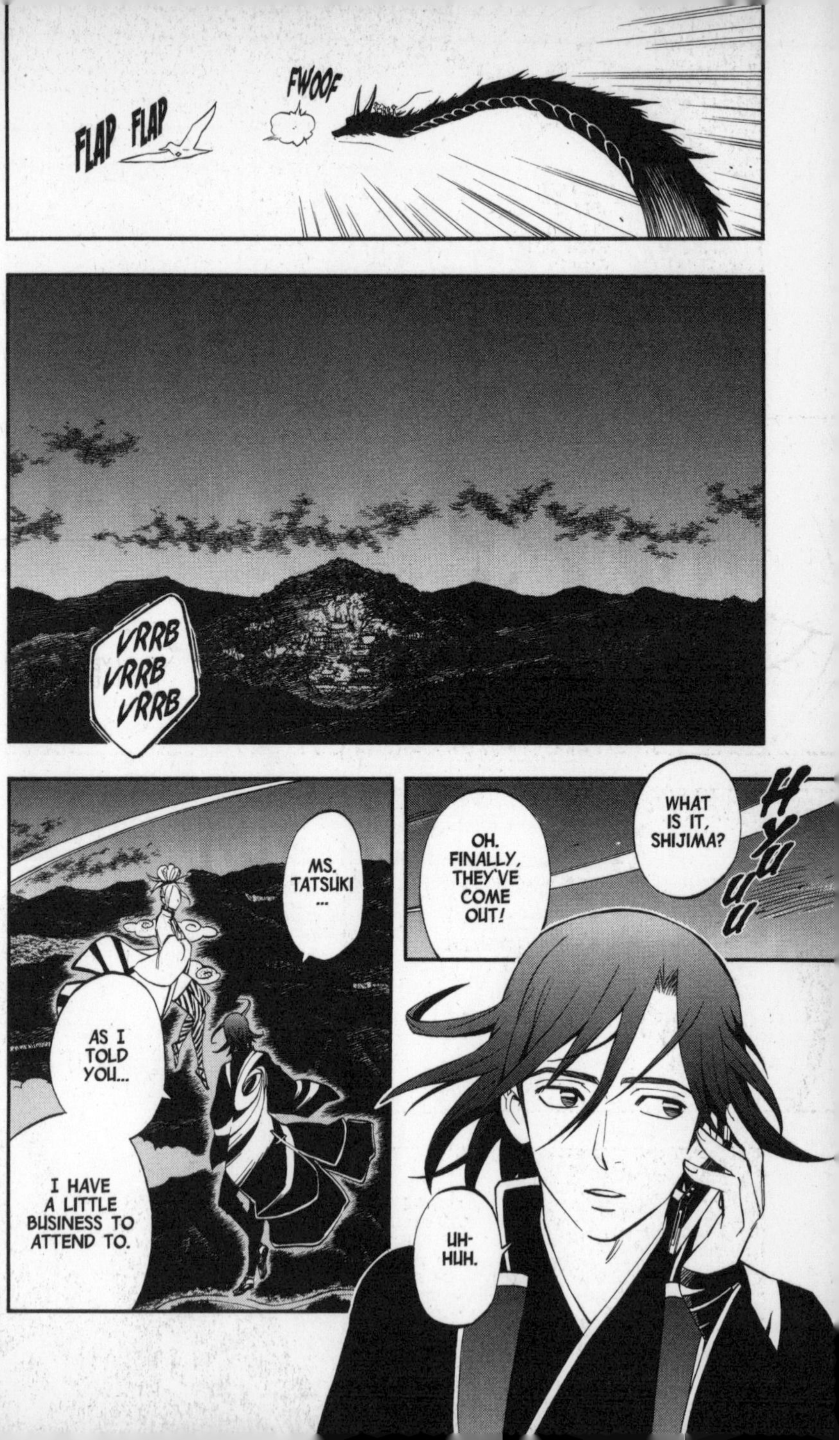
FWOOF
FLAP FLAP
VRRB VRRB VRRB
HYUUUU
WHAT IS IT, SHIJIMA?
OH. FINALLY, THEY'VE COME OUT!
UH-HUH.
MS. TATSUKI ...
AS I TOLD YOU...
I HAVE A LITTLE BUSINESS TO ATTEND TO.

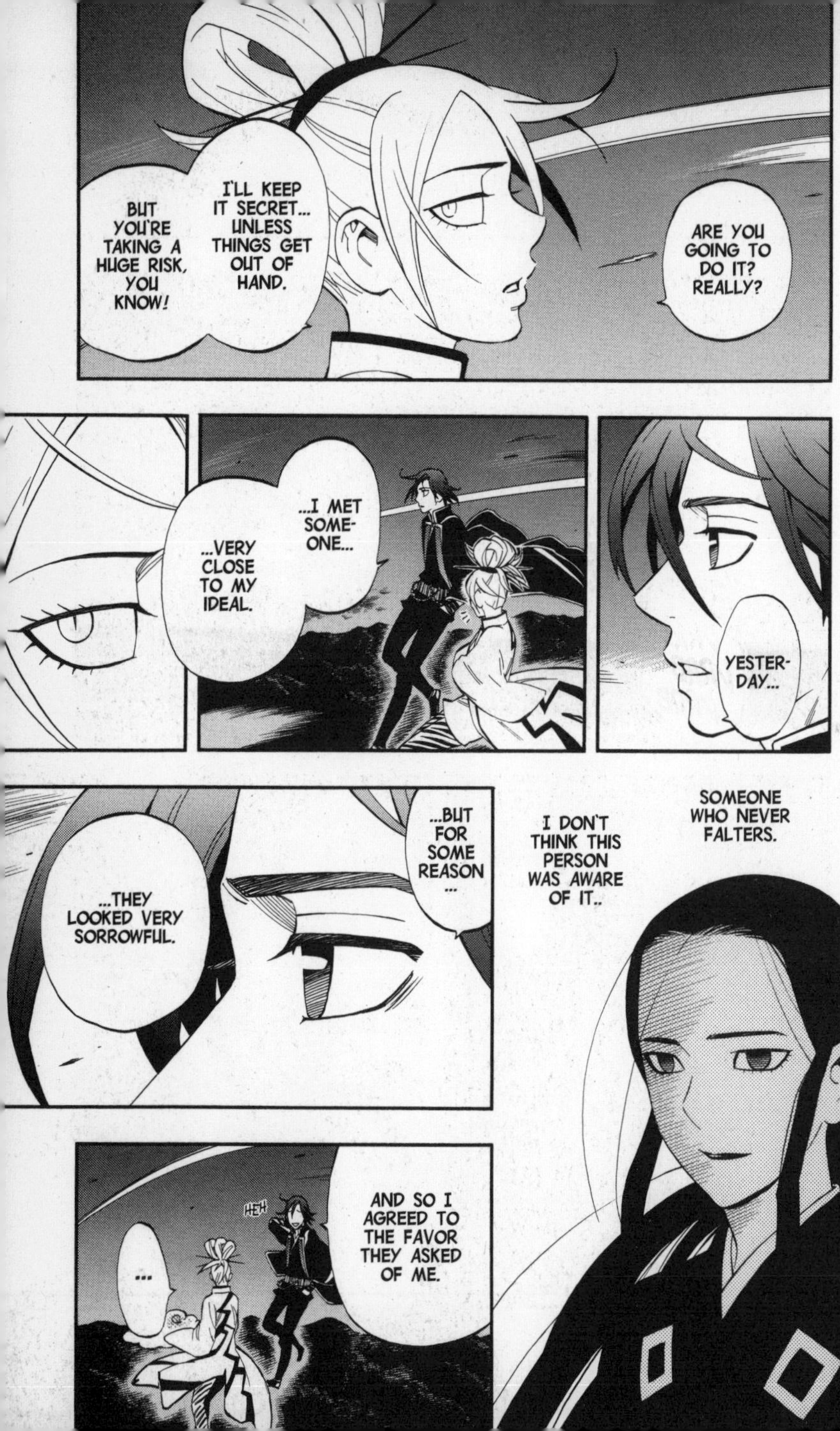
ARE YOU GOING TO DO IT? REALLY?
I'LL KEEP IT SECRET... UNLESS THINGS GET OUT OF HAND.
BUT YOU'RE TAKING A HUGE RISK, YOU KNOW!
YESTER-DAY...
...I MET SOME-ONE...
...VERY CLOSE TO MY IDEAL.
SOMEONE WHO NEVER FALTERS.
I DON'T THINK THIS PERSON WAS AWARE OF IT..
...BUT FOR SOME REASON ...
...THEY LOOKED VERY SORROWFUL.
AND SO I AGREED TO THE FAVOR THEY ASKED OF ME.
HEH
...

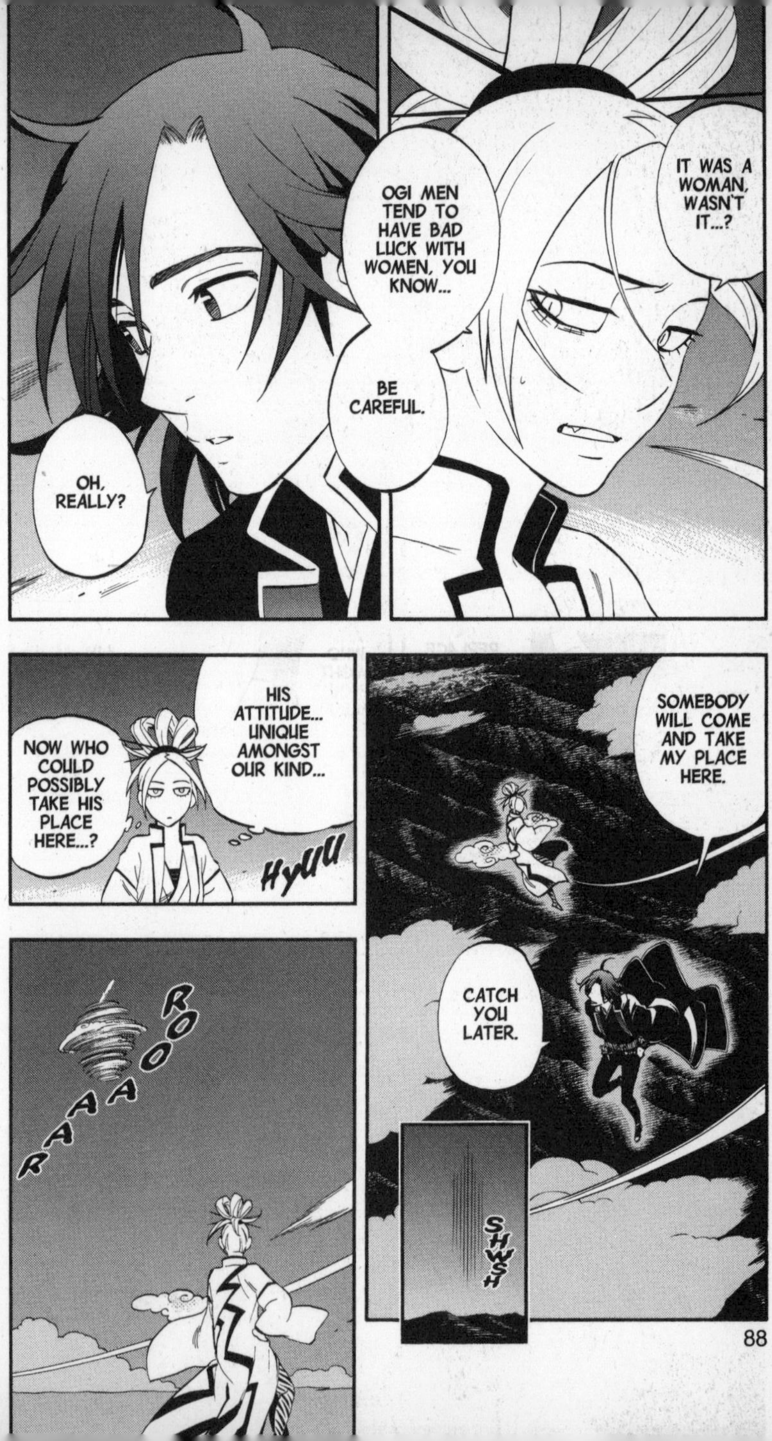
IT WAS A WOMAN, WASN'T IT...?
OGI MEN TEND TO HAVE BAD LUCK WITH WOMEN, YOU KNOW...
BE CAREFUL.
OH, REALLY?
SOMEBODY WILL COME AND TAKE MY PLACE HERE.
CATCH YOU LATER.
SHWSH
HIS ATTITUDE... UNIQUE AMONGST OUR KIND...
NOW WHO COULD POSSIBLY TAKE HIS PLACE HERE...?
HYUU
RAAAOOR

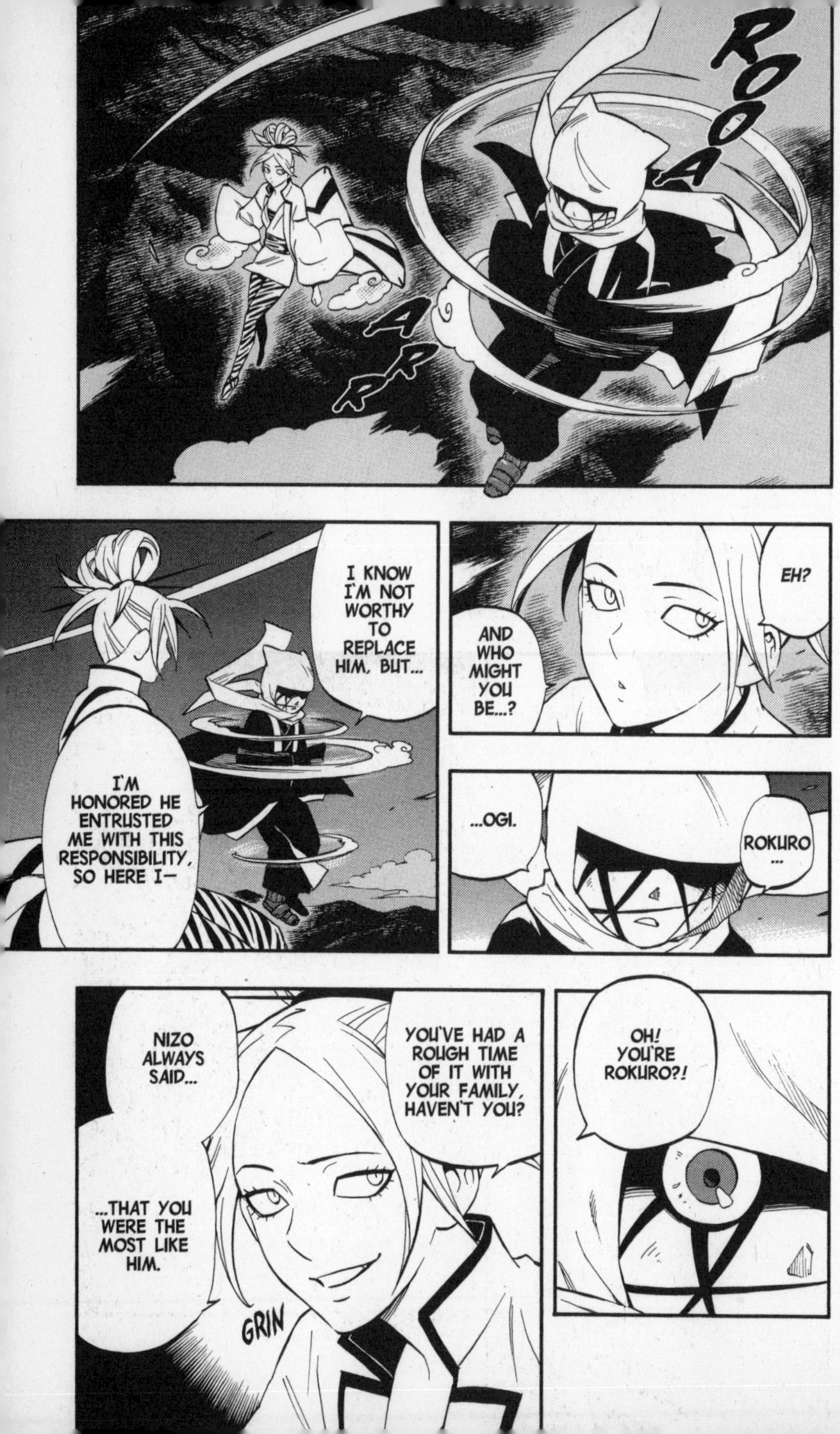
ROOOA
ARR
EH?
AND WHO MIGHT YOU BE...?
ROKURO...
...OGI.
I KNOW I'M NOT WORTHY TO REPLACE HIM, BUT...
I'M HONORED HE ENTRUSTED ME WITH THIS RESPONSIBILITY, SO HERE I—
OH! YOU'RE ROKURO?!
YOU'VE HAD A ROUGH TIME OF IT WITH YOUR FAMILY, HAVEN'T YOU?
NIZO ALWAYS SAID...
...THAT YOU WERE THE MOST LIKE HIM.
GRIN

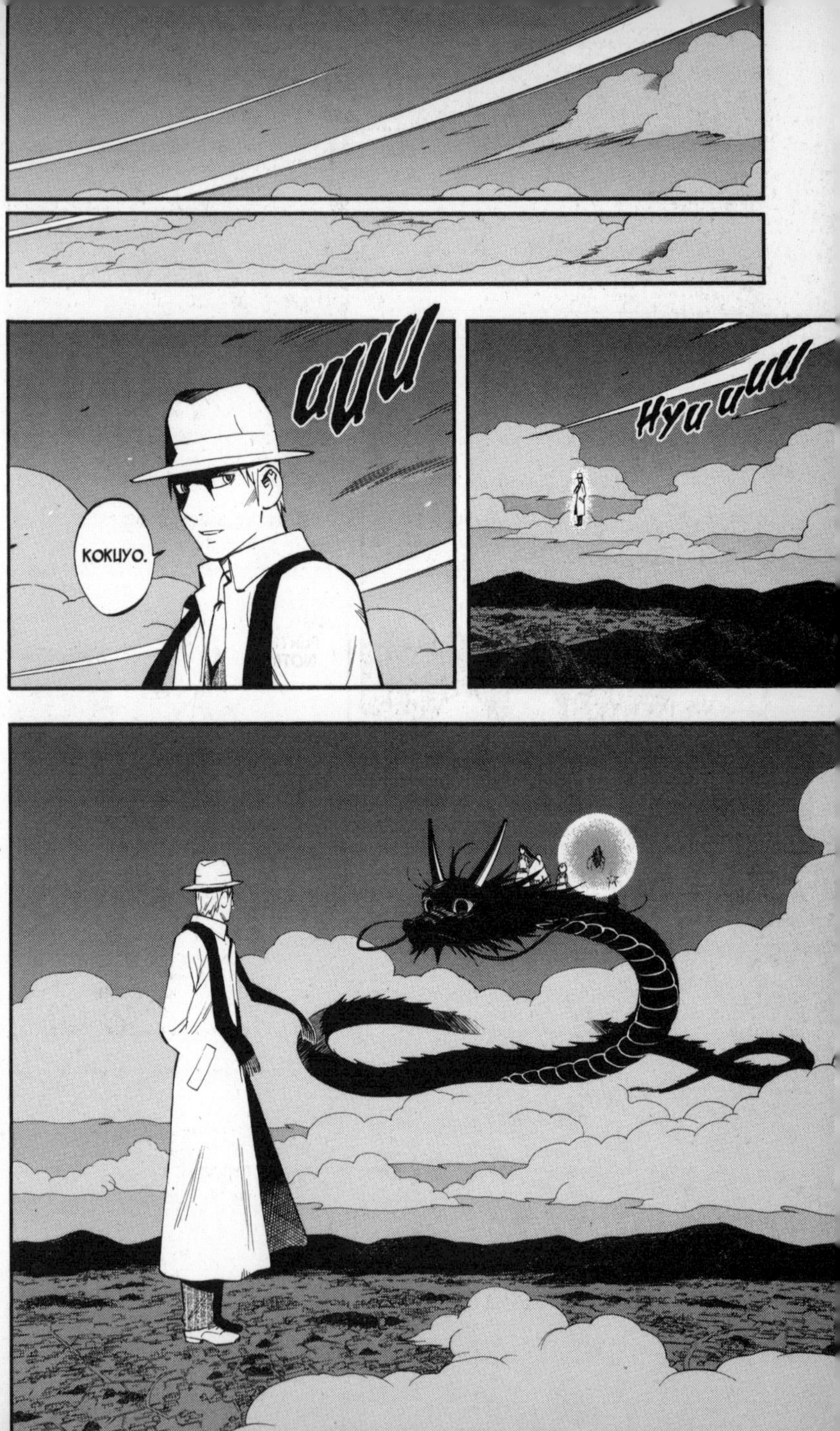
Hyu uuu
UUU
KOKUYO.

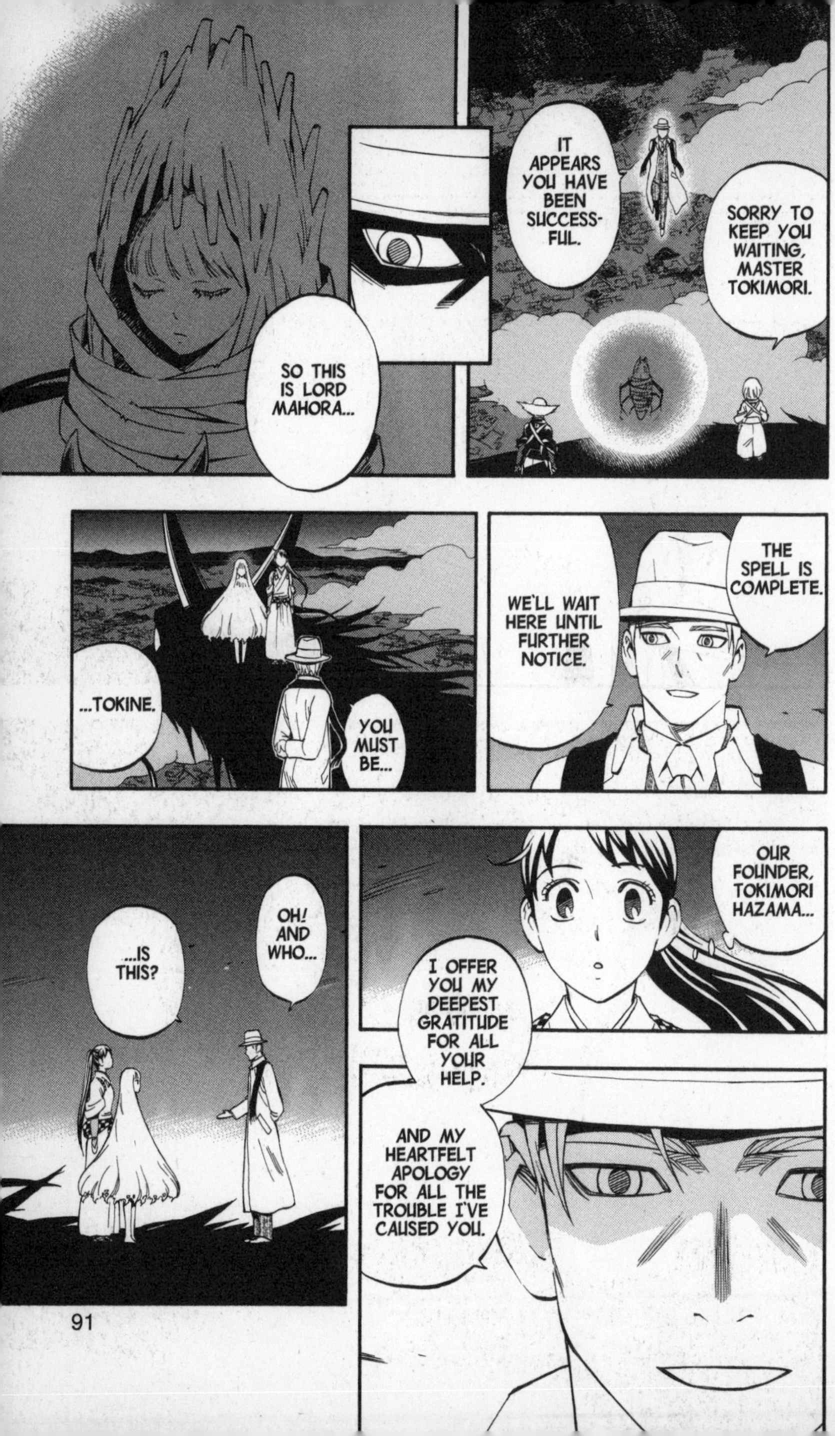
SORRY TO KEEP YOU WAITING, MASTER TOKIMORI.
IT APPEARS YOU HAVE BEEN SUCCESSFUL.
SO THIS IS LORD MAHORA...
THE SPELL IS COMPLETE.
WE'LL WAIT HERE UNTIL FURTHER NOTICE.
YOU MUST BE...
...TOKINE.
OUR FOUNDER, TOKIMORI HAZAMA...
I OFFER YOU MY DEEPEST GRATITUDE FOR ALL YOUR HELP.
AND MY HEARTFELT APOLOGY FOR ALL THE TROUBLE I'VE CAUSED YOU.
OH! AND WHO...
...IS THIS?

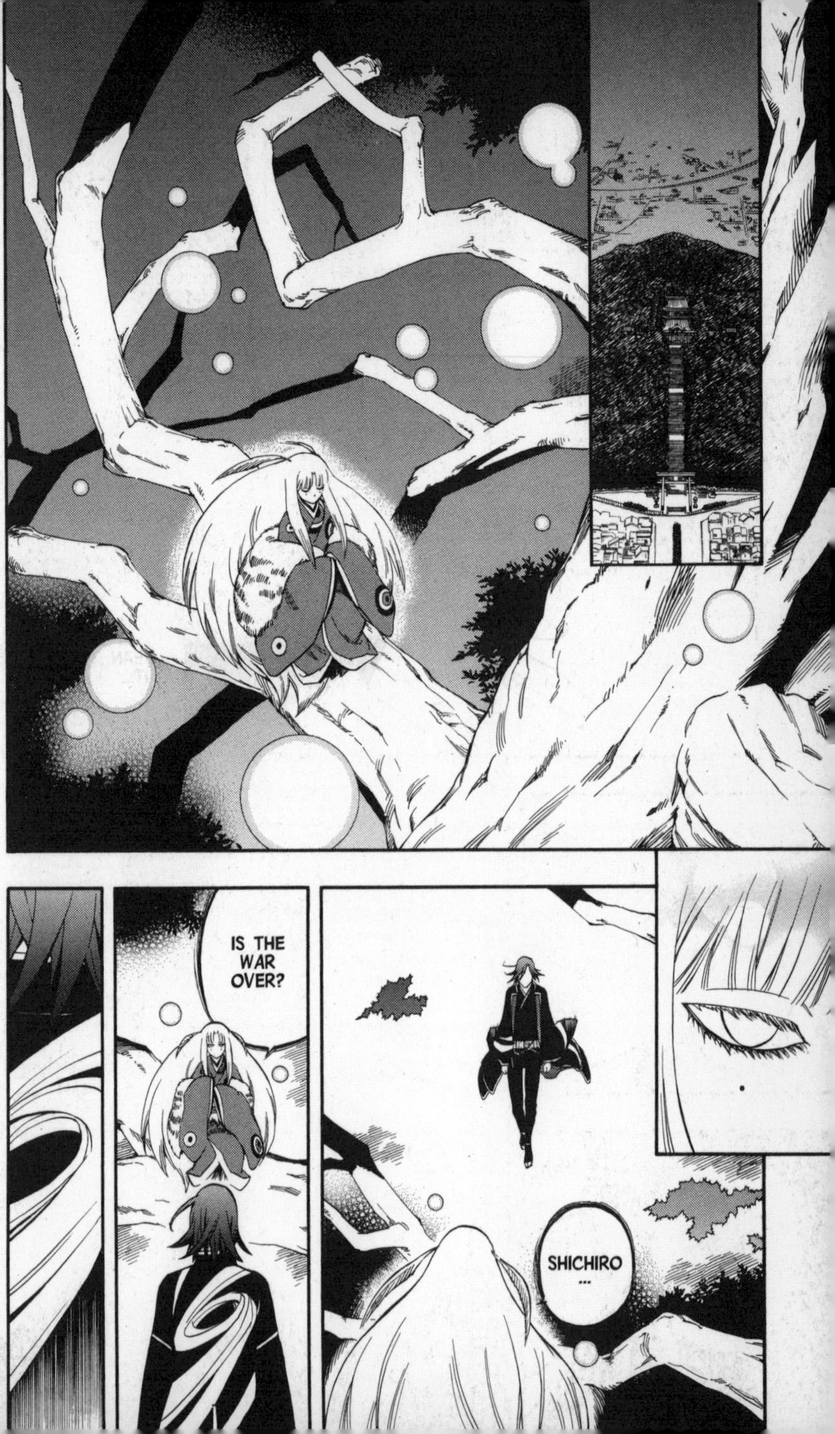
SHICHIRO ...
IS THE WAR OVER?

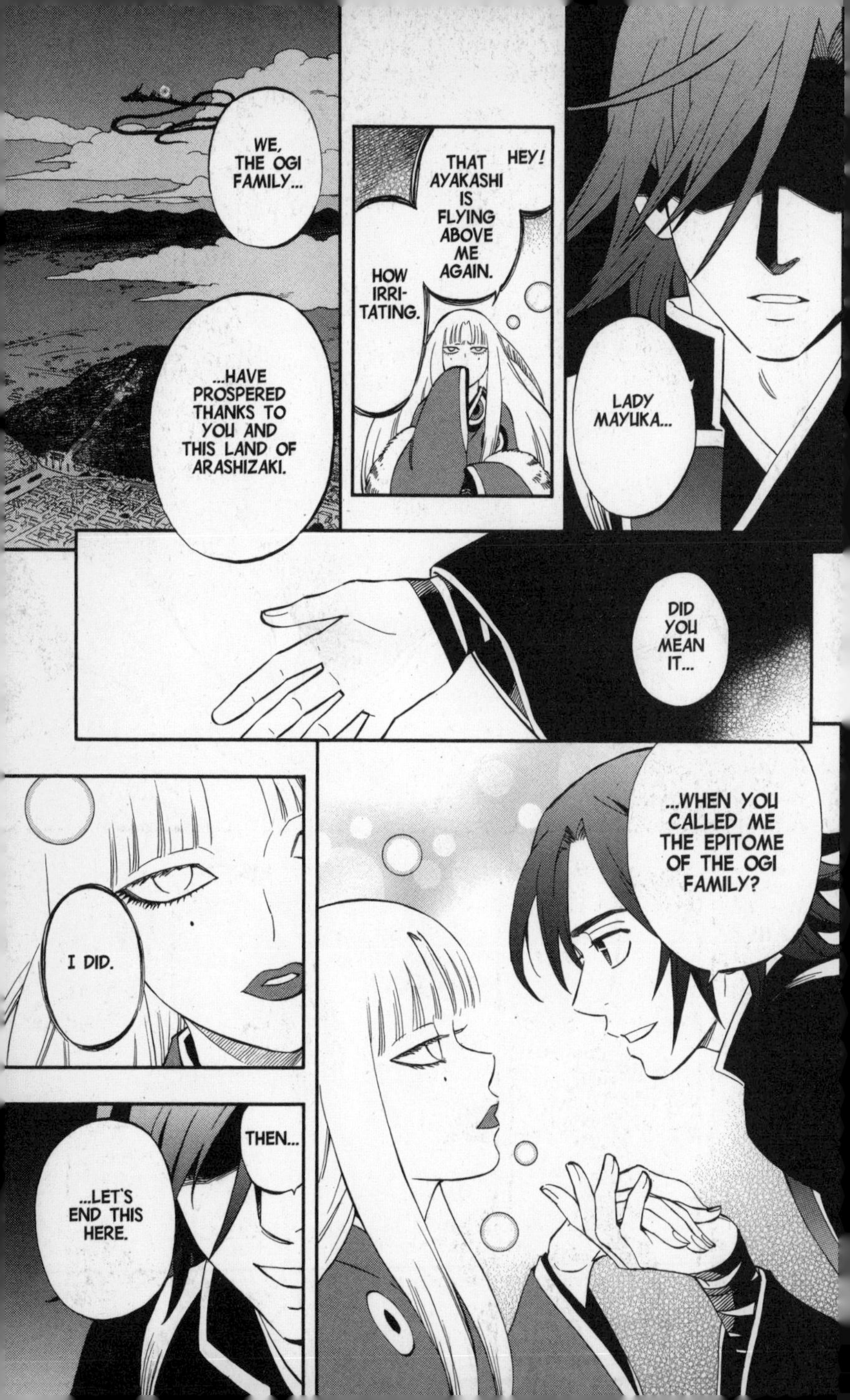
LADY MAYUKA...
HEY!
THAT AYAKASHI IS FLYING ABOVE ME AGAIN.
HOW IRRITATING.
WE, THE OGI FAMILY...
...HAVE PROSPERED THANKS TO YOU AND THIS LAND OF ARASHIZAKI.
DID YOU MEAN IT...
...WHEN YOU CALLED ME THE EPITOME OF THE OGI FAMILY?
I DID.
THEN...
...LET'S END THIS HERE.

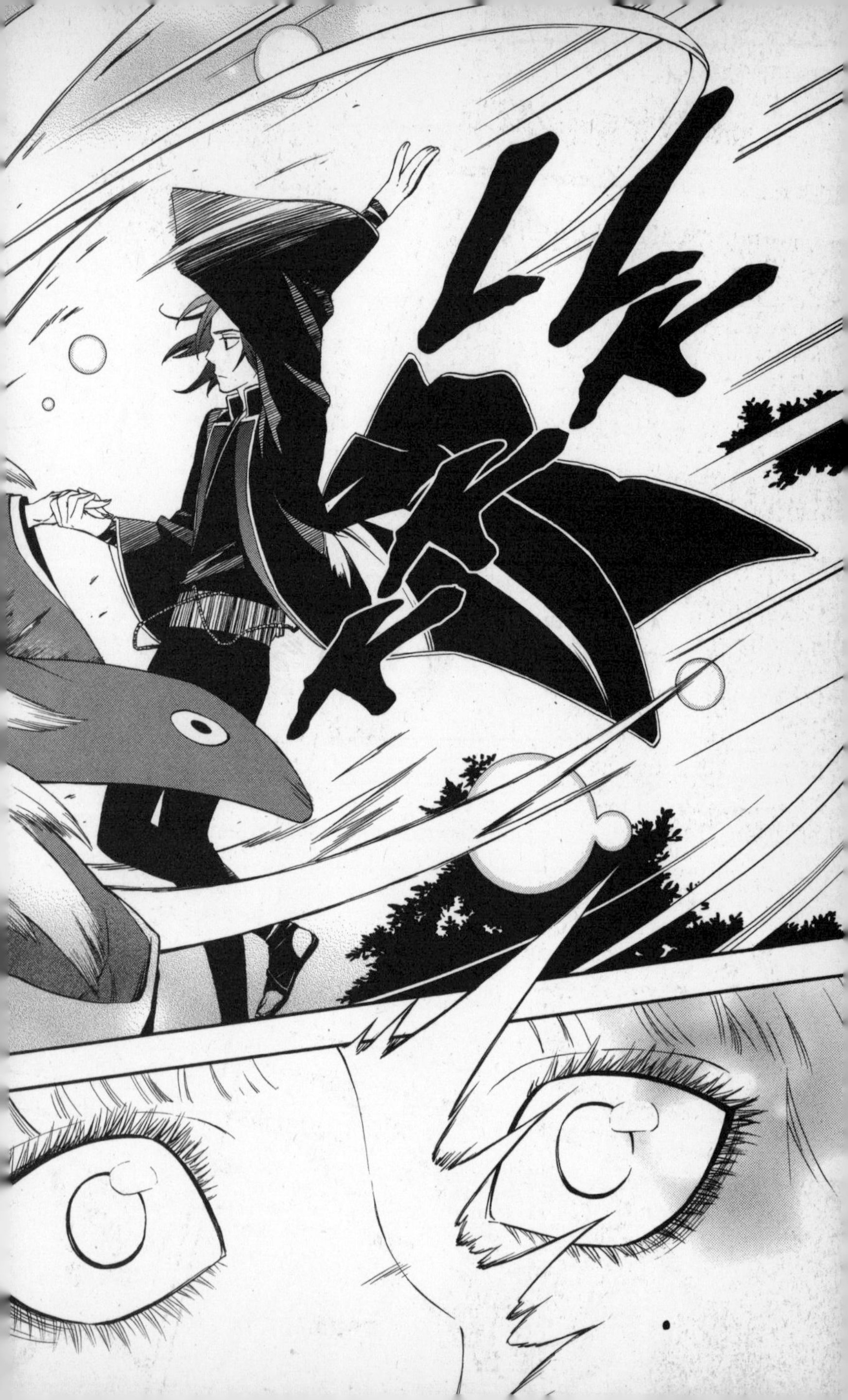

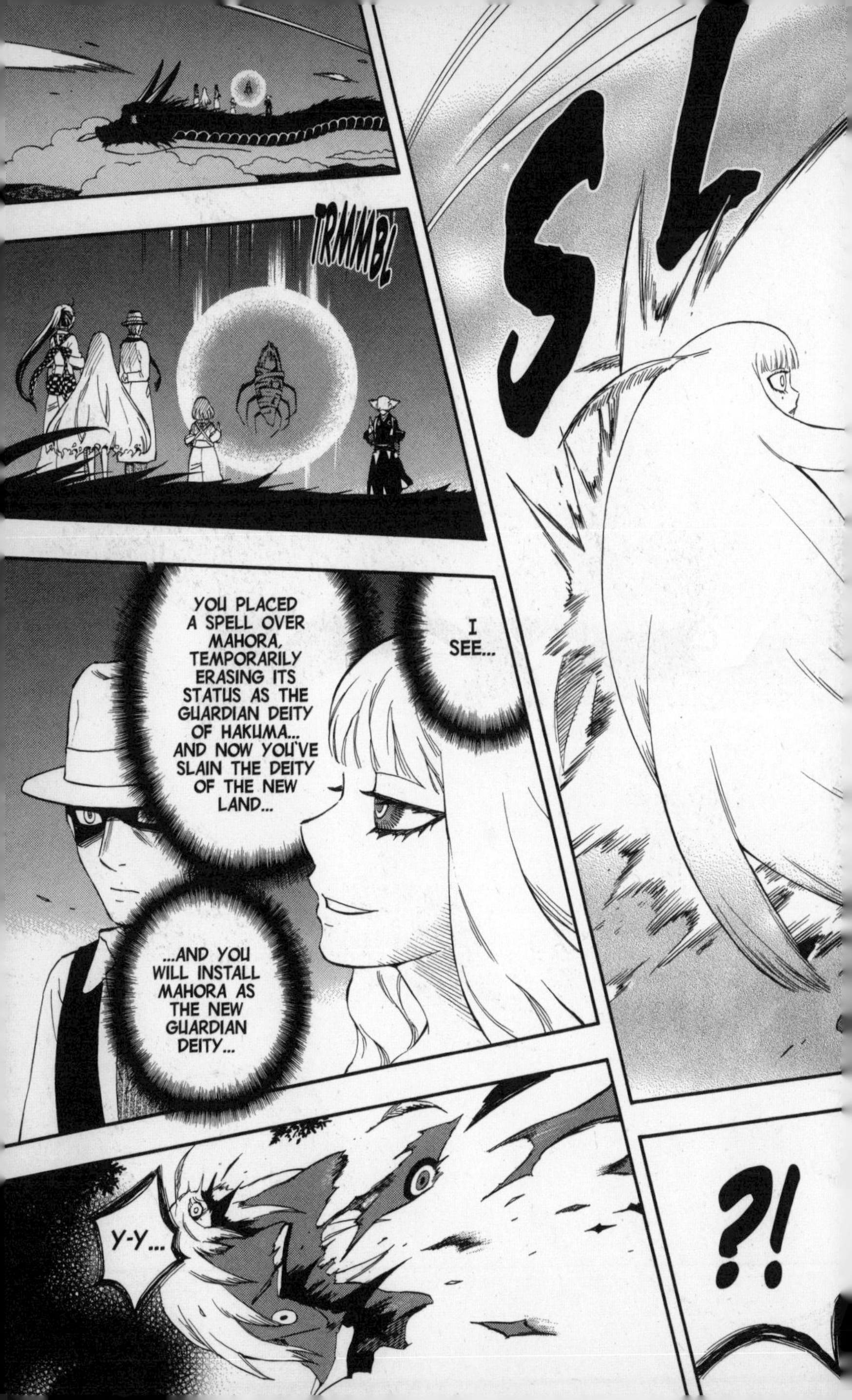
SL
TRMMBL
I SEE...
YOU PLACED A SPELL OVER MAHORA, TEMPORARILY ERASING ITS STATUS AS THE GUARDIAN DEITY OF HAKUMA... AND NOW YOU'VE SLAIN THE DEITY OF THE NEW LAND...
...AND YOU WILL INSTALL MAHORA AS THE NEW GUARDIAN DEITY...
?!
Y-Y...

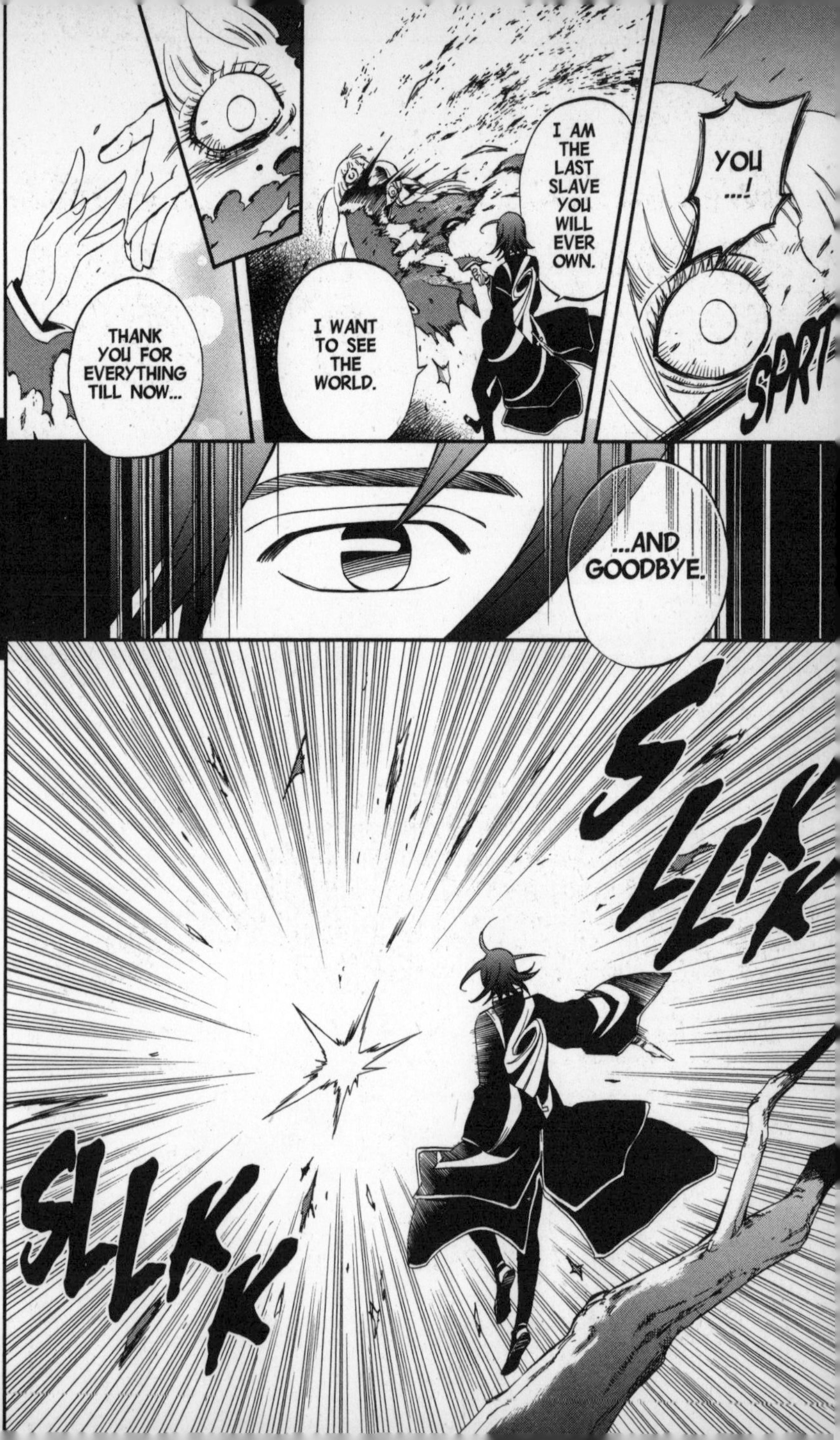
YOU ...!
SPRT
I AM THE LAST SLAVE YOU WILL EVER OWN.
I WANT TO SEE THE WORLD.
THANK YOU FOR EVERYTHING TILL NOW...
...AND GOODBYE.
SLLK
SLLKK

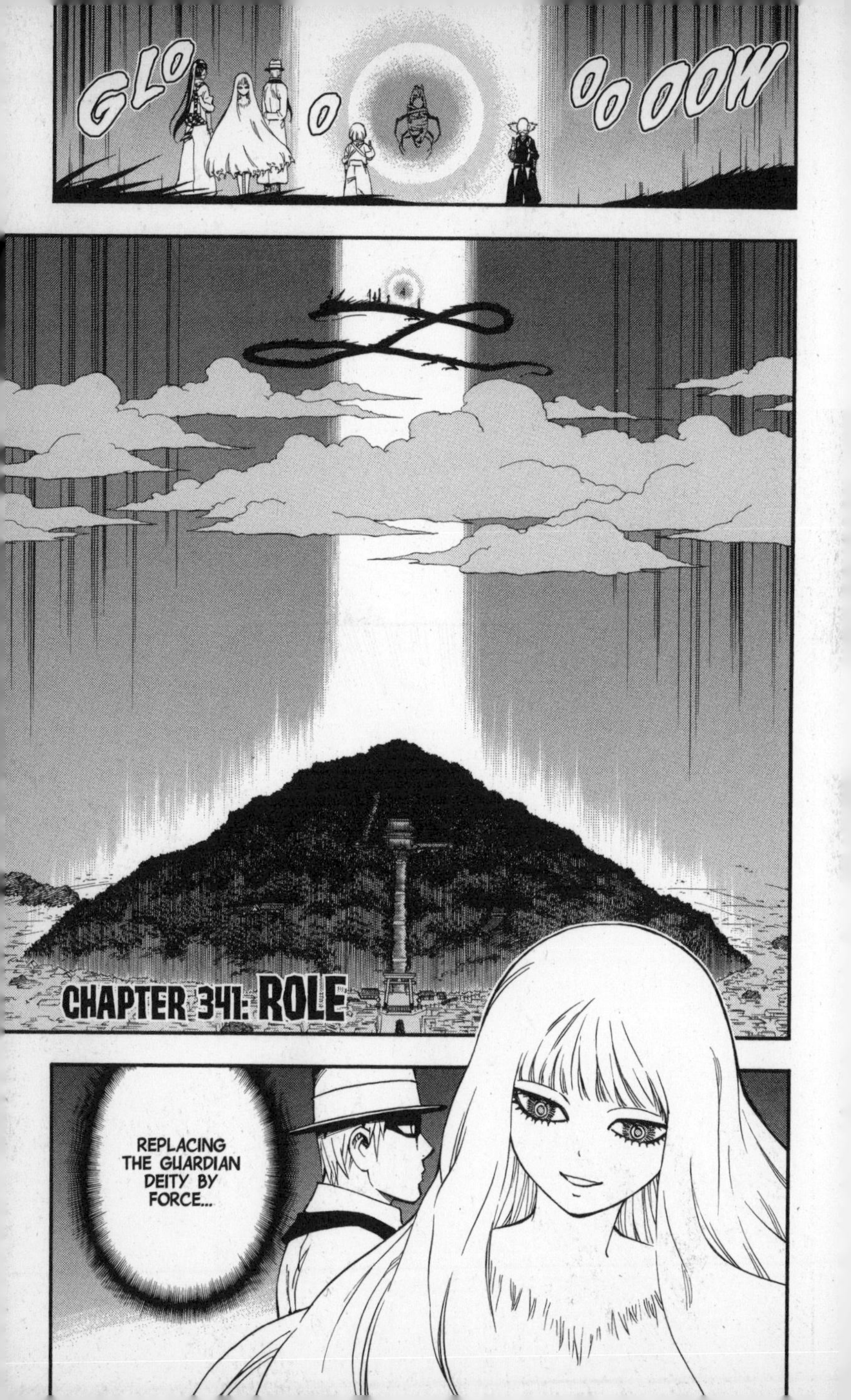
GLO O OO OOW
CHAPTER 341: ROLE
REPLACING THE GUARDIAN DEITY BY FORCE...

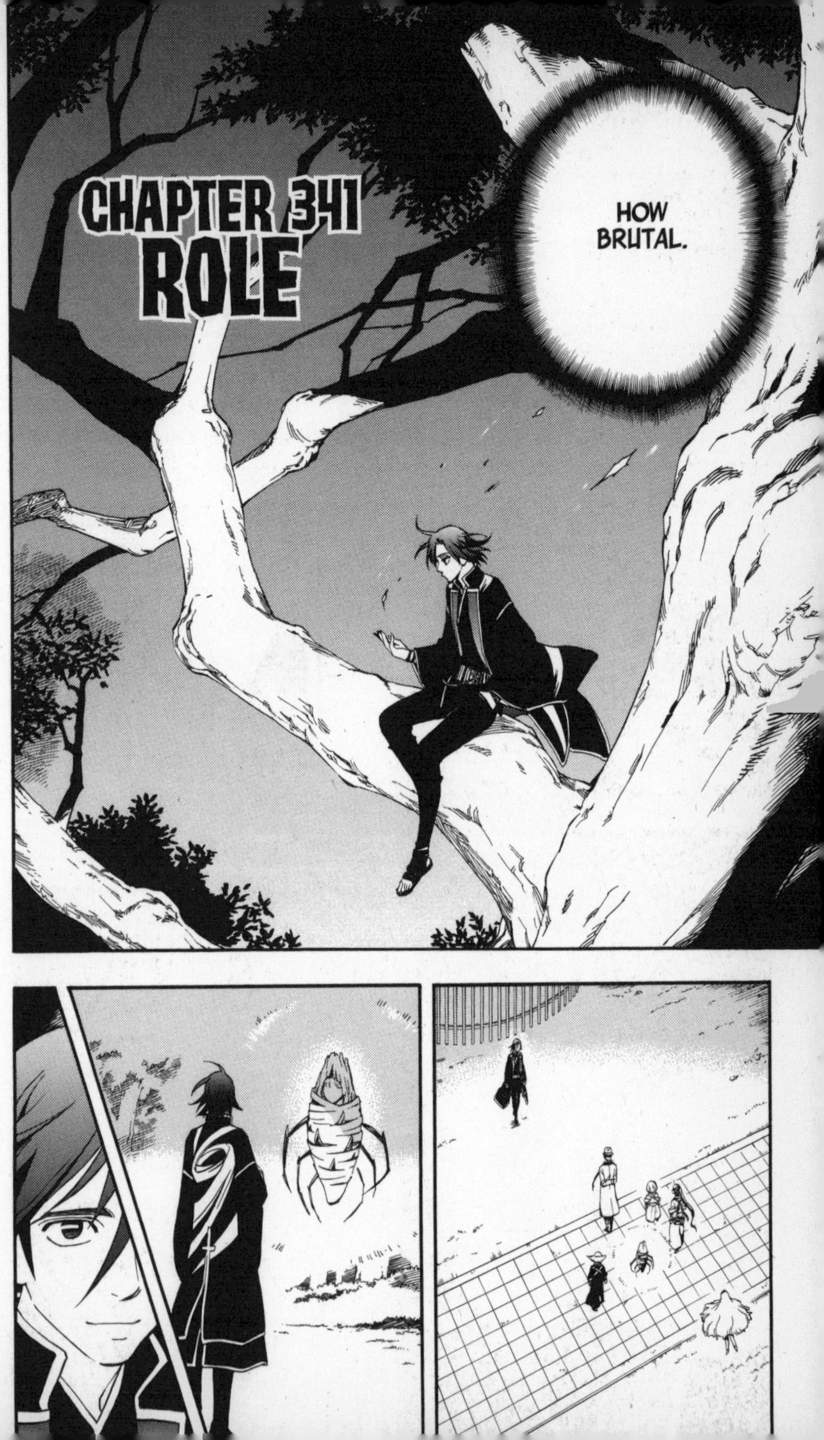
HOW BRUTAL.
CHAPTER 341
ROLE

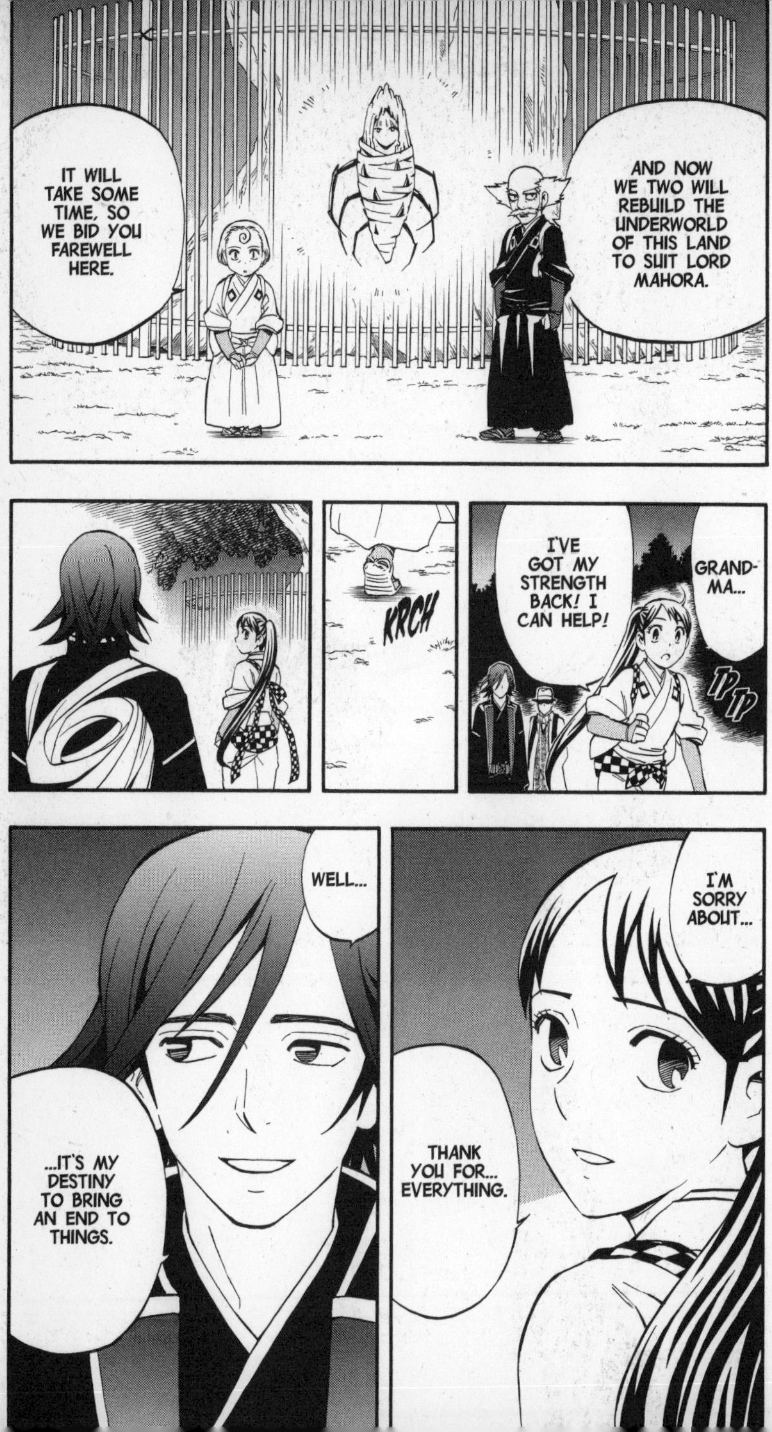
AND NOW WE TWO WILL REBUILD THE UNDERWORLD OF THIS LAND TO SUIT LORD MAHORA.
IT WILL TAKE SOME TIME, SO WE BID YOU FAREWELL HERE.
GRAND-MA...
I'VE GOT MY STRENGTH BACK! I CAN HELP!
TP TP
KRCH
I'M SORRY ABOUT...
THANK YOU FOR... EVERYTHING.
WELL...
...IT'S MY DESTINY TO BRING AN END TO THINGS.

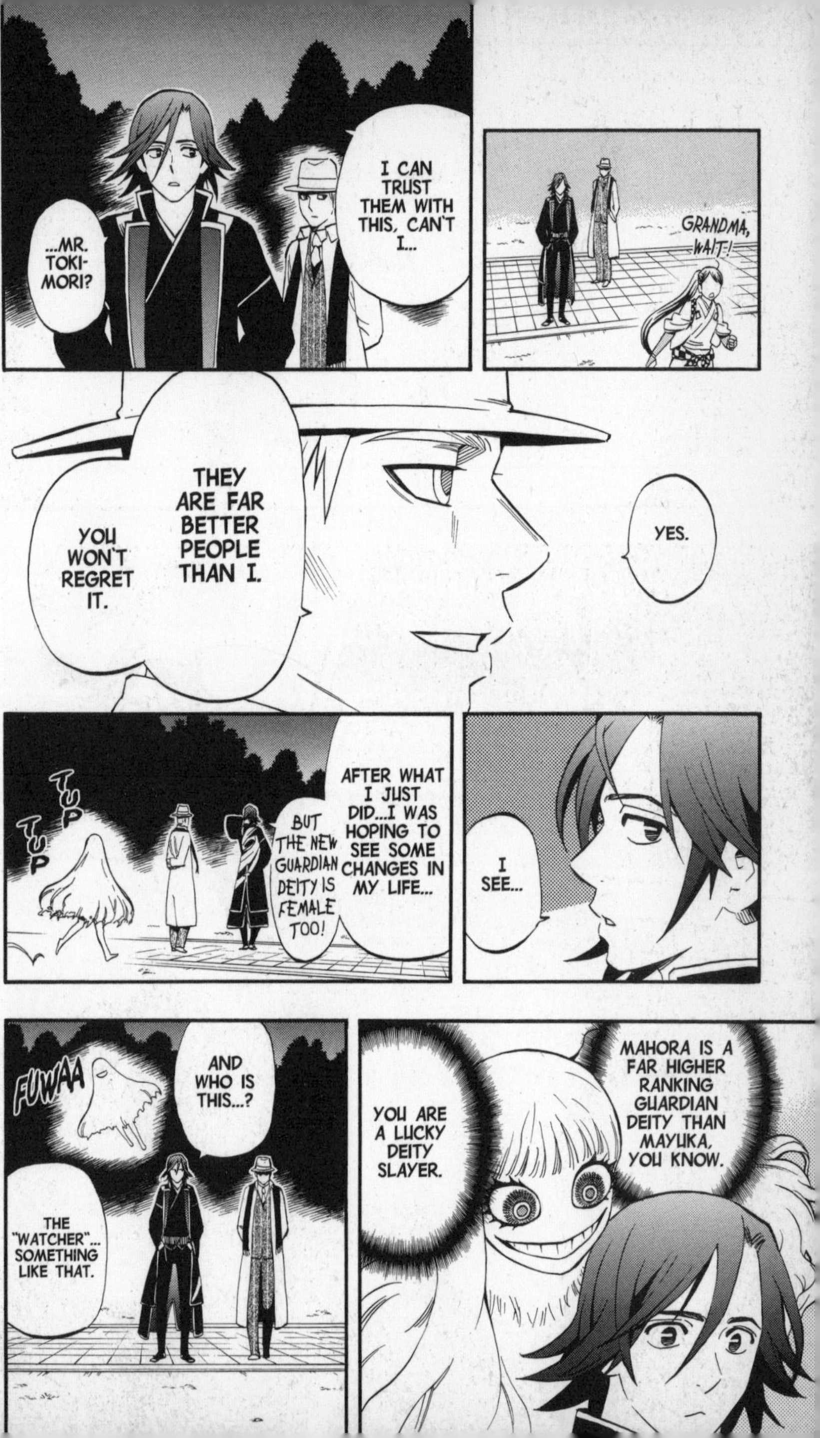
GRANDMA, WAIT!
I CAN TRUST THEM WITH THIS, CAN'T I...
...MR. TOKI-MORI?
YES.
THEY ARE FAR BETTER PEOPLE THAN I.
YOU WON'T REGRET IT.
I SEE...
AFTER WHAT I JUST DID...I WAS HOPING TO SEE SOME CHANGES IN MY LIFE...
BUT THE NEW GUARDIAN DEITY IS FEMALE TOO!
TUP TUP TUP
MAHORA IS A FAR HIGHER RANKING GUARDIAN DEITY THAN MAYUKA, YOU KNOW.
YOU ARE A LUCKY DEITY SLAYER.
AND WHO IS THIS...?
FUWAA
THE "WATCHER"... SOMETHING LIKE THAT.

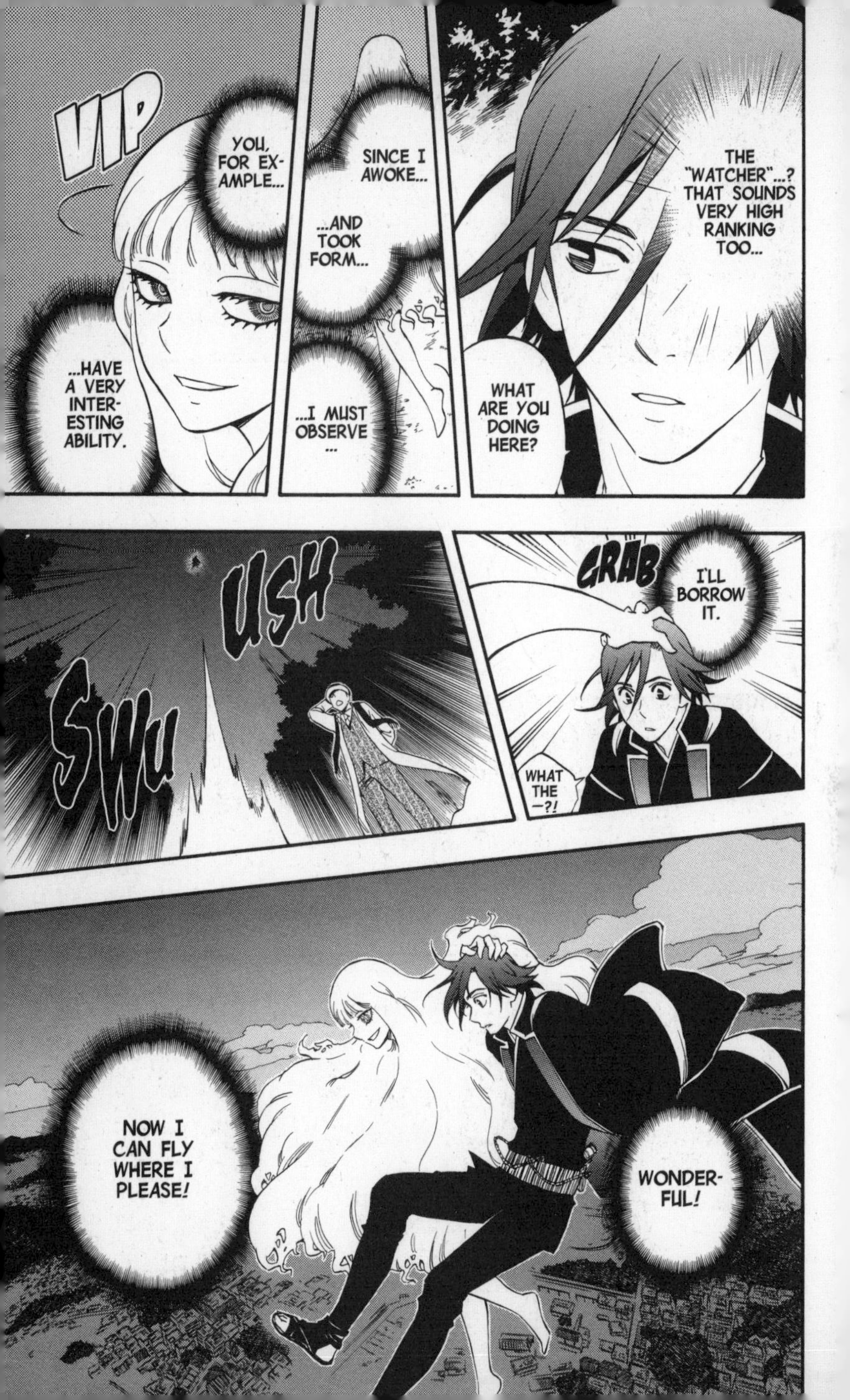
THE "WATCHER"...? THAT SOUNDS VERY HIGH RANKING TOO...
WHAT ARE YOU DOING HERE?
SINCE I AWOKE...
...AND TOOK FORM...
...I MUST OBSERVE ...
VIP
YOU, FOR EX-AMPLE...
...HAVE A VERY INTER-ESTING ABILITY.
GRAB
I'LL BORROW IT.
WHAT THE —?!
SWU USH
WONDER-FUL!
NOW I CAN FLY WHERE I PLEASE!

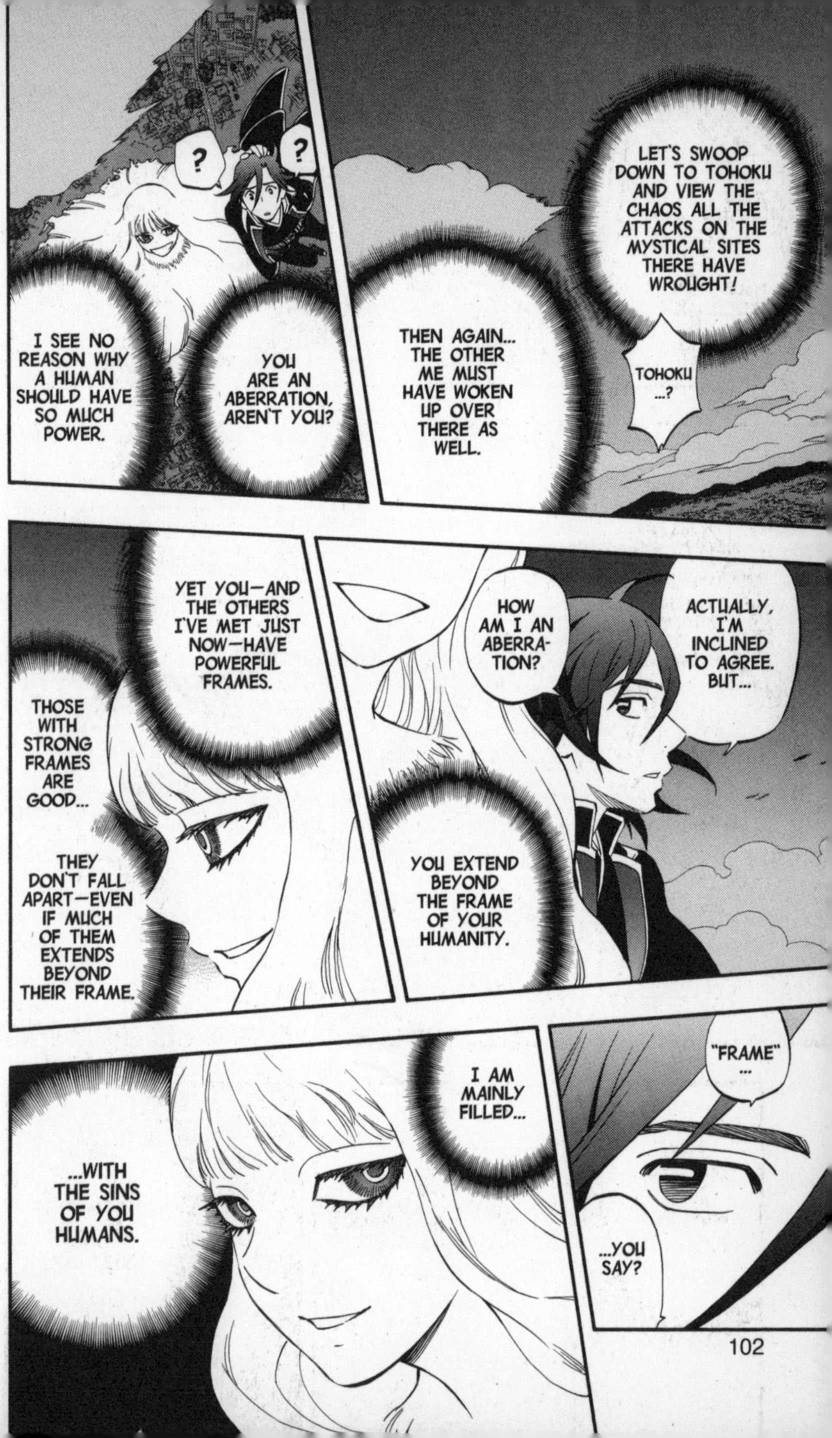
LET'S SWOOP DOWN TO TOHOKU AND VIEW THE CHAOS ALL THE ATTACKS ON THE MYSTICAL SITES THERE HAVE WROUGHT!
TOHOKU ...?
THEN AGAIN... THE OTHER ME MUST HAVE WOKEN UP OVER THERE AS WELL.
?
?
YOU ARE AN ABERRATION, AREN'T YOU?
I SEE NO REASON WHY A HUMAN SHOULD HAVE SO MUCH POWER.
ACTUALLY, I'M INCLINED TO AGREE. BUT...
HOW AM I AN ABERRATION?
YOU EXTEND BEYOND THE FRAME OF YOUR HUMANITY.
YET YOU—AND THE OTHERS I'VE MET JUST NOW—HAVE POWERFUL FRAMES.
THOSE WITH STRONG FRAMES ARE GOOD...
THEY DON'T FALL APART—EVEN IF MUCH OF THEM EXTENDS BEYOND THEIR FRAME.
"FRAME" ...
...YOU SAY?
I AM MAINLY FILLED...
...WITH THE SINS OF YOU HUMANS.

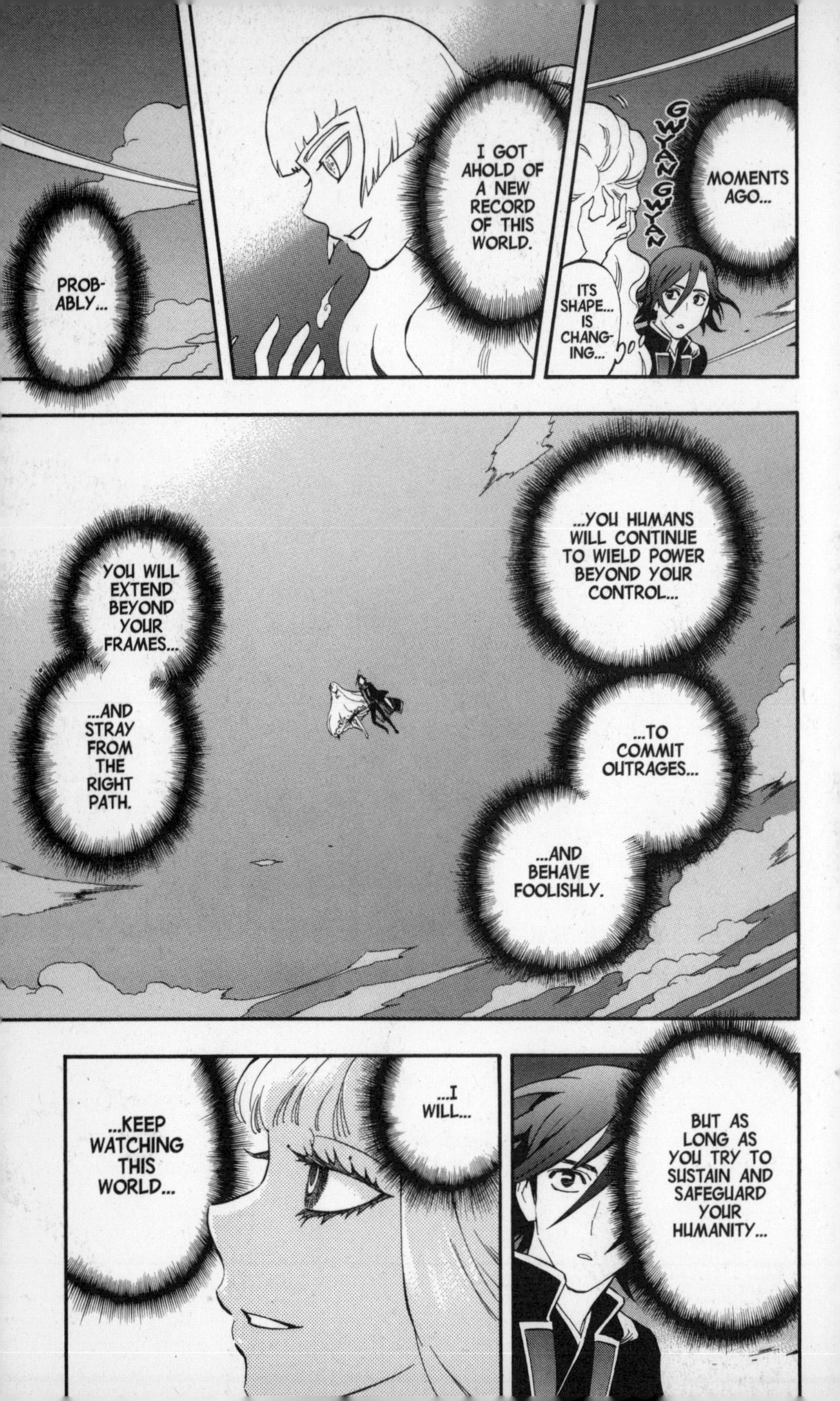
MOMENTS AGO...
GWYAN GWYAN
ITS SHAPE... IS CHANGING...
I GOT AHOLD OF A NEW RECORD OF THIS WORLD.
PROBABLY...
...YOU HUMANS WILL CONTINUE TO WIELD POWER BEYOND YOUR CONTROL...
...TO COMMIT OUTRAGES...
...AND BEHAVE FOOLISHLY.
YOU WILL EXTEND BEYOND YOUR FRAMES...
...AND STRAY FROM THE RIGHT PATH.
BUT AS LONG AS YOU TRY TO SUSTAIN AND SAFEGUARD YOUR HUMANITY...
...I WILL...
...KEEP WATCHING THIS WORLD...

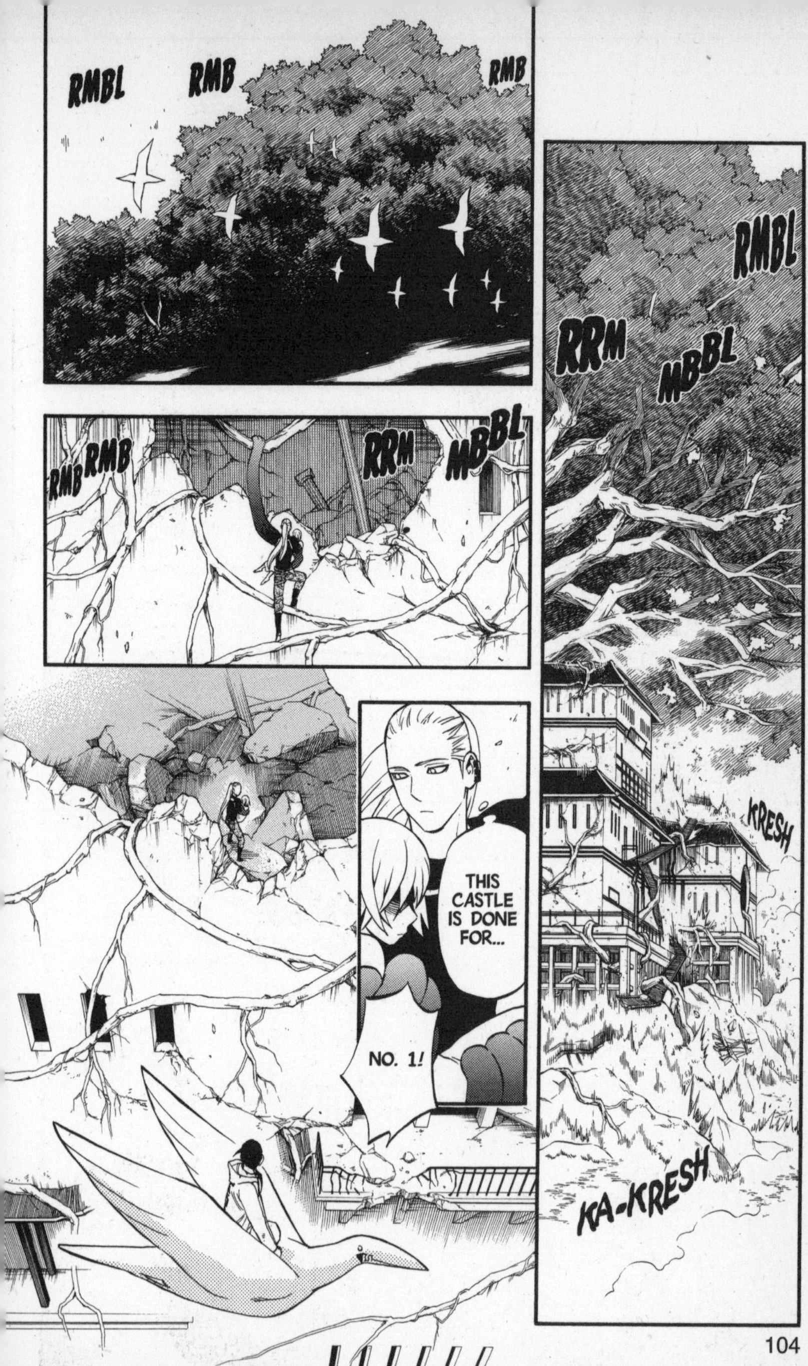

RMBL
RRM
MBBL
KRESH
KA-KRESH
RMB
RMB
RMBL
MBBL
RRM
RMB
RMB
THIS CASTLE IS DONE FOR...
NO. 1!

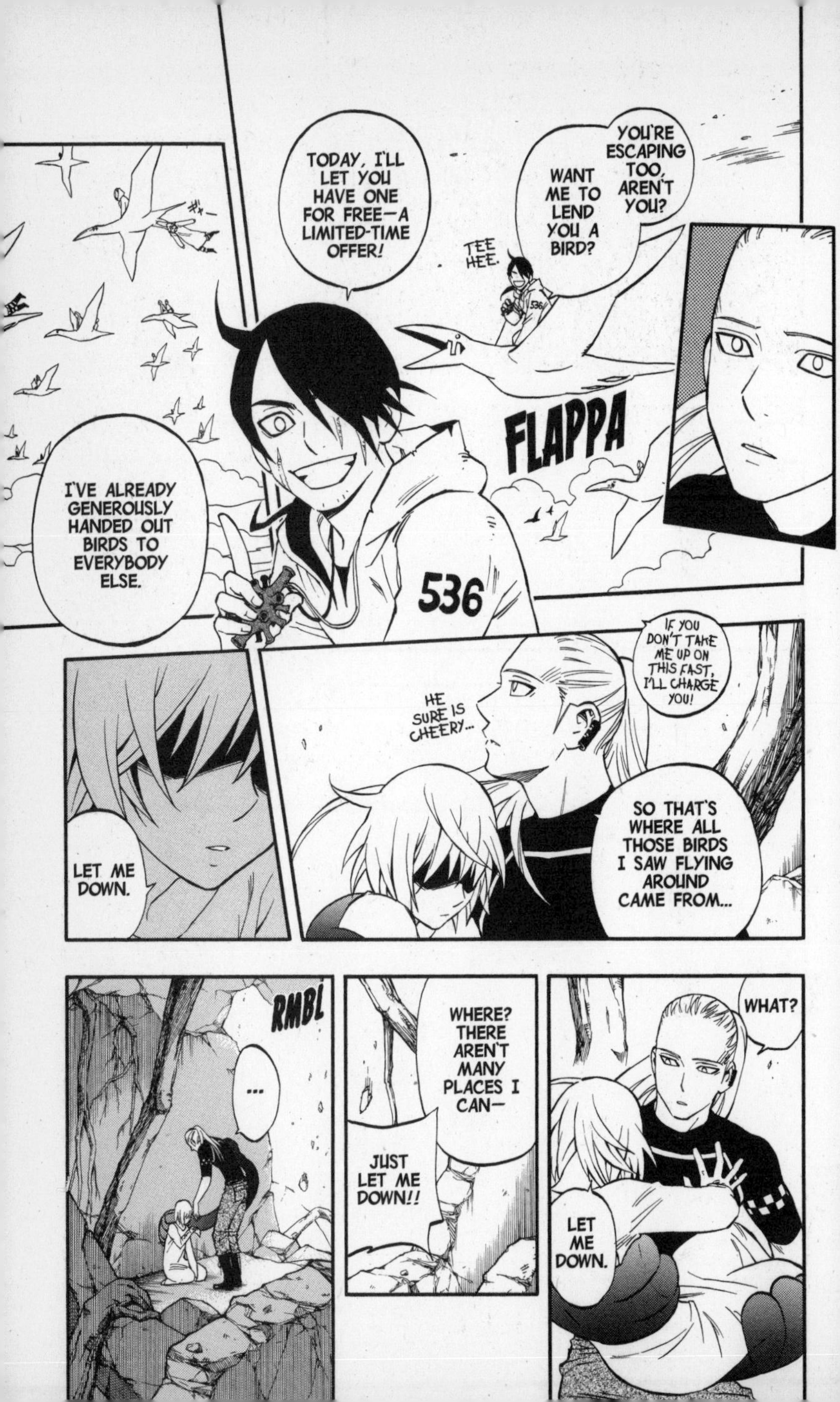
YOU'RE ESCAPING TOO, AREN'T YOU?
WANT ME TO LEND YOU A BIRD?
TEE HEE.
TODAY, I'LL LET YOU HAVE ONE FOR FREE—A LIMITED-TIME OFFER!
FLAPPA
536
I'VE ALREADY GENEROUSLY HANDED OUT BIRDS TO EVERYBODY ELSE.
IF YOU DON'T TAKE ME UP ON THIS FAST, I'LL CHARGE YOU!
HE SURE IS CHEERY...
SO THAT'S WHERE ALL THOSE BIRDS I SAW FLYING AROUND CAME FROM...
LET ME DOWN.
WHAT?
LET ME DOWN.
WHERE? THERE AREN'T MANY PLACES I CAN—
JUST LET ME DOWN!!
RMBL
...

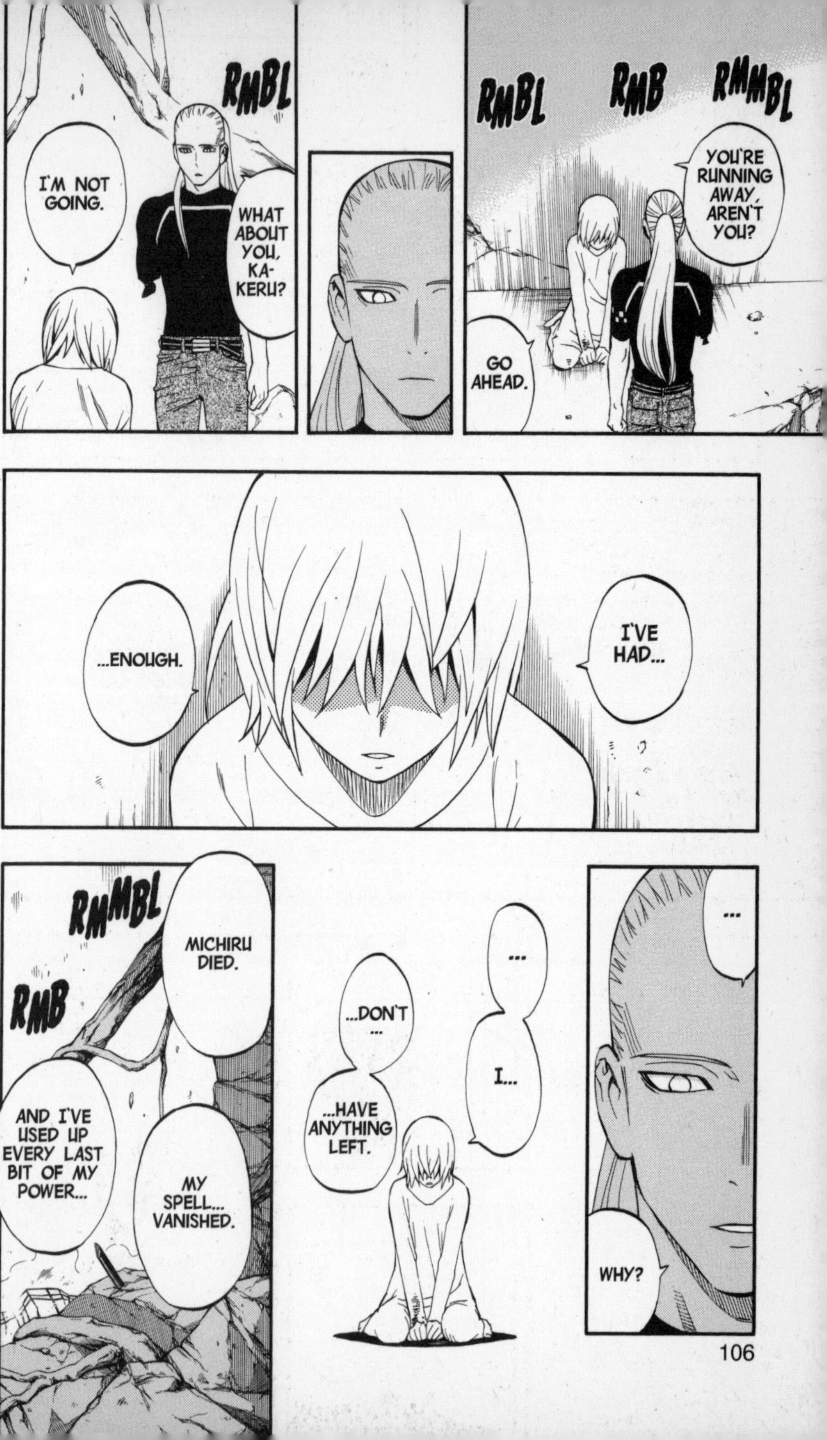
RMBL
RMB
RMMBL
YOU'RE RUNNING AWAY, AREN'T YOU?
GO AHEAD.
RMBL
I'M NOT GOING.
WHAT ABOUT YOU, KA-KERU?
I'VE HAD...
...ENOUGH.
...
WHY?
...
I...
...DON'T ...
...HAVE ANYTHING LEFT.
RMMBL
RMB
MICHIRU DIED.
MY SPELL... VANISHED.
AND I'VE USED UP EVERY LAST BIT OF MY POWER...

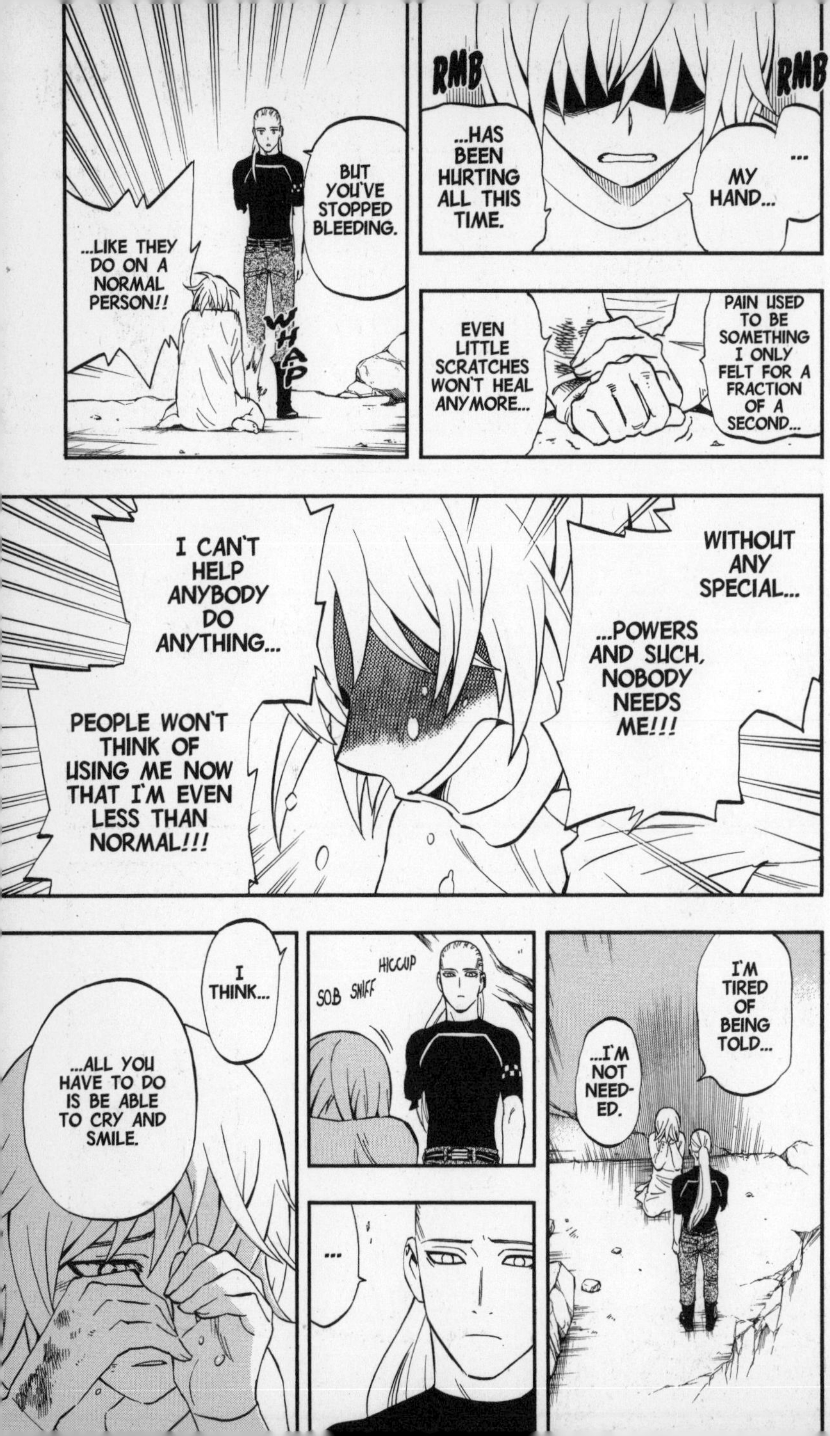
RMB
...
MY HAND...
...HAS BEEN HURTING ALL THIS TIME.
RMB
PAIN USED TO BE SOMETHING I ONLY FELT FOR A FRACTION OF A SECOND...
EVEN LITTLE SCRATCHES WON'T HEAL ANYMORE...
BUT YOU'VE STOPPED BLEEDING.
...LIKE THEY DO ON A NORMAL PERSON!!
WHAP
WITHOUT ANY SPECIAL...
...POWERS AND SUCH, NOBODY NEEDS ME!!!
I CAN'T HELP ANYBODY DO ANYTHING...
PEOPLE WON'T THINK OF USING ME NOW THAT I'M EVEN LESS THAN NORMAL!!!
I'M TIRED OF BEING TOLD...
...I'M NOT NEEDED.
HICCUP
SNIFF
SOB
...
I THINK...
...ALL YOU HAVE TO DO IS BE ABLE TO CRY AND SMILE.

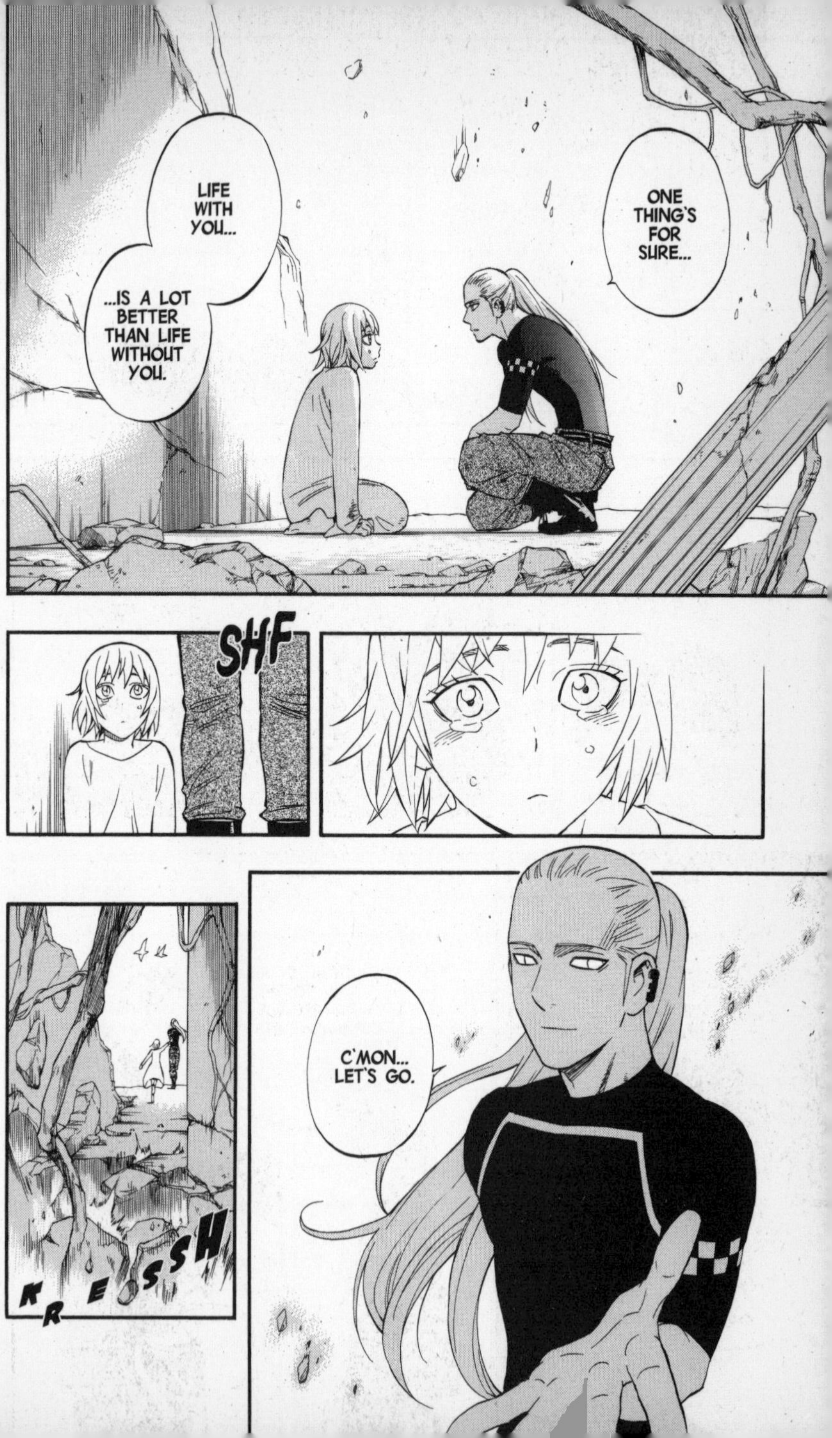
ONE THING'S FOR SURE...
LIFE WITH YOU...
...IS A LOT BETTER THAN LIFE WITHOUT YOU.
SHF
C'MON... LET'S GO.
KRESSH

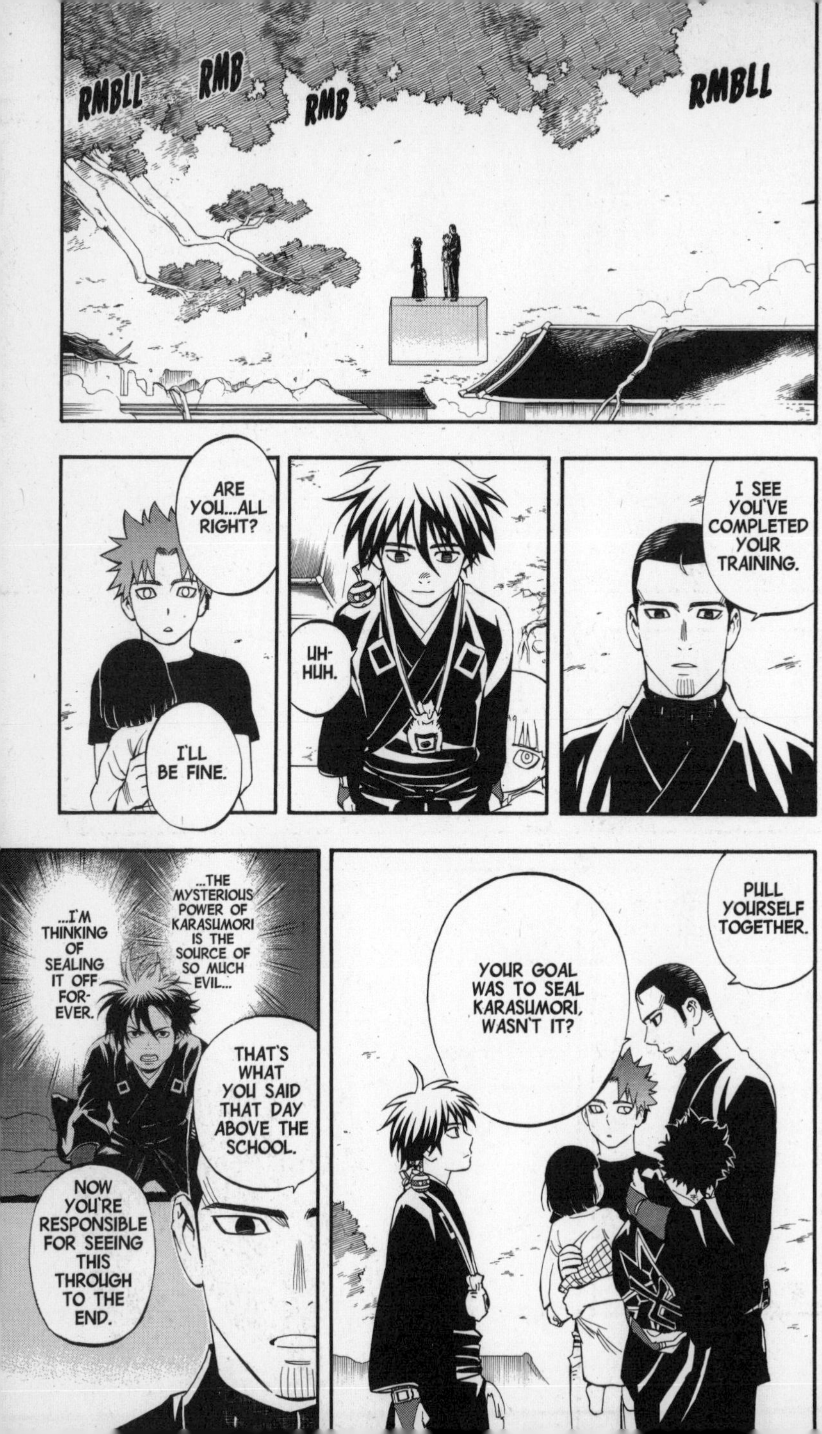
RMBLL
RMB
RMB
RMBLL
I SEE YOU'VE COMPLETED YOUR TRAINING.
UH-HUH.
ARE YOU...ALL RIGHT?
I'LL BE FINE.
PULL YOURSELF TOGETHER.
YOUR GOAL WAS TO SEAL KARASUMORI, WASN'T IT?
...THE MYSTERIOUS POWER OF KARASUMORI IS THE SOURCE OF SO MUCH EVIL...
...I'M THINKING OF SEALING IT OFF FOR-EVER.
THAT'S WHAT YOU SAID THAT DAY ABOVE THE SCHOOL.
NOW YOU'RE RESPONSIBLE FOR SEEING THIS THROUGH TO THE END.

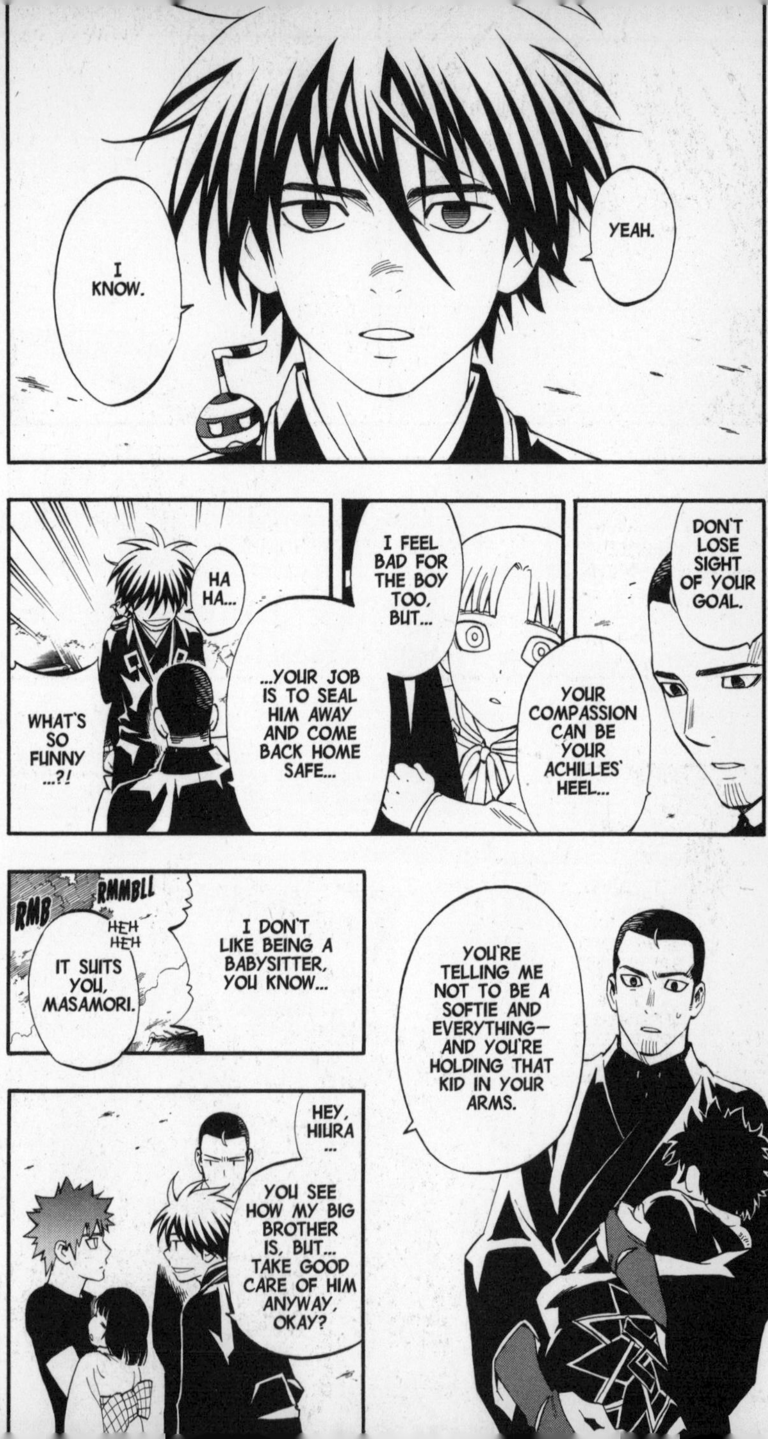
YEAH.
I KNOW.
DON'T LOSE SIGHT OF YOUR GOAL.
YOUR COMPASSION CAN BE YOUR ACHILLES' HEEL...
I FEEL BAD FOR THE BOY TOO, BUT...
...YOUR JOB IS TO SEAL HIM AWAY AND COME BACK HOME SAFE...
HA HA...
WHAT'S SO FUNNY ...?!
YOU'RE TELLING ME NOT TO BE A SOFTIE AND EVERYTHING— AND YOU'RE HOLDING THAT KID IN YOUR ARMS.
RMMBLL
I DON'T LIKE BEING A BABYSITTER, YOU KNOW...
RMB
HEH HEH
IT SUITS YOU, MASAMORI.
HEY, HIURA ...
YOU SEE HOW MY BIG BROTHER IS, BUT... TAKE GOOD CARE OF HIM ANYWAY, OKAY?

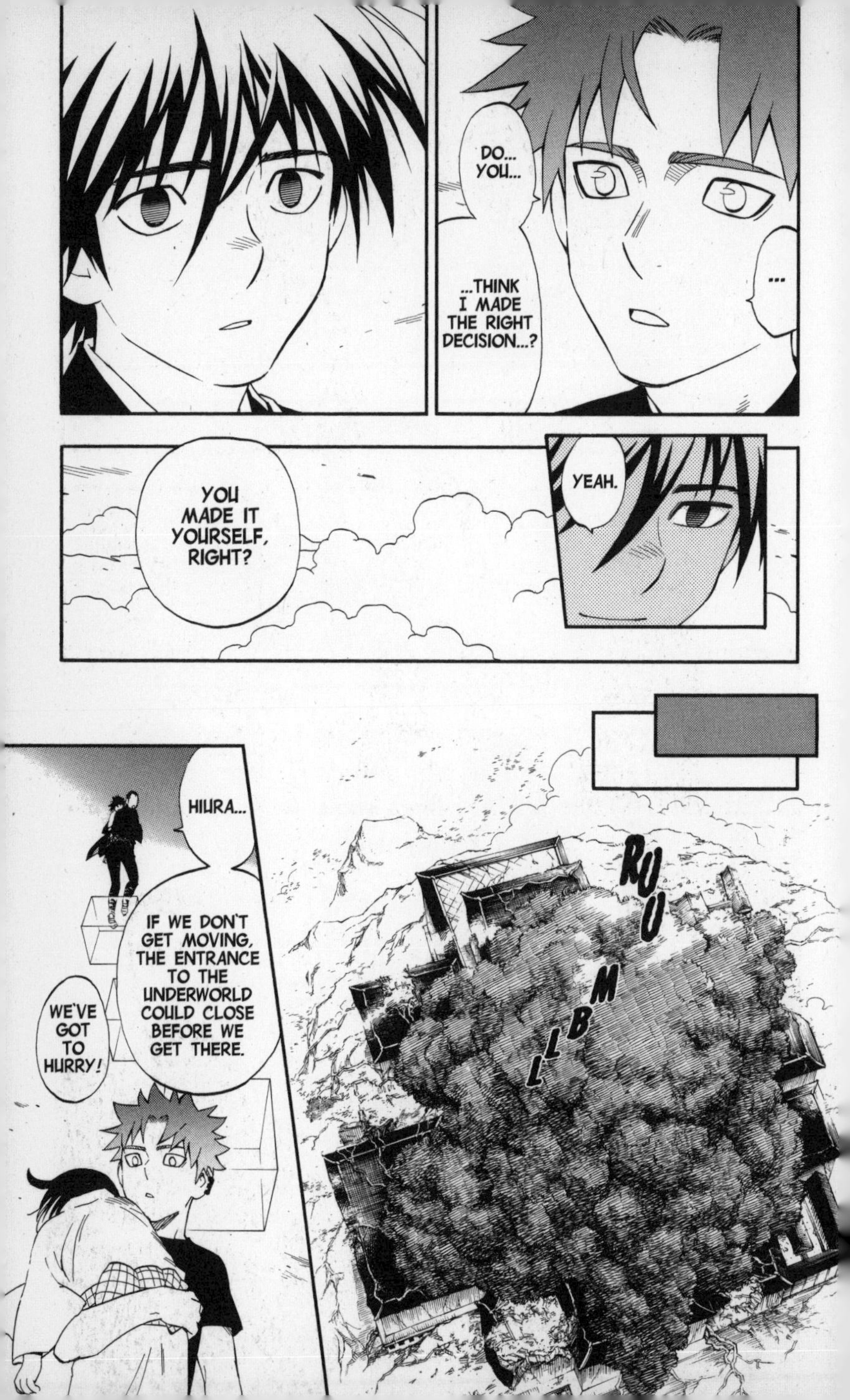

DO... YOU...
...THINK I MADE THE RIGHT DECISION...?
...
YOU MADE IT YOURSELF, RIGHT?
YEAH.
RUUMBLL
HIURA...
IF WE DON'T GET MOVING, THE ENTRANCE TO THE UNDERWORLD COULD CLOSE BEFORE WE GET THERE.
WE'VE GOT TO HURRY!

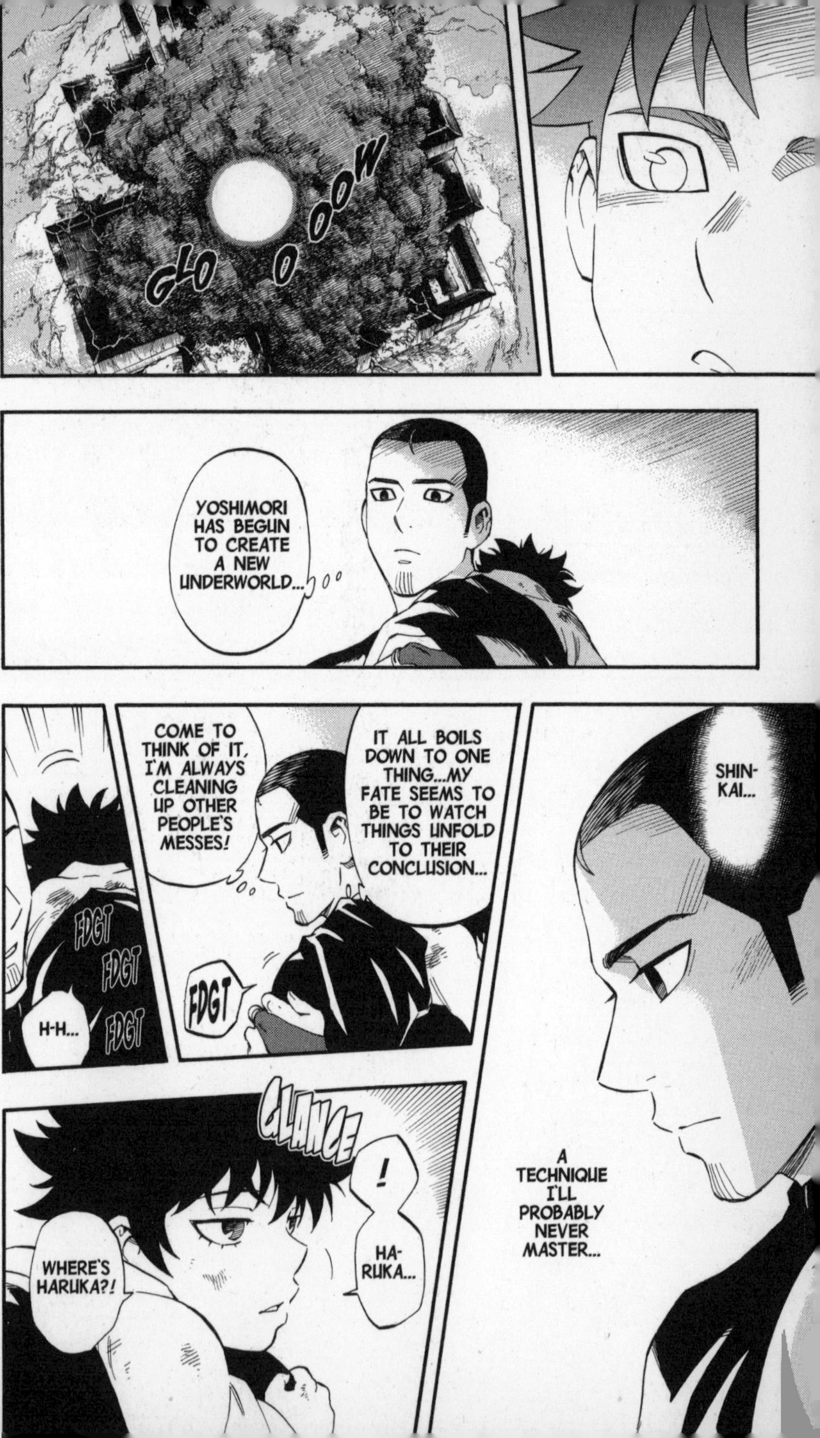
GLO O OOW
YOSHIMORI HAS BEGUN TO CREATE A NEW UNDERWORLD...
SHIN-KAI...
A TECHNIQUE I'LL PROBABLY NEVER MASTER...
IT ALL BOILS DOWN TO ONE THING...MY FATE SEEMS TO BE TO WATCH THINGS UNFOLD TO THEIR CONCLUSION...
COME TO THINK OF IT, I'M ALWAYS CLEANING UP OTHER PEOPLE'S MESSES!
FDGT
FDGT
FDGT
FDGT
H-H...
GLANCE
!
HA-RUKA...
WHERE'S HARUKA?!

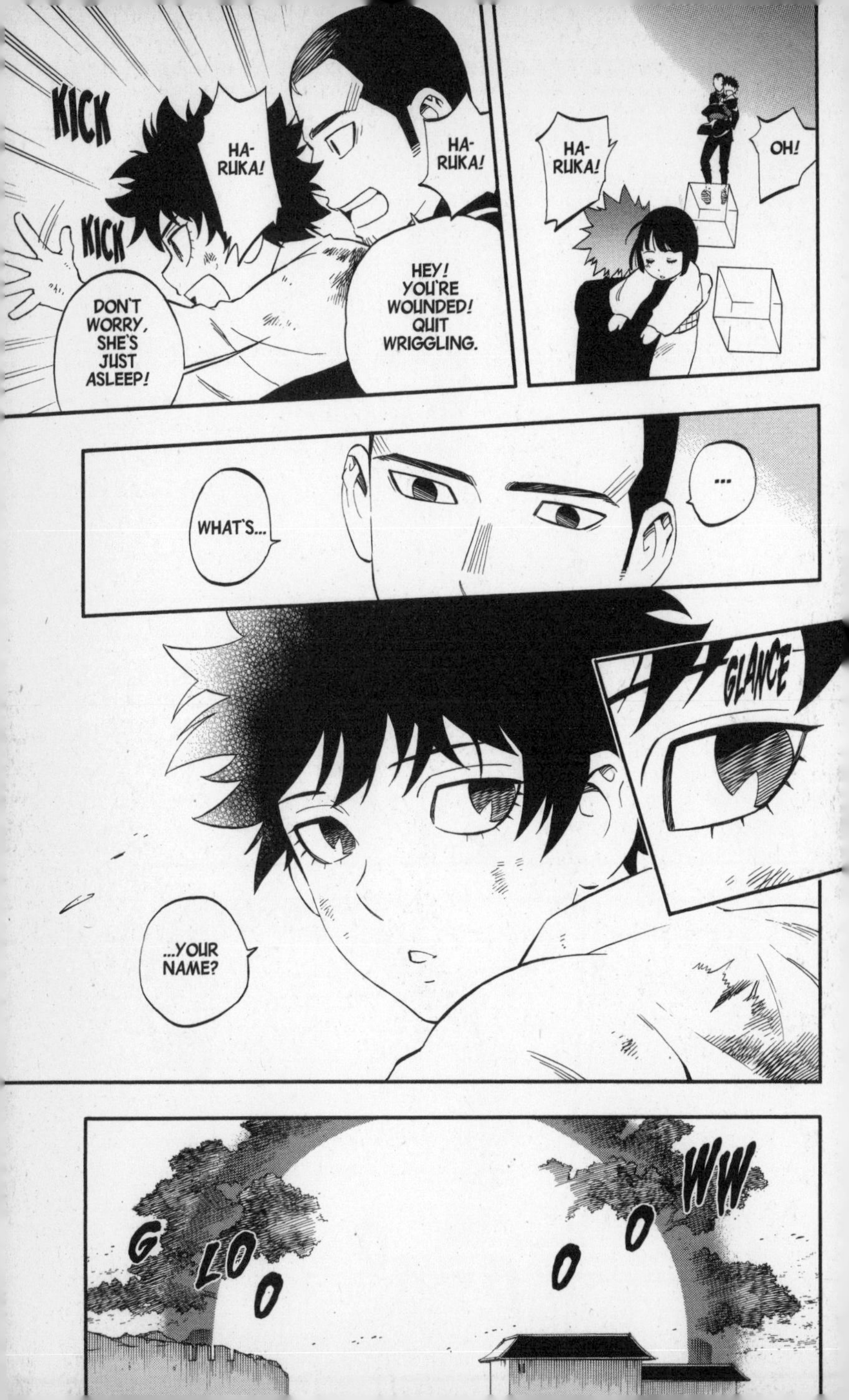
OH!
HA-RUKA!
HA-RUKA!
HA-RUKA!
HEY! YOU'RE WOUNDED! QUIT WRIGGLING.
KICK
KICK
DON'T WORRY, SHE'S JUST ASLEEP!
...
WHAT'S...
GLANCE
...YOUR NAME?
G LO O O O WW

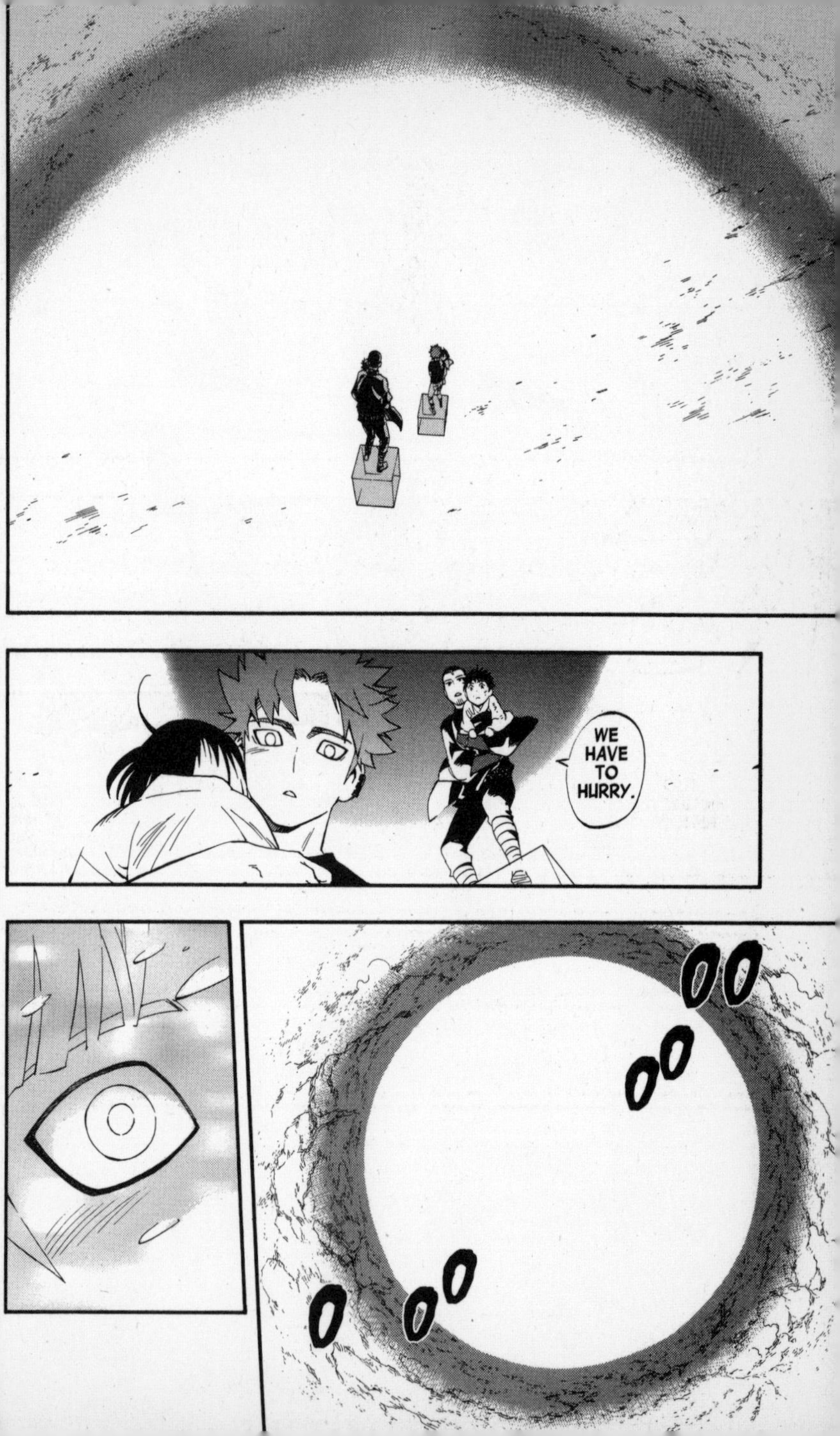
WE HAVE TO HURRY.

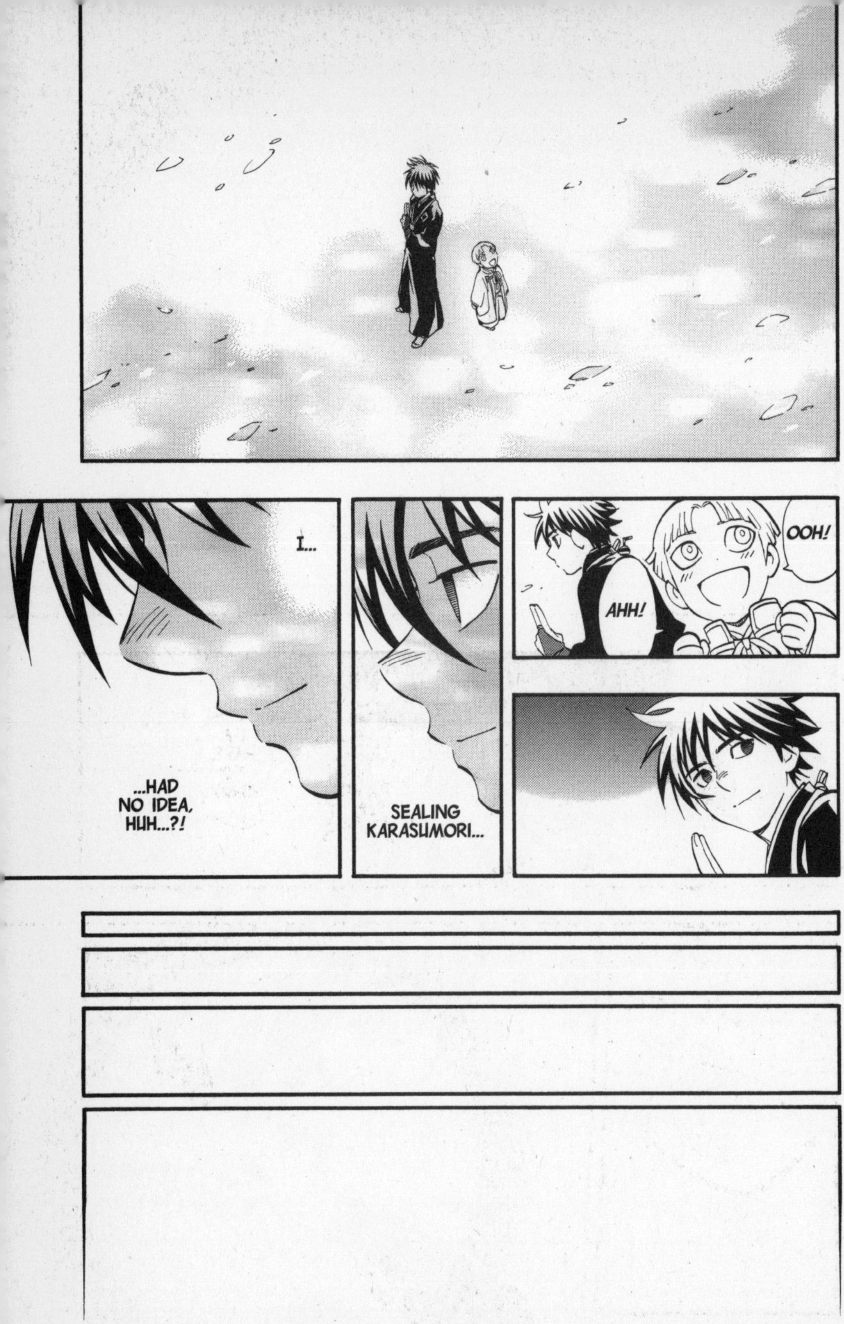
OOH!
AHH!
SEALING KARASUMORI...
I...
...HAD NO IDEA, HUH...?!

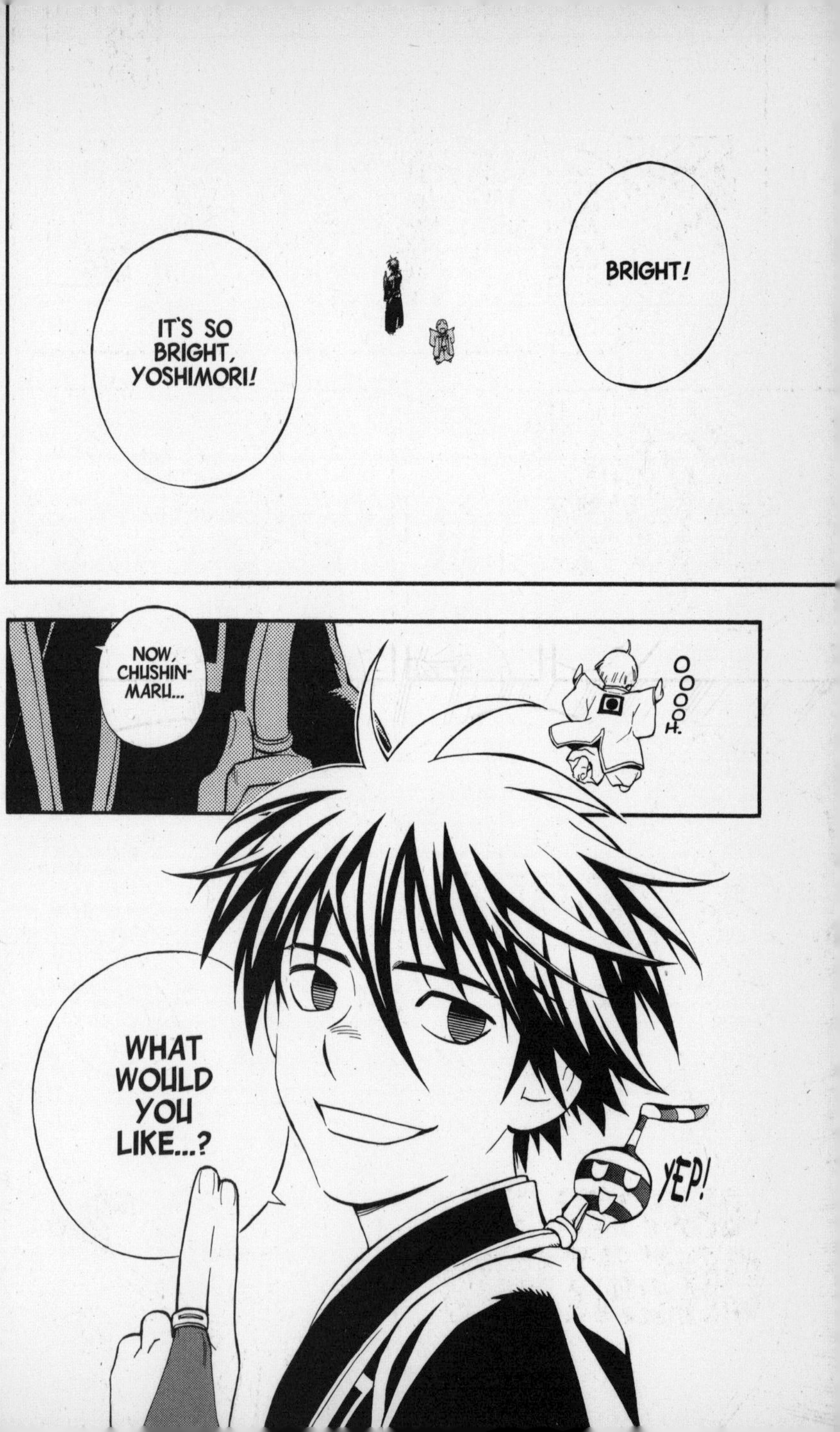
BRIGHT!
IT'S SO BRIGHT, YOSHIMORI!
OOOOH.
NOW, CHUSHIN-MARU...
WHAT WOULD YOU LIKE...?
YEP!

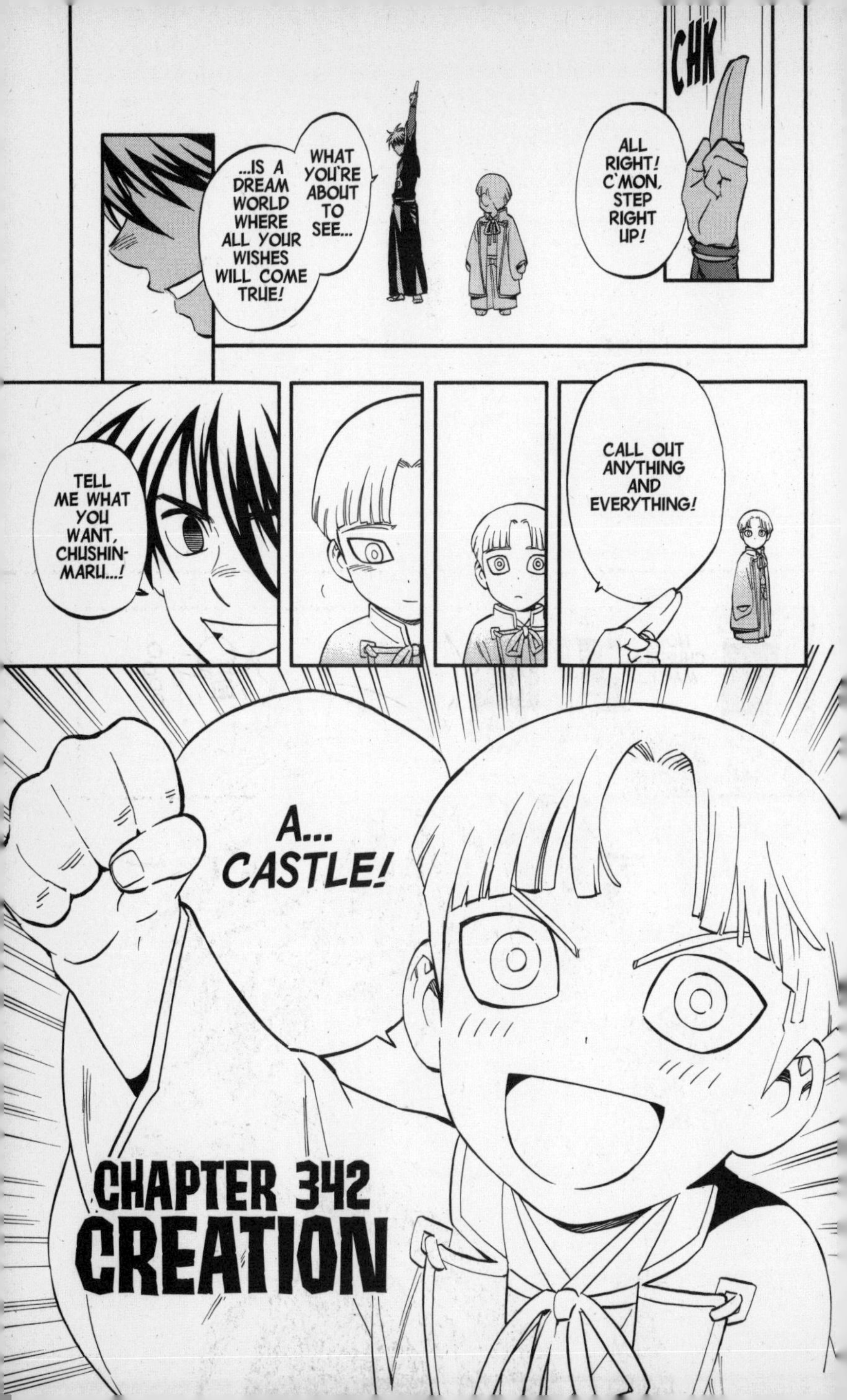
CHK
ALL RIGHT! C'MON, STEP RIGHT UP!
WHAT YOU'RE ABOUT TO SEE...
...IS A DREAM WORLD WHERE ALL YOUR WISHES WILL COME TRUE!
CALL OUT ANYTHING AND EVERYTHING!
TELL ME WHAT YOU WANT, CHUSHIN-MARU...!
A... CASTLE!

CHAPTER 342
CREATION

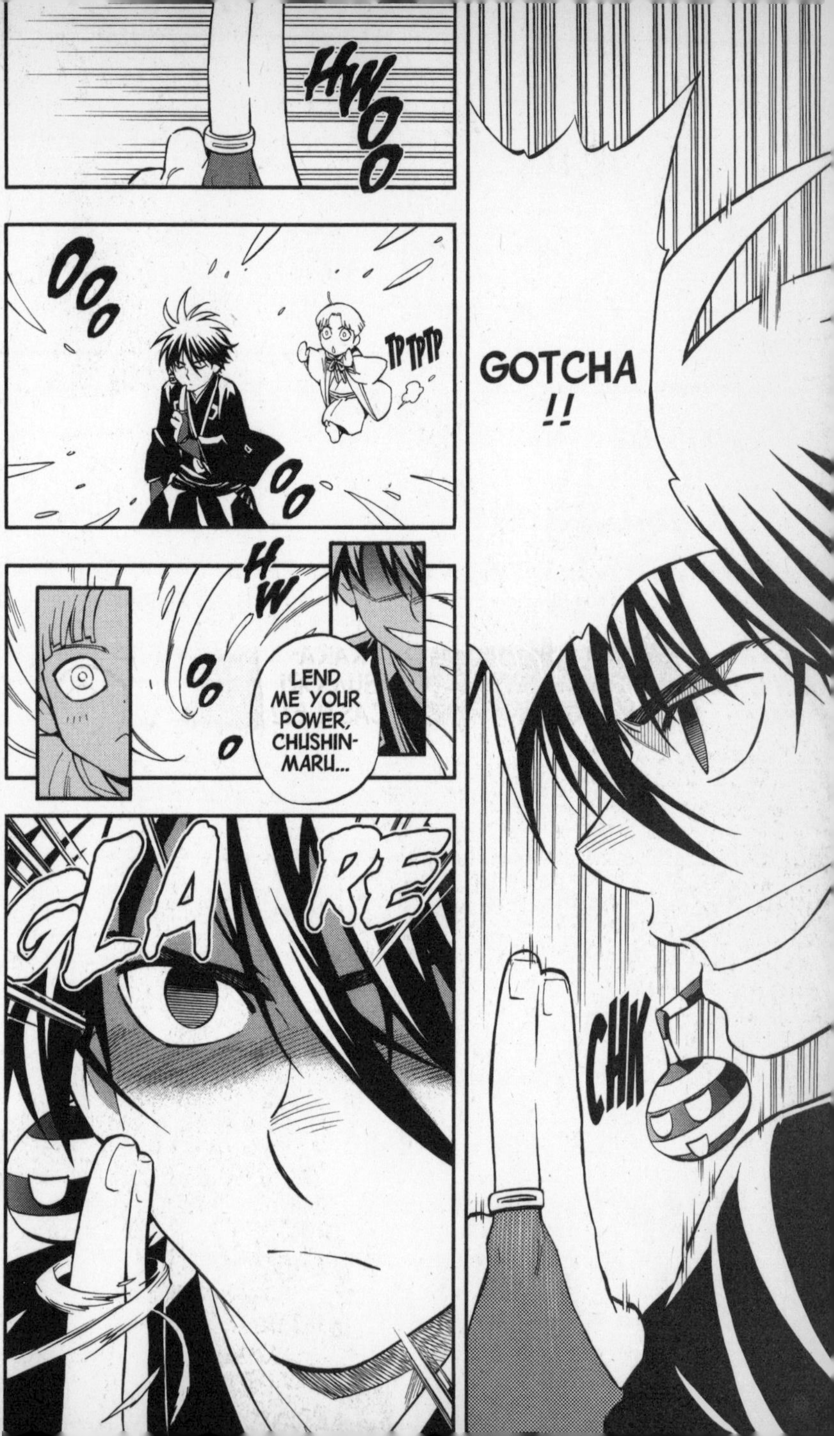
GOTCHA!!
CHK
HWOO
TP TP TP
OOO
OOO
HW
OOO
LEND ME YOUR POWER, CHUSHIN-MARU...
GLARE

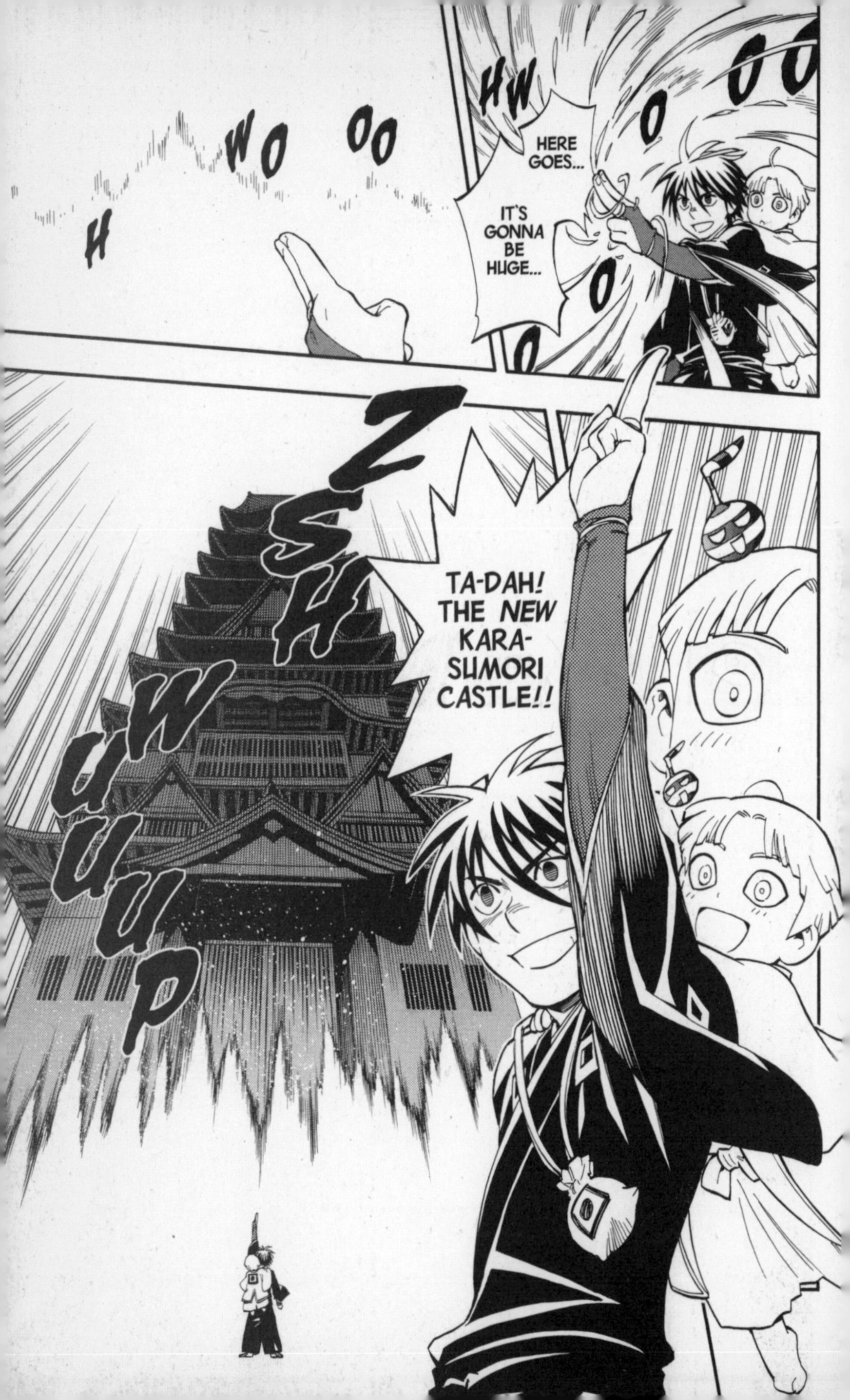
HWOOOOOO
HERE GOES...
IT'S GONNA BE HUGE...
HWOOO
TA-DAH! THE NEW KARA-SUMORI CASTLE!!
ZSHWUUUUP

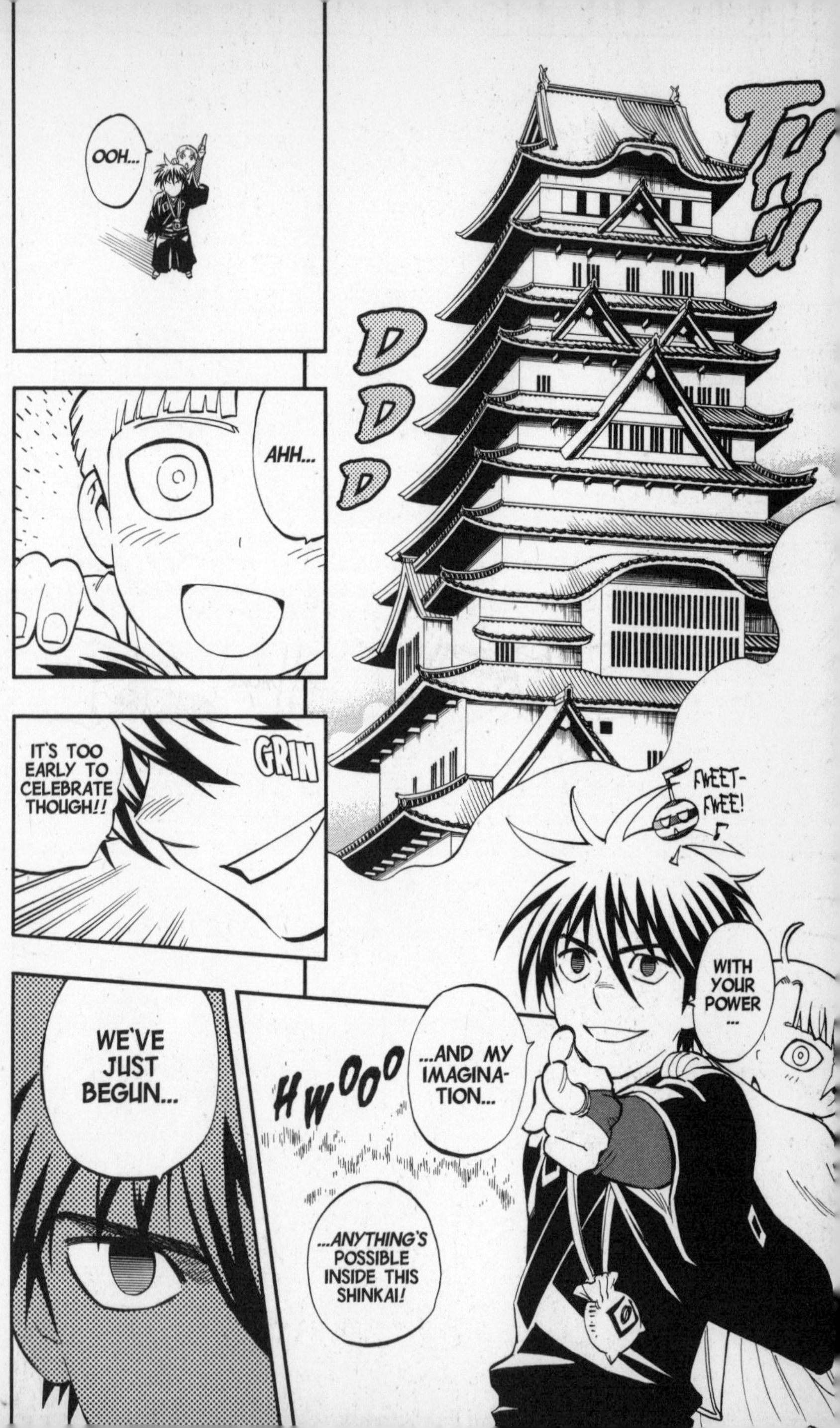

THU
DDD
OOH...
AHH...
IT'S TOO EARLY TO CELEBRATE THOUGH!!
GRIN
FWEET-FWEE!
WITH YOUR POWER...
...AND MY IMAGINATION...
HWOOO
...ANYTHING'S POSSIBLE INSIDE THIS SHINKAI!
WE'VE JUST BEGUN...

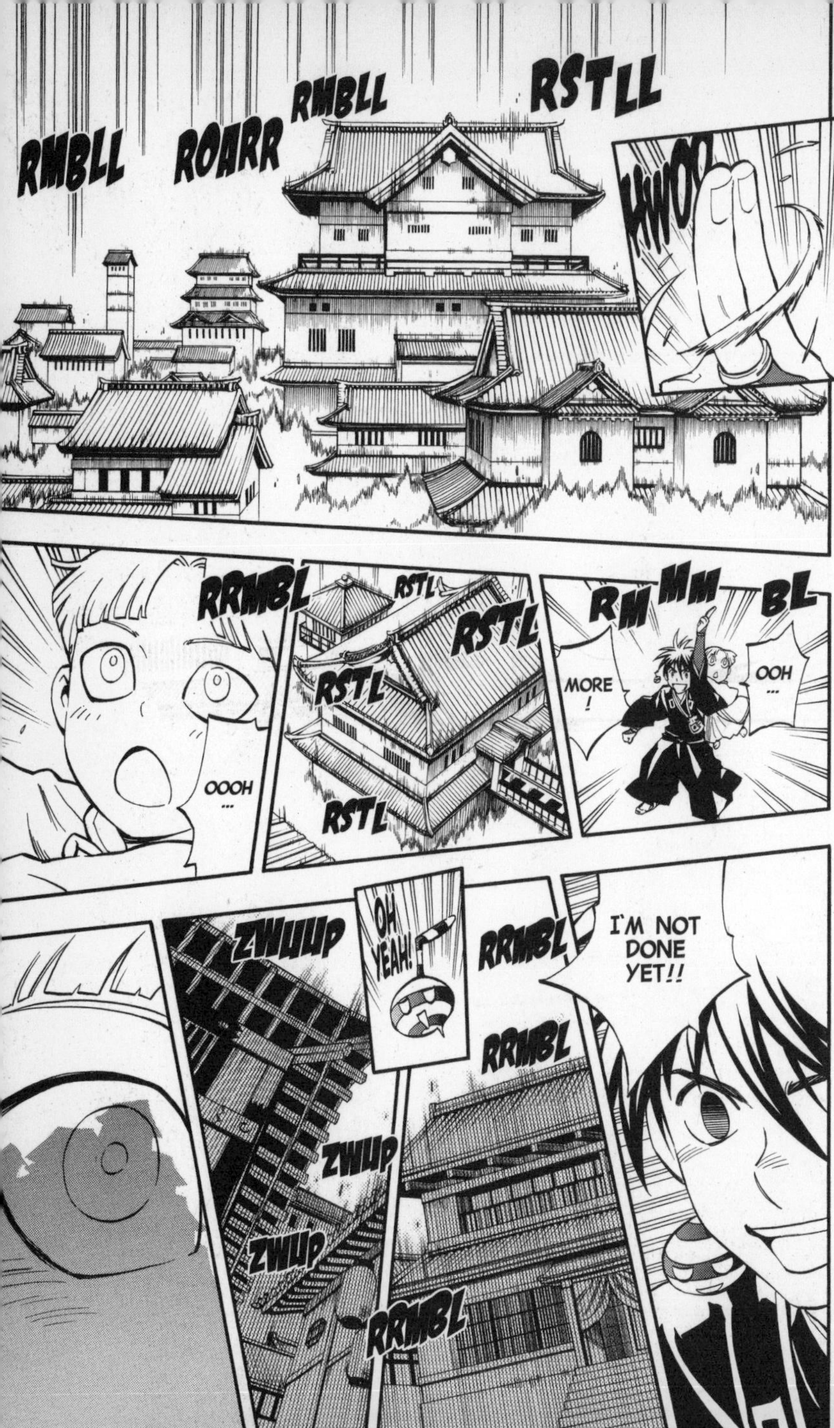
RSTLL
HWOO
RMBLL
ROARR
RMBLL
RM MM BL
OOH ...
MORE!
RSTL
RSTL
RSTL
RSTL
RRMBL
OOOH ...
I'M NOT DONE YET!!
RRMBL
RRMBL
RRMBL
OH YEAH!
ZWUUP
ZWUP
ZWUP

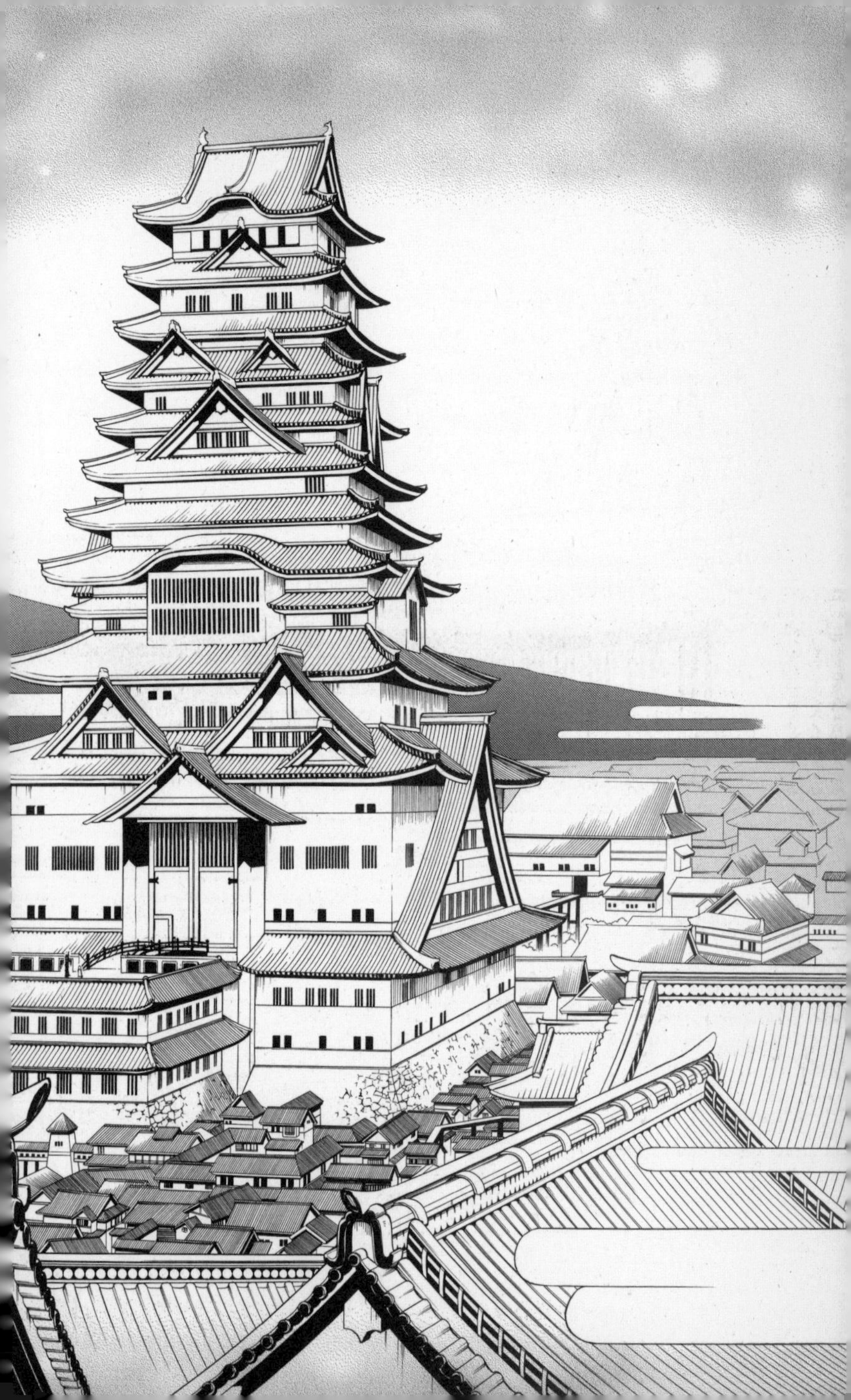

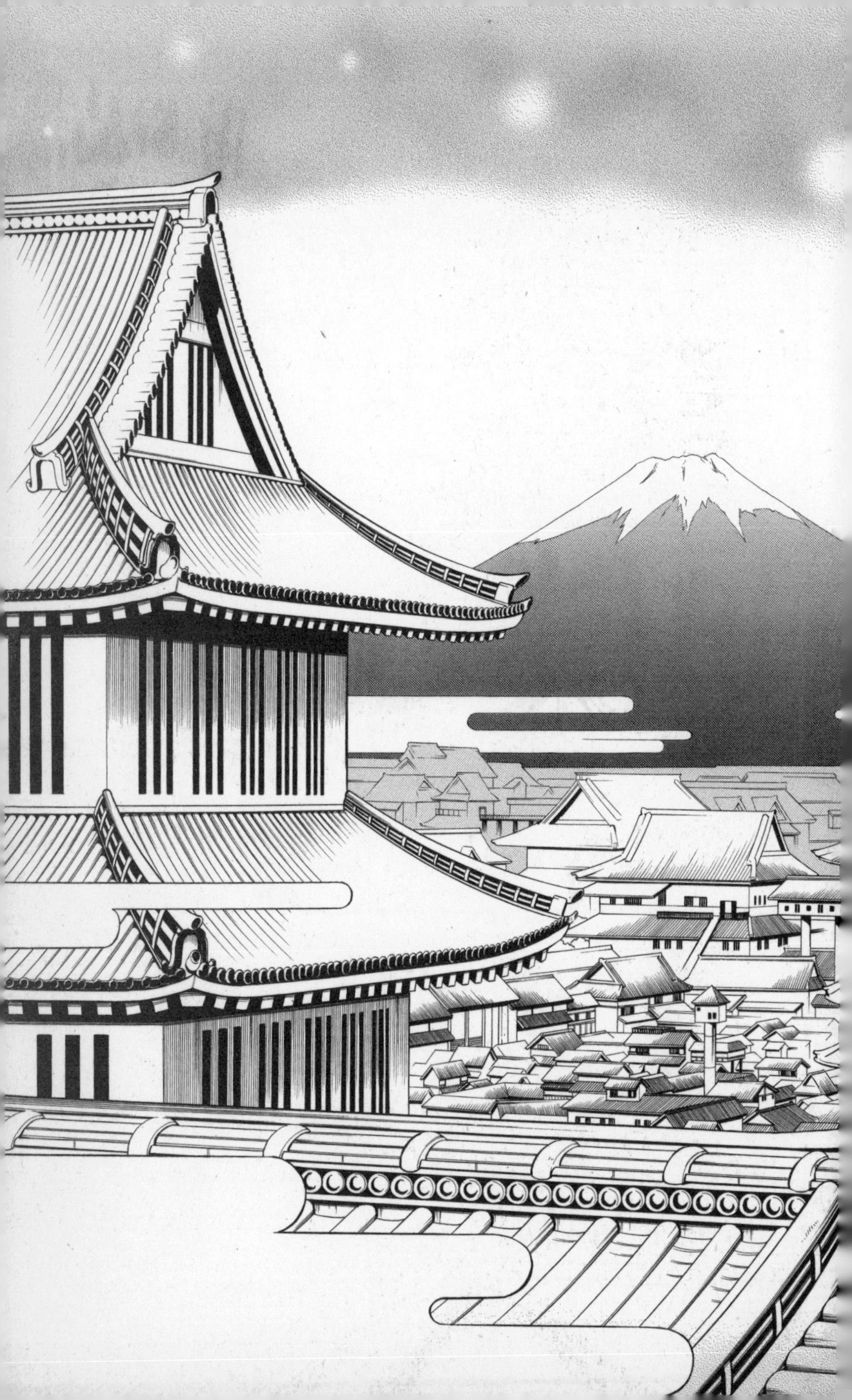

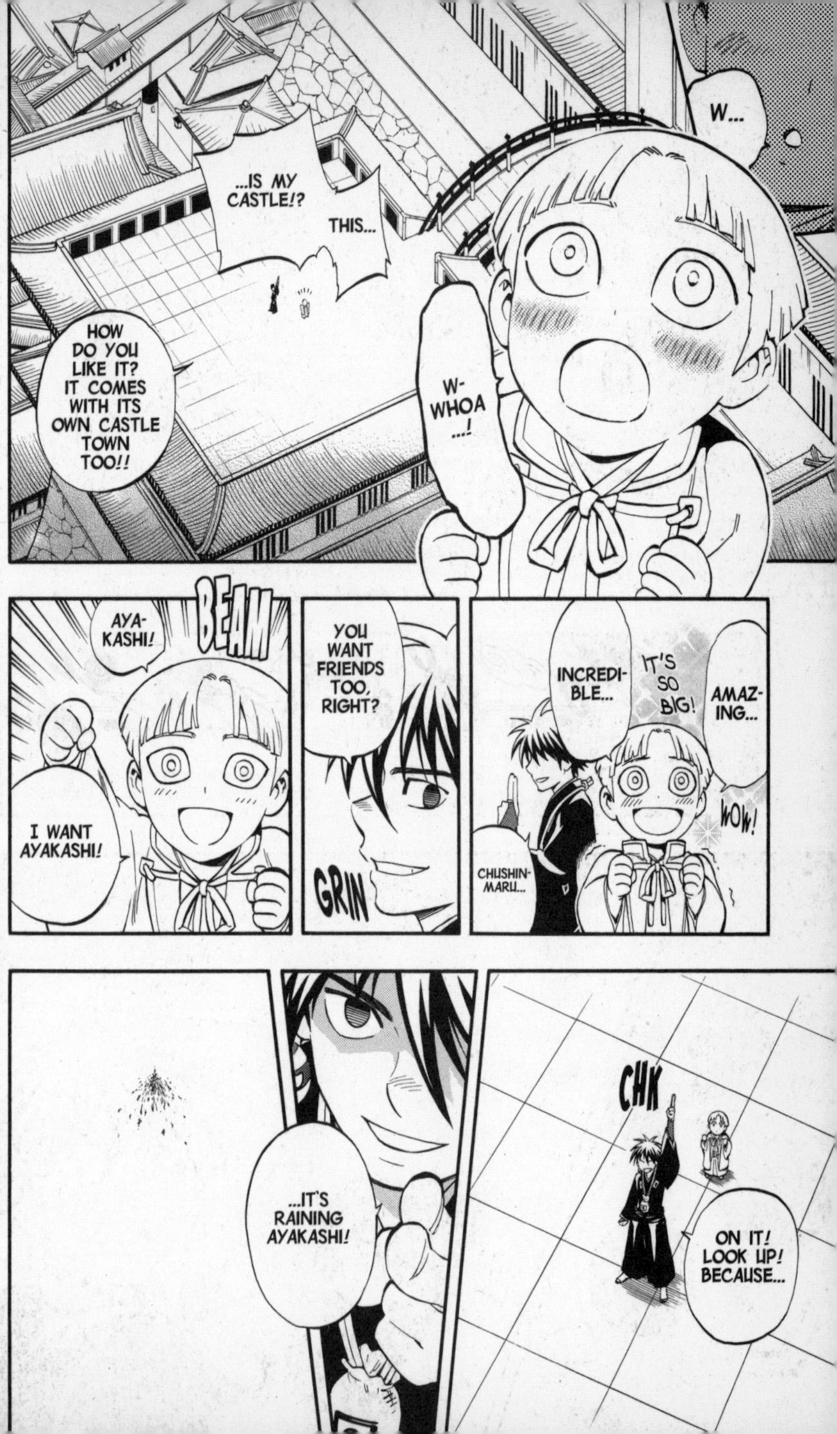
W...
W-WHOA...!
THIS...
...IS MY CASTLE!?
HOW DO YOU LIKE IT? IT COMES WITH ITS OWN CASTLE TOWN TOO!!
AMAZ-ING...
WOW!
IT'S SO BIG!
INCREDI-BLE...
CHUSHIN-MARU...
YOU WANT FRIENDS TOO, RIGHT?
GRIN
BEAM
AYA-KASHI!
I WANT AYAKASHI!
CHK
ON IT! LOOK UP! BECAUSE...
...IT'S RAINING AYAKASHI!

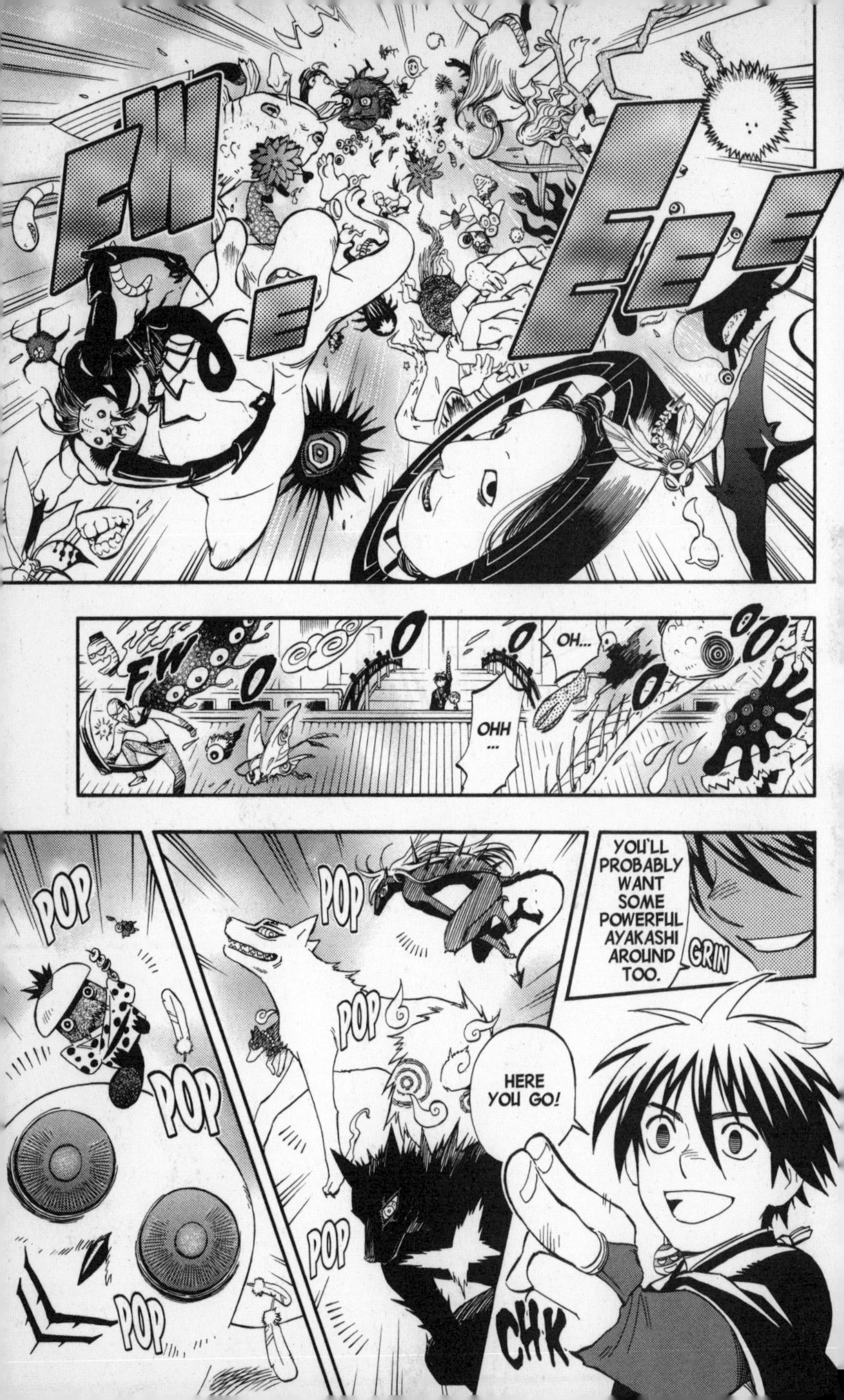
OH...
OHH ...
FW
YOU'LL PROBABLY WANT SOME POWERFUL AYAKASHI AROUND TOO.
GRIN
HERE YOU GO!
POP
POP
POP
CHK
POP
POP
POP

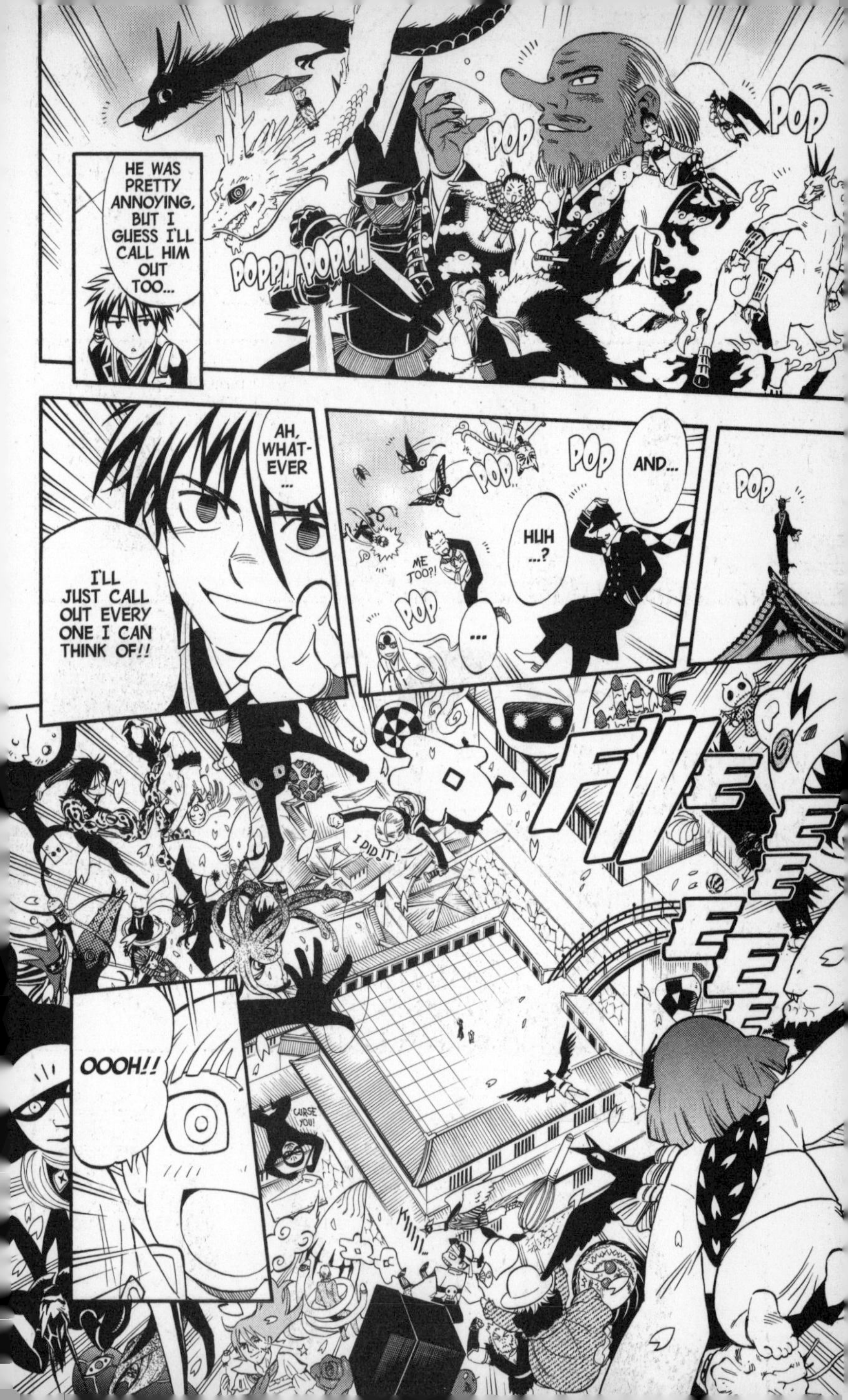
POP
POP
HE WAS PRETTY ANNOYING, BUT I GUESS I'LL CALL HIM OUT TOO...
POPPA POPPA
POP
AND...
POP
POP
HUH ...?
ME TOO?!
POP
...
AH, WHATEVER ...
I'LL JUST CALL OUT EVERY ONE I CAN THINK OF!!
FWEEEEEEE
I DID IT!
OOOH!!
CURSE YOU!

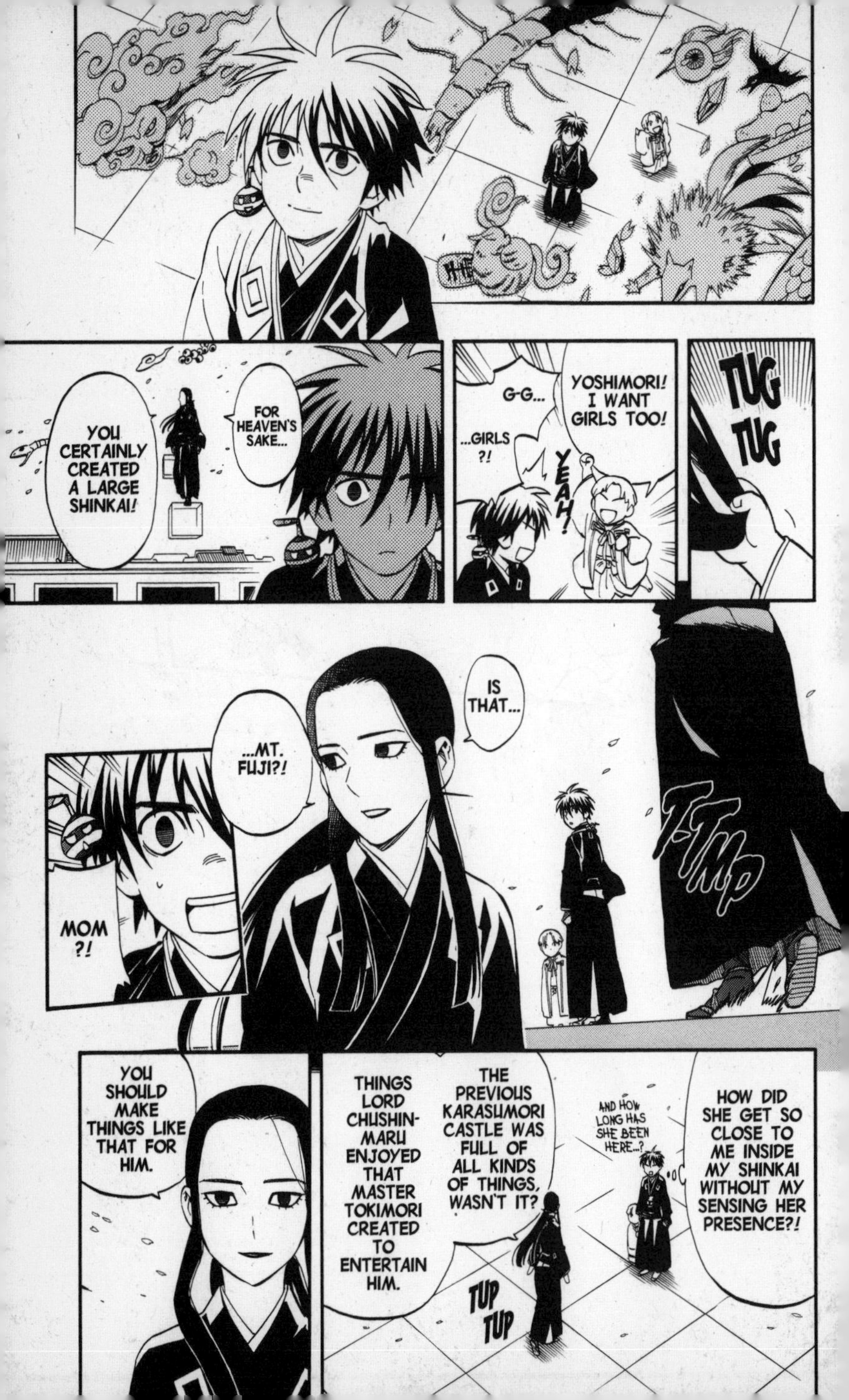
TUG TUG
YOSHIMORI! I WANT GIRLS TOO!
YEAH!
G-G...
...GIRLS ?!
FOR HEAVEN'S SAKE...
YOU CERTAINLY CREATED A LARGE SHINKAI!
T-TMP
IS THAT...
...MT. FUJI?!
MOM ?!
HOW DID SHE GET SO CLOSE TO ME INSIDE MY SHINKAI WITHOUT MY SENSING HER PRESENCE?!
AND HOW LONG HAS SHE BEEN HERE...?
THE PREVIOUS KARASUMORI CASTLE WAS FULL OF ALL KINDS OF THINGS, WASN'T IT?
THINGS LORD CHUSHIN-MARU ENJOYED THAT MASTER TOKIMORI CREATED TO ENTERTAIN HIM.
TUP TUP
YOU SHOULD MAKE THINGS LIKE THAT FOR HIM.

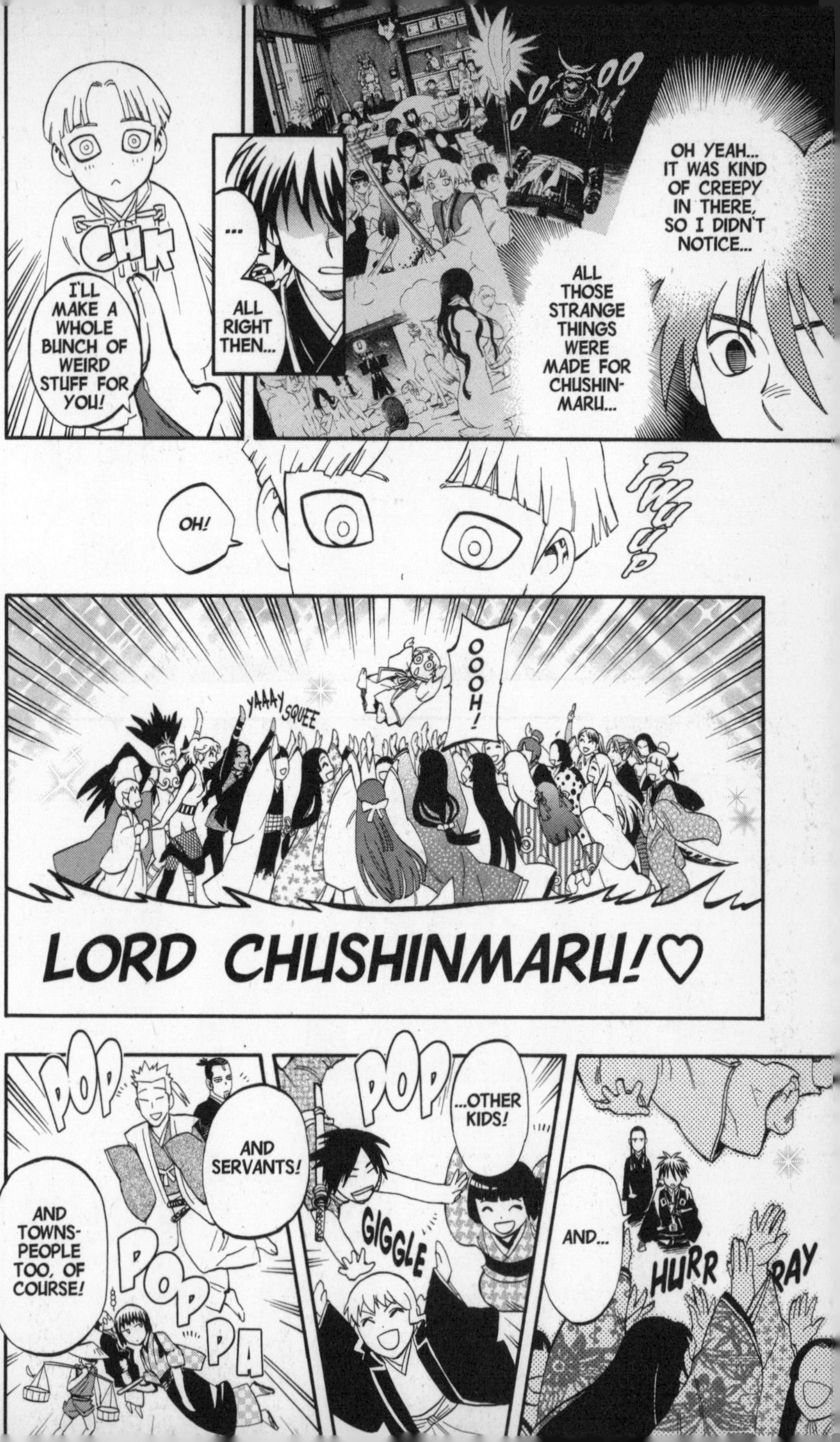
OOOO
OH YEAH... IT WAS KIND OF CREEPY IN THERE, SO I DIDN'T NOTICE...
ALL THOSE STRANGE THINGS WERE MADE FOR CHUSHIN-MARU...
...
ALL RIGHT THEN...
CHK
I'LL MAKE A WHOLE BUNCH OF WEIRD STUFF FOR YOU!
FWUP
OH!
OOOH!
YAAAY
SQUEE
LORD CHUSHINMARU! ♡
AND...
HURR
RAY
POP
...OTHER KIDS!
GIGGLE
AND SERVANTS!
POP
AND TOWNS-PEOPLE TOO, OF COURSE!
POP
POP
PA

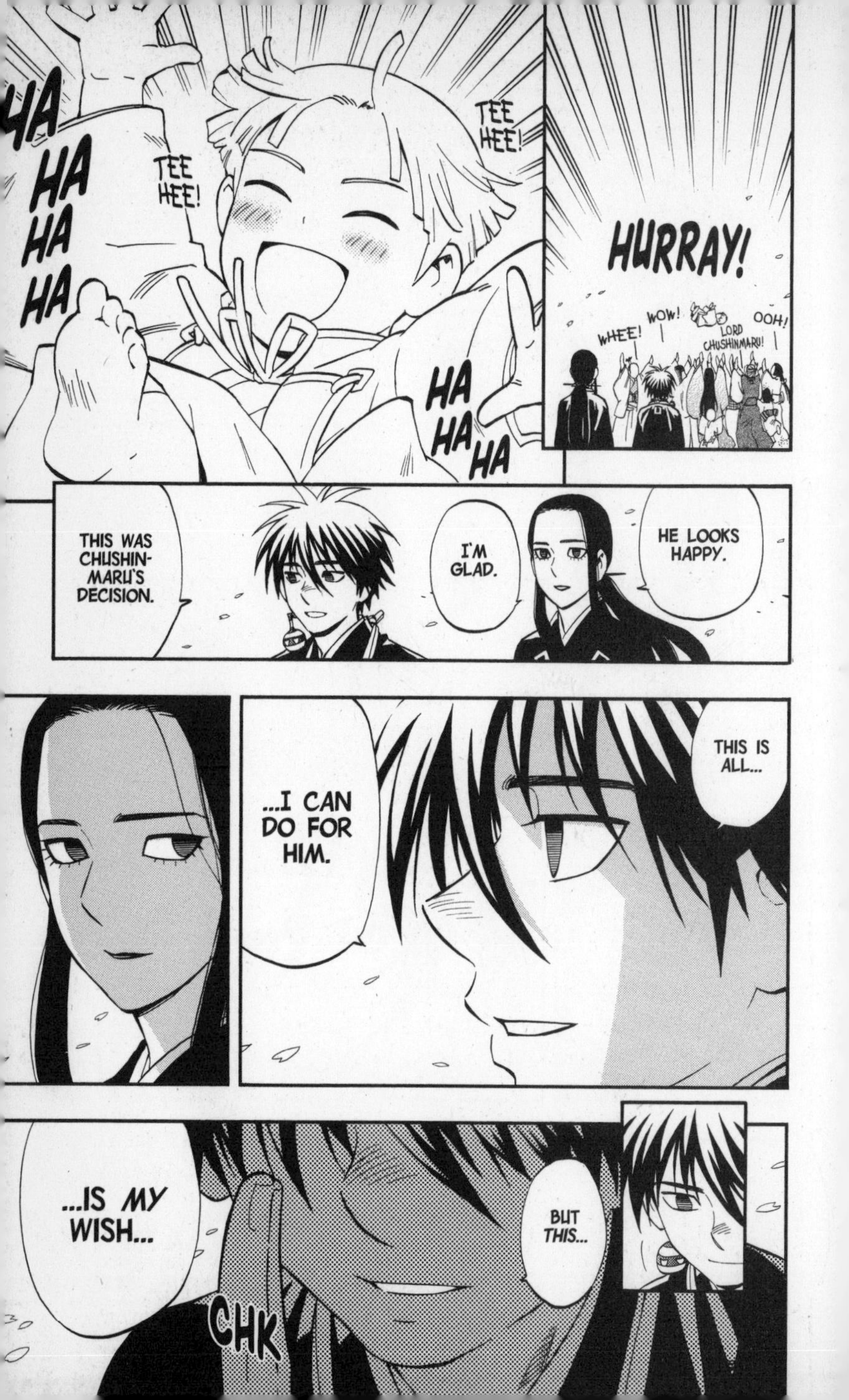
HURRAY!
OOH!
LORD CHUSHINMARU!
WOW!
WHEE!
TEE HEE!
TEE HEE!
HA HA HA HA HA
HA HA HA
HE LOOKS HAPPY.
I'M GLAD.
THIS WAS CHUSHINMARU'S DECISION.
THIS IS ALL...
...I CAN DO FOR HIM.
BUT THIS...
...IS MY WISH...
CHK

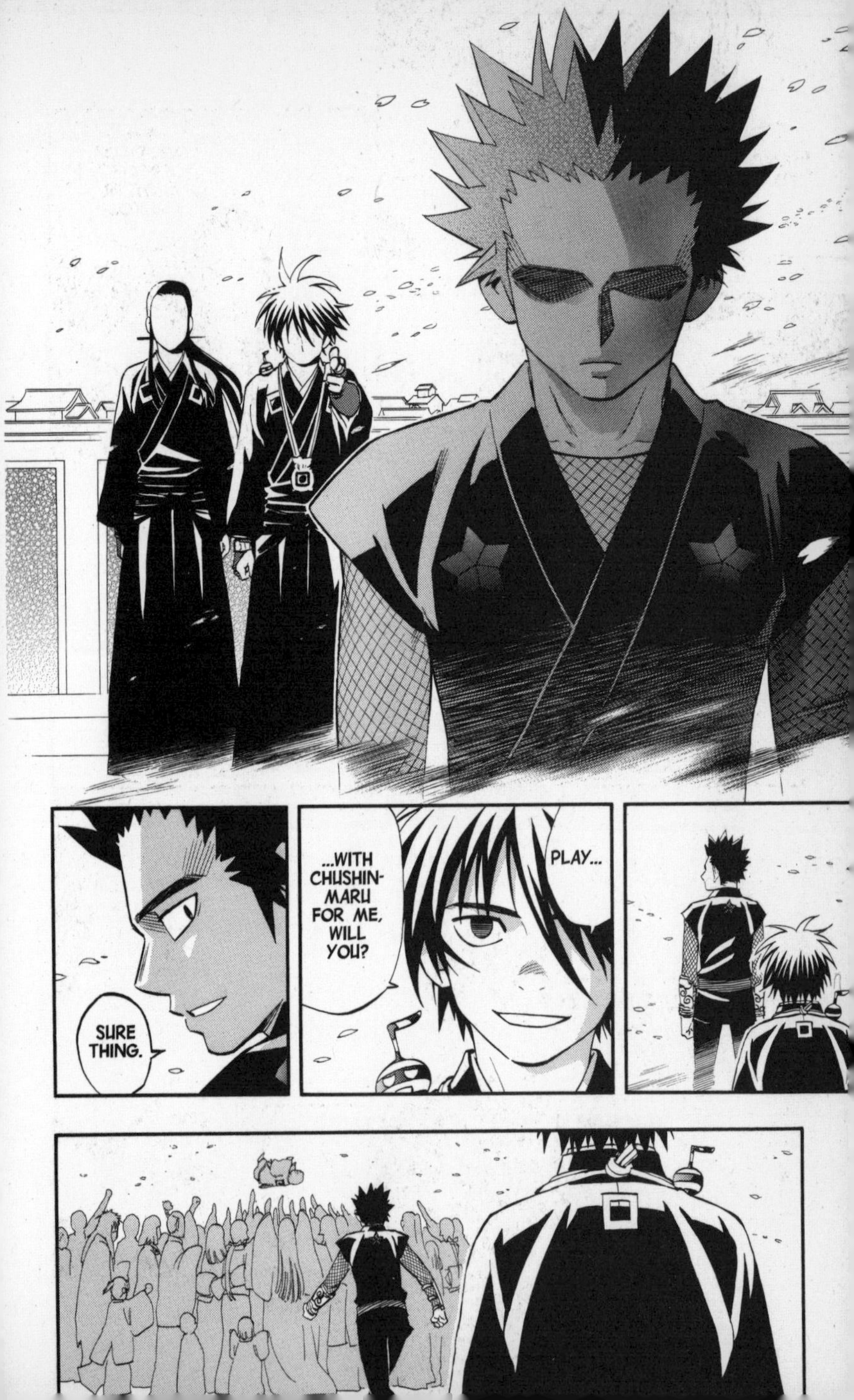
PLAY...
...WITH CHUSHIN-MARU FOR ME, WILL YOU?
SURE THING.

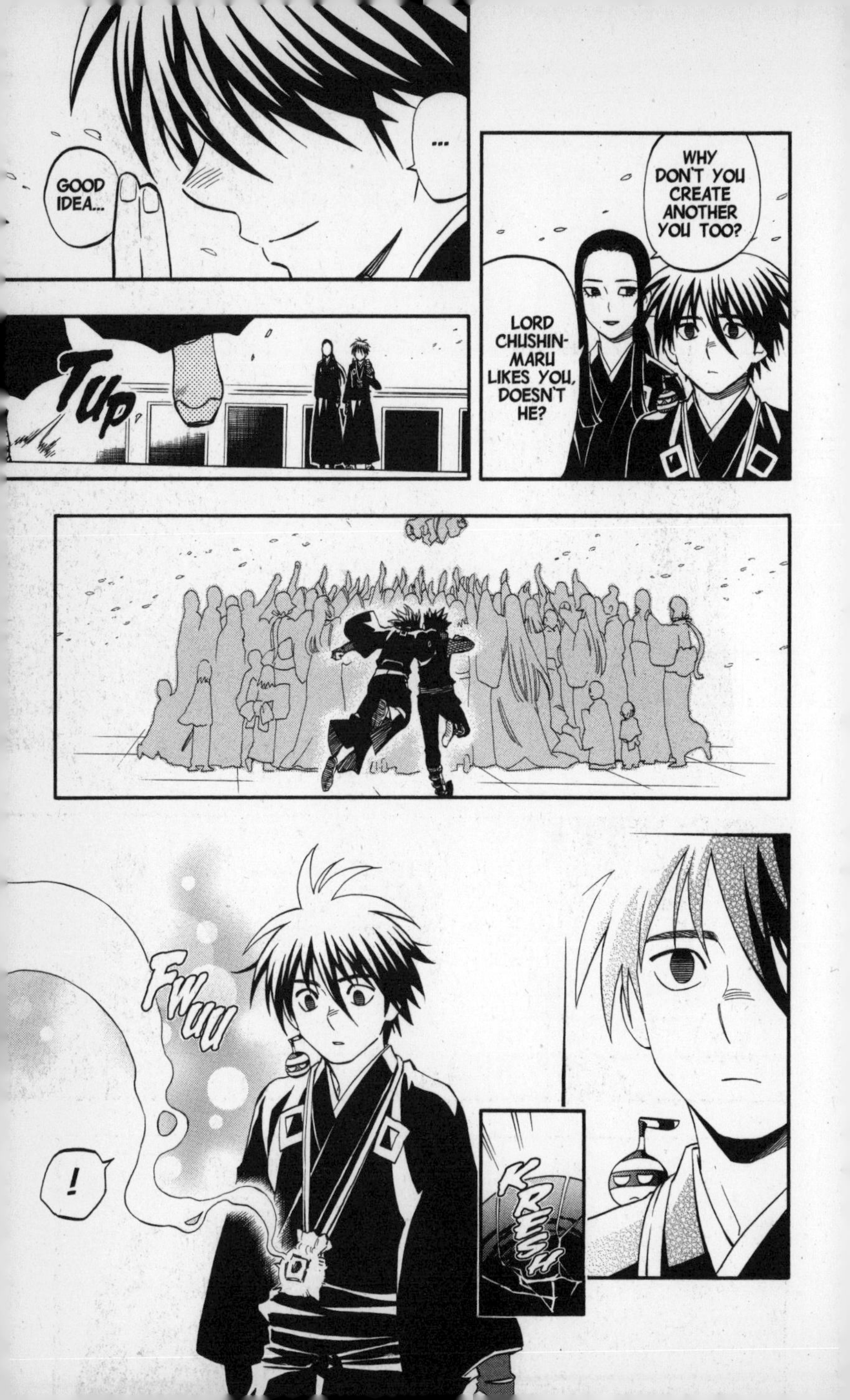
WHY DON'T YOU CREATE ANOTHER YOU TOO?
LORD CHUSHIN-MARU LIKES YOU, DOESN'T HE?
...
GOOD IDEA...
TUP
KRESH
FWUU
!

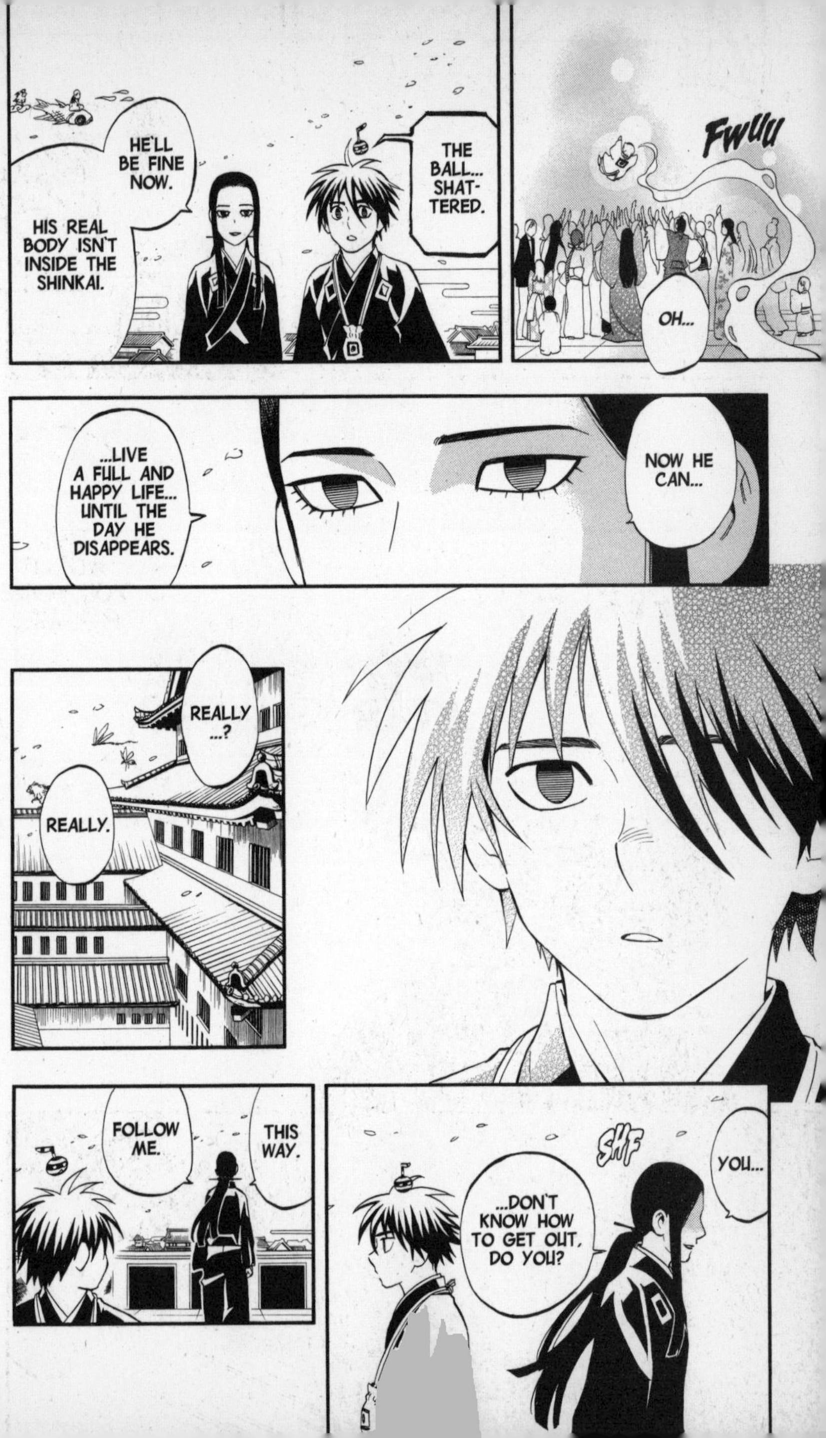
FWUU
OH...
THE BALL... SHATTERED.
HE'LL BE FINE NOW.
HIS REAL BODY ISN'T INSIDE THE SHINKAI.
NOW HE CAN...
...LIVE A FULL AND HAPPY LIFE... UNTIL THE DAY HE DISAPPEARS.
REALLY ...?
REALLY.
YOU...
SHF
...DON'T KNOW HOW TO GET OUT, DO YOU?
THIS WAY.
FOLLOW ME.

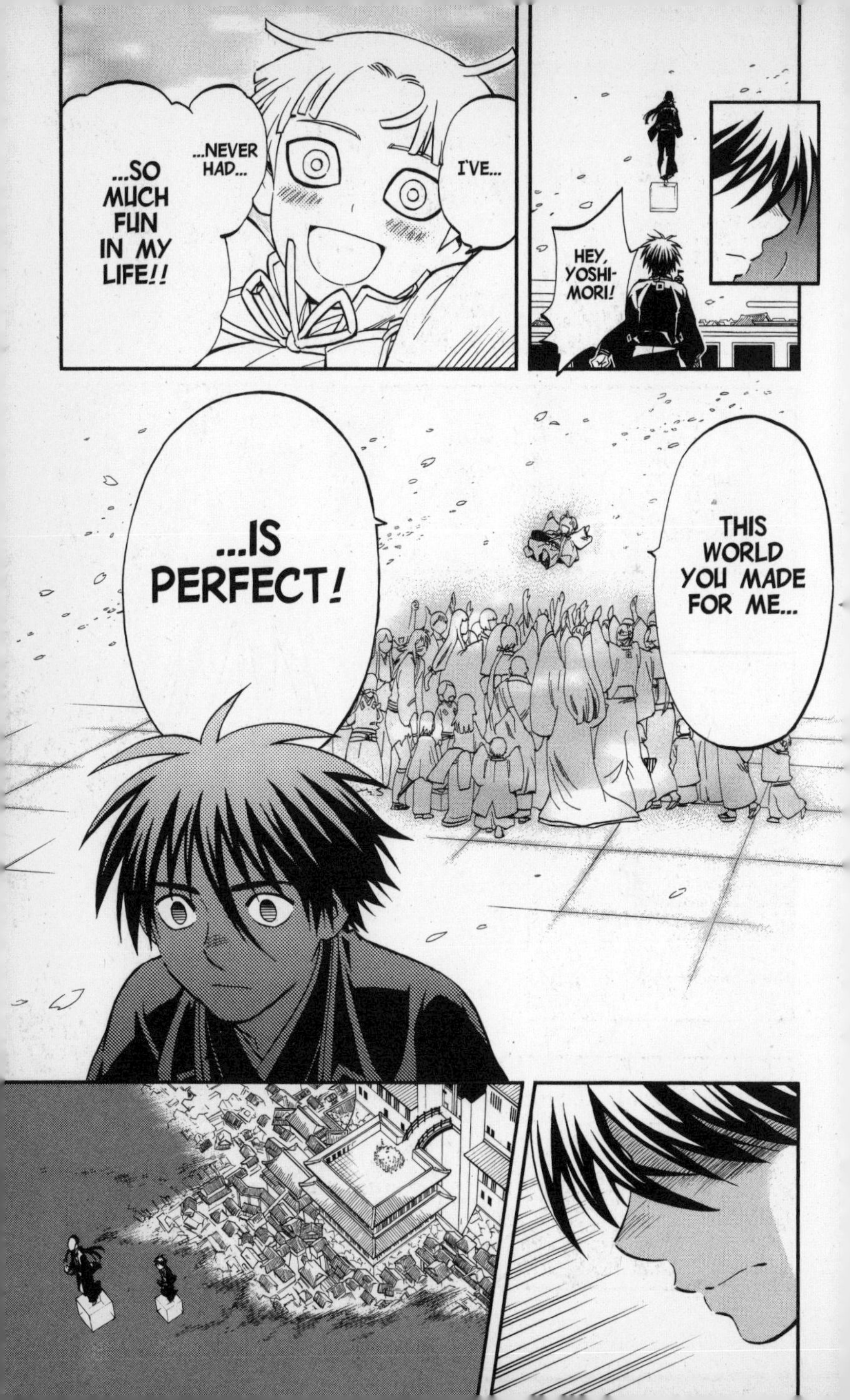
HEY, YOSHIMORI!
I'VE...
...NEVER HAD...
...SO MUCH FUN IN MY LIFE!!
THIS WORLD YOU MADE FOR ME...
...IS PERFECT!

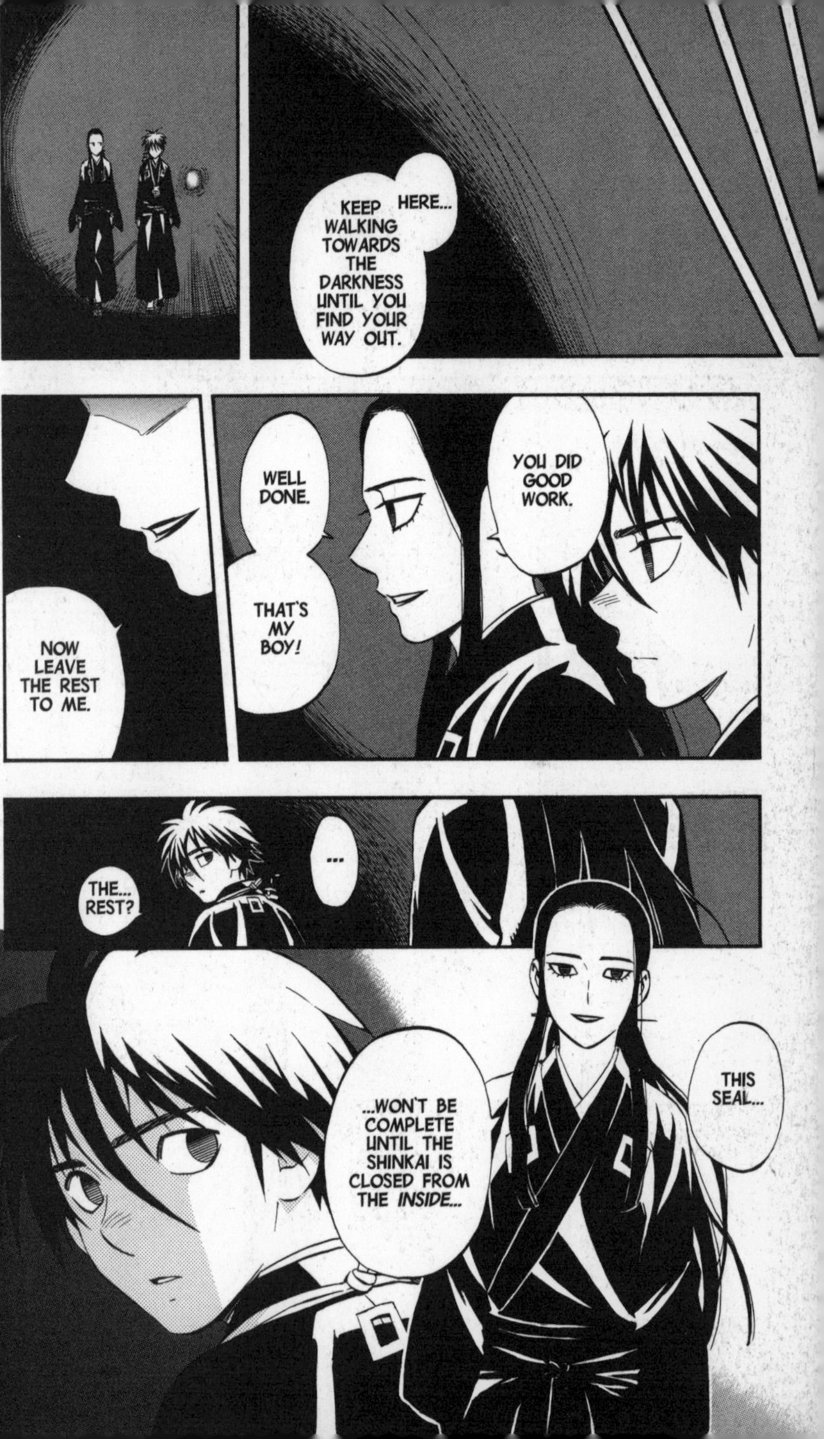
HERE...
KEEP WALKING TOWARDS THE DARKNESS UNTIL YOU FIND YOUR WAY OUT.
YOU DID GOOD WORK.
WELL DONE.
THAT'S MY BOY!
NOW LEAVE THE REST TO ME.
...
THE... REST?
THIS SEAL...
...WON'T BE COMPLETE UNTIL THE SHINKAI IS CLOSED FROM THE *INSIDE*...

CHAPTER 343: SUMIKO

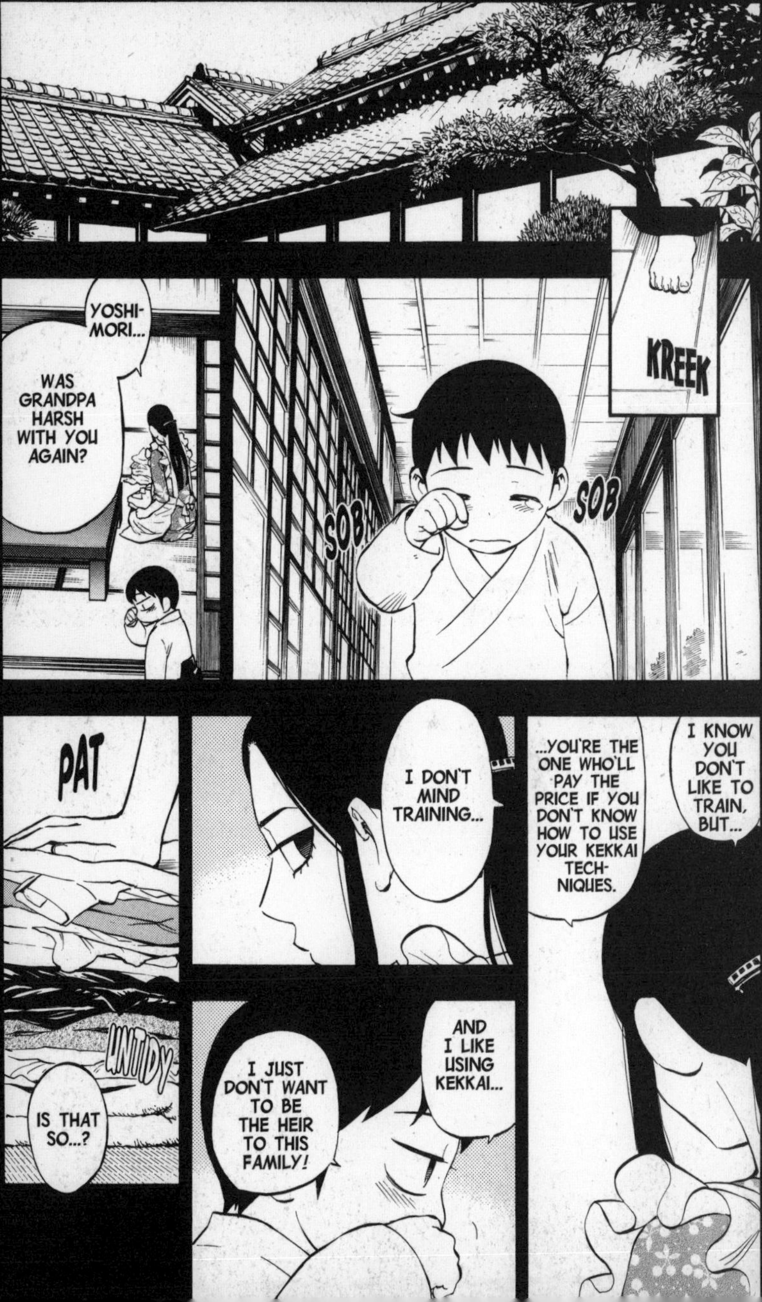
KREEK
SOB
SOB
YOSHI-MORI...
WAS GRANDPA HARSH WITH YOU AGAIN?
I KNOW YOU DON'T LIKE TO TRAIN, BUT...
...YOU'RE THE ONE WHO'LL PAY THE PRICE IF YOU DON'T KNOW HOW TO USE YOUR KEKKAI TECH-NIQUES.
I DON'T MIND TRAINING...
AND I LIKE USING KEKKAI...
I JUST DON'T WANT TO BE THE HEIR TO THIS FAMILY!
PAT
UNTIDY
IS THAT SO...?

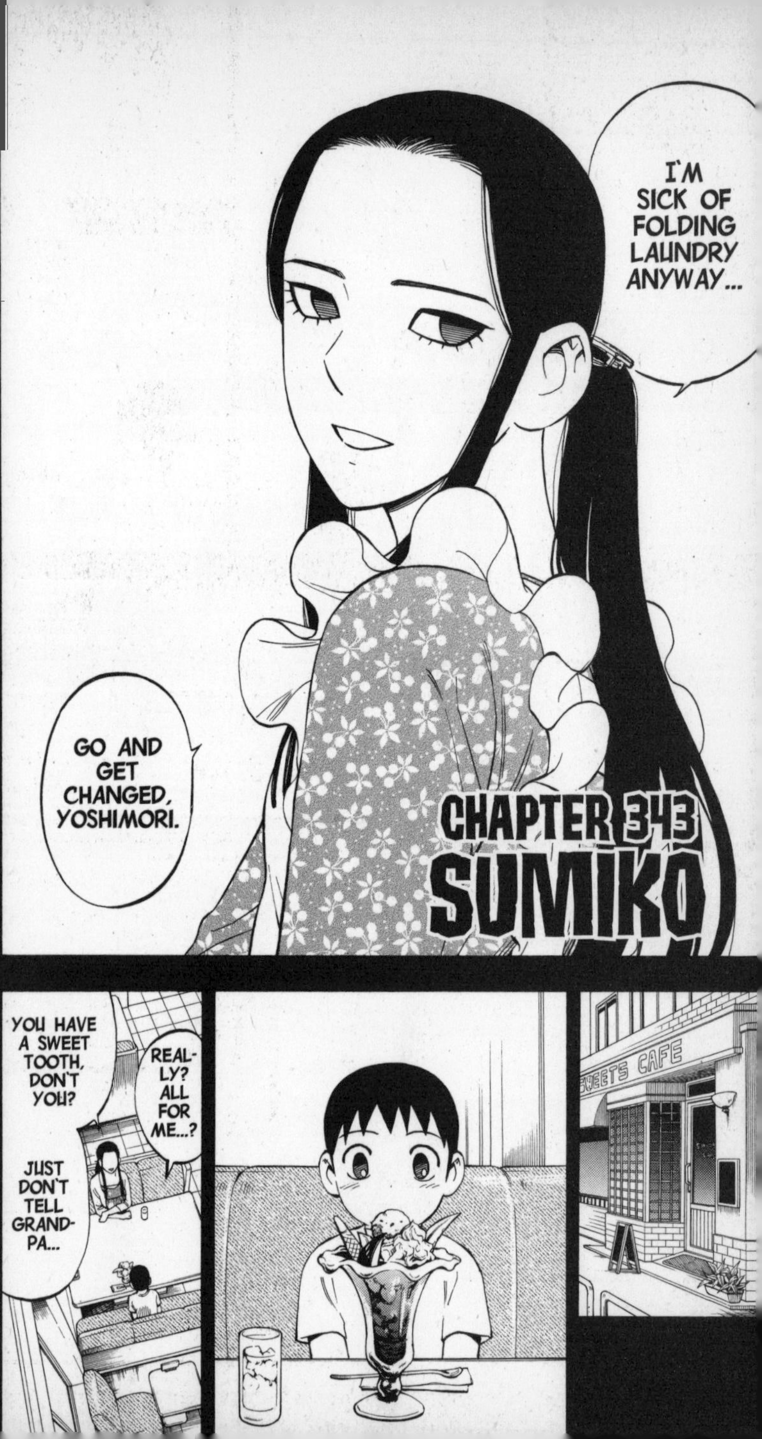
I'M SICK OF FOLDING LAUNDRY ANYWAY...
GO AND GET CHANGED, YOSHIMORI.
CHAPTER 343
SUMIKO
SWEETS CAFE
REAL-LY? ALL FOR ME...?
YOU HAVE A SWEET TOOTH, DON'T YOU?
JUST DON'T TELL GRAND-PA...

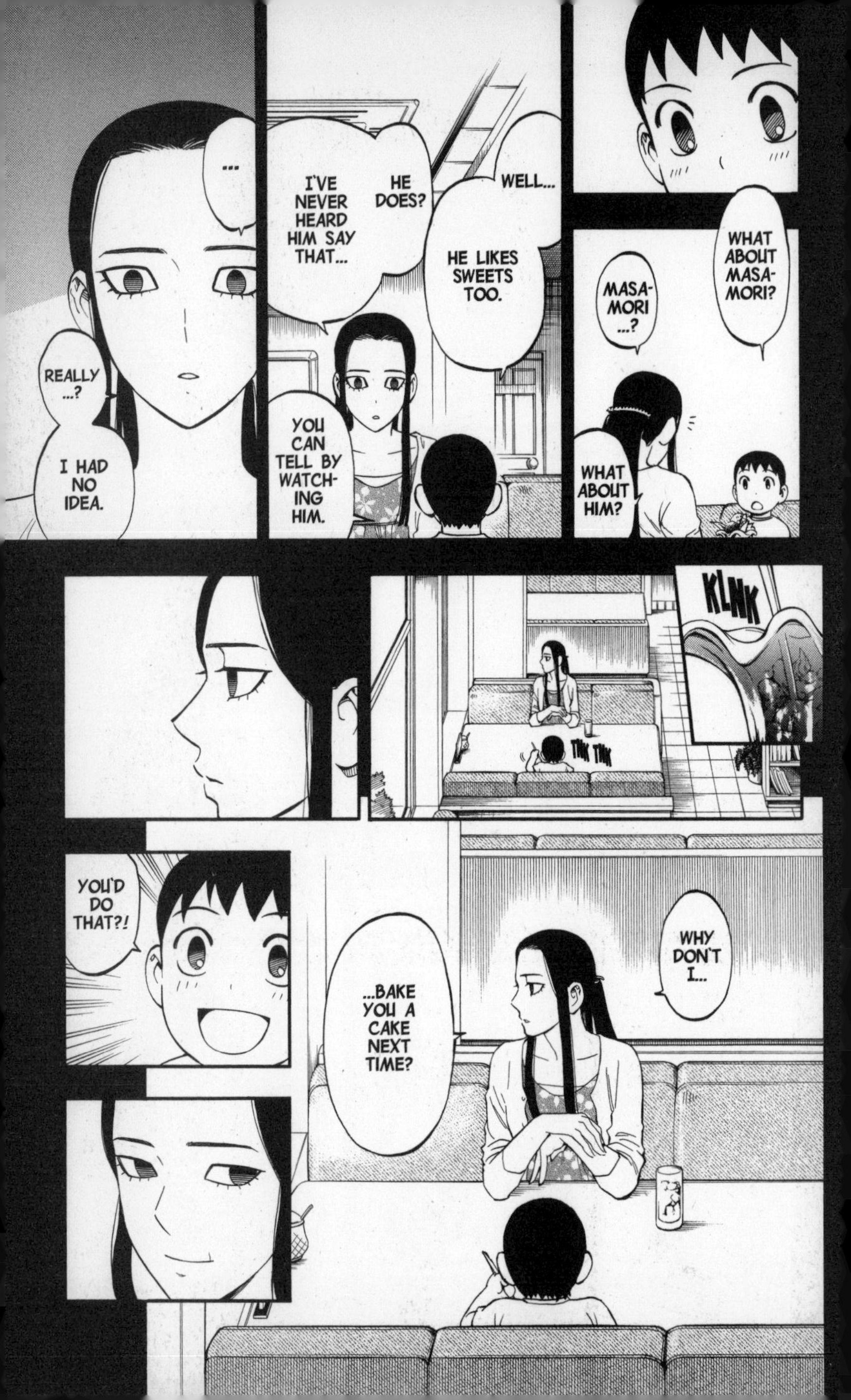
WHAT ABOUT MASA-MORI?
MASA-MORI ...?
WHAT ABOUT HIM?
WELL...
HE LIKES SWEETS TOO.
HE DOES?
I'VE NEVER HEARD HIM SAY THAT...
YOU CAN TELL BY WATCH-ING HIM.
...
REALLY ...?
I HAD NO IDEA.
KLNK
TIK TIK
WHY DON'T I...
...BAKE YOU A CAKE NEXT TIME?
YOU'D DO THAT?!

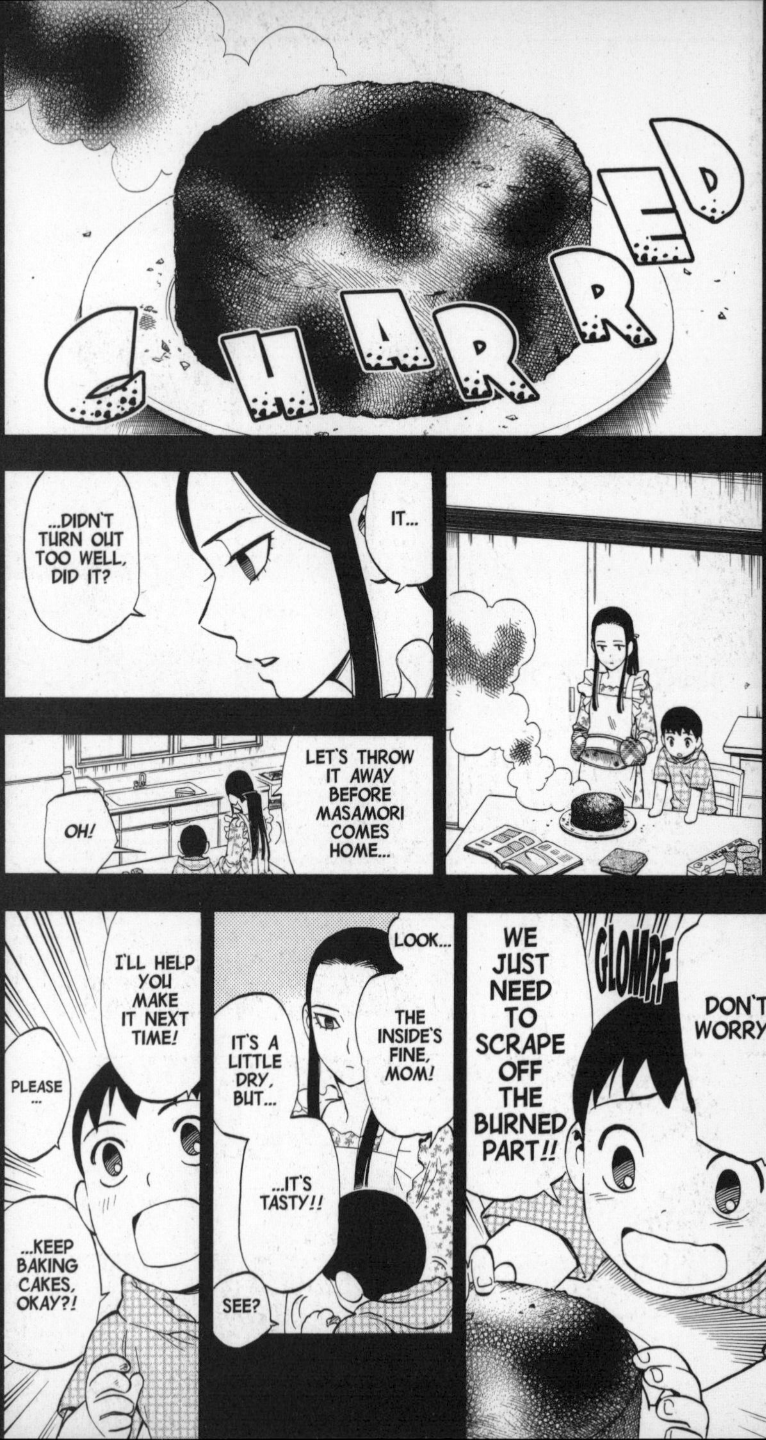
CHARRED
IT...
...DIDN'T TURN OUT TOO WELL, DID IT?
LET'S THROW IT AWAY BEFORE MASAMORI COMES HOME...
OH!
GLOMPF
DON'T WORRY!
WE JUST NEED TO SCRAPE OFF THE BURNED PART!!
LOOK...
THE INSIDE'S FINE, MOM!
IT'S A LITTLE DRY, BUT...
...IT'S TASTY!!
SEE?
I'LL HELP YOU MAKE IT NEXT TIME!
PLEASE...
...KEEP BAKING CAKES, OKAY?!

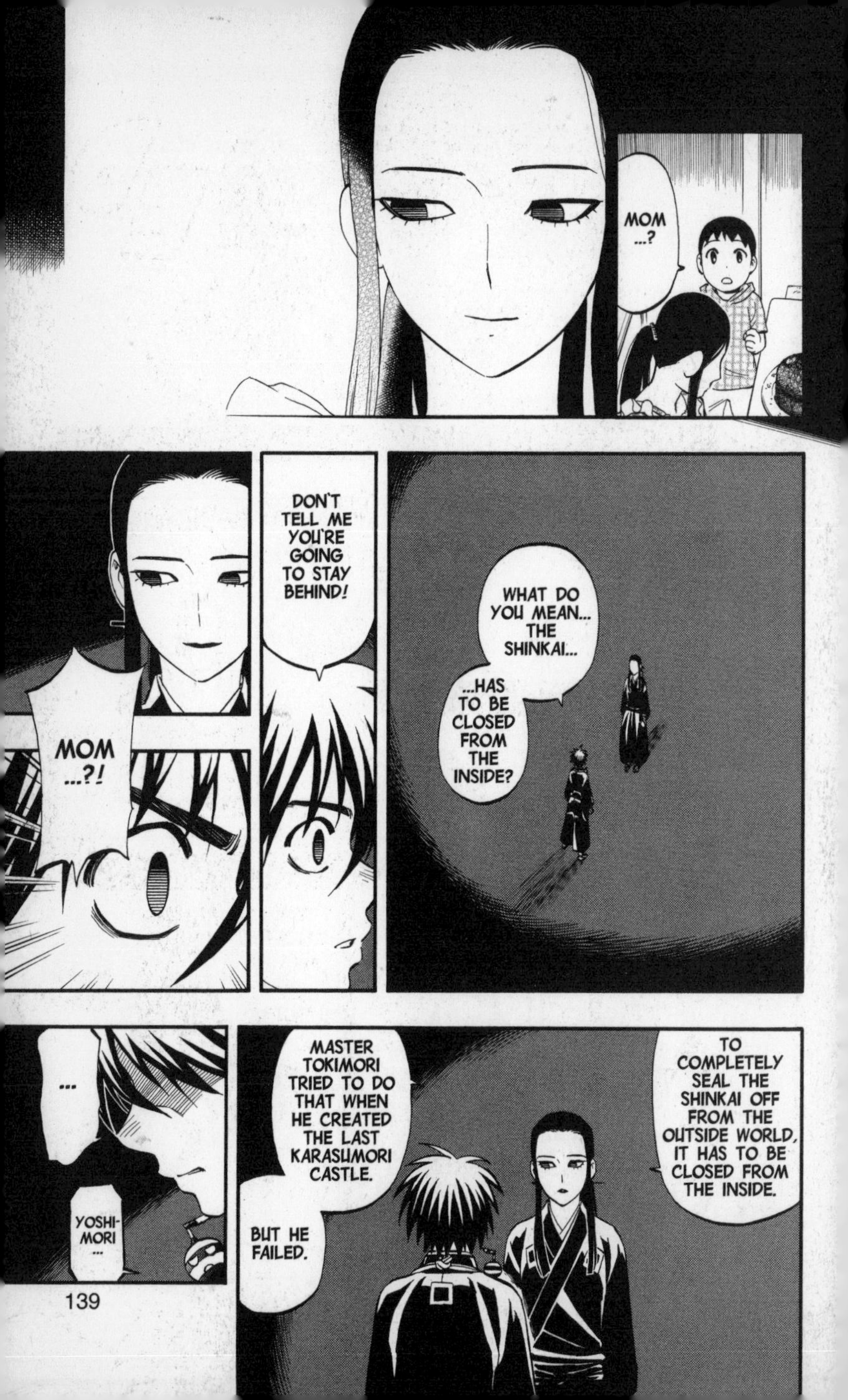
MOM ...?
WHAT DO YOU MEAN... THE SHINKAI...
...HAS TO BE CLOSED FROM THE INSIDE?
DON'T TELL ME YOU'RE GOING TO STAY BEHIND!
MOM ...?!
TO COMPLETELY SEAL THE SHINKAI OFF FROM THE OUTSIDE WORLD, IT HAS TO BE CLOSED FROM THE INSIDE.
MASTER TOKIMORI TRIED TO DO THAT WHEN HE CREATED THE LAST KARASUMORI CASTLE.
BUT HE FAILED.
...
YOSHIMORI ...

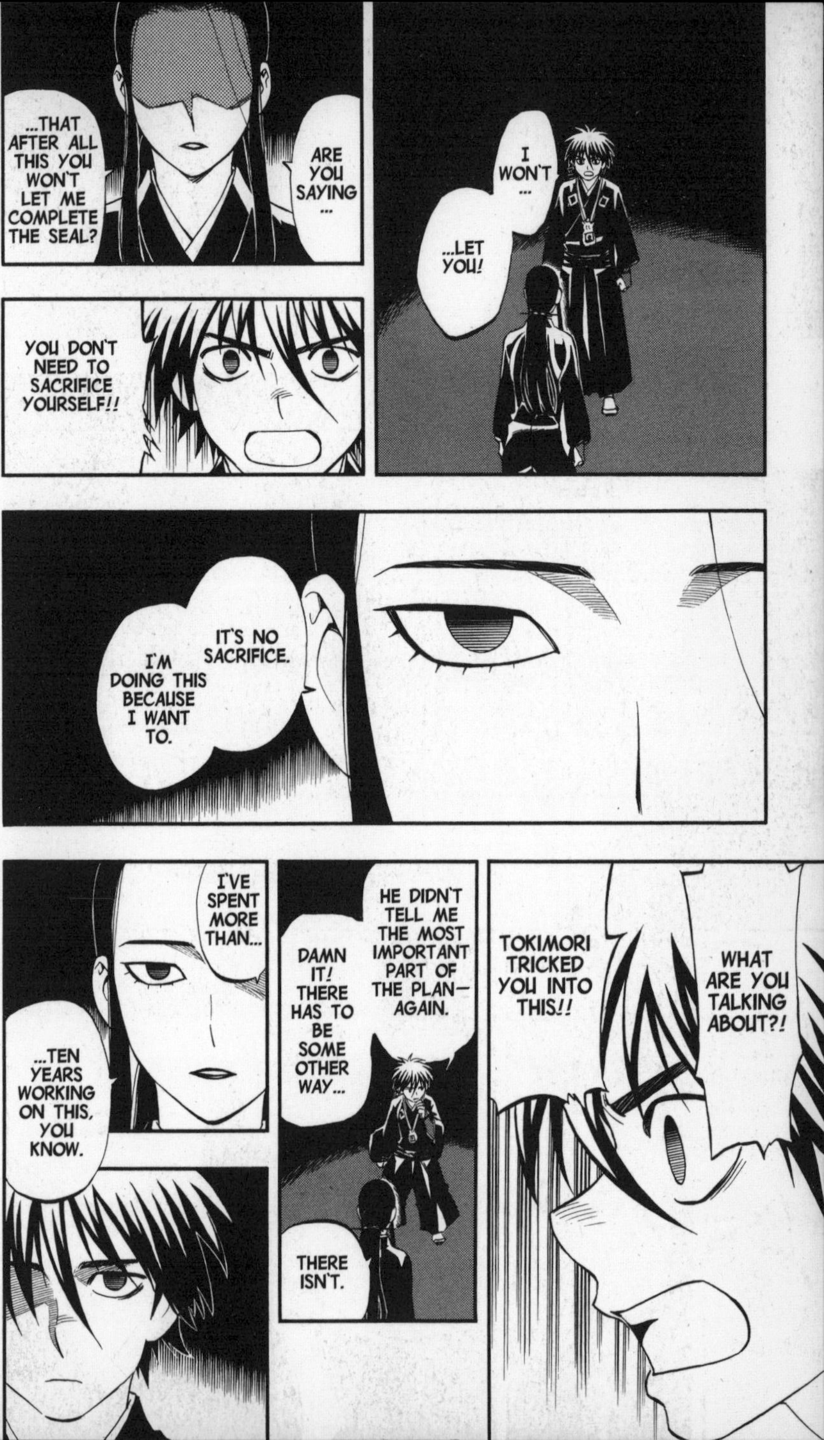
I WON'T ...
...LET YOU!
ARE YOU SAYING ...
...THAT AFTER ALL THIS YOU WON'T LET ME COMPLETE THE SEAL?
YOU DON'T NEED TO SACRIFICE YOURSELF!!
IT'S NO SACRIFICE.
I'M DOING THIS BECAUSE I WANT TO.
WHAT ARE YOU TALKING ABOUT?!
TOKIMORI TRICKED YOU INTO THIS!!
HE DIDN'T TELL ME THE MOST IMPORTANT PART OF THE PLAN—AGAIN.
DAMN IT! THERE HAS TO BE SOME OTHER WAY...
THERE ISN'T.
I'VE SPENT MORE THAN...
...TEN YEARS WORKING ON THIS, YOU KNOW.

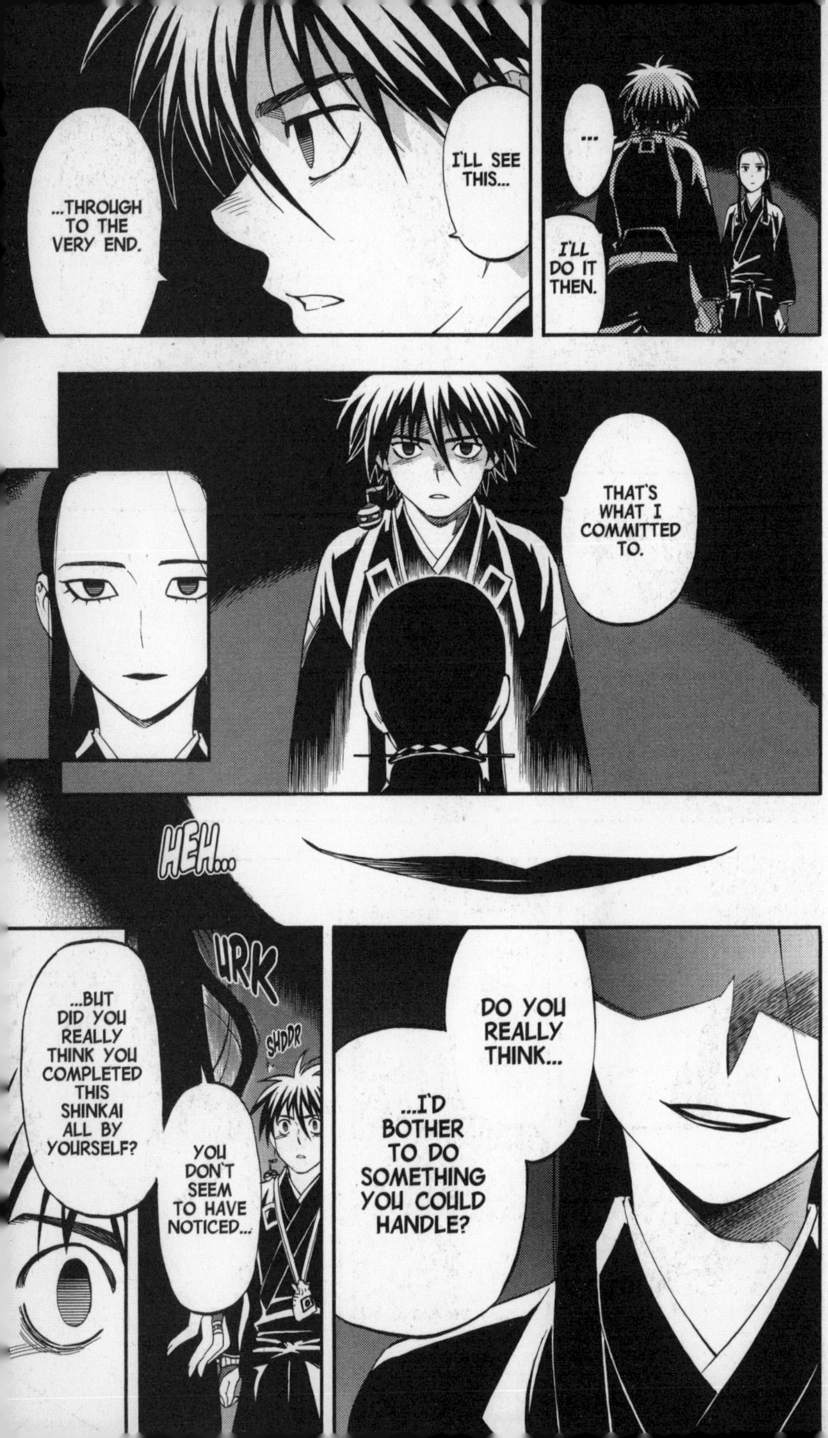
...
I'LL DO IT THEN.
I'LL SEE THIS...
...THROUGH TO THE VERY END.
THAT'S WHAT I COMMITTED TO.
HEH...
DO YOU REALLY THINK...
...I'D BOTHER TO DO SOMETHING YOU COULD HANDLE?
URK
SHDDR
YOU DON'T SEEM TO HAVE NOTICED...
...BUT DID YOU REALLY THINK YOU COMPLETED THIS SHINKAI ALL BY YOURSELF?

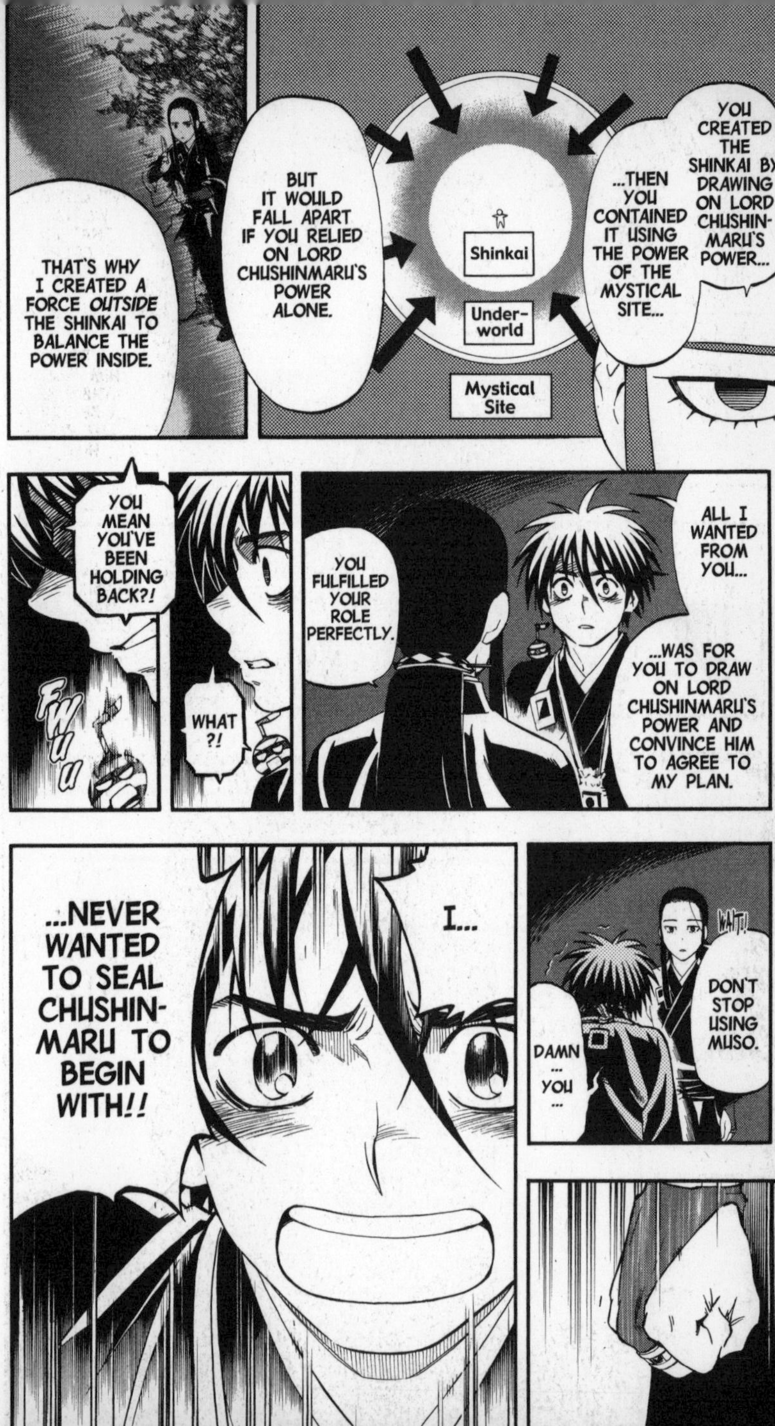
YOU CREATED THE SHINKAI BY DRAWING ON LORD CHUSHINMARU'S POWER...
...THEN YOU CONTAINED IT USING THE POWER OF THE MYSTICAL SITE...
Shinkai
Underworld
Mystical Site
BUT IT WOULD FALL APART IF YOU RELIED ON LORD CHUSHINMARU'S POWER ALONE.
THAT'S WHY I CREATED A FORCE *OUTSIDE* THE SHINKAI TO BALANCE THE POWER INSIDE.
ALL I WANTED FROM YOU...
...WAS FOR YOU TO DRAW ON LORD CHUSHINMARU'S POWER AND CONVINCE HIM TO AGREE TO MY PLAN.
YOU FULFILLED YOUR ROLE PERFECTLY.
WHAT?!
YOU MEAN YOU'VE BEEN HOLDING BACK?!
FWUU
WAIT!
DON'T STOP USING MUSO.
DAMN... YOU...
I...
...NEVER WANTED TO SEAL CHUSHINMARU TO BEGIN WITH!!

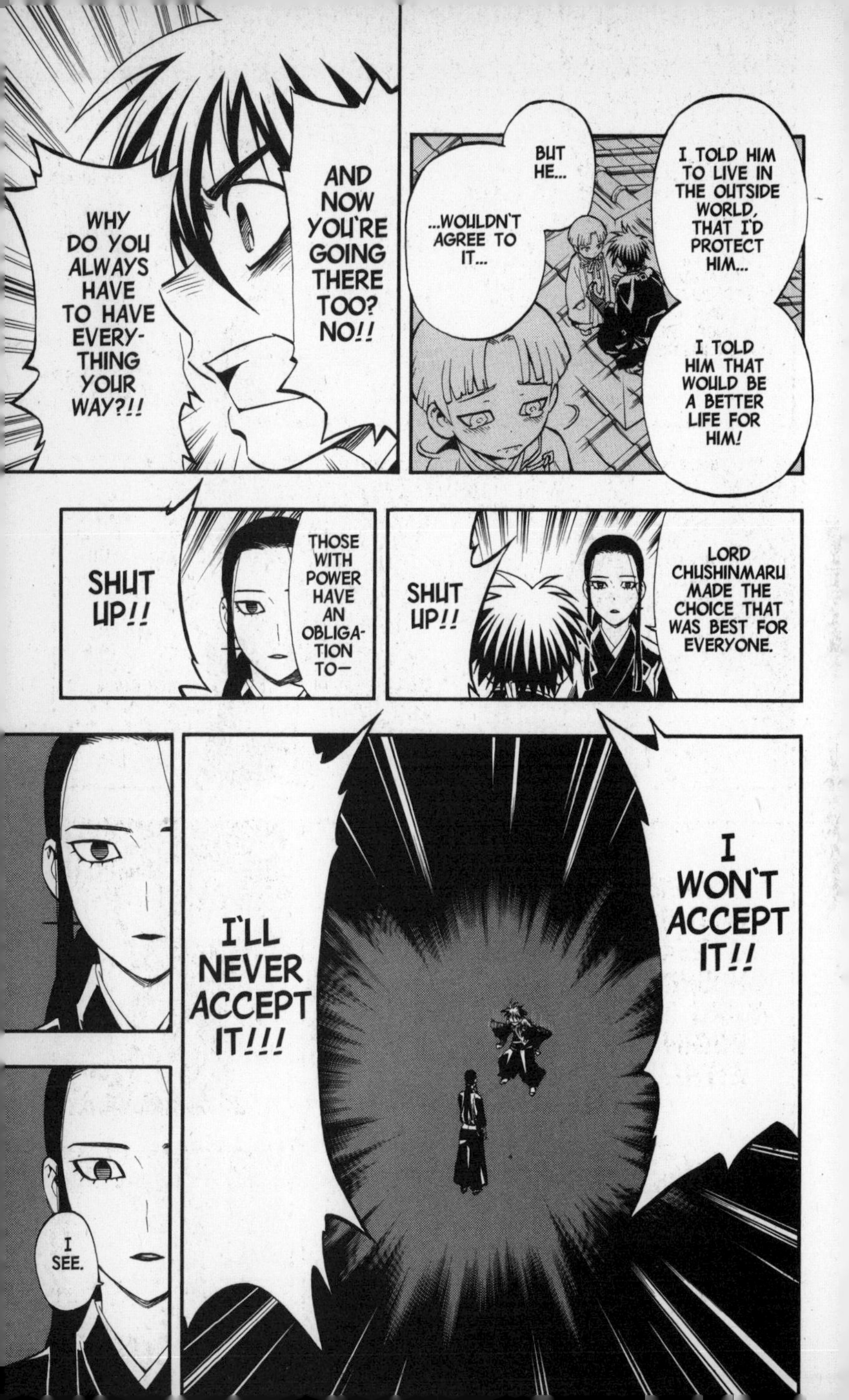
I TOLD HIM TO LIVE IN THE OUTSIDE WORLD, THAT I'D PROTECT HIM...
I TOLD HIM THAT WOULD BE A BETTER LIFE FOR HIM!
BUT HE...
...WOULDN'T AGREE TO IT...
AND NOW YOU'RE GOING THERE TOO? NO!!
WHY DO YOU ALWAYS HAVE TO HAVE EVERY-THING YOUR WAY?!!
LORD CHUSHINMARU MADE THE CHOICE THAT WAS BEST FOR EVERYONE.
SHUT UP!!
THOSE WITH POWER HAVE AN OBLIGA-TION TO—
SHUT UP!!
I WON'T ACCEPT IT!!
I'LL NEVER ACCEPT IT!!!
I SEE.

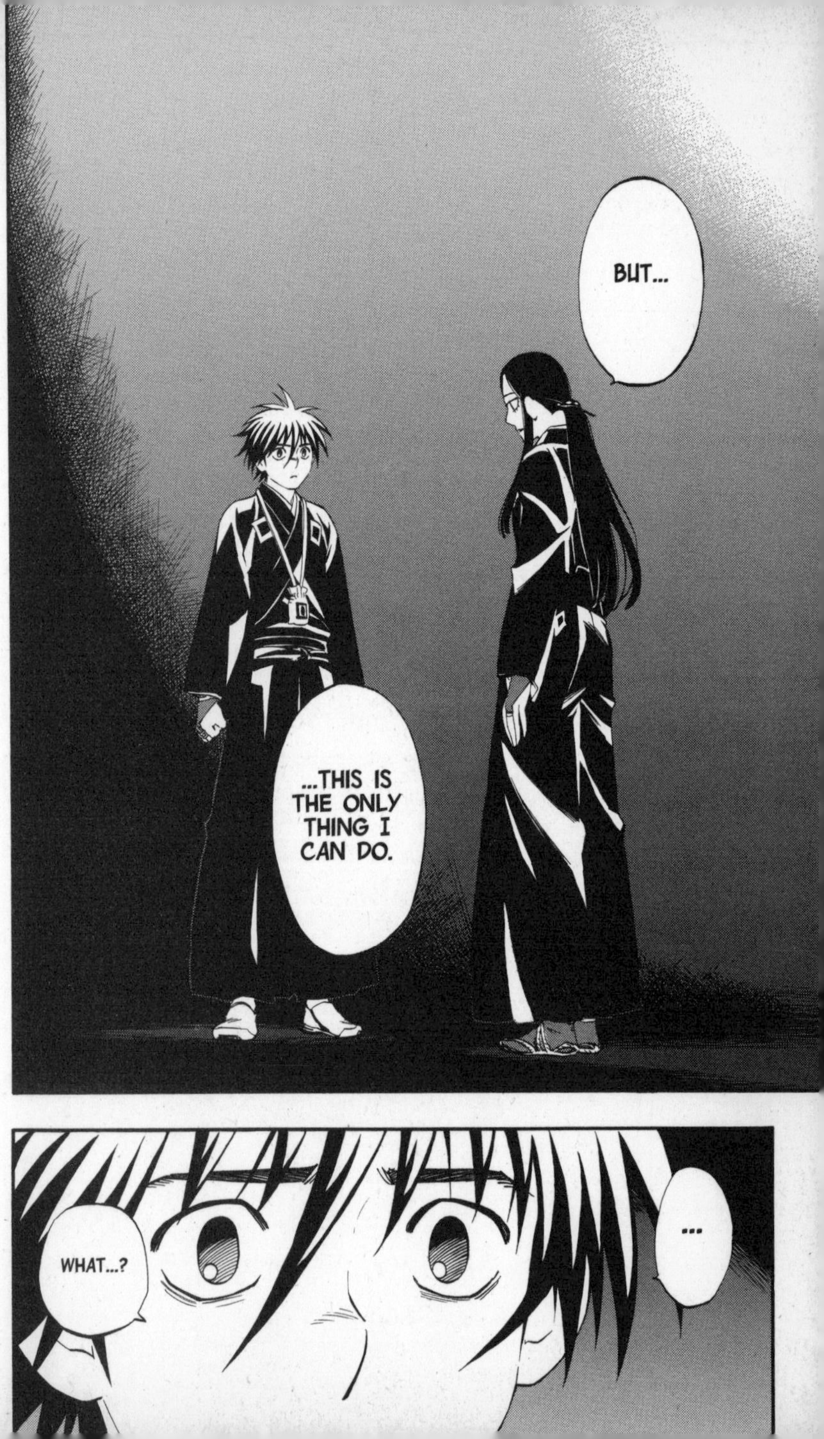
BUT...
...THIS IS THE ONLY THING I CAN DO.
...
WHAT...?

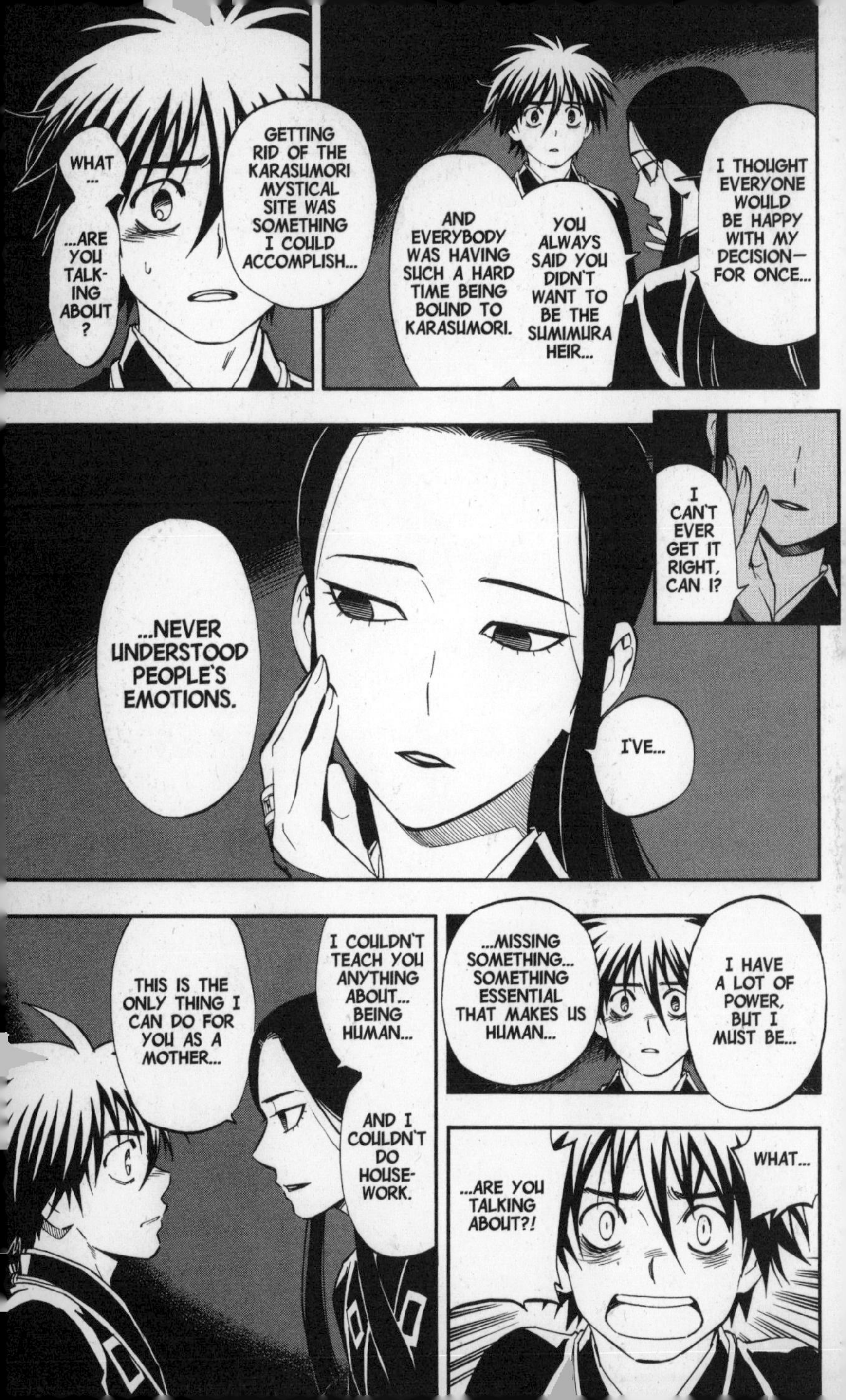
I THOUGHT EVERYONE WOULD BE HAPPY WITH MY DECISION—FOR ONCE...
YOU ALWAYS SAID YOU DIDN'T WANT TO BE THE SUMIMURA HEIR...
AND EVERYBODY WAS HAVING SUCH A HARD TIME BEING BOUND TO KARASUMORI.
GETTING RID OF THE KARASUMORI MYSTICAL SITE WAS SOMETHING I COULD ACCOMPLISH...
WHAT...
...ARE YOU TALKING ABOUT?
I CAN'T EVER GET IT RIGHT, CAN I?
I'VE...
...NEVER UNDERSTOOD PEOPLE'S EMOTIONS.
I HAVE A LOT OF POWER, BUT I MUST BE...
...MISSING SOMETHING... SOMETHING ESSENTIAL THAT MAKES US HUMAN...
WHAT...
...ARE YOU TALKING ABOUT?!
I COULDN'T TEACH YOU ANYTHING ABOUT... BEING HUMAN...
AND I COULDN'T DO HOUSEWORK.
THIS IS THE ONLY THING I CAN DO FOR YOU AS A MOTHER...

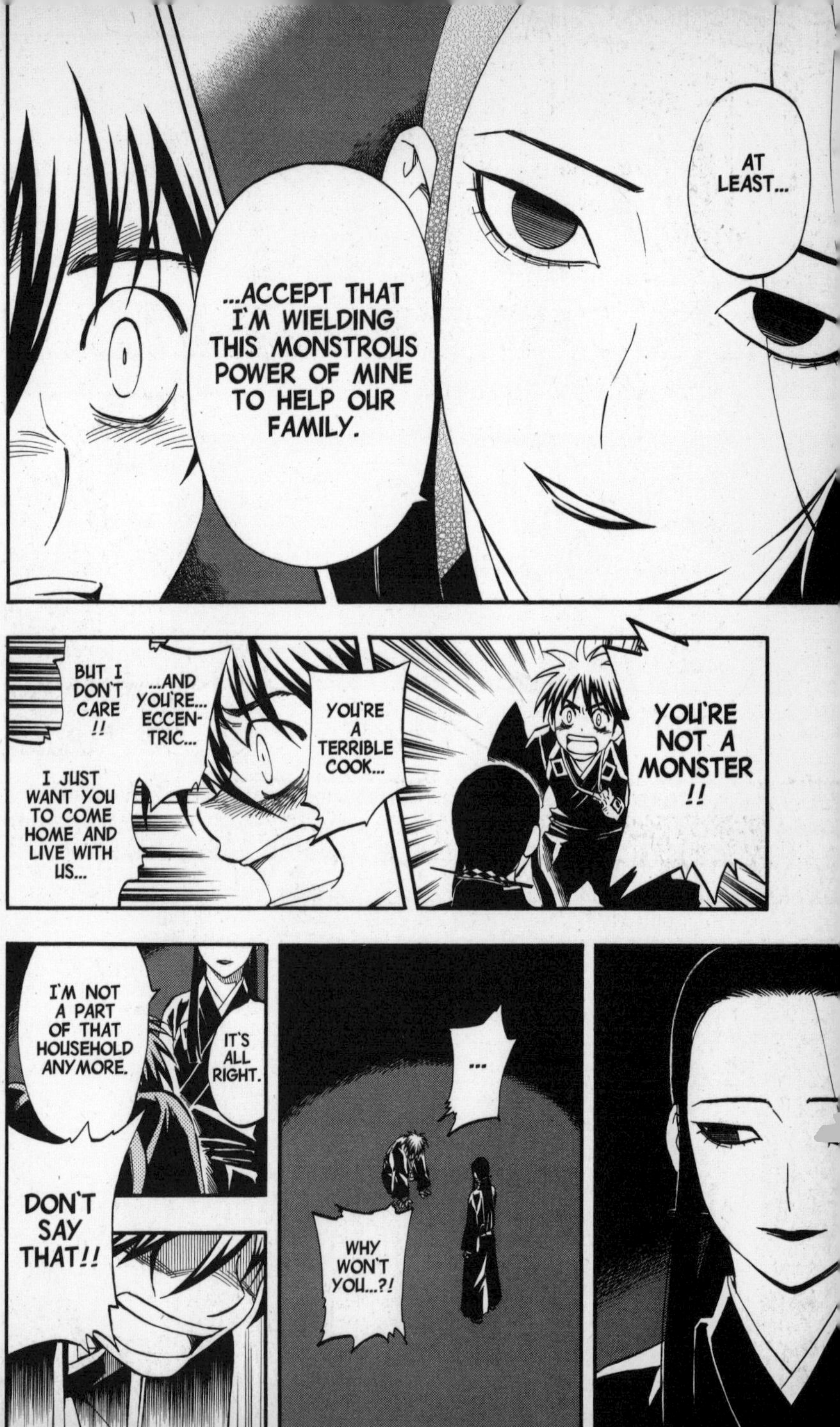
AT LEAST...
...ACCEPT THAT I'M WIELDING THIS MONSTROUS POWER OF MINE TO HELP OUR FAMILY.
YOU'RE NOT A MONSTER!!
YOU'RE A TERRIBLE COOK...
...AND YOU'RE... ECCENTRIC...
BUT I DON'T CARE!!
I JUST WANT YOU TO COME HOME AND LIVE WITH US...
...
WHY WON'T YOU...?!
IT'S ALL RIGHT.
I'M NOT A PART OF THAT HOUSEHOLD ANYMORE.
DON'T SAY THAT!!

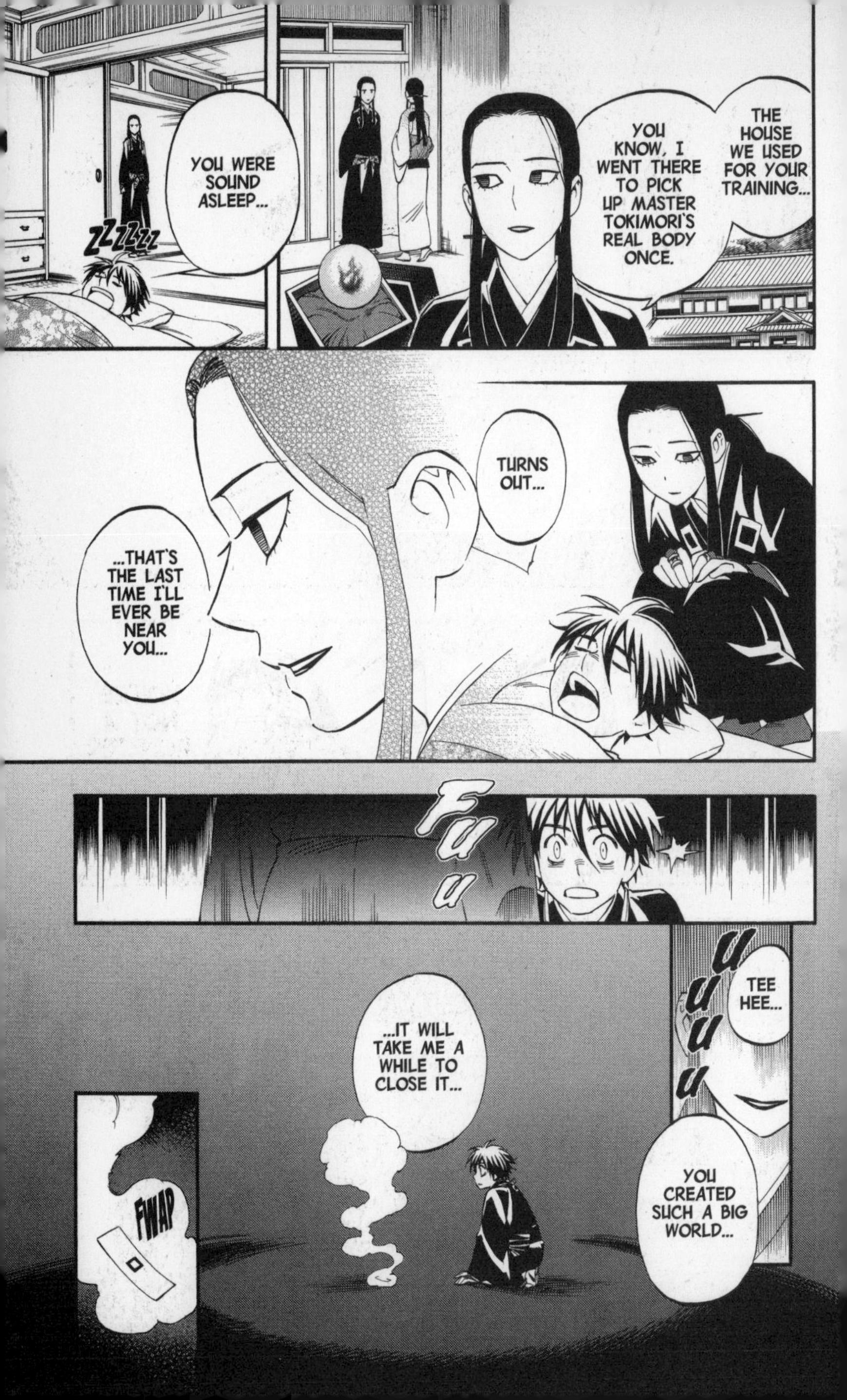
THE HOUSE WE USED FOR YOUR TRAINING...
YOU KNOW, I WENT THERE TO PICK UP MASTER TOKIMORI'S REAL BODY ONCE.
YOU WERE SOUND ASLEEP...
ZZZZZZ
TURNS OUT...
...THAT'S THE LAST TIME I'LL EVER BE NEAR YOU...
FUUU
UUUUU
TEE HEE...
YOU CREATED SUCH A BIG WORLD...
...IT WILL TAKE ME A WHILE TO CLOSE IT...
FWAP

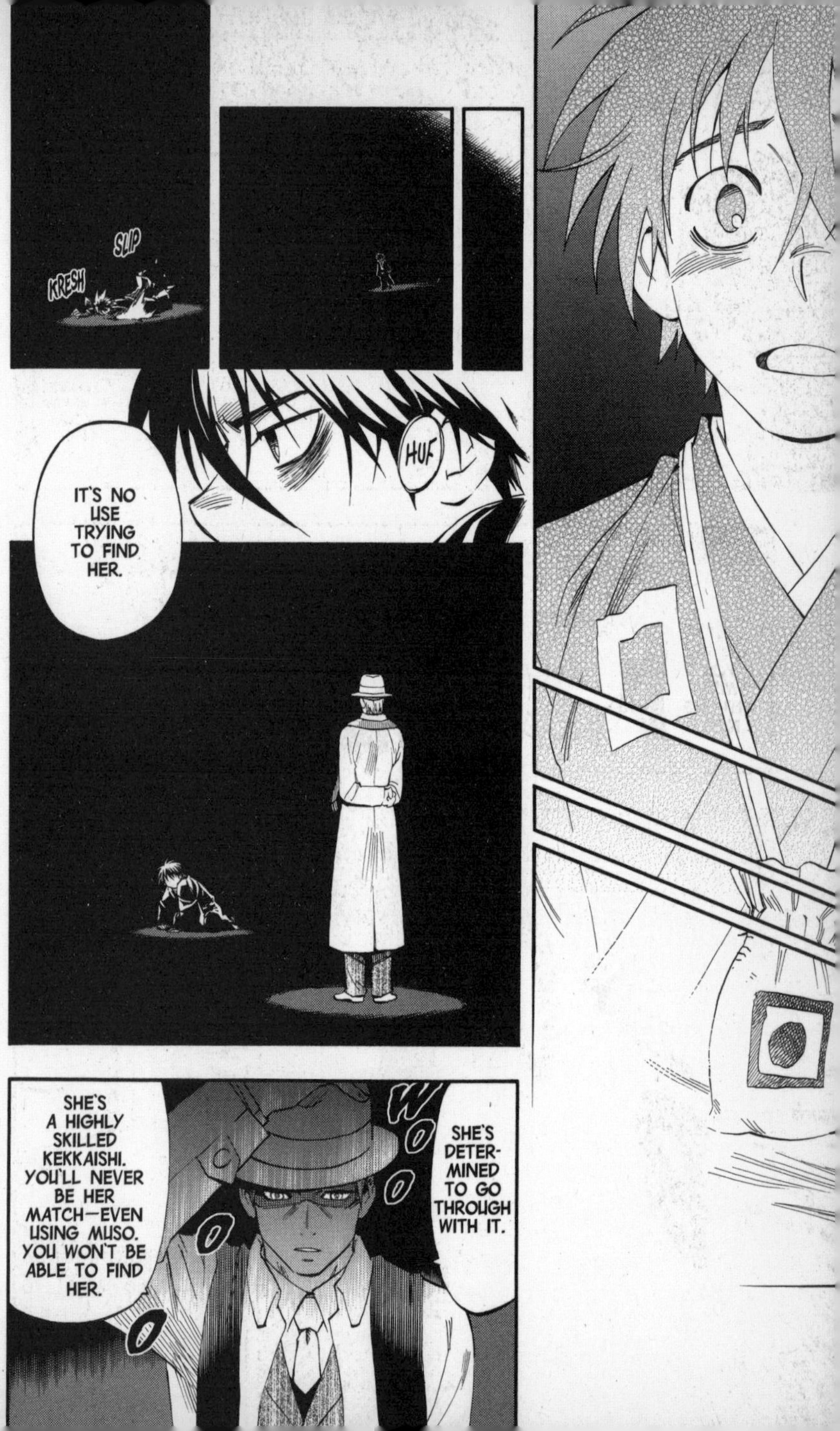
SLIP
KRESH
HUF
IT'S NO USE TRYING TO FIND HER.
SHE'S DETERMINED TO GO THROUGH WITH IT.
SHE'S A HIGHLY SKILLED KEKKAISHI. YOU'LL NEVER BE HER MATCH—EVEN USING MUSO. YOU WON'T BE ABLE TO FIND HER.

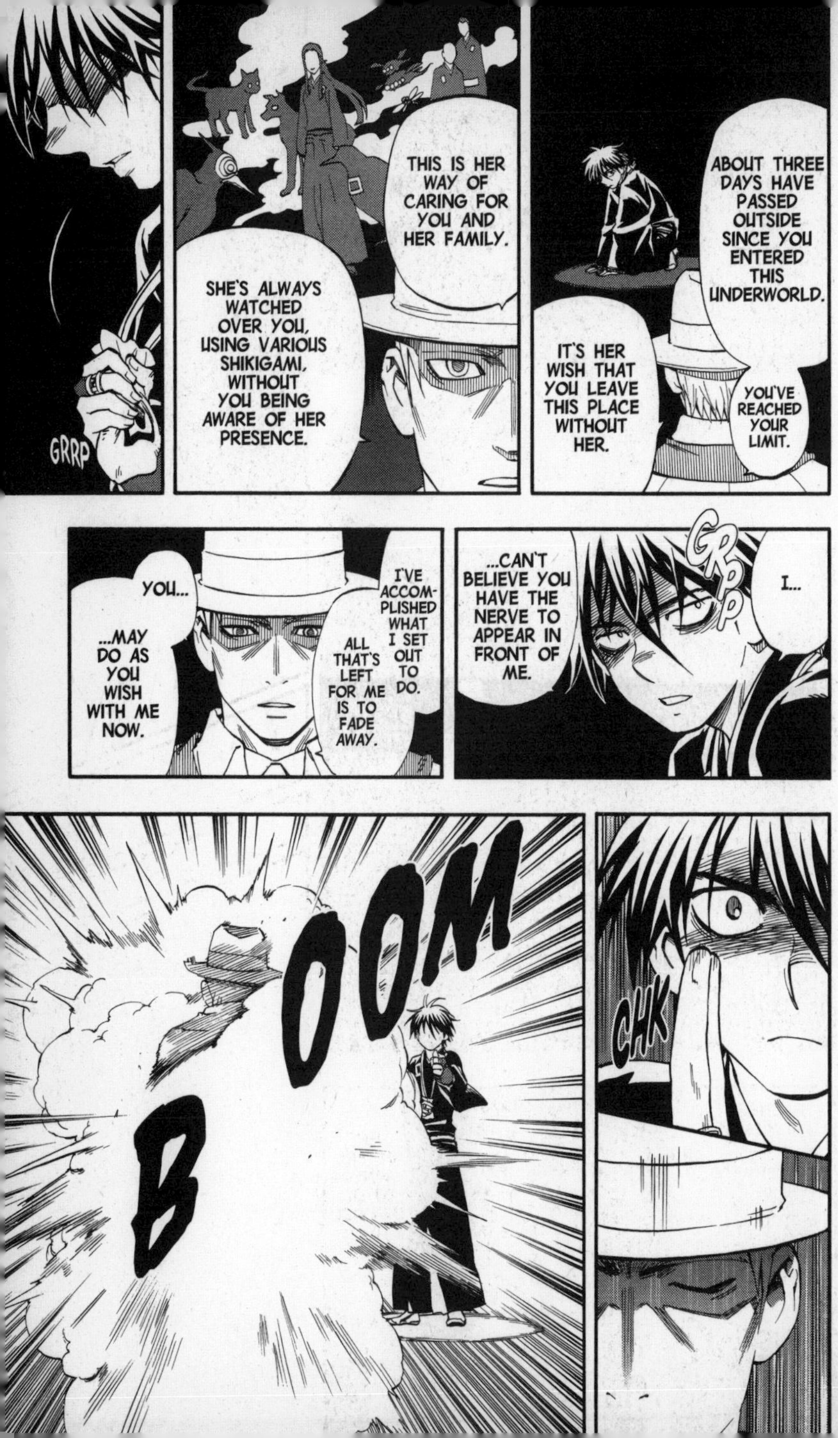
ABOUT THREE DAYS HAVE PASSED OUTSIDE SINCE YOU ENTERED THIS UNDERWORLD.
YOU'VE REACHED YOUR LIMIT.
IT'S HER WISH THAT YOU LEAVE THIS PLACE WITHOUT HER.
THIS IS HER WAY OF CARING FOR YOU AND HER FAMILY.
SHE'S ALWAYS WATCHED OVER YOU, USING VARIOUS SHIKIGAMI, WITHOUT YOU BEING AWARE OF HER PRESENCE.
GRRP
I...
GRRP
...CAN'T BELIEVE YOU HAVE THE NERVE TO APPEAR IN FRONT OF ME.
I'VE ACCOMPLISHED WHAT I SET OUT TO DO.
ALL THAT'S LEFT FOR ME IS TO FADE AWAY.
YOU...
...MAY DO AS YOU WISH WITH ME NOW.
CHK
BOOM

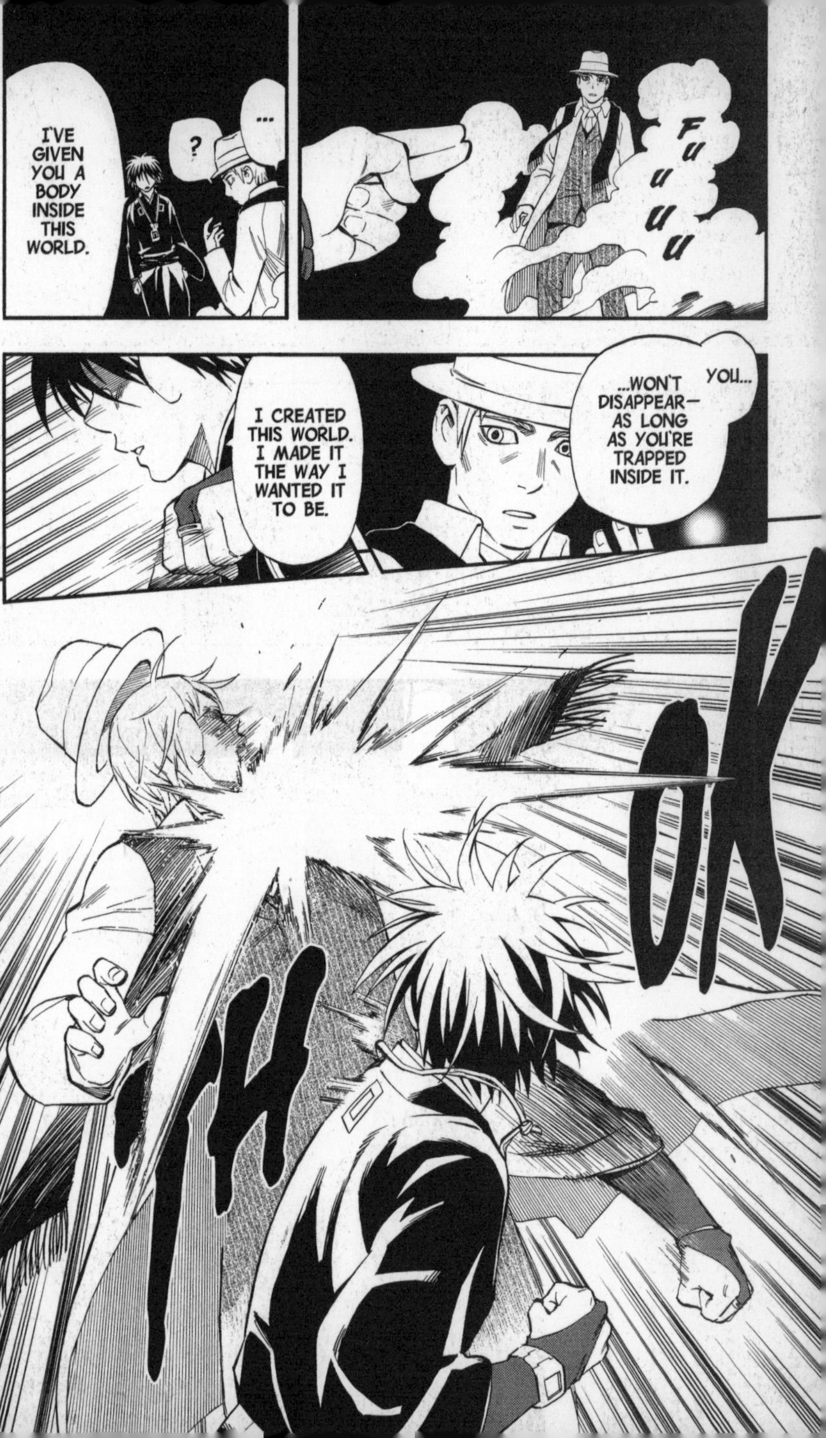
Fuuuu
...
?
I'VE GIVEN YOU A BODY INSIDE THIS WORLD.
YOU...
...WON'T DISAPPEAR— AS LONG AS YOU'RE TRAPPED INSIDE IT.
I CREATED THIS WORLD. I MADE IT THE WAY I WANTED IT TO BE.
OK

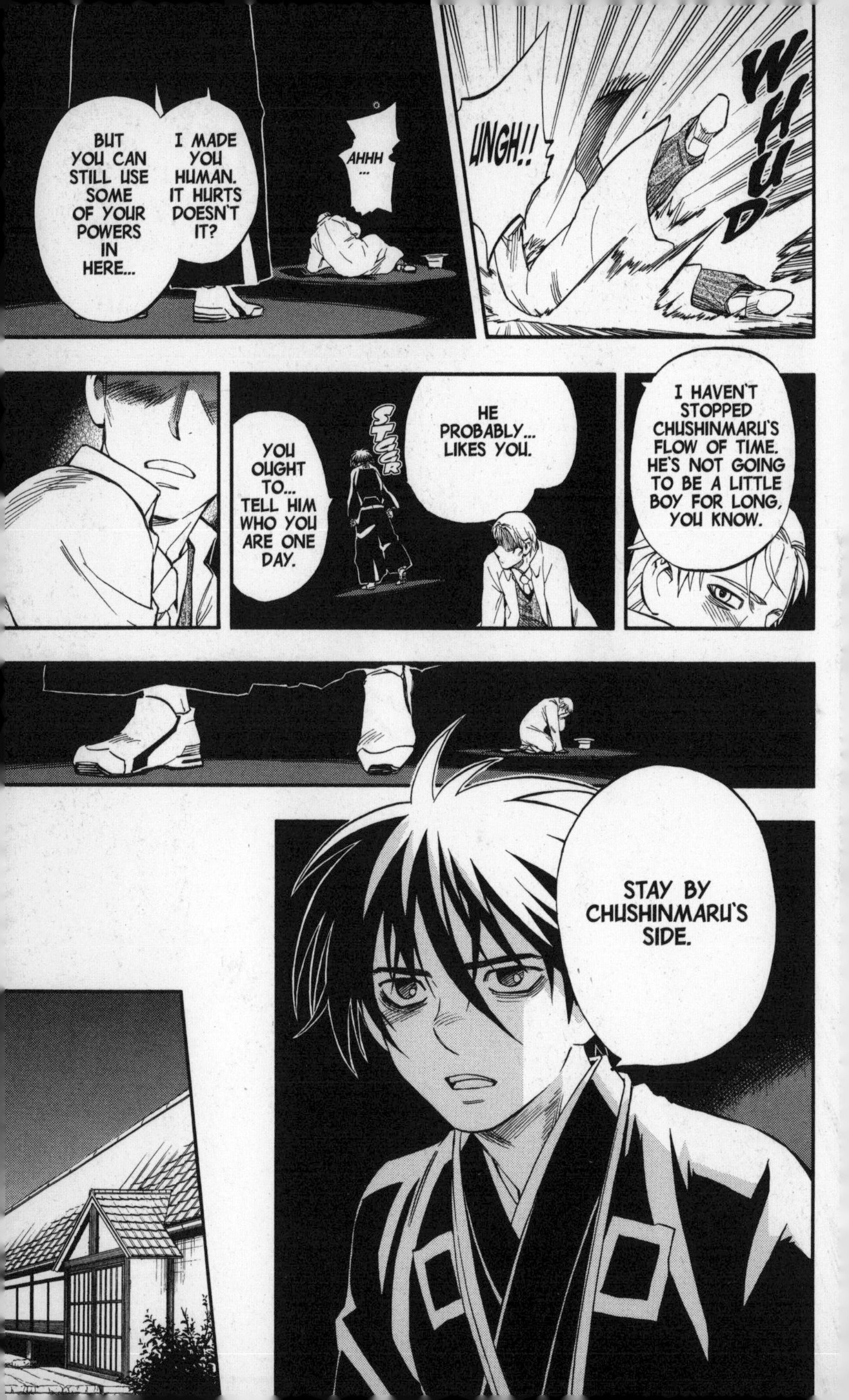
WHUD
UNGH!!
AHHH...
I MADE YOU HUMAN. IT HURTS DOESN'T IT?
BUT YOU CAN STILL USE SOME OF YOUR POWERS IN HERE...
I HAVEN'T STOPPED CHUSHINMARU'S FLOW OF TIME. HE'S NOT GOING TO BE A LITTLE BOY FOR LONG, YOU KNOW.
HE PROBABLY... LIKES YOU.
STGGR
YOU OUGHT TO... TELL HIM WHO YOU ARE ONE DAY.
STAY BY CHUSHINMARU'S SIDE.

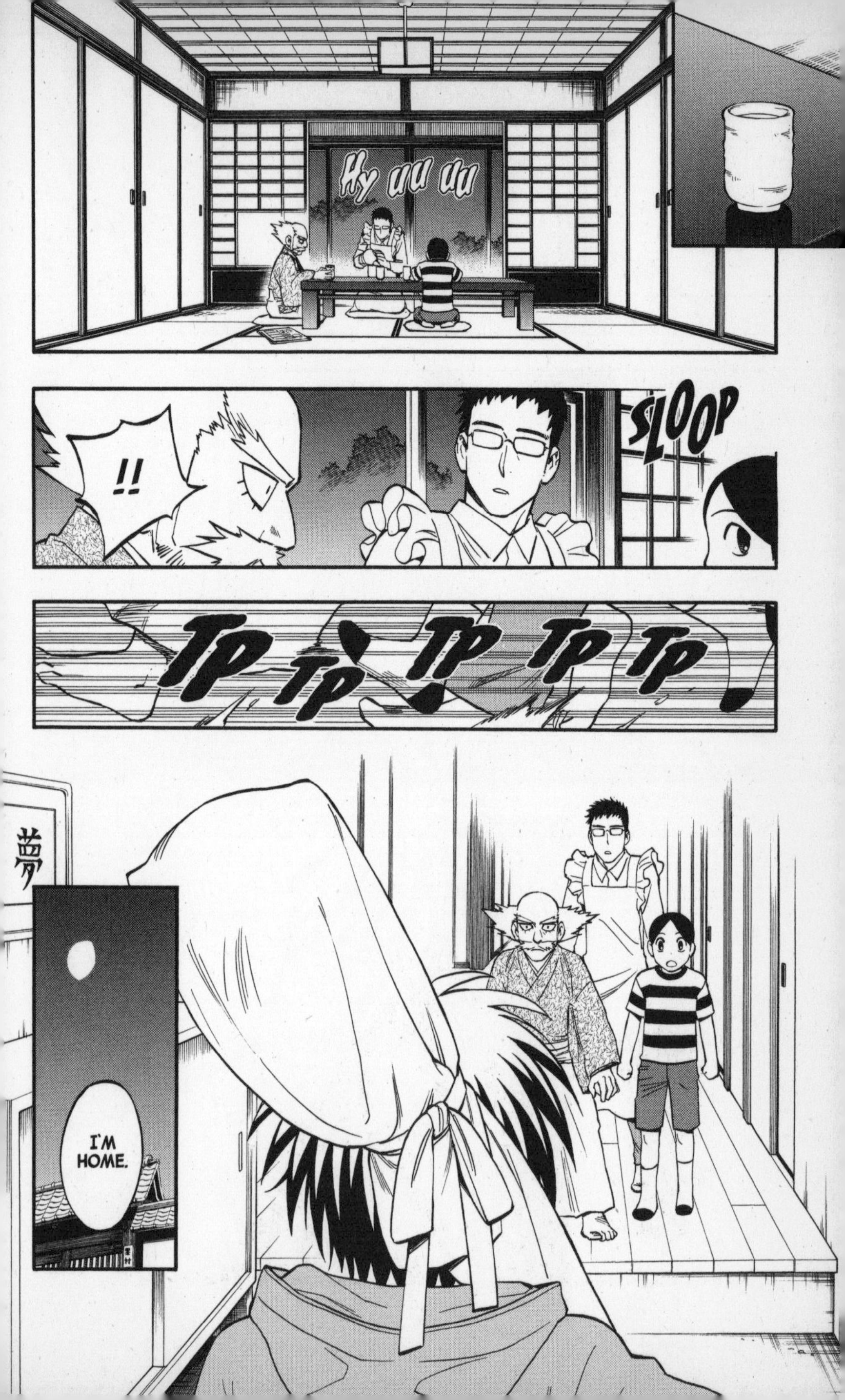
Hy uu uu
SLOOP
!!
TP TP TP TP TP
夢
I'M HOME.

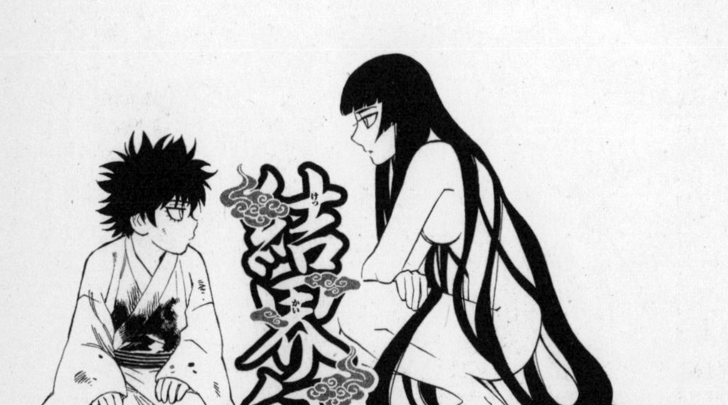
結界師

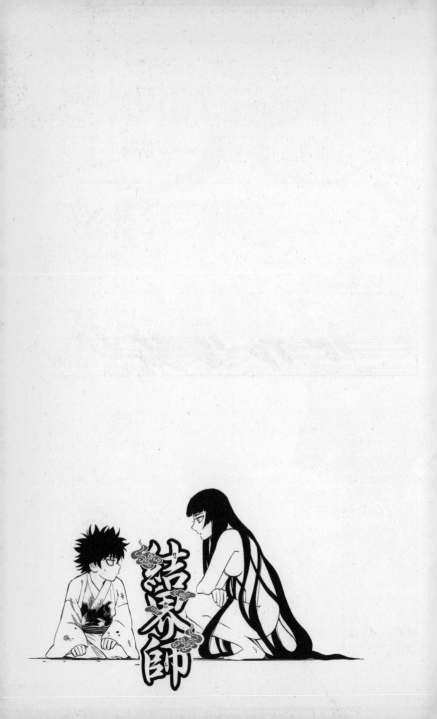

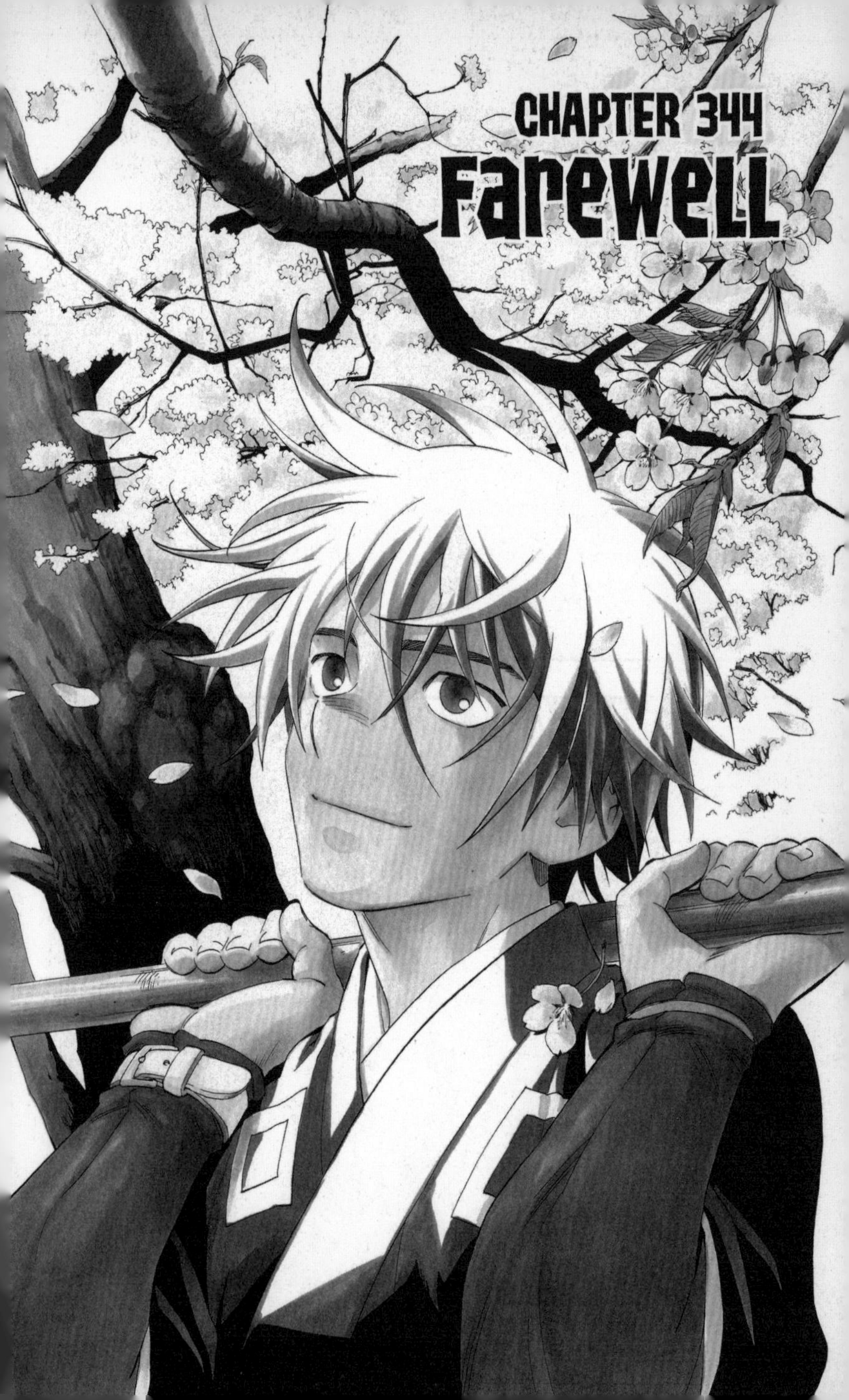
CHAPTER 344
Farewell

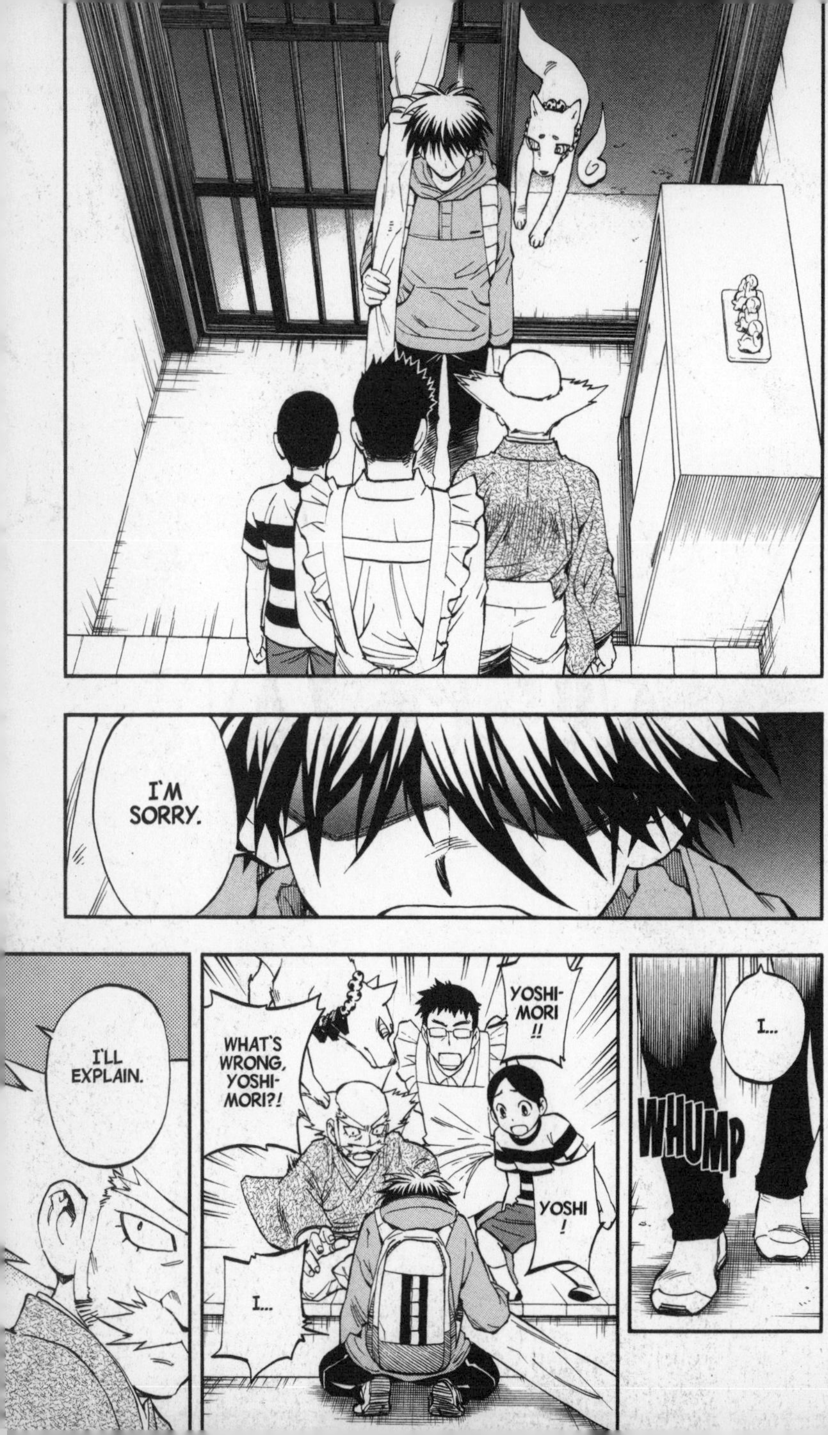
I'M SORRY.
I...
WHUMP
YOSHI-MORI!!
WHAT'S WRONG, YOSHI-MORI?!
YOSHI!
I...
I'LL EXPLAIN.

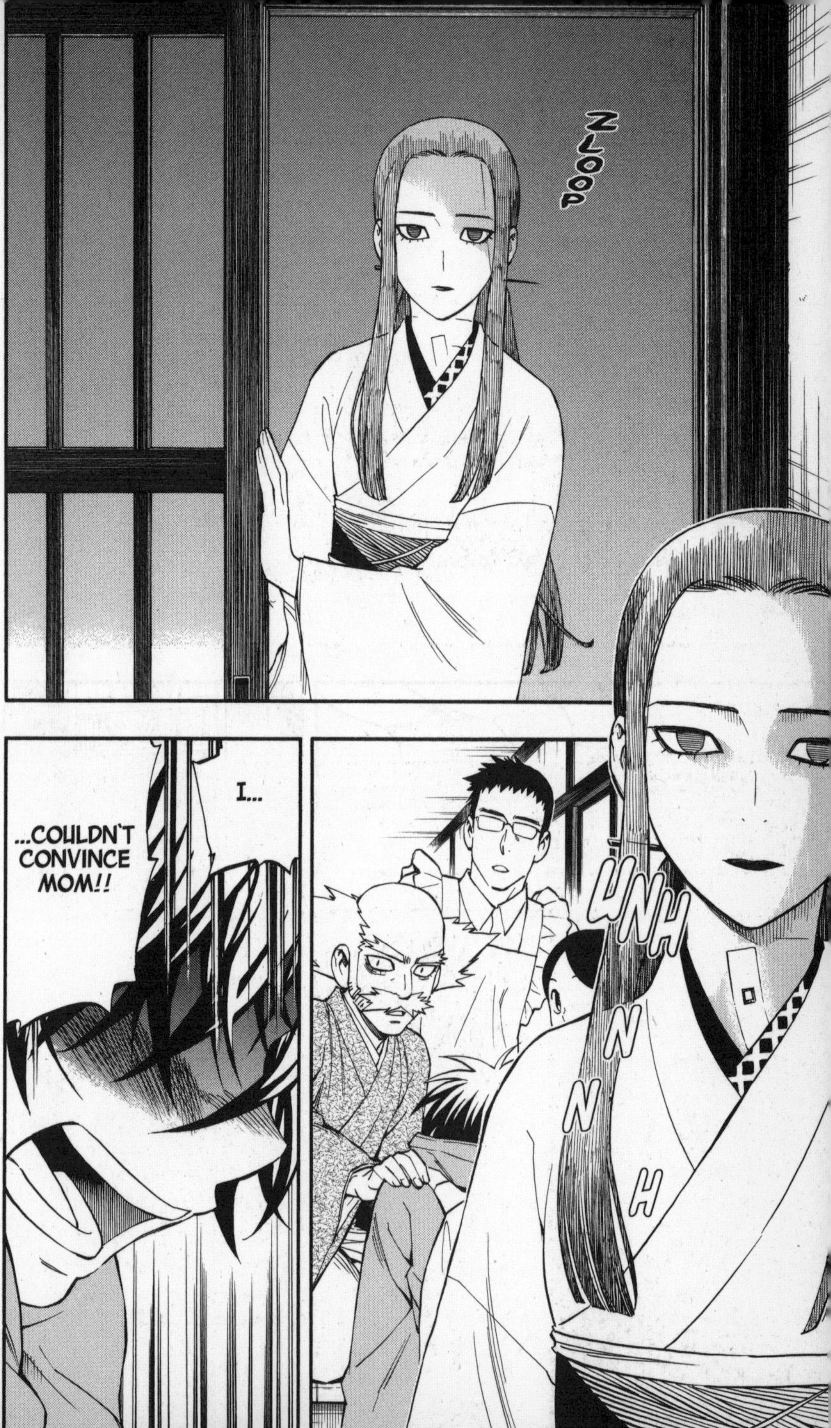
ZLOOP
UNH NNNH
I...
...COULDN'T CONVINCE MOM!!

CHAPTER 344: FAREWELL

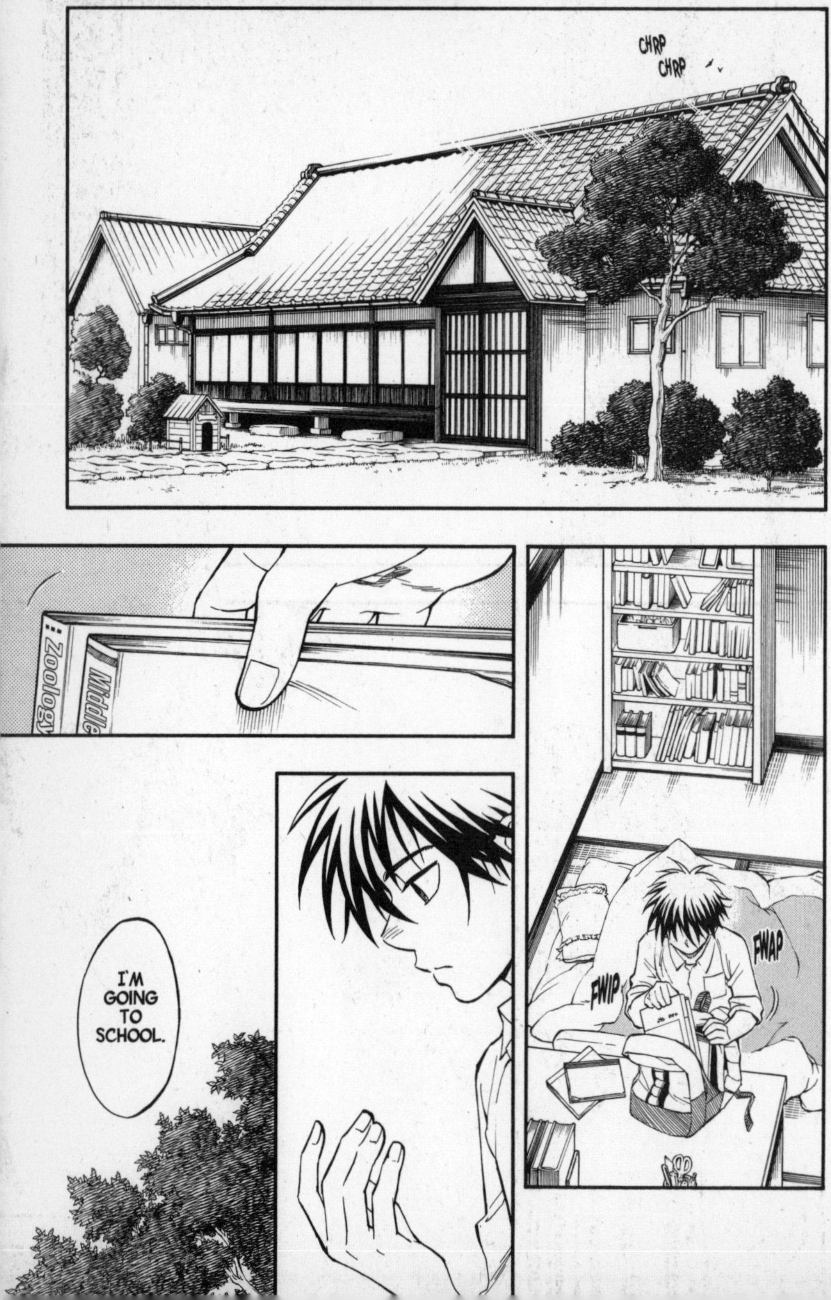
CHRP
CHRP
FWAP
FWIP
Zoology
Middle
I'M GOING TO SCHOOL.

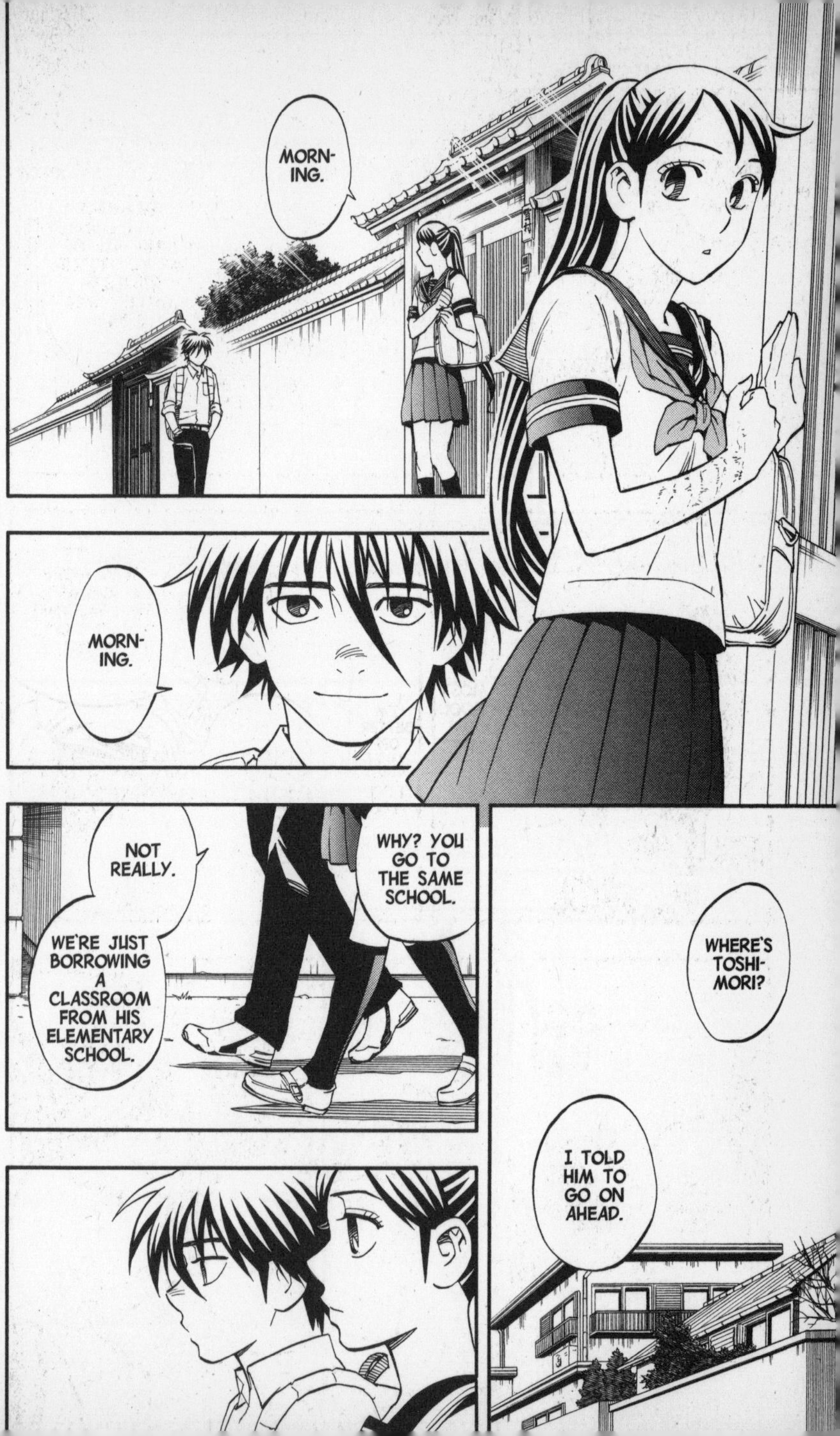
MORN-ING.
MORN-ING.
WHERE'S TOSHI-MORI?
I TOLD HIM TO GO ON AHEAD.
WHY? YOU GO TO THE SAME SCHOOL.
NOT REALLY.
WE'RE JUST BORROWING A CLASSROOM FROM HIS ELEMENTARY SCHOOL.

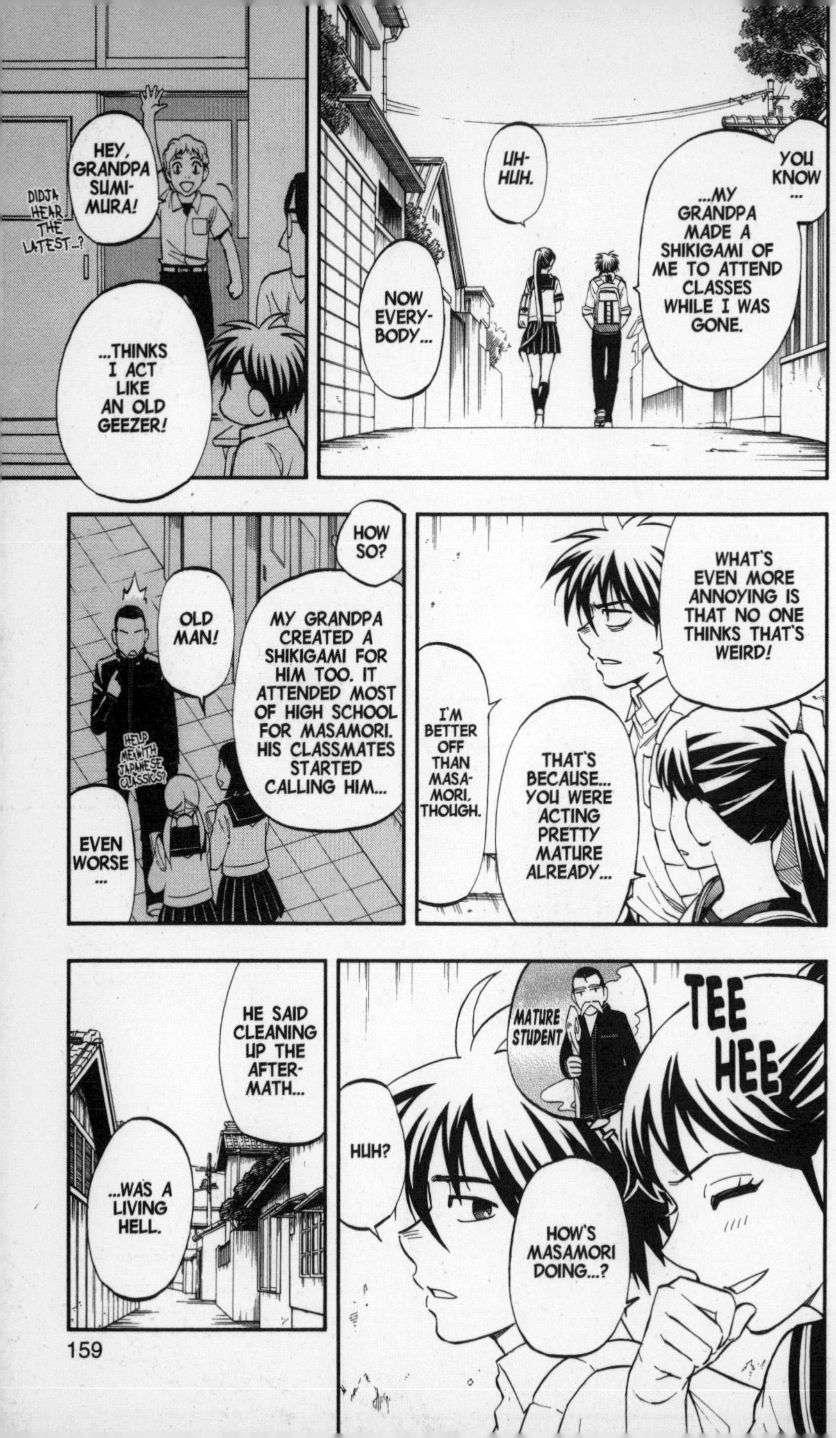
YOU KNOW...
...MY GRANDPA MADE A SHIKIGAMI OF ME TO ATTEND CLASSES WHILE I WAS GONE.
UH-HUH.
NOW EVERYBODY...
HEY, GRANDPA SUMIMURA!
DIDJA HEAR THE LATEST...?
...THINKS I ACT LIKE AN OLD GEEZER!
WHAT'S EVEN MORE ANNOYING IS THAT NO ONE THINKS THAT'S WEIRD!
THAT'S BECAUSE... YOU WERE ACTING PRETTY MATURE ALREADY...
I'M BETTER OFF THAN MASAMORI, THOUGH.
HOW SO?
MY GRANDPA CREATED A SHIKIGAMI FOR HIM TOO. IT ATTENDED MOST OF HIGH SCHOOL FOR MASAMORI. HIS CLASSMATES STARTED CALLING HIM...
OLD MAN!
HELP ME WITH JAPANESE CLASSICS?
EVEN WORSE...
TEE HEE
MATURE STUDENT
HUH?
HOW'S MASAMORI DOING...?
HE SAID CLEANING UP THE AFTERMATH...
...WAS A LIVING HELL.

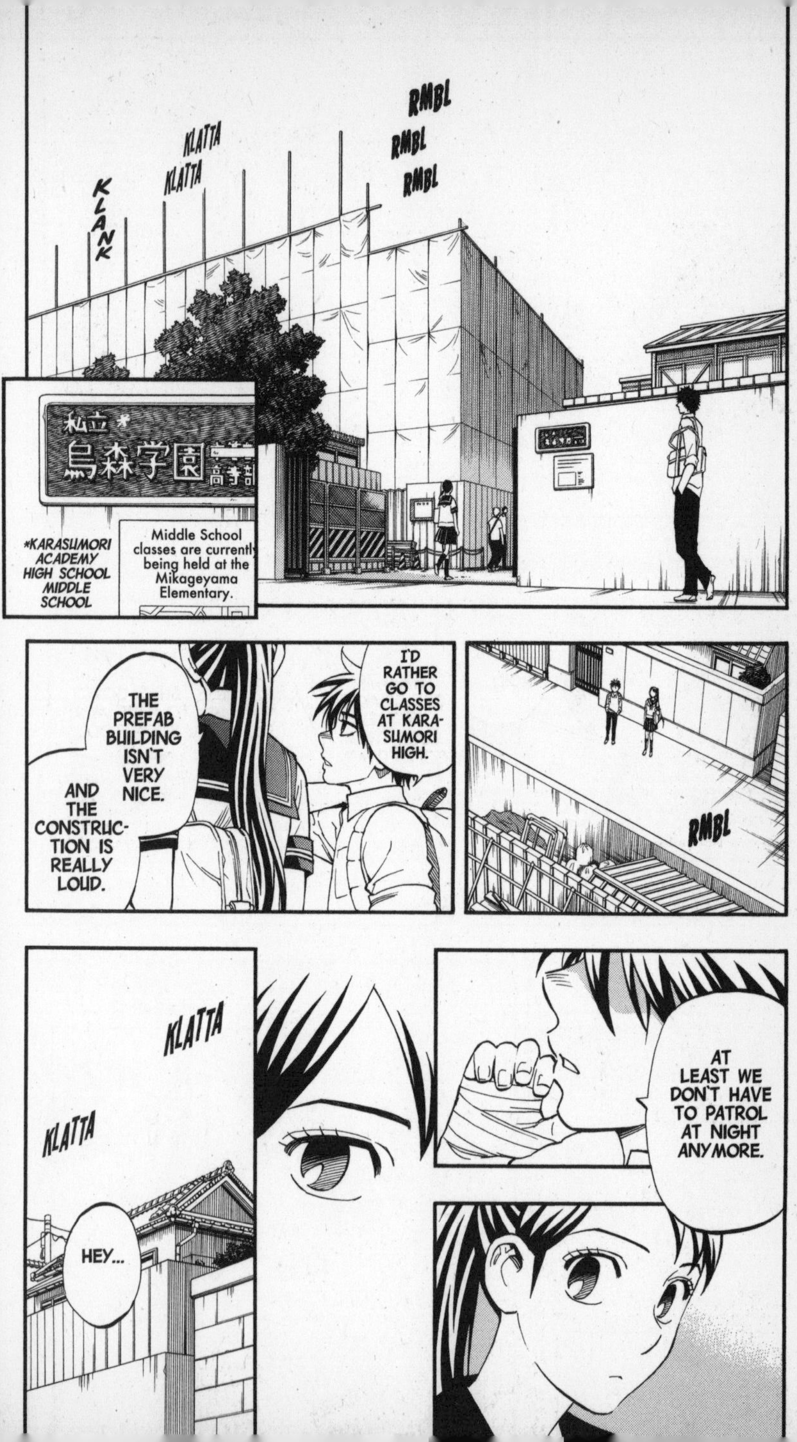
RMBL
RMBL
RMBL
KLATTA
KLATTA
KLANK
私立*
鳥森学園 高等部
*KARASUMORI ACADEMY HIGH SCHOOL MIDDLE SCHOOL
Middle School classes are currently being held at the Mikageyama Elementary.
RMBL
I'D RATHER GO TO CLASSES AT KARA-SUMORI HIGH.
THE PREFAB BUILDING ISN'T VERY NICE.
AND THE CONSTRUC-TION IS REALLY LOUD.
AT LEAST WE DON'T HAVE TO PATROL AT NIGHT ANYMORE.
KLATTA
KLATTA
HEY...

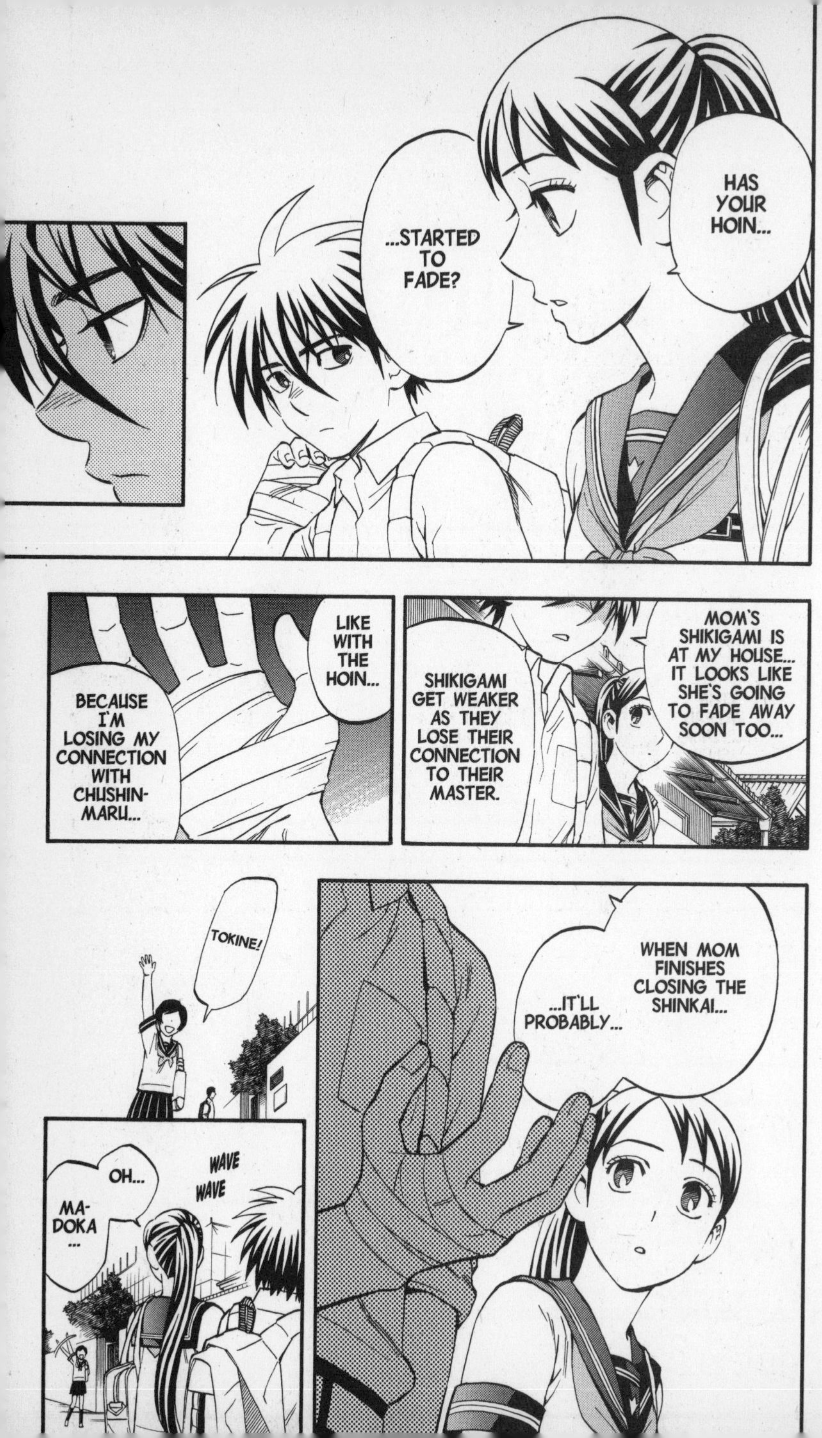
HAS YOUR HOIN...
...STARTED TO FADE?
MOM'S SHIKIGAMI IS AT MY HOUSE... IT LOOKS LIKE SHE'S GOING TO FADE AWAY SOON TOO...
SHIKIGAMI GET WEAKER AS THEY LOSE THEIR CONNECTION TO THEIR MASTER.
LIKE WITH THE HOIN...
BECAUSE I'M LOSING MY CONNECTION WITH CHUSHIN-MARU...
WHEN MOM FINISHES CLOSING THE SHINKAI...
...IT'LL PROBABLY...
TOKINE!
WAVE WAVE
OH...
MA-DOKA...

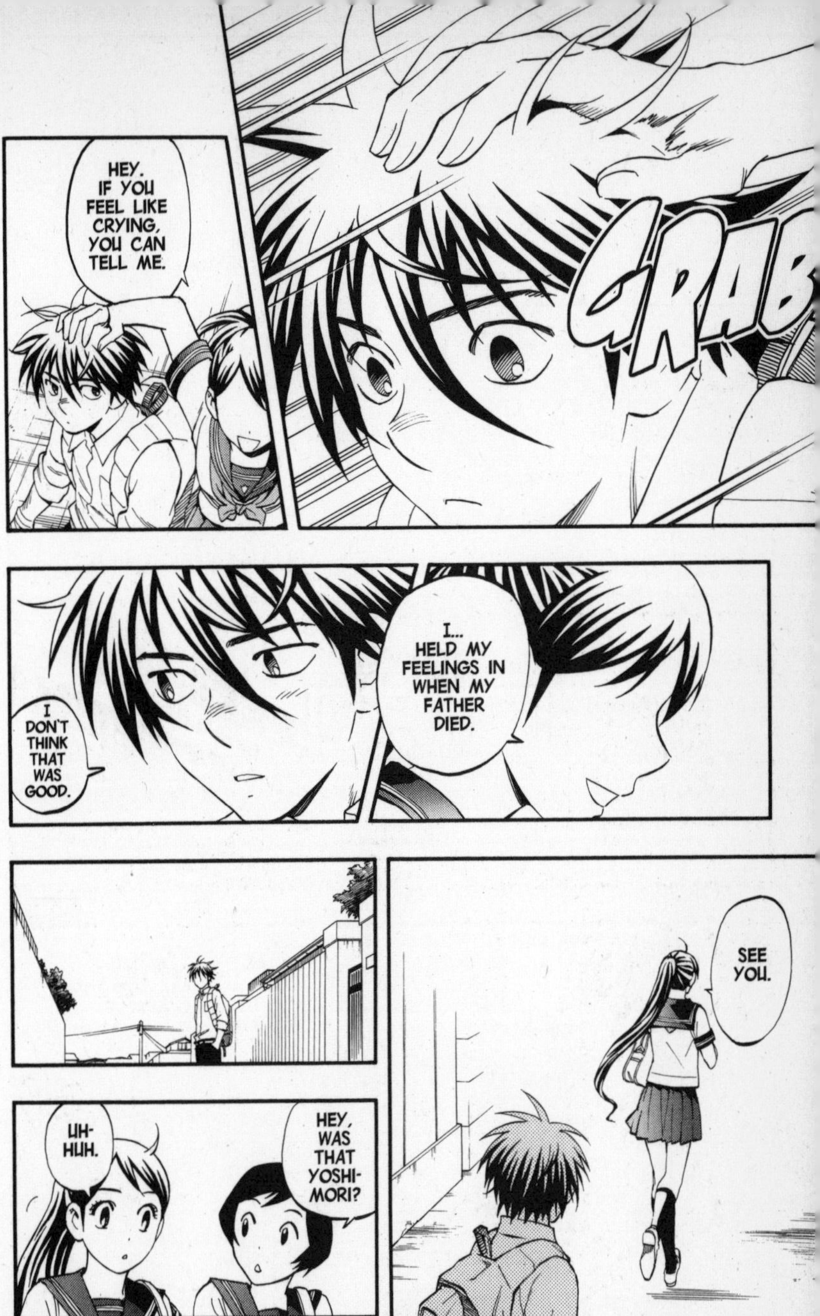
GRAB
HEY. IF YOU FEEL LIKE CRYING, YOU CAN TELL ME.
I... HELD MY FEELINGS IN WHEN MY FATHER DIED.
I DON'T THINK THAT WAS GOOD.
SEE YOU.
HEY, WAS THAT YOSHIMORI?
UH-HUH.

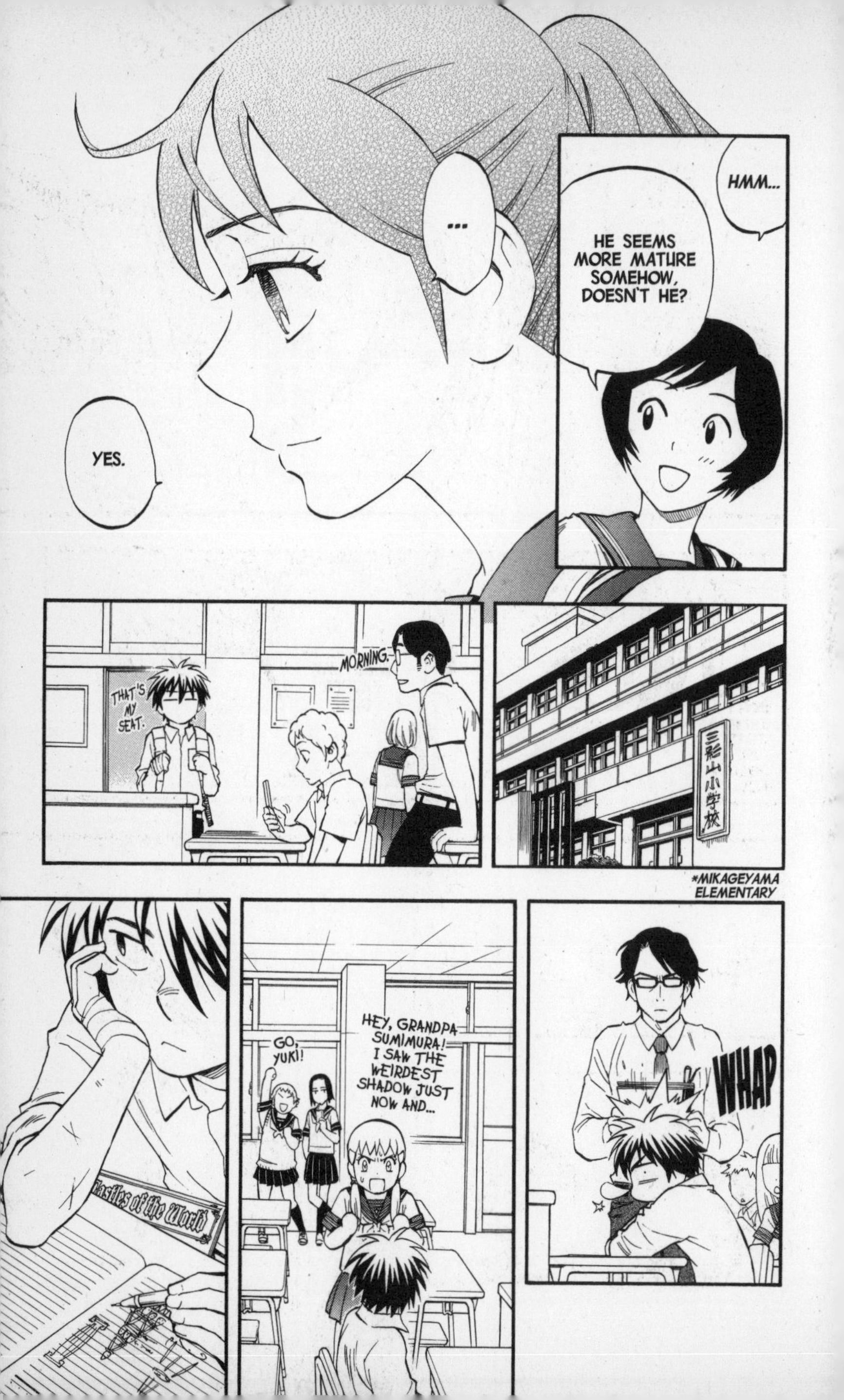
HMM...
HE SEEMS MORE MATURE SOMEHOW, DOESN'T HE?
...
YES.
三影山小学校
*MIKAGEYAMA ELEMENTARY
MORNING.
THAT'S MY SEAT.
WHAP
HEY, GRANDPA SUMIMURA! I SAW THE WEIRDEST SHADOW JUST NOW AND...
GO, YUKI!
Castles of the World

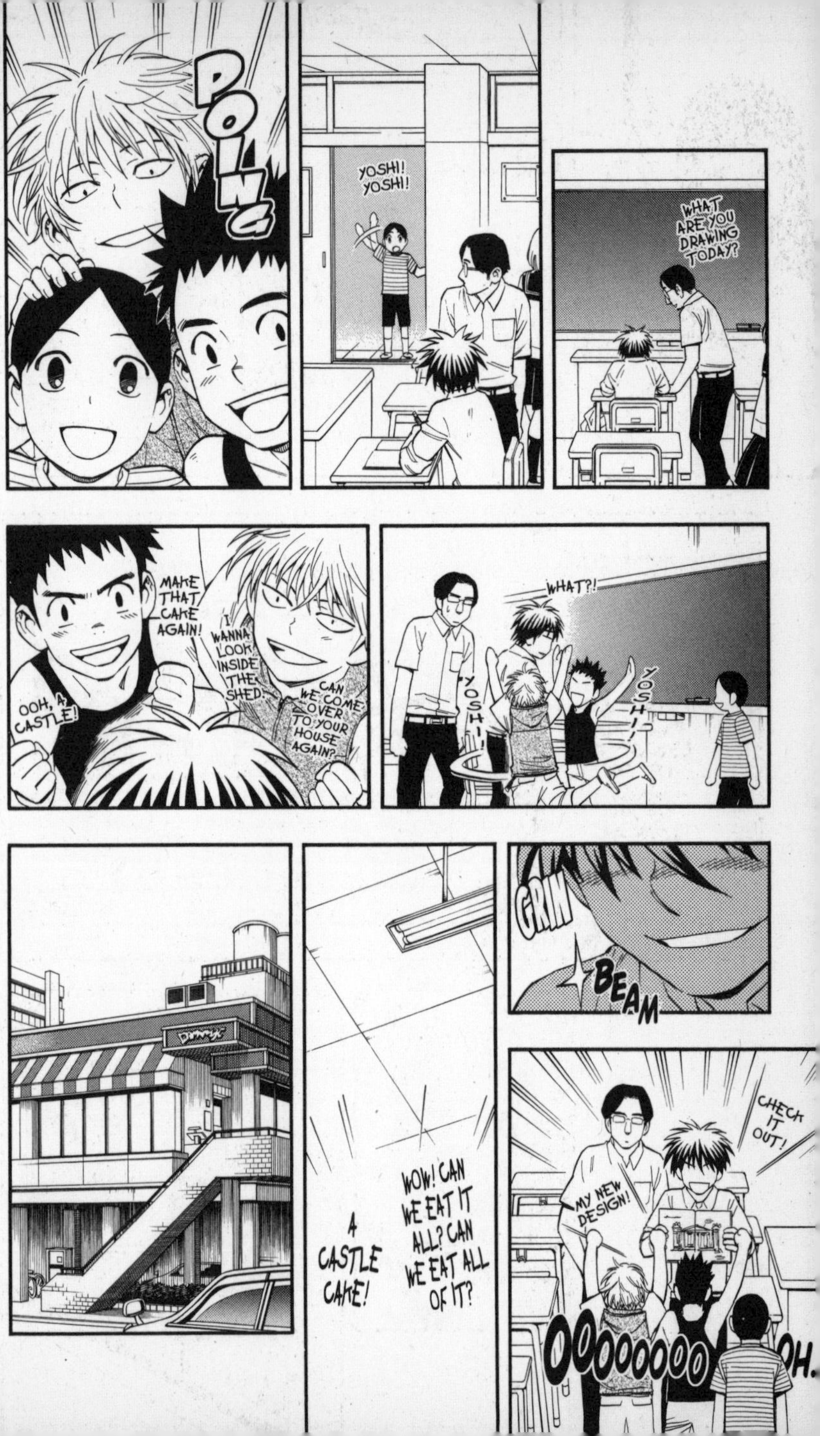
WHAT ARE YOU DRAWING TODAY?
YOSHI! YOSHI!
POING
WHAT?!
YOSHI!
YOSHI!
CAN WE COME OVER TO YOUR HOUSE AGAIN?
I WANNA LOOK INSIDE THE SHED.
MAKE THAT CAKE AGAIN!
OOH, A CASTLE!
GRIN
BEAM
CHECK IT OUT!
MY NEW DESIGN!
OOOOOOOOH.
WOW! CAN WE EAT IT ALL? CAN WE EAT ALL OF IT?
A CASTLE CAKE!

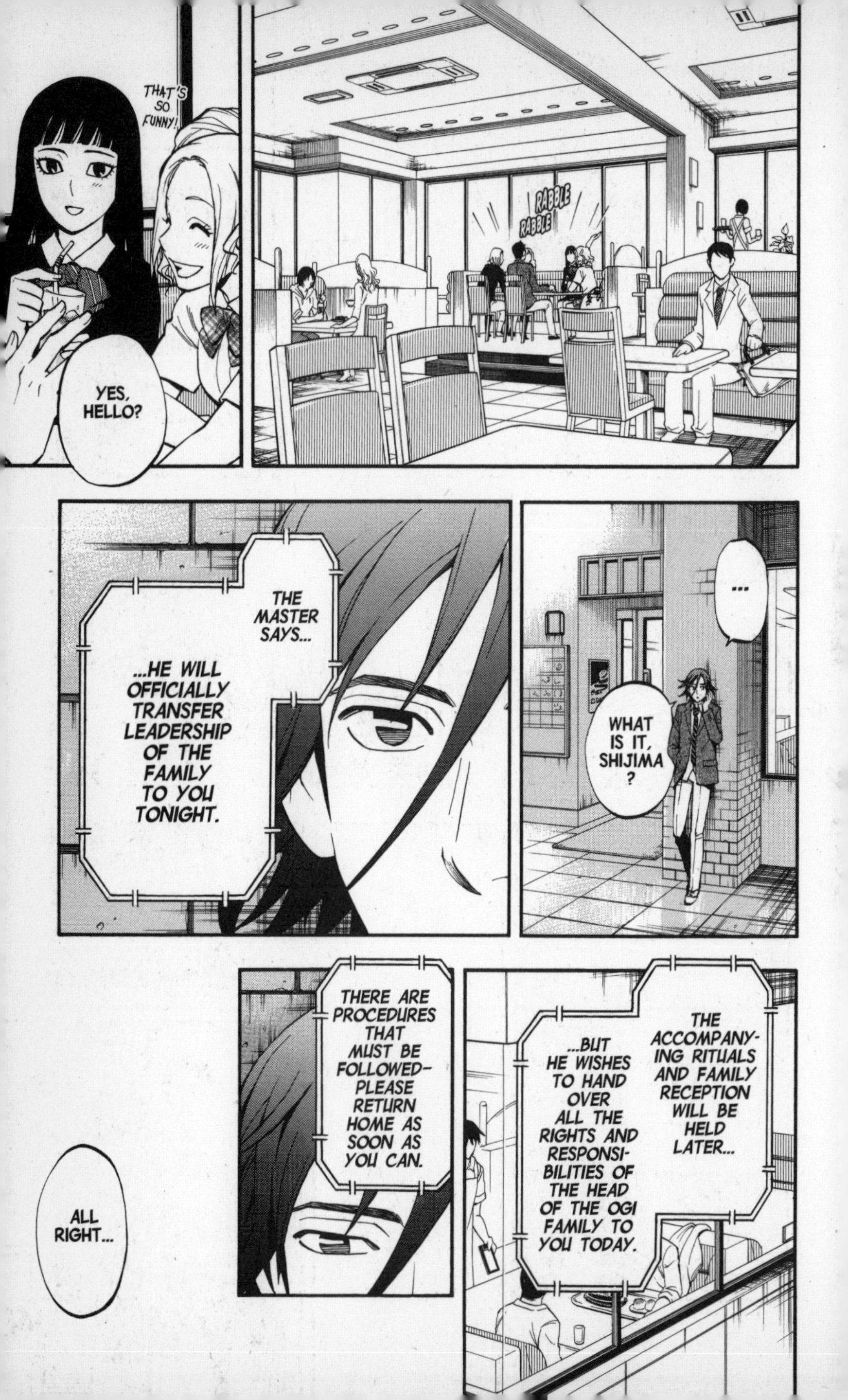
RABBLE RABBLE
THAT'S SO FUNNY!
YES, HELLO?
...
WHAT IS IT, SHIJIMA?
THE MASTER SAYS...
...HE WILL OFFICIALLY TRANSFER LEADERSHIP OF THE FAMILY TO YOU TONIGHT.
THE ACCOMPANYING RITUALS AND FAMILY RECEPTION WILL BE HELD LATER...
...BUT HE WISHES TO HAND OVER ALL THE RIGHTS AND RESPONSIBILITIES OF THE HEAD OF THE OGI FAMILY TO YOU TODAY.
THERE ARE PROCEDURES THAT MUST BE FOLLOWED—PLEASE RETURN HOME AS SOON AS YOU CAN.
ALL RIGHT...

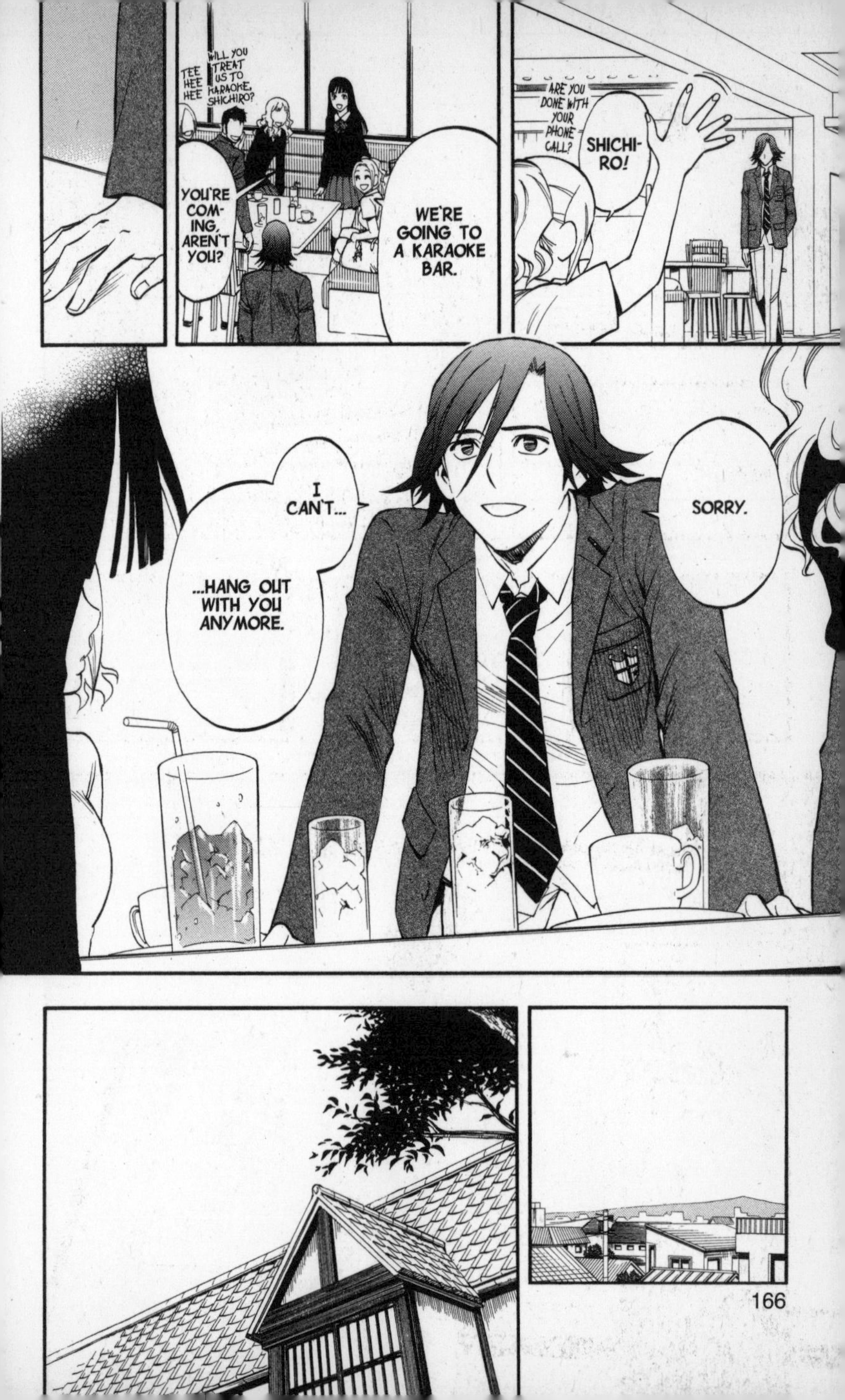
SHICHI-RO!
ARE YOU DONE WITH YOUR PHONE CALL?
WE'RE GOING TO A KARAOKE BAR.
YOU'RE COM-ING, AREN'T YOU?
WILL YOU TREAT US TO KARAOKE, SHICHIRO?
TEE HEE HEE
SORRY.
I CAN'T...
...HANG OUT WITH YOU ANYMORE.

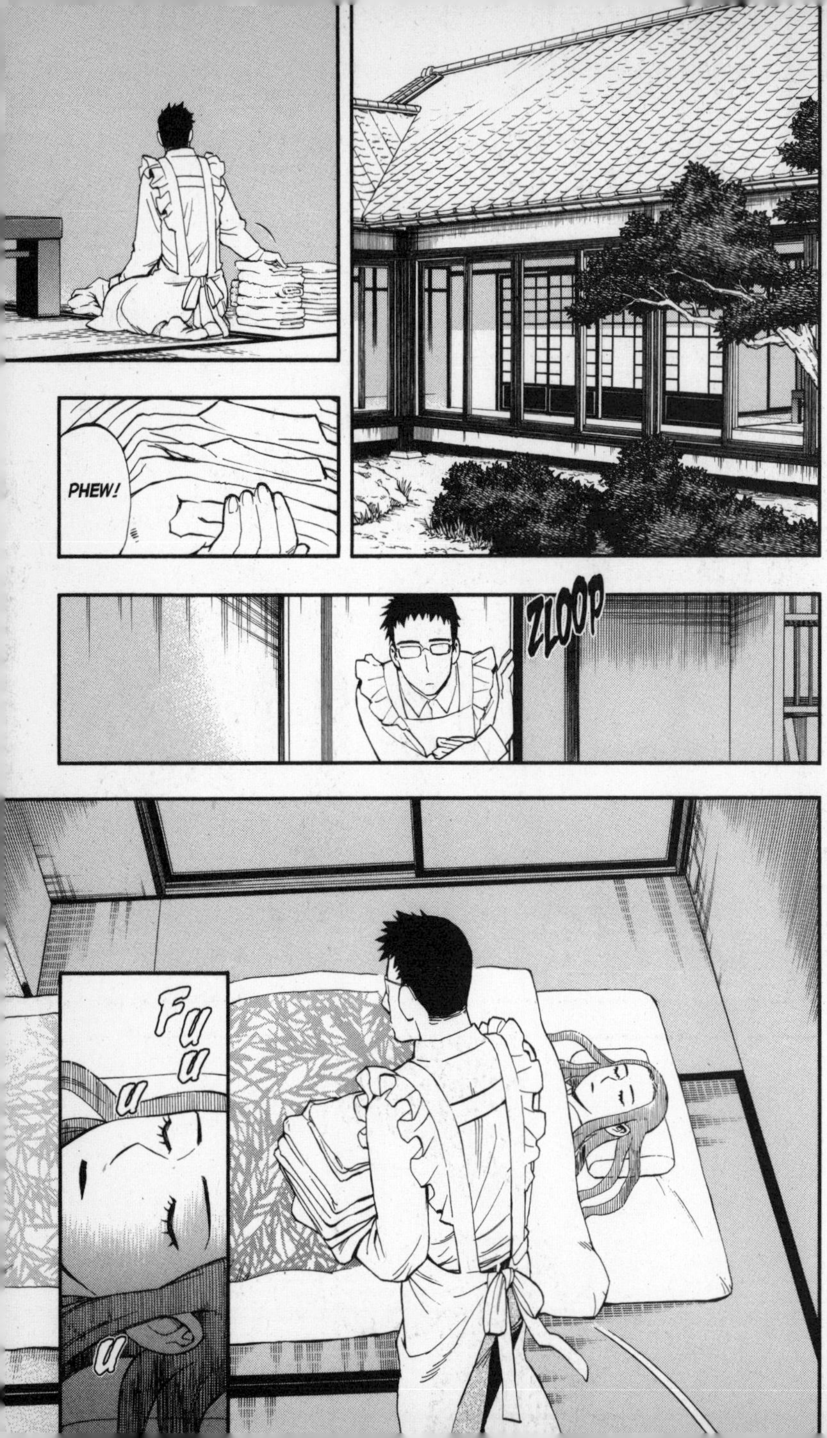
PHEW!
ZLOOP
Fuuuu

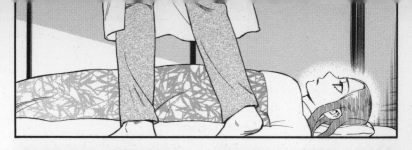

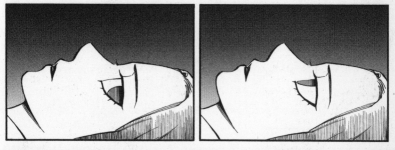

...

YES.

I HAVE A MESSAGE FOR YOU... FROM MY MISTRESS.

WOULD YOU LIKE TO HEAR IT?

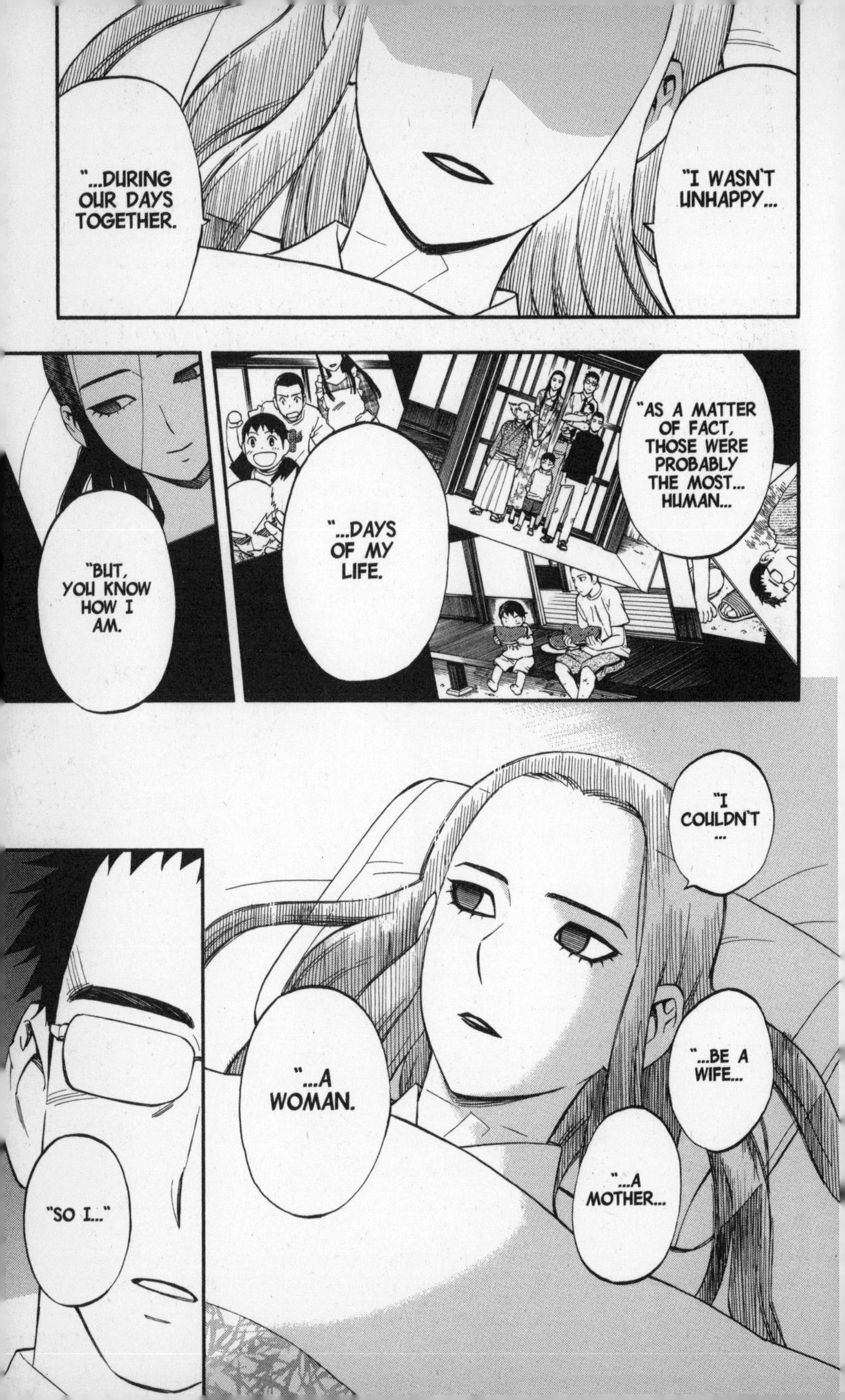
"I WASN'T UNHAPPY...
"...DURING OUR DAYS TOGETHER.
"AS A MATTER OF FACT, THOSE WERE PROBABLY THE MOST... HUMAN...
"...DAYS OF MY LIFE.
"BUT, YOU KNOW HOW I AM.
"I COULDN'T ...
"...BE A WIFE...
"...A MOTHER...
"...A WOMAN.
"SO I..."

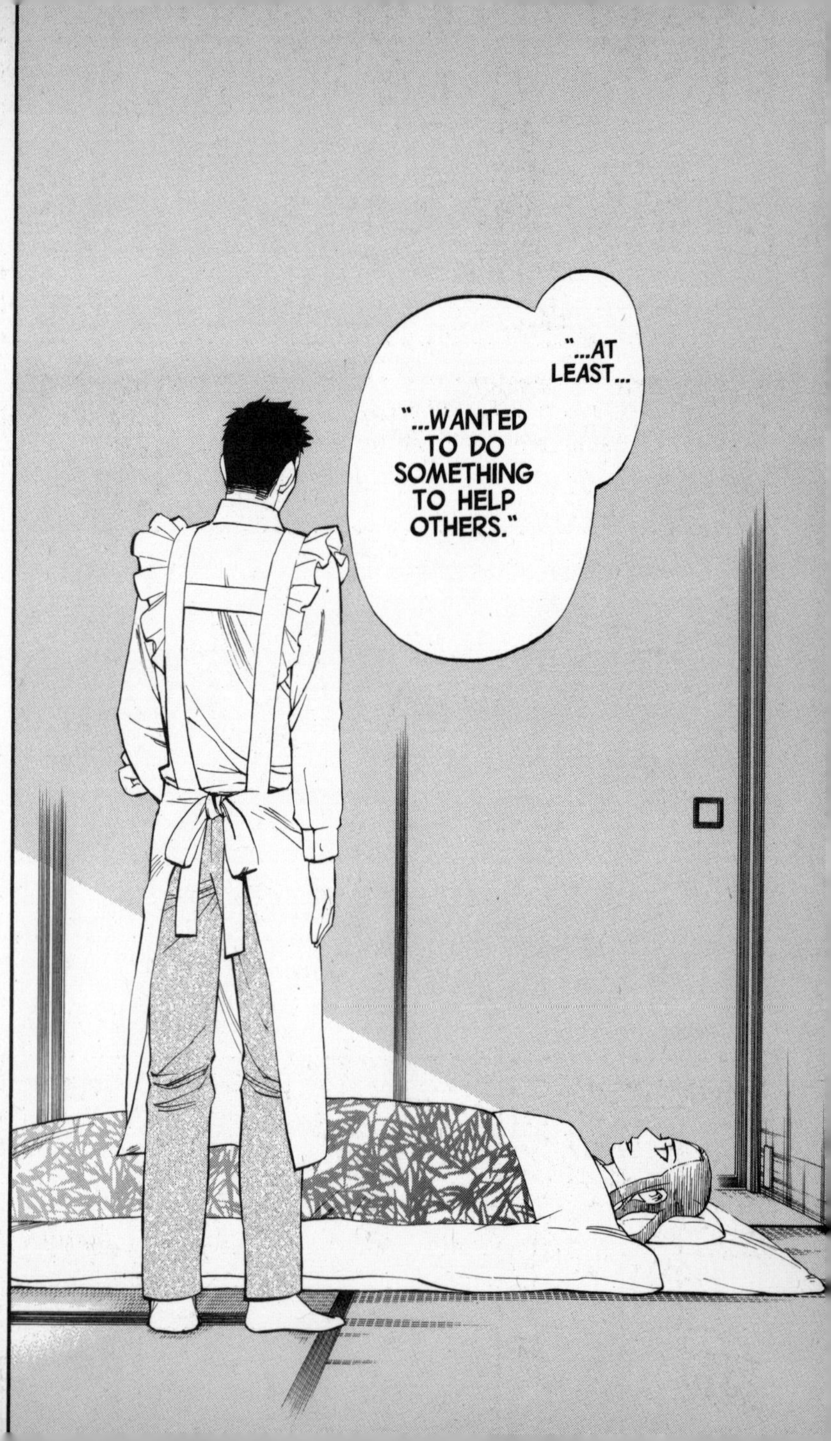
"...AT LEAST...
"...WANTED TO DO SOMETHING TO HELP OTHERS."

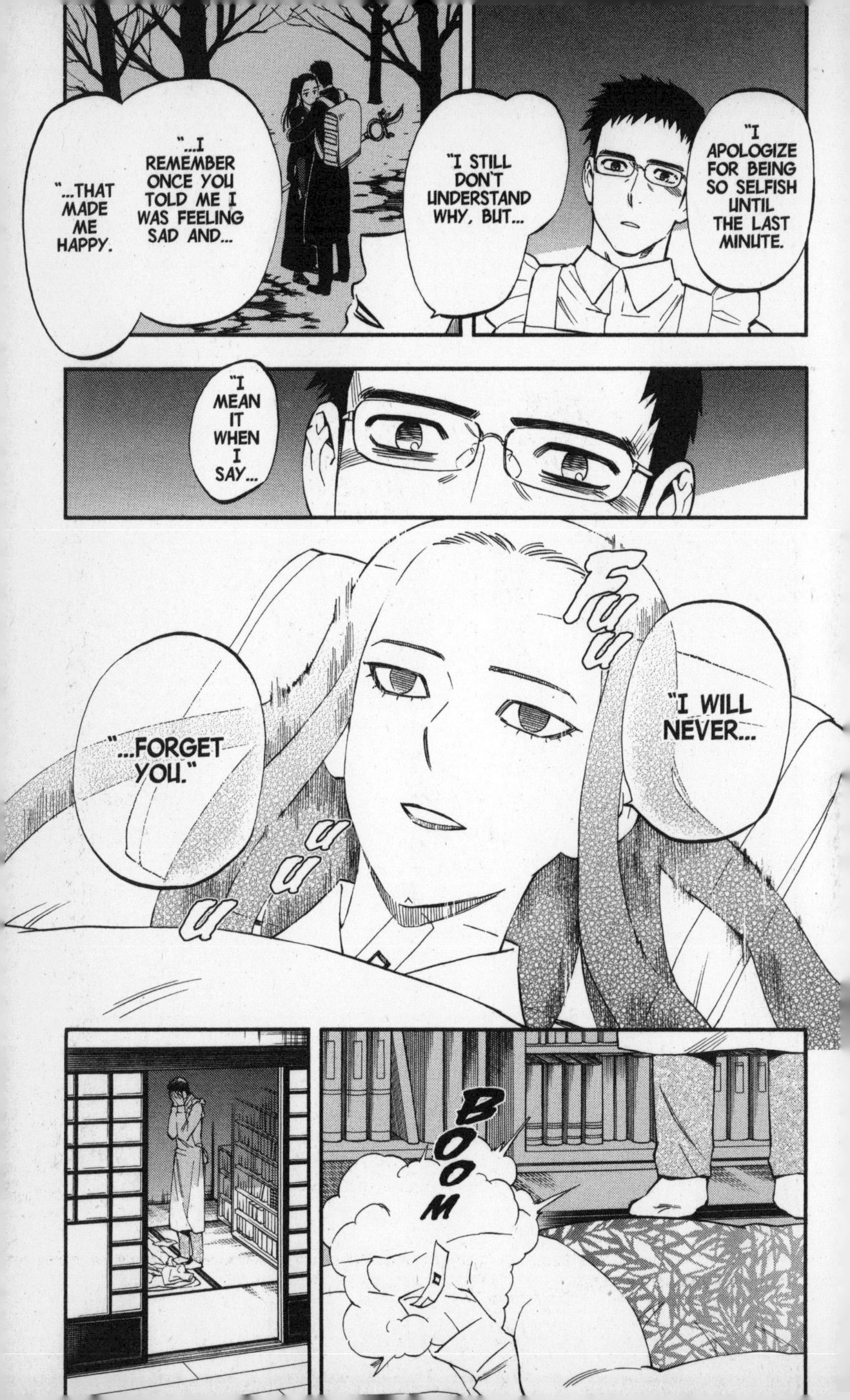
"I APOLOGIZE FOR BEING SO SELFISH UNTIL THE LAST MINUTE.
"I STILL DON'T UNDERSTAND WHY, BUT...
"...I REMEMBER ONCE YOU TOLD ME I WAS FEELING SAD AND...
"...THAT MADE ME HAPPY.
"I MEAN IT WHEN I SAY...
"I WILL NEVER...
FUUUUU
"...FORGET YOU."
BOOM

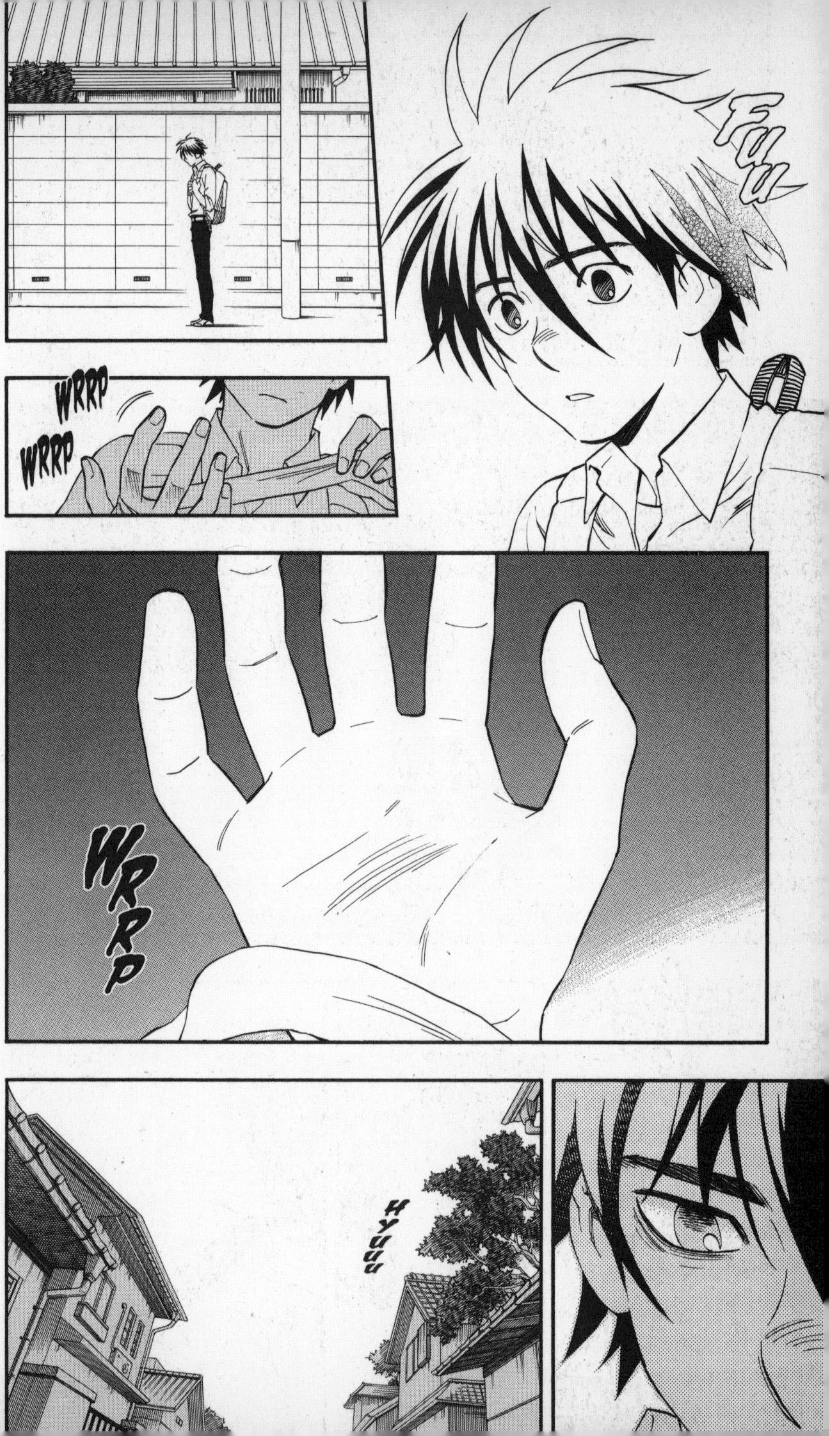
FUU
WRRP
WRRP
WRRP
HYUUU

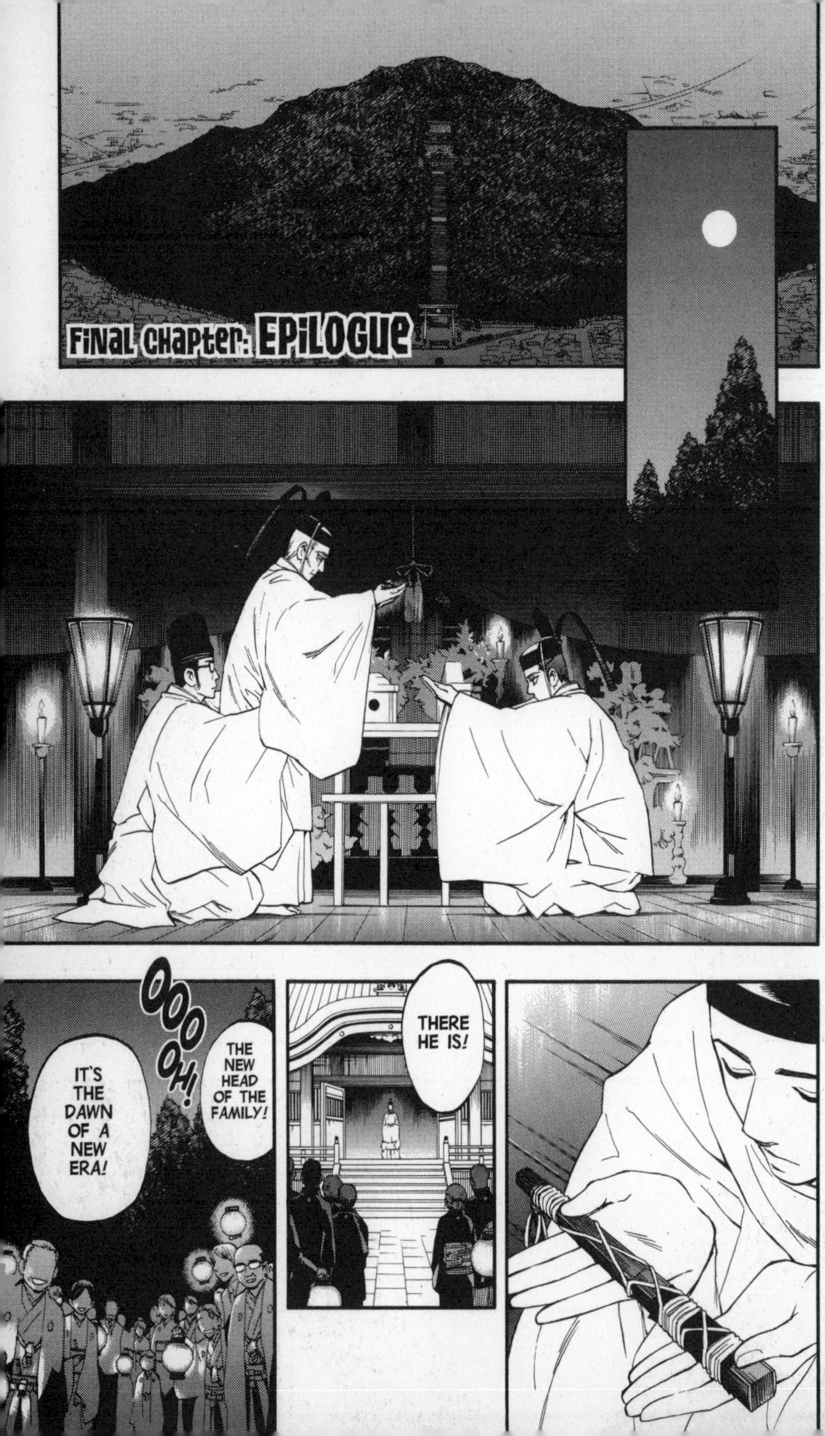
FINAL CHAPTER: EPILOGUE
THERE HE IS!
OOOOH!
THE NEW HEAD OF THE FAMILY!
IT'S THE DAWN OF A NEW ERA!

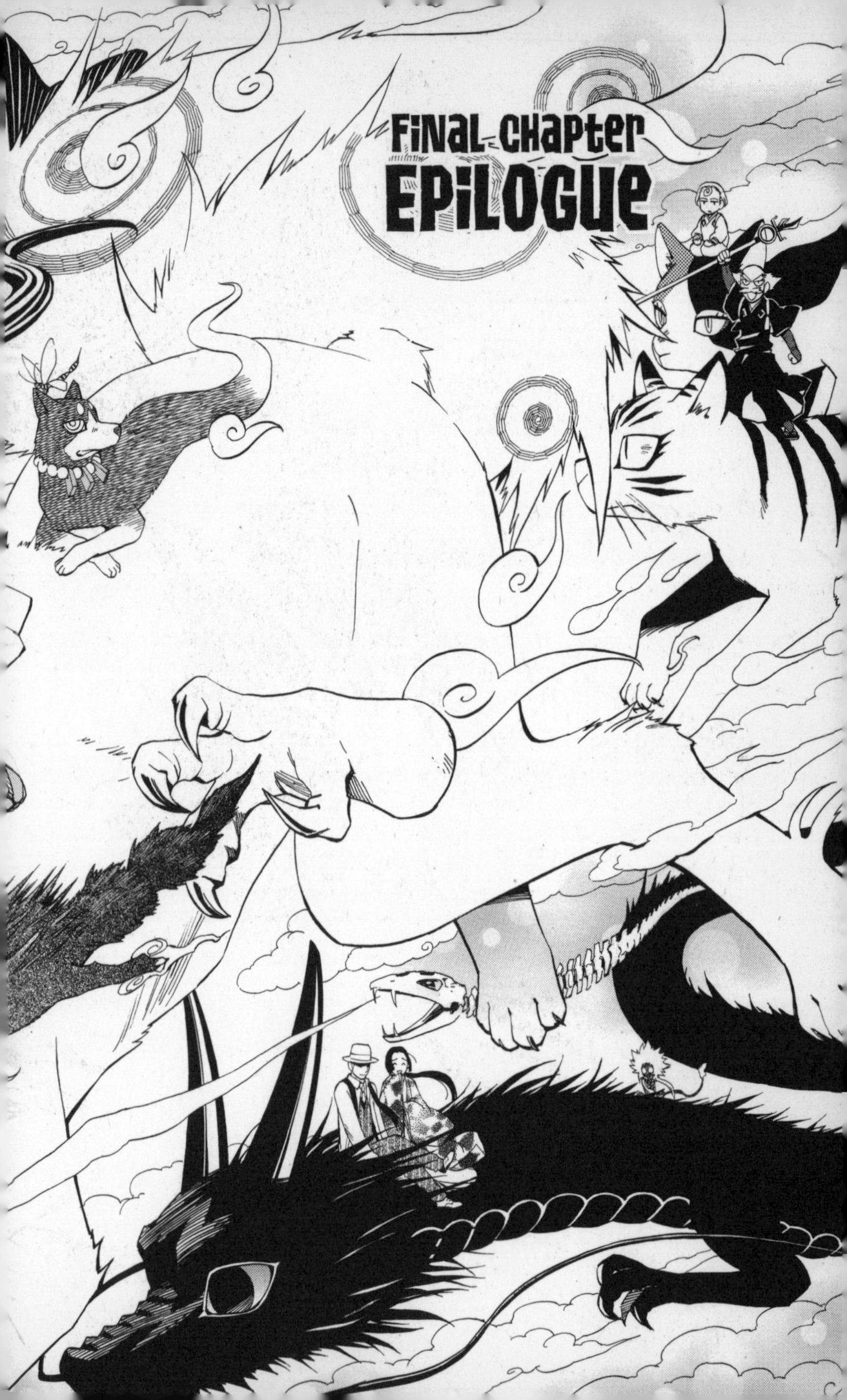
Final Chapter
Epilogue

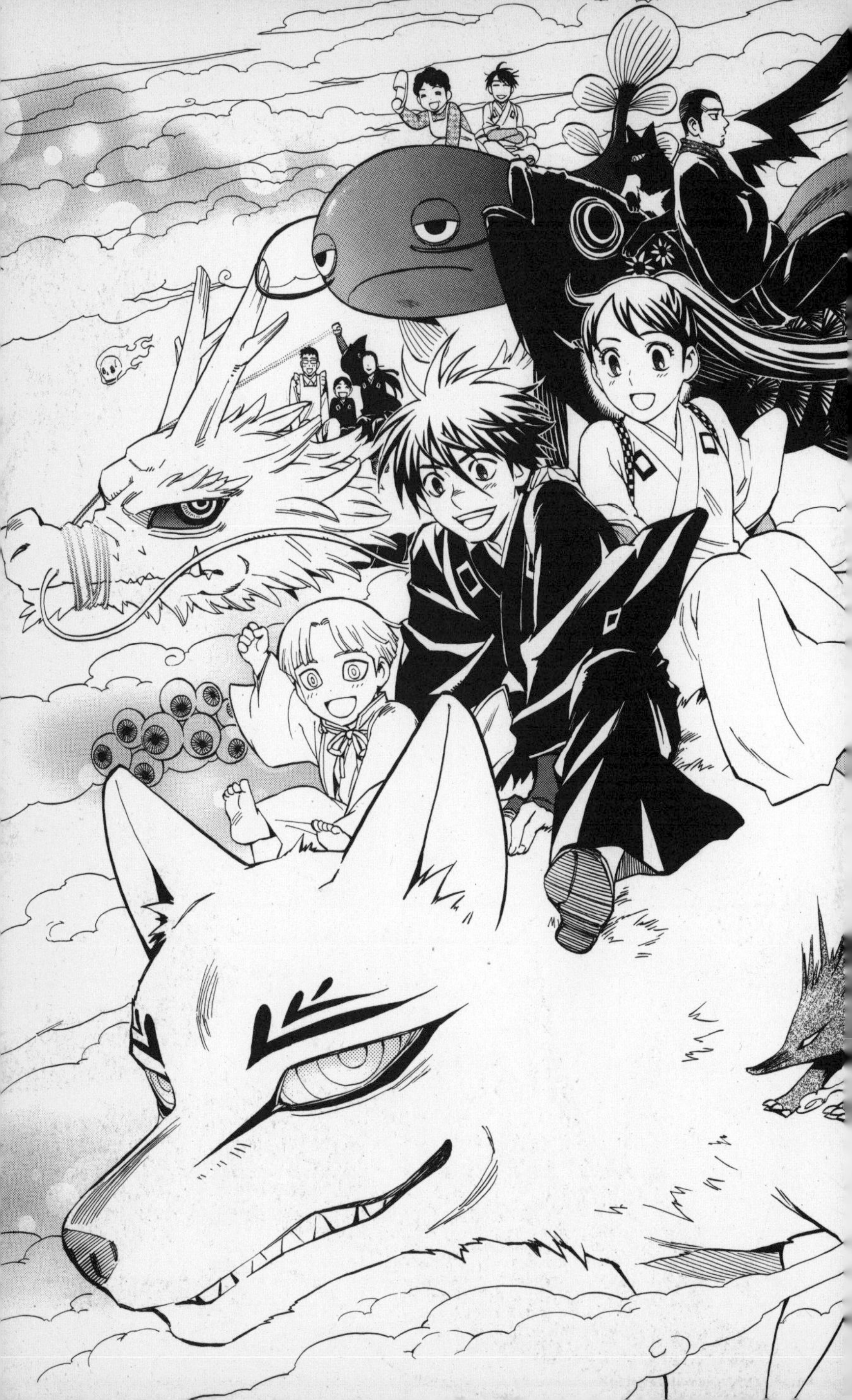

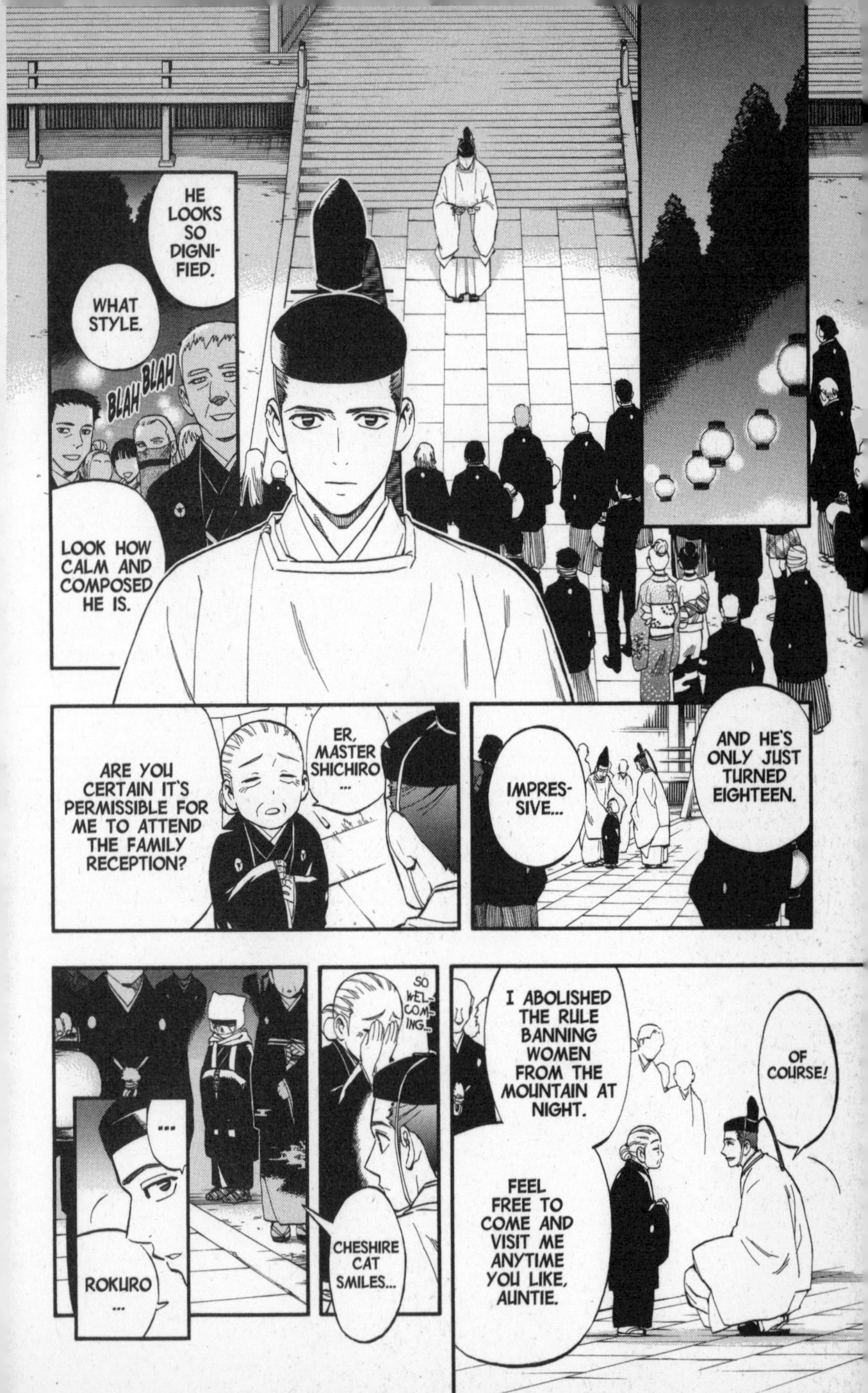
HE LOOKS SO DIGNIFIED.
WHAT STYLE.
BLAH BLAH
LOOK HOW CALM AND COMPOSED HE IS.
AND HE'S ONLY JUST TURNED EIGHTEEN.
IMPRESSIVE...
ER, MASTER SHICHIRO ...
ARE YOU CERTAIN IT'S PERMISSIBLE FOR ME TO ATTEND THE FAMILY RECEPTION?
OF COURSE!
I ABOLISHED THE RULE BANNING WOMEN FROM THE MOUNTAIN AT NIGHT.
FEEL FREE TO COME AND VISIT ME ANYTIME YOU LIKE, AUNTIE.
SO WELCOMING...
CHESHIRE CAT SMILES...
...
ROKURO ...

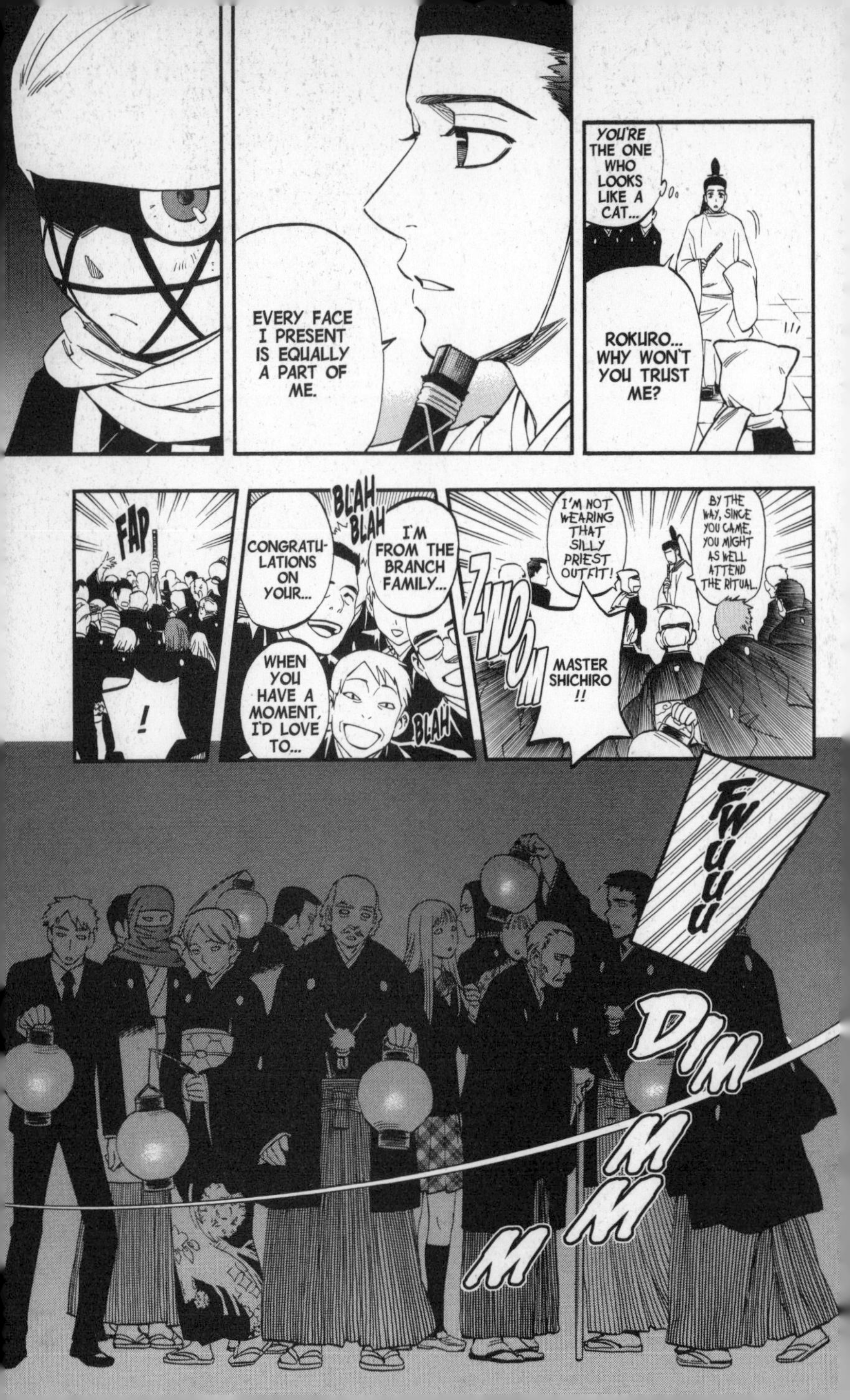
YOU'RE THE ONE WHO LOOKS LIKE A CAT...
ROKURO... WHY WON'T YOU TRUST ME?
EVERY FACE I PRESENT IS EQUALLY A PART OF ME.
BY THE WAY, SINCE YOU CAME, YOU MIGHT AS WELL ATTEND THE RITUAL.
I'M NOT WEARING THAT SILLY PRIEST OUTFIT!
ZWOOM
MASTER SHICHIRO !!
BLAH BLAH
I'M FROM THE BRANCH FAMILY...
CONGRATU-LATIONS ON YOUR...
WHEN YOU HAVE A MOMENT, I'D LOVE TO...
BLAH
FAP
!
FWUUUU
DIMMMM

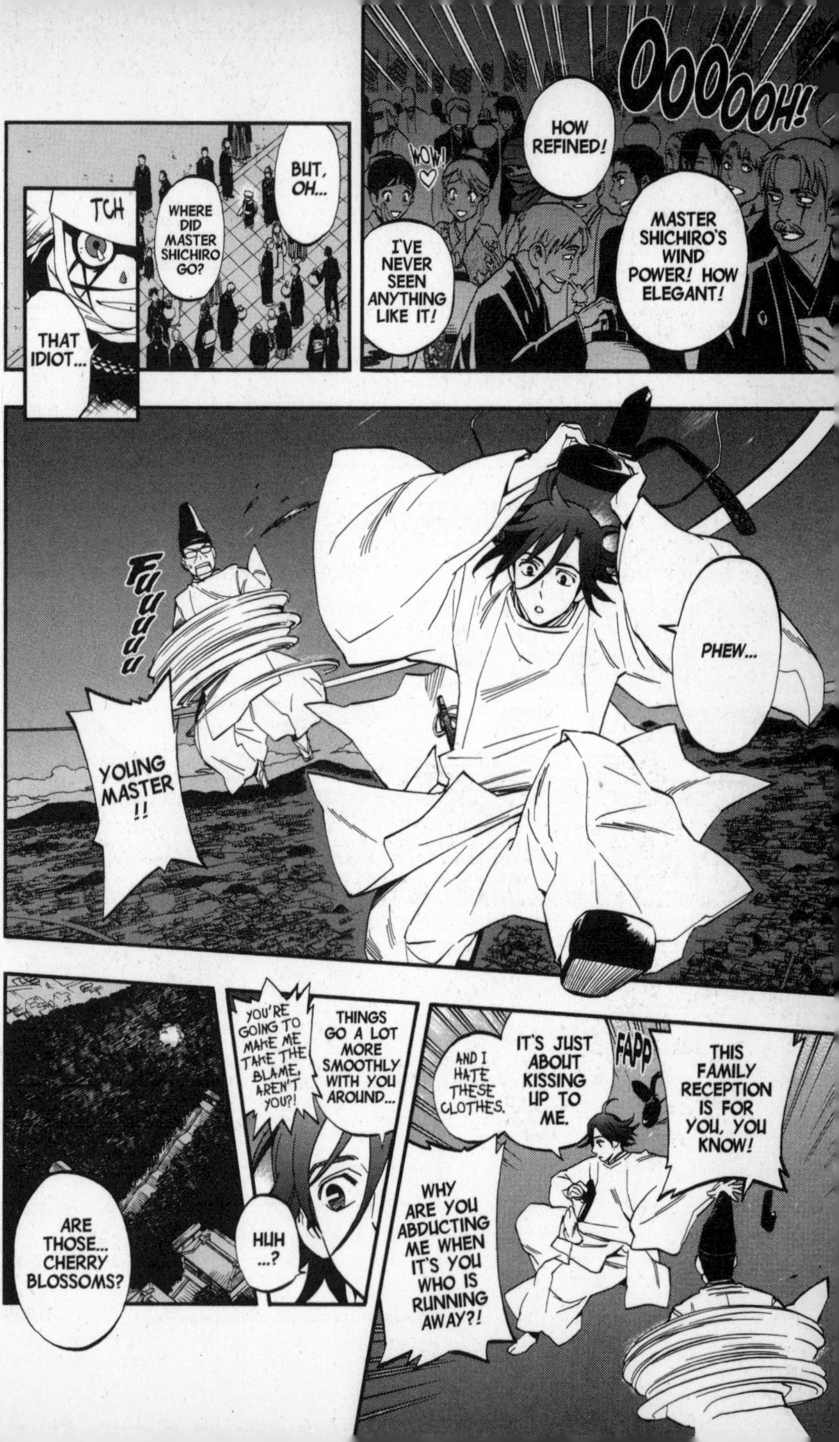
OOOOOOH!
HOW REFINED!
MASTER SHICHIRO'S WIND POWER! HOW ELEGANT!
WOW! ♡
I'VE NEVER SEEN ANYTHING LIKE IT!
BUT, OH...
WHERE DID MASTER SHICHIRO GO?
TCH
THAT IDIOT...
PHEW...
FUUUUUU
YOUNG MASTER !!
THIS FAMILY RECEPTION IS FOR YOU, YOU KNOW!
FAPP
IT'S JUST ABOUT KISSING UP TO ME.
AND I HATE THESE CLOTHES.
WHY ARE YOU ABDUCTING ME WHEN IT'S YOU WHO IS RUNNING AWAY?!
THINGS GO A LOT MORE SMOOTHLY WITH YOU AROUND...
YOU'RE GOING TO MAKE ME TAKE THE BLAME, AREN'T YOU?!
HUH ...?
ARE THOSE... CHERRY BLOSSOMS?

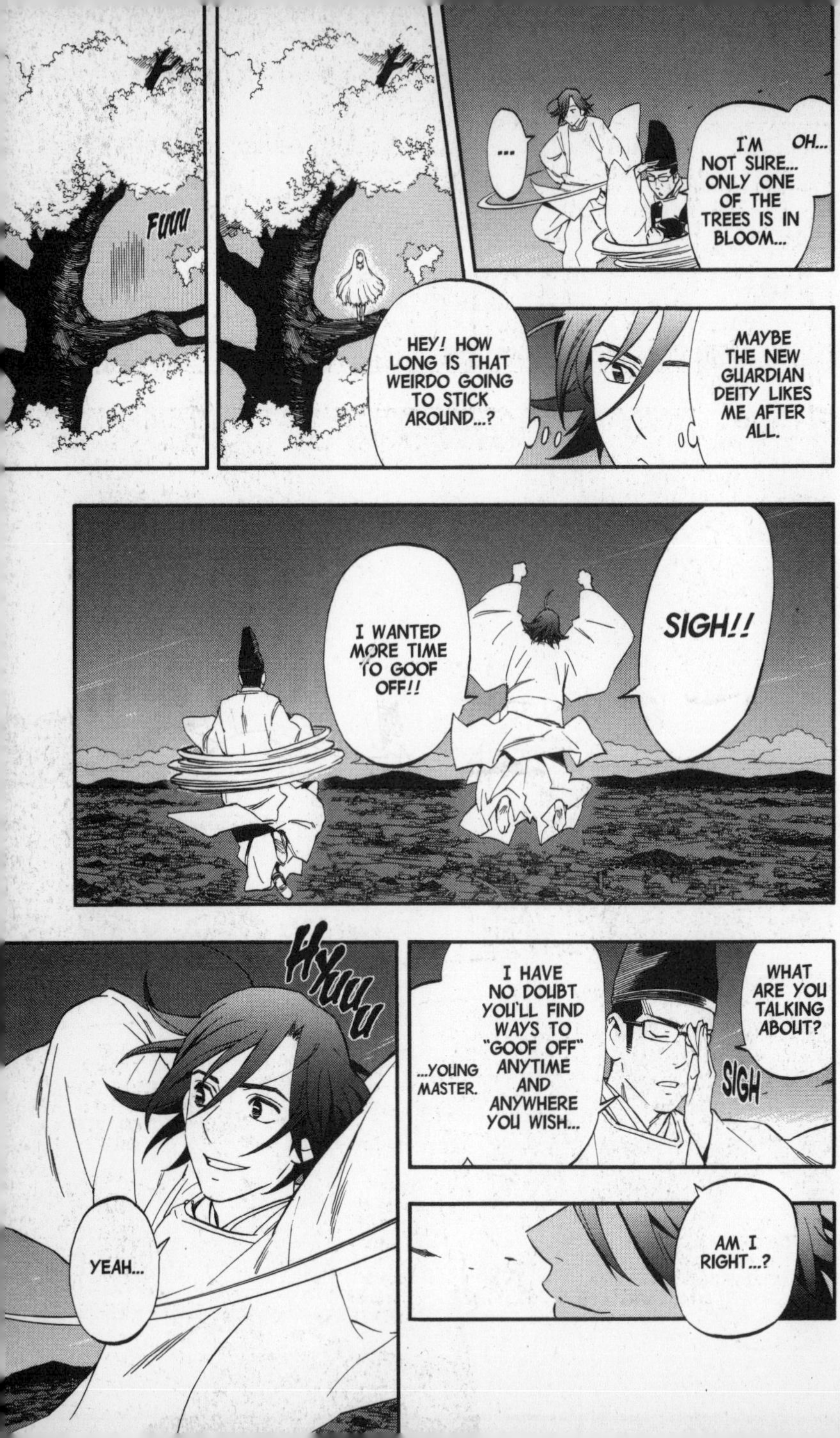
OH...
I'M NOT SURE... ONLY ONE OF THE TREES IS IN BLOOM...
...
MAYBE THE NEW GUARDIAN DEITY LIKES ME AFTER ALL.
HEY! HOW LONG IS THAT WEIRDO GOING TO STICK AROUND...?
FUUU
SIGH!!
I WANTED MORE TIME TO GOOF OFF!!
WHAT ARE YOU TALKING ABOUT?
SIGH
I HAVE NO DOUBT YOU'LL FIND WAYS TO "GOOF OFF" ANYTIME AND ANYWHERE YOU WISH...
...YOUNG MASTER.
AM I RIGHT...?
HYUUU
YEAH...

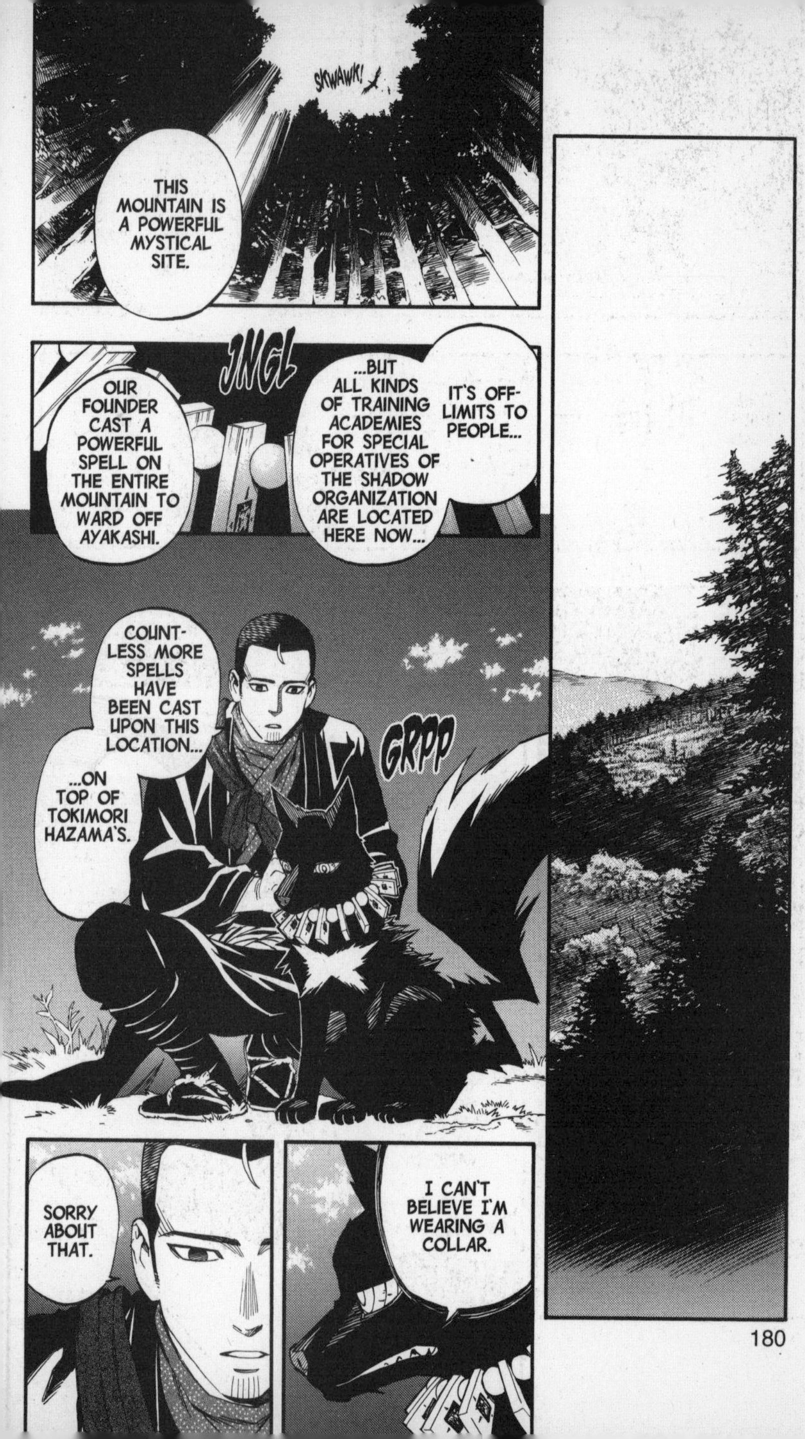
SKWAWK!
THIS MOUNTAIN IS A POWERFUL MYSTICAL SITE.
IT'S OFF-LIMITS TO PEOPLE...
...BUT ALL KINDS OF TRAINING ACADEMIES FOR SPECIAL OPERATIVES OF THE SHADOW ORGANIZATION ARE LOCATED HERE NOW...
JNGL
OUR FOUNDER CAST A POWERFUL SPELL ON THE ENTIRE MOUNTAIN TO WARD OFF AYAKASHI.
GRPP
COUNT-LESS MORE SPELLS HAVE BEEN CAST UPON THIS LOCATION...
...ON TOP OF TOKIMORI HAZAMA'S.
I CAN'T BELIEVE I'M WEARING A COLLAR.
SORRY ABOUT THAT.

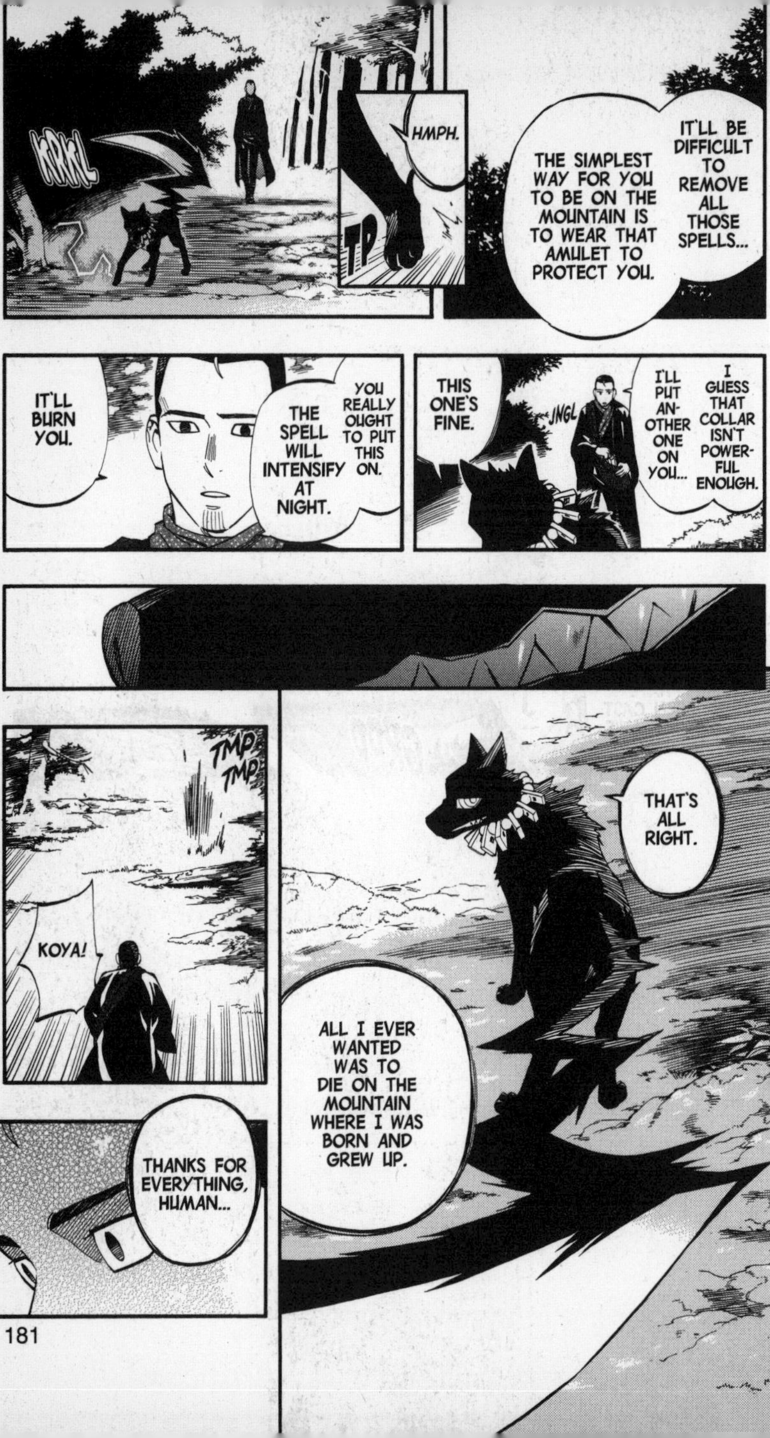
IT'LL BE DIFFICULT TO REMOVE ALL THOSE SPELLS...
THE SIMPLEST WAY FOR YOU TO BE ON THE MOUNTAIN IS TO WEAR THAT AMULET TO PROTECT YOU.
HMPH.
TP
KRRKL
I GUESS THAT COLLAR ISN'T POWERFUL ENOUGH.
I'LL PUT ANOTHER ONE ON YOU...
JNGL
THIS ONE'S FINE.
YOU REALLY OUGHT TO PUT THIS ON.
THE SPELL WILL INTENSIFY AT NIGHT.
IT'LL BURN YOU.
THAT'S ALL RIGHT.
ALL I EVER WANTED WAS TO DIE ON THE MOUNTAIN WHERE I WAS BORN AND GREW UP.
TMP TMP
KOYA!
THANKS FOR EVERYTHING, HUMAN...

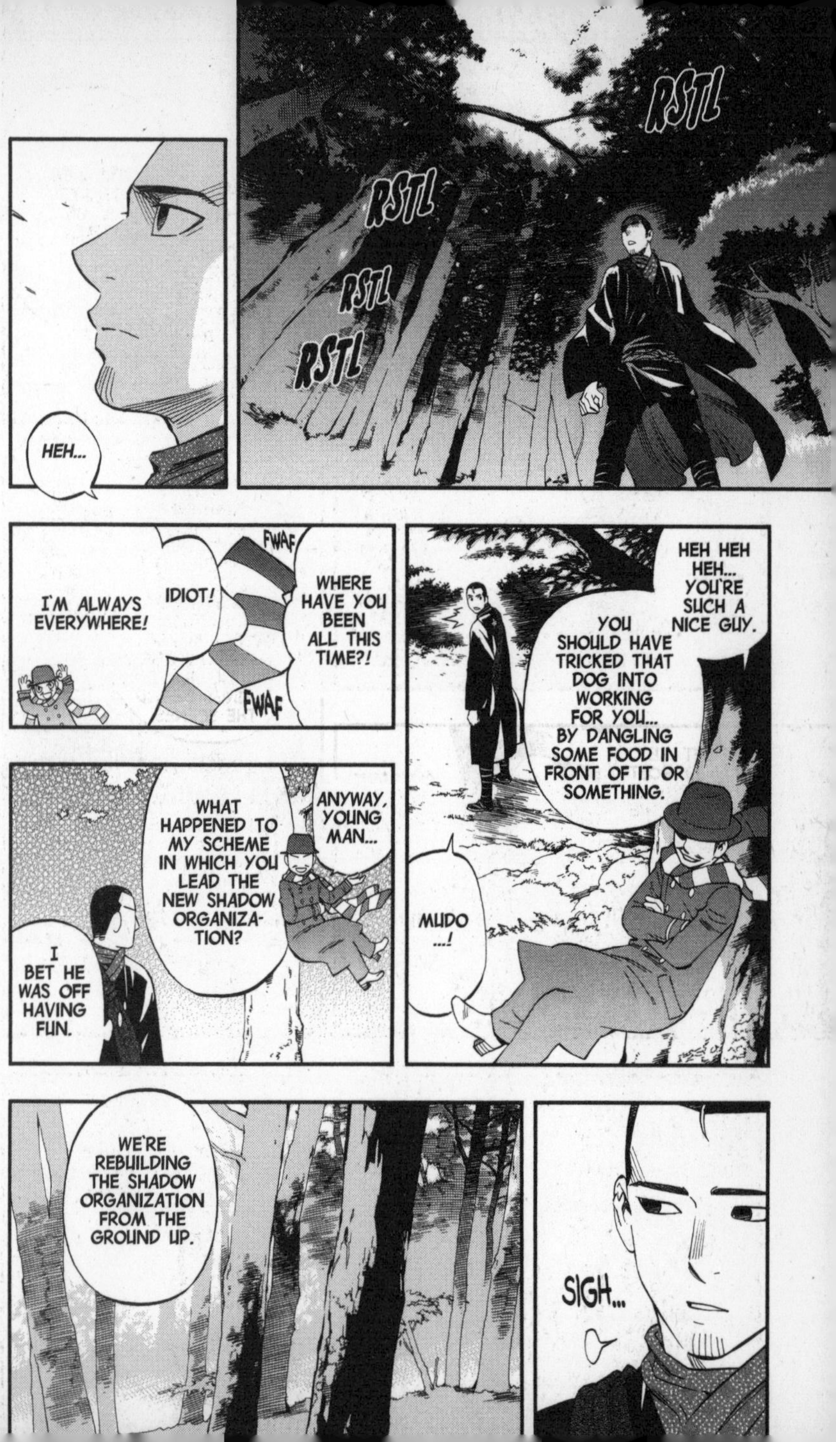
RSTL
RSTL
RSTL
RSTL
HEH...
HEH HEH HEH... YOU'RE SUCH A NICE GUY.
YOU SHOULD HAVE TRICKED THAT DOG INTO WORKING FOR YOU... BY DANGLING SOME FOOD IN FRONT OF IT OR SOMETHING.
MUDO ...!
FWAF
WHERE HAVE YOU BEEN ALL THIS TIME?!
FWAF
IDIOT!
I'M ALWAYS EVERYWHERE!
ANYWAY, YOUNG MAN...
WHAT HAPPENED TO MY SCHEME IN WHICH YOU LEAD THE NEW SHADOW ORGANIZA-TION?
I BET HE WAS OFF HAVING FUN.
SIGH...
WE'RE REBUILDING THE SHADOW ORGANIZATION FROM THE GROUND UP.

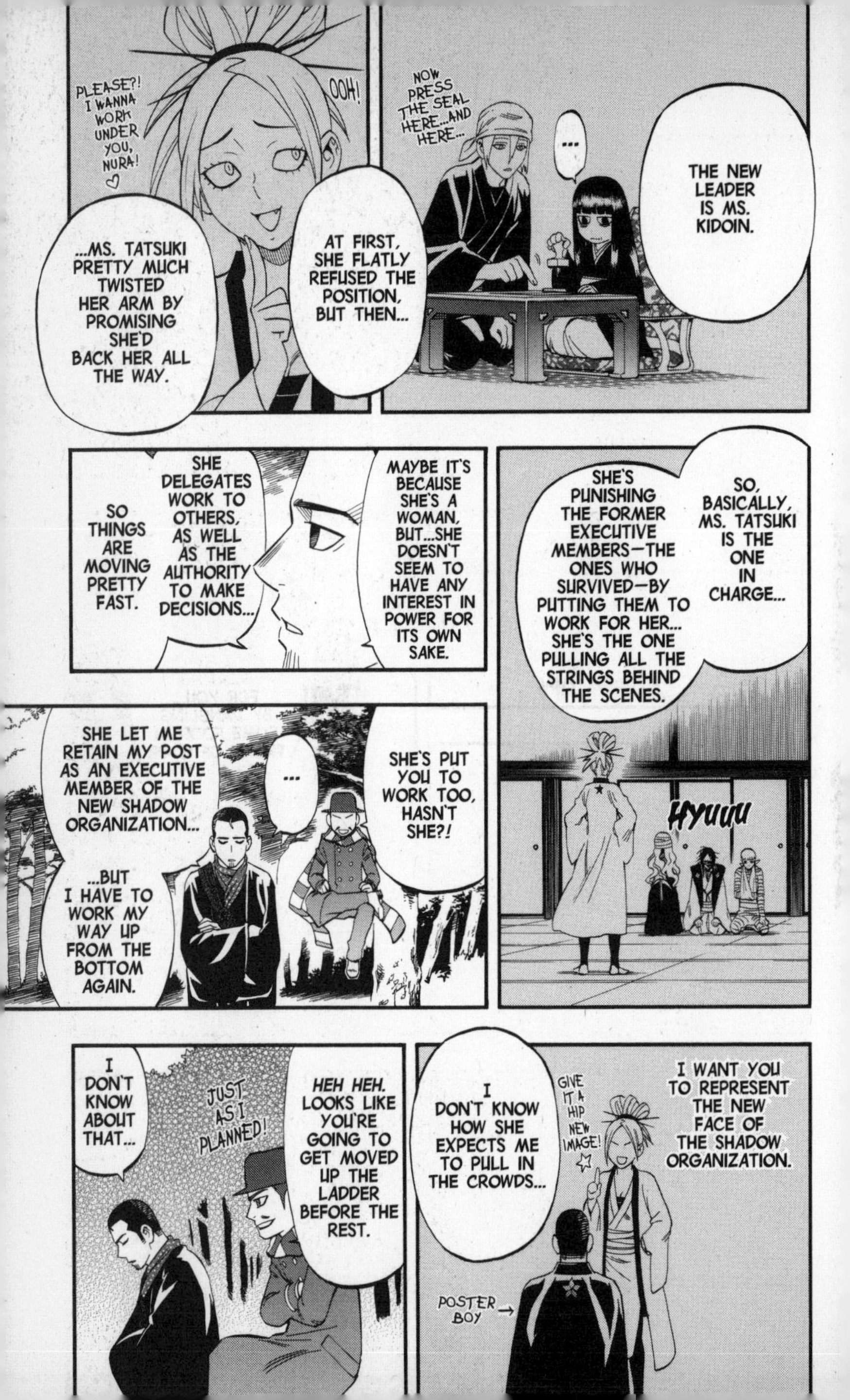
THE NEW LEADER IS MS. KIDOIN.
...
NOW PRESS THE SEAL HERE...AND HERE...
OOH!
PLEASE?! I WANNA WORK UNDER YOU, NURA! ♡
AT FIRST, SHE FLATLY REFUSED THE POSITION, BUT THEN...
...MS. TATSUKI PRETTY MUCH TWISTED HER ARM BY PROMISING SHE'D BACK HER ALL THE WAY.
SO, BASICALLY, MS. TATSUKI IS THE ONE IN CHARGE...
SHE'S PUNISHING THE FORMER EXECUTIVE MEMBERS—THE ONES WHO SURVIVED—BY PUTTING THEM TO WORK FOR HER... SHE'S THE ONE PULLING ALL THE STRINGS BEHIND THE SCENES.
MAYBE IT'S BECAUSE SHE'S A WOMAN, BUT...SHE DOESN'T SEEM TO HAVE ANY INTEREST IN POWER FOR ITS OWN SAKE.
SHE DELEGATES WORK TO OTHERS, AS WELL AS THE AUTHORITY TO MAKE DECISIONS...
SO THINGS ARE MOVING PRETTY FAST.
HYUUU
SHE'S PUT YOU TO WORK TOO, HASN'T SHE?!
...
SHE LET ME RETAIN MY POST AS AN EXECUTIVE MEMBER OF THE NEW SHADOW ORGANIZATION...
...BUT I HAVE TO WORK MY WAY UP FROM THE BOTTOM AGAIN.
I WANT YOU TO REPRESENT THE NEW FACE OF THE SHADOW ORGANIZATION.
GIVE IT A HIP NEW IMAGE!
I DON'T KNOW HOW SHE EXPECTS ME TO PULL IN THE CROWDS...
POSTER BOY →
HEH HEH. LOOKS LIKE YOU'RE GOING TO GET MOVED UP THE LADDER BEFORE THE REST.
JUST AS I PLANNED!
I DON'T KNOW ABOUT THAT...

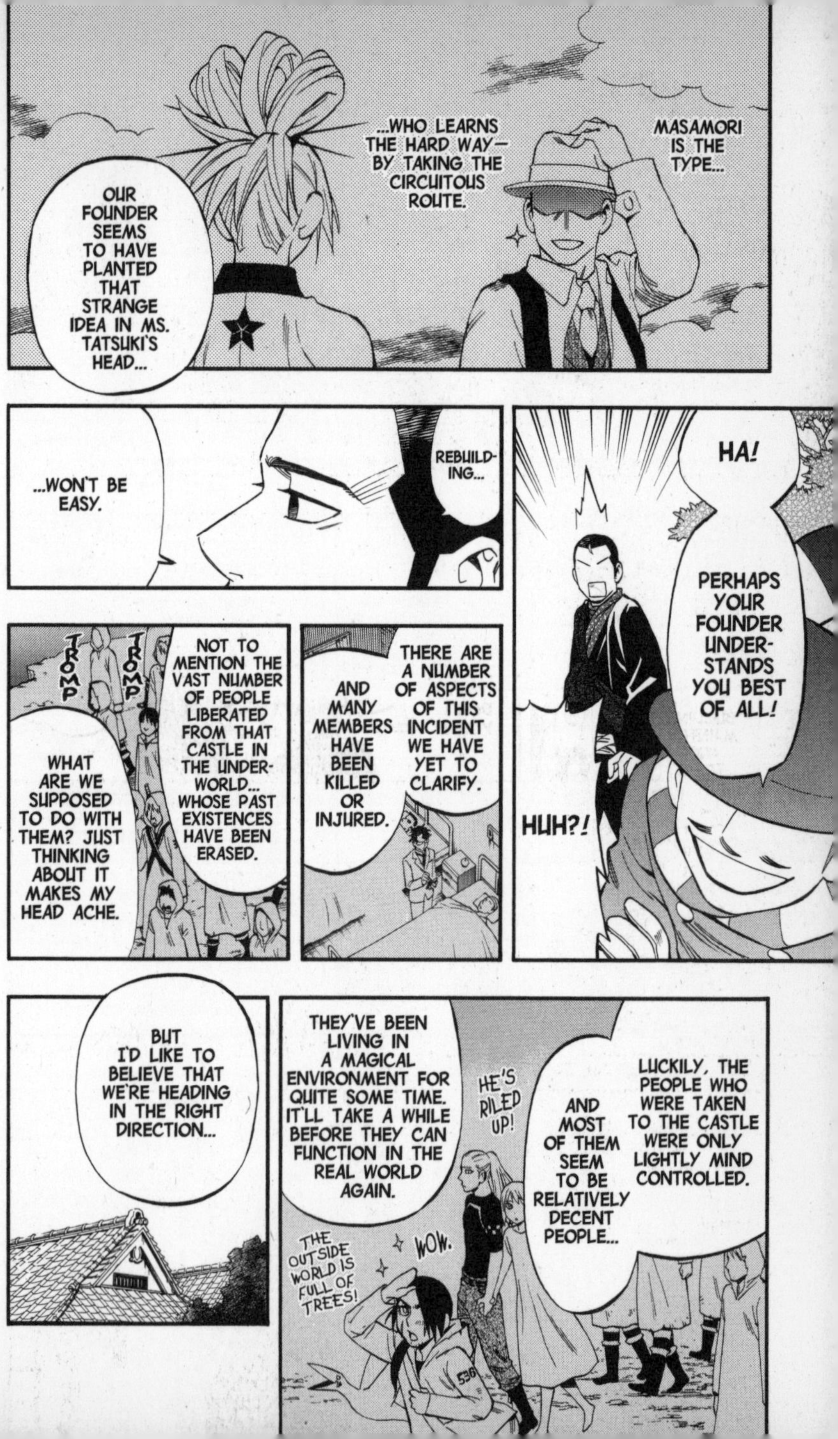
MASAMORI IS THE TYPE...
...WHO LEARNS THE HARD WAY— BY TAKING THE CIRCUITOUS ROUTE.
OUR FOUNDER SEEMS TO HAVE PLANTED THAT STRANGE IDEA IN MS. TATSUKI'S HEAD...
HA!
PERHAPS YOUR FOUNDER UNDER-STANDS YOU BEST OF ALL!
HUH?!
REBUILD-ING...
...WON'T BE EASY.
THERE ARE A NUMBER OF ASPECTS OF THIS INCIDENT WE HAVE YET TO CLARIFY.
AND MANY MEMBERS HAVE BEEN KILLED OR INJURED.
NOT TO MENTION THE VAST NUMBER OF PEOPLE LIBERATED FROM THAT CASTLE IN THE UNDER-WORLD... WHOSE PAST EXISTENCES HAVE BEEN ERASED.
TROMP
TROMP
WHAT ARE WE SUPPOSED TO DO WITH THEM? JUST THINKING ABOUT IT MAKES MY HEAD ACHE.
LUCKILY, THE PEOPLE WHO WERE TAKEN TO THE CASTLE WERE ONLY LIGHTLY MIND CONTROLLED.
AND MOST OF THEM SEEM TO BE RELATIVELY DECENT PEOPLE...
HE'S RILED UP!
THEY'VE BEEN LIVING IN A MAGICAL ENVIRONMENT FOR QUITE SOME TIME. IT'LL TAKE A WHILE BEFORE THEY CAN FUNCTION IN THE REAL WORLD AGAIN.
WOW.
THE OUTSIDE WORLD IS FULL OF TREES!
BUT I'D LIKE TO BELIEVE THAT WE'RE HEADING IN THE RIGHT DIRECTION...

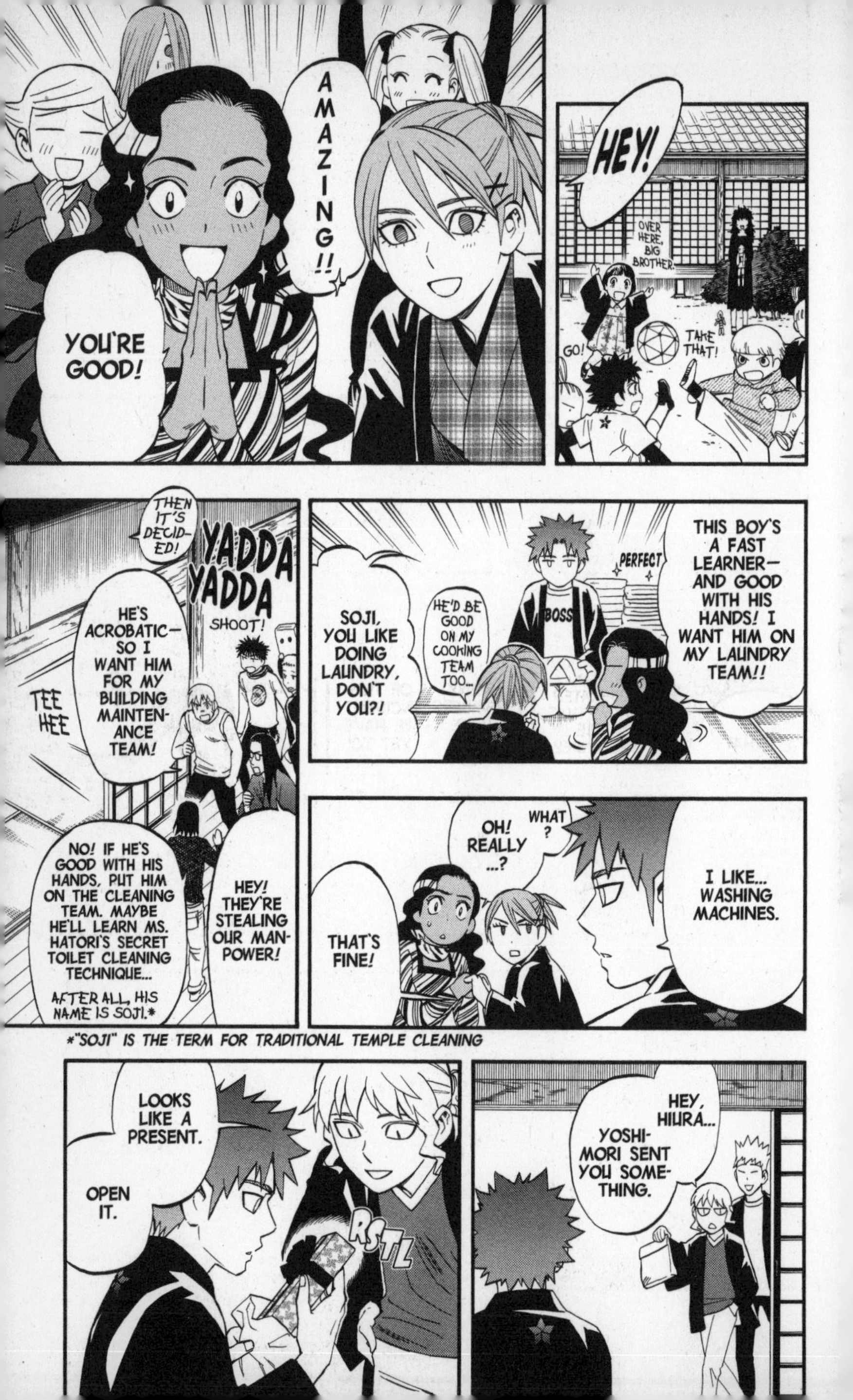

HEY!
OVER HERE, BIG BROTHER.
TAKE THAT!
GO!
AMAZING!!
YOU'RE GOOD!
THIS BOY'S A FAST LEARNER—AND GOOD WITH HIS HANDS! I WANT HIM ON MY LAUNDRY TEAM!!
PERFECT
HE'D BE GOOD ON MY COOKING TEAM TOO...
SOJI, YOU LIKE DOING LAUNDRY, DON'T YOU?!
BOSS
I LIKE... WASHING MACHINES.
WHAT?
OH! REALLY...?
THAT'S FINE!
THEN IT'S DECIDED!
YADDA YADDA
HE'S ACROBATIC—SO I WANT HIM FOR MY BUILDING MAINTENANCE TEAM!
SHOOT!
TEE HEE
HEY! THEY'RE STEALING OUR MANPOWER!
NO! IF HE'S GOOD WITH HIS HANDS, PUT HIM ON THE CLEANING TEAM. MAYBE HE'LL LEARN MS. HATORI'S SECRET TOILET CLEANING TECHNIQUE...
AFTER ALL, HIS NAME IS SOJI.*
HEY, HIURA... YOSHIMORI SENT YOU SOMETHING.
LOOKS LIKE A PRESENT.
RSTL
OPEN IT.

*"SOJI" IS THE TERM FOR TRADITIONAL TEMPLE CLEANING

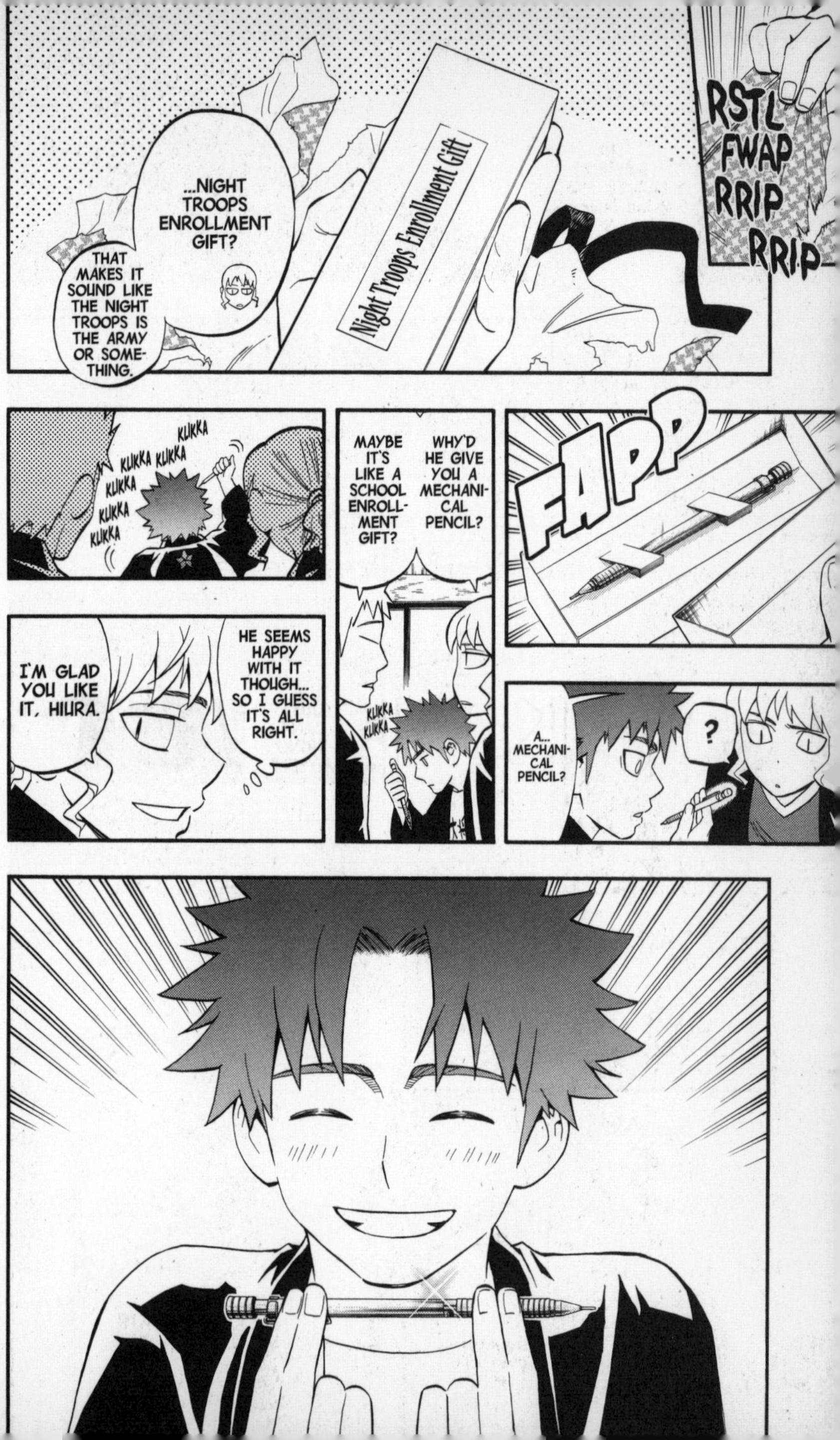
RSTL
FWAP
RRIP
RRIP
Night Troops Enrollment Gift
...NIGHT TROOPS ENROLLMENT GIFT?
THAT MAKES IT SOUND LIKE THE NIGHT TROOPS IS THE ARMY OR SOMETHING.
FAPP
?
A... MECHANICAL PENCIL?
WHY'D HE GIVE YOU A MECHANICAL PENCIL?
MAYBE IT'S LIKE A SCHOOL ENROLLMENT GIFT?
KLIKKA KLIKKA
KLIKKA KLIKKA KLIKKA KLIKKA KLIKKA KLIKKA
HE SEEMS HAPPY WITH IT THOUGH... SO I GUESS IT'S ALL RIGHT.
I'M GLAD YOU LIKE IT, HIURA.

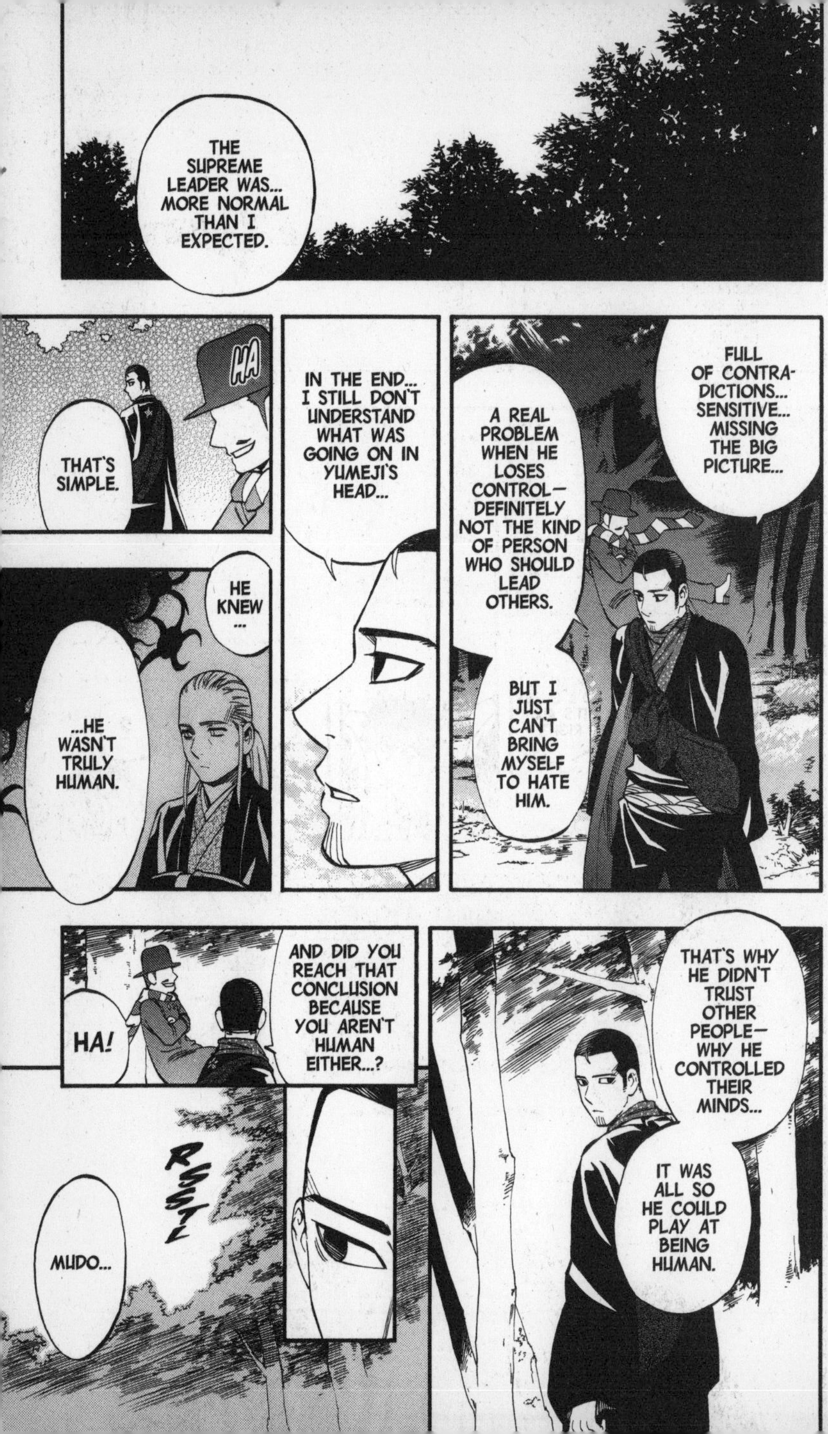
THE SUPREME LEADER WAS... MORE NORMAL THAN I EXPECTED.
FULL OF CONTRA-DICTIONS... SENSITIVE... MISSING THE BIG PICTURE...
A REAL PROBLEM WHEN HE LOSES CONTROL— DEFINITELY NOT THE KIND OF PERSON WHO SHOULD LEAD OTHERS.
BUT I JUST CAN'T BRING MYSELF TO HATE HIM.
IN THE END... I STILL DON'T UNDERSTAND WHAT WAS GOING ON IN YUMEJI'S HEAD...
HA
THAT'S SIMPLE.
HE KNEW...
...HE WASN'T TRULY HUMAN.
THAT'S WHY HE DIDN'T TRUST OTHER PEOPLE— WHY HE CONTROLLED THEIR MINDS...
IT WAS ALL SO HE COULD PLAY AT BEING HUMAN.
AND DID YOU REACH THAT CONCLUSION BECAUSE YOU AREN'T HUMAN EITHER...?
HA!
RSSTL
MUDO...

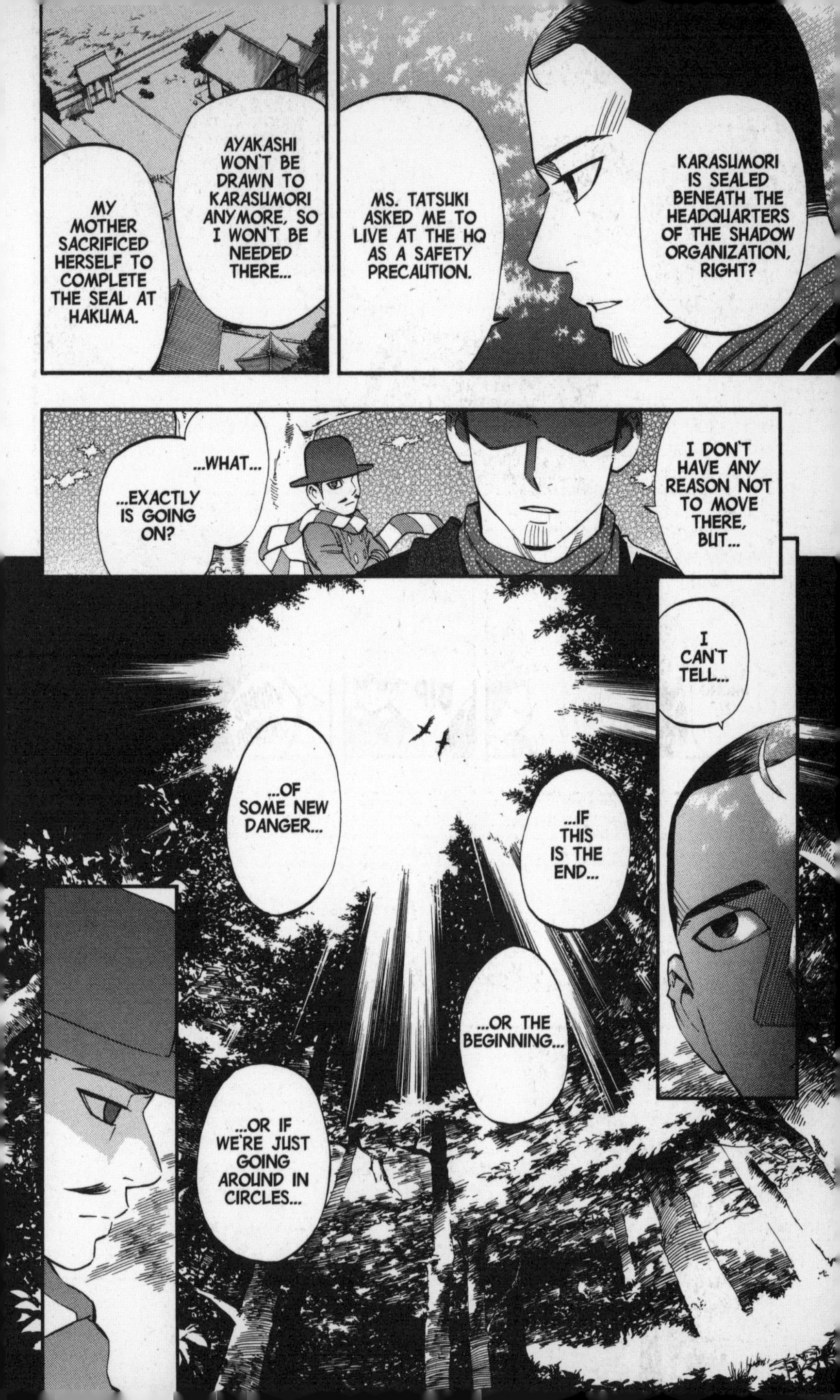
KARASUMORI IS SEALED BENEATH THE HEADQUARTERS OF THE SHADOW ORGANIZATION, RIGHT?
MS. TATSUKI ASKED ME TO LIVE AT THE HQ AS A SAFETY PRECAUTION.
AYAKASHI WON'T BE DRAWN TO KARASUMORI ANYMORE, SO I WON'T BE NEEDED THERE...
MY MOTHER SACRIFICED HERSELF TO COMPLETE THE SEAL AT HAKUMA.
I DON'T HAVE ANY REASON NOT TO MOVE THERE, BUT...
...WHAT...
...EXACTLY IS GOING ON?
I CAN'T TELL...
...IF THIS IS THE END...
...OR THE BEGINNING...
...OF SOME NEW DANGER...
...OR IF WE'RE JUST GOING AROUND IN CIRCLES...

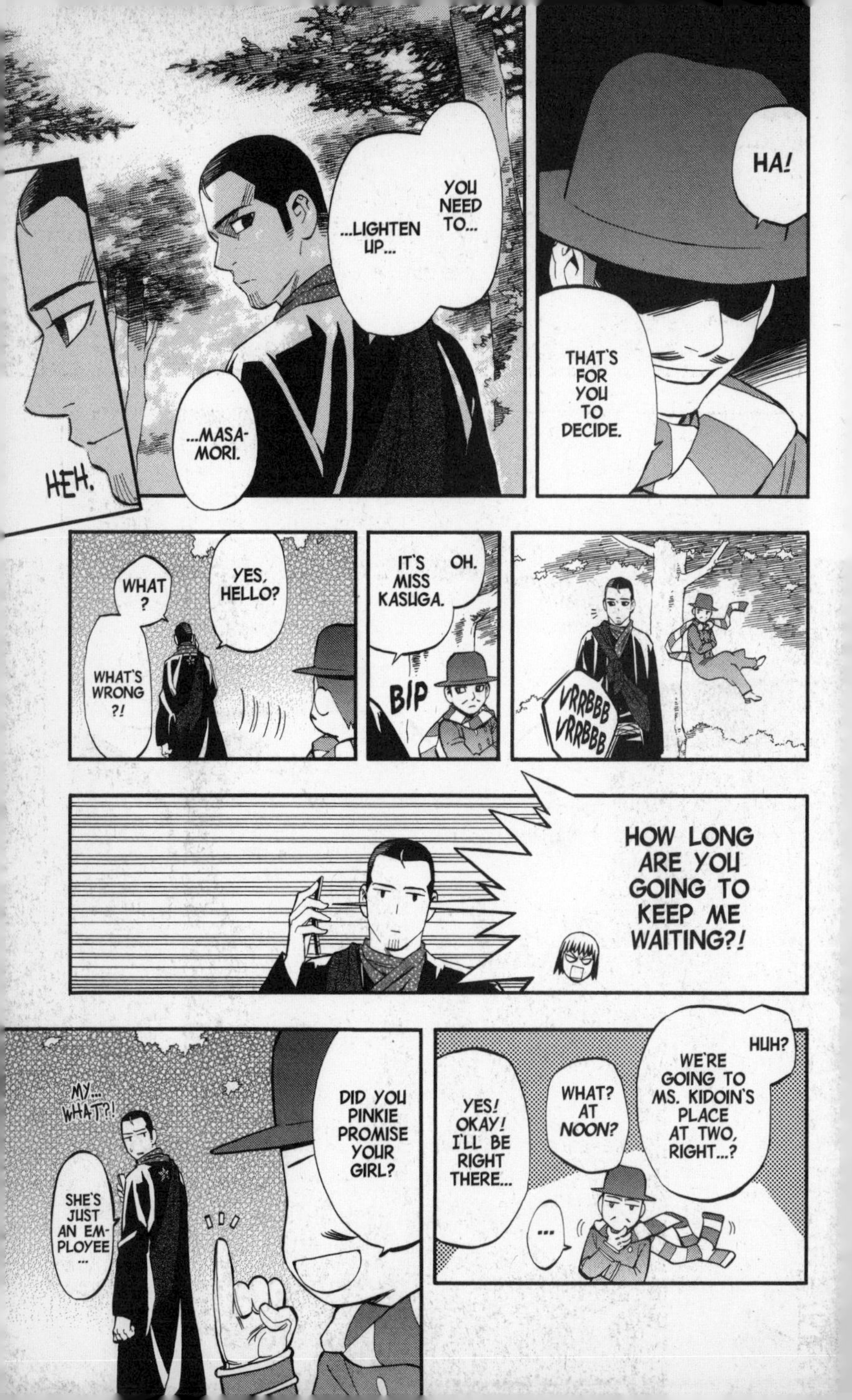
HA!
THAT'S FOR YOU TO DECIDE.
YOU NEED TO...
...LIGHTEN UP...
...MASA-MORI.
HEH.
VRRBBB VRRBBB
OH.
IT'S MISS KASUGA.
BIP
YES, HELLO?
WHAT?
WHAT'S WRONG?!
HOW LONG ARE YOU GOING TO KEEP ME WAITING?!
HUH?
WE'RE GOING TO MS. KIDOIN'S PLACE AT TWO, RIGHT...?
WHAT? AT NOON?
YES! OKAY! I'LL BE RIGHT THERE...
...
DID YOU PINKIE PROMISE YOUR GIRL?
MY... WHAT?!
SHE'S JUST AN EM-PLOYEE...

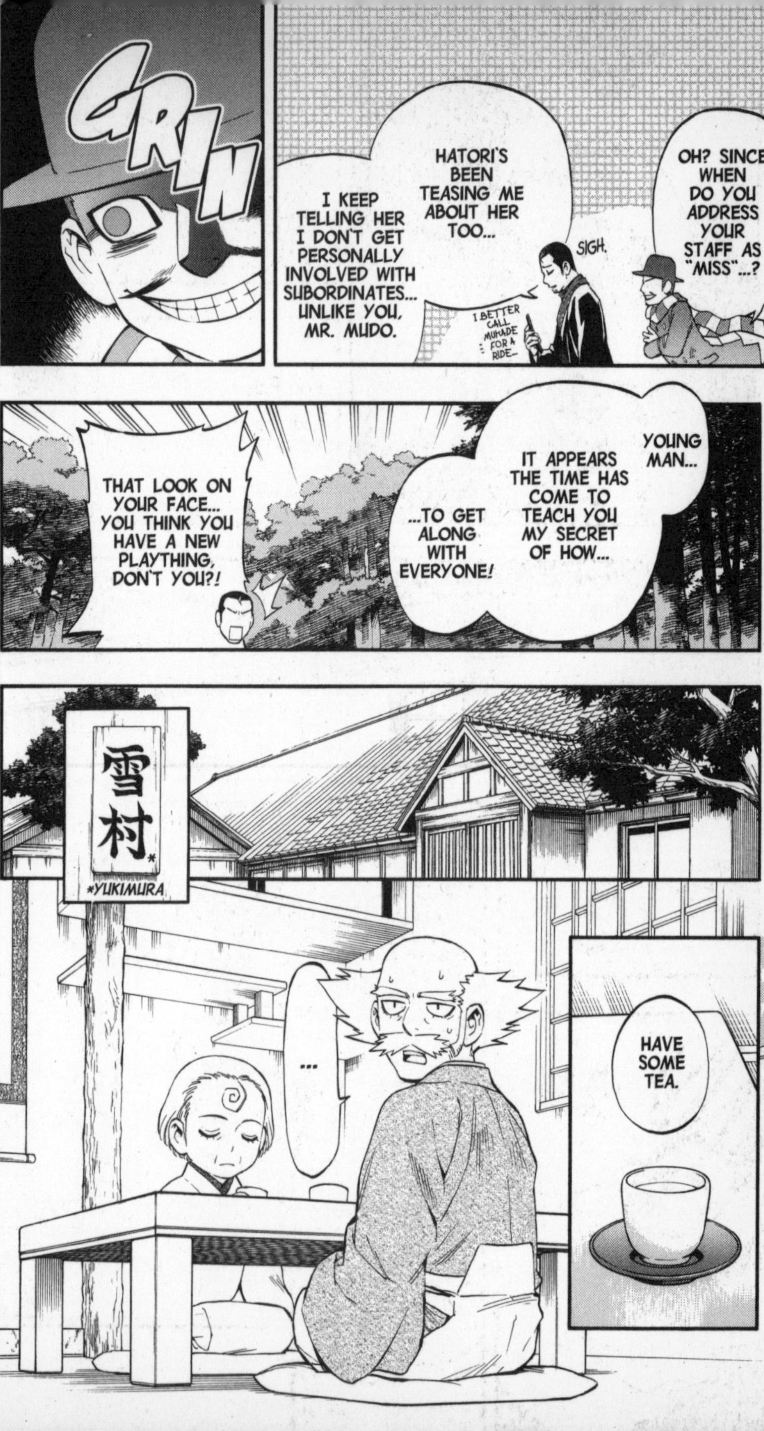
OH? SINCE WHEN DO YOU ADDRESS YOUR STAFF AS "MISS"...?
SIGH.
HATORI'S BEEN TEASING ME ABOUT HER TOO...
I KEEP TELLING HER I DON'T GET PERSONALLY INVOLVED WITH SUBORDINATES... UNLIKE YOU, MR. MUDO.
I BETTER CALL MUKADE FOR A RIDE...
GRIN
YOUNG MAN...
IT APPEARS THE TIME HAS COME TO TEACH YOU MY SECRET OF HOW...
...TO GET ALONG WITH EVERYONE!
THAT LOOK ON YOUR FACE... YOU THINK YOU HAVE A NEW PLAYTHING, DON'T YOU?!
雪村*
*YUKIMURA
HAVE SOME TEA.
...

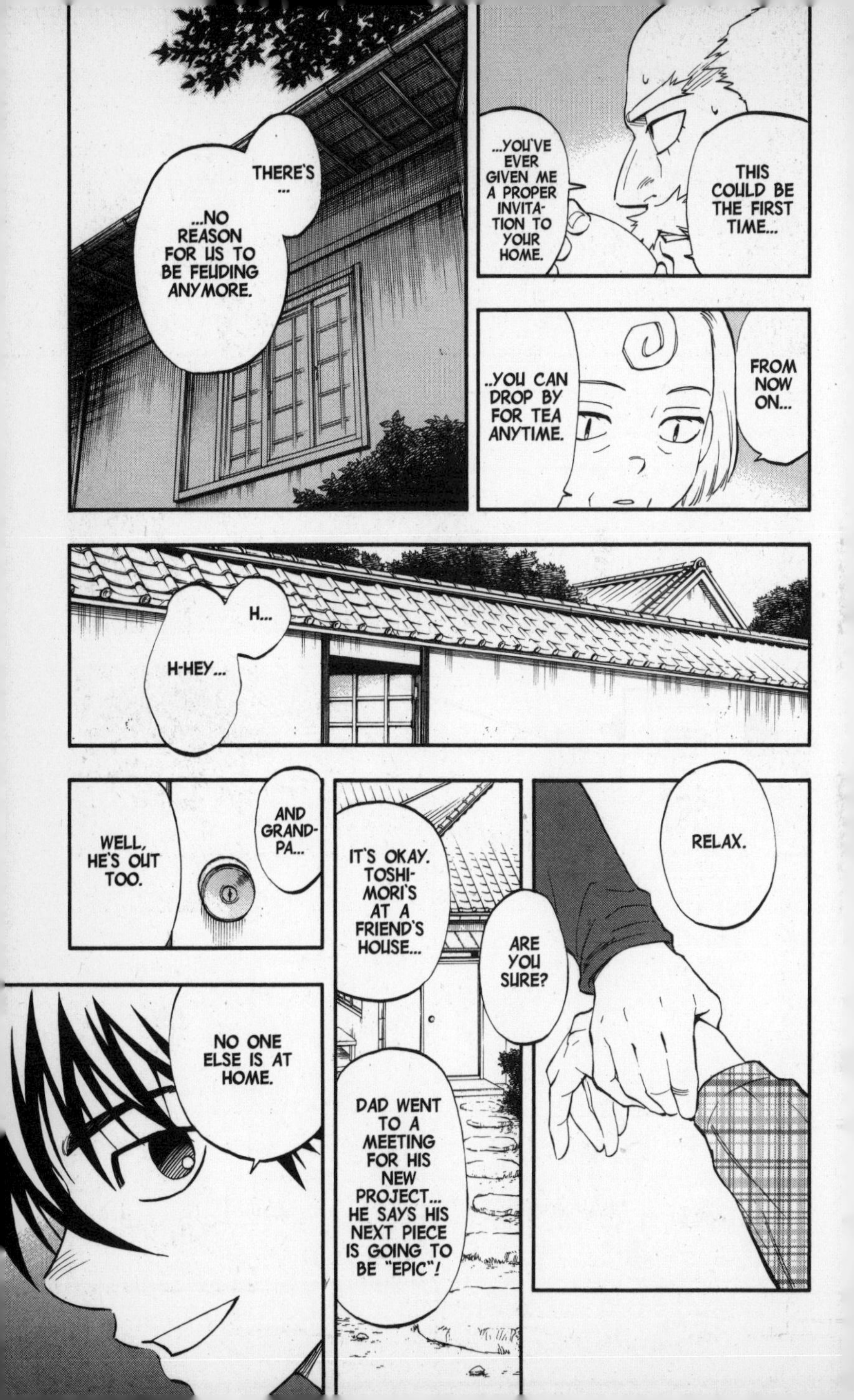
THIS COULD BE THE FIRST TIME...
...YOU'VE EVER GIVEN ME A PROPER INVITATION TO YOUR HOME.
FROM NOW ON...
..YOU CAN DROP BY FOR TEA ANYTIME.
THERE'S...
...NO REASON FOR US TO BE FEUDING ANYMORE.
H...
H-HEY...
RELAX.
ARE YOU SURE?
IT'S OKAY. TOSHIMORI'S AT A FRIEND'S HOUSE...
DAD WENT TO A MEETING FOR HIS NEW PROJECT... HE SAYS HIS NEXT PIECE IS GOING TO BE "EPIC"!
AND GRANDPA...
WELL, HE'S OUT TOO.
NO ONE ELSE IS AT HOME.

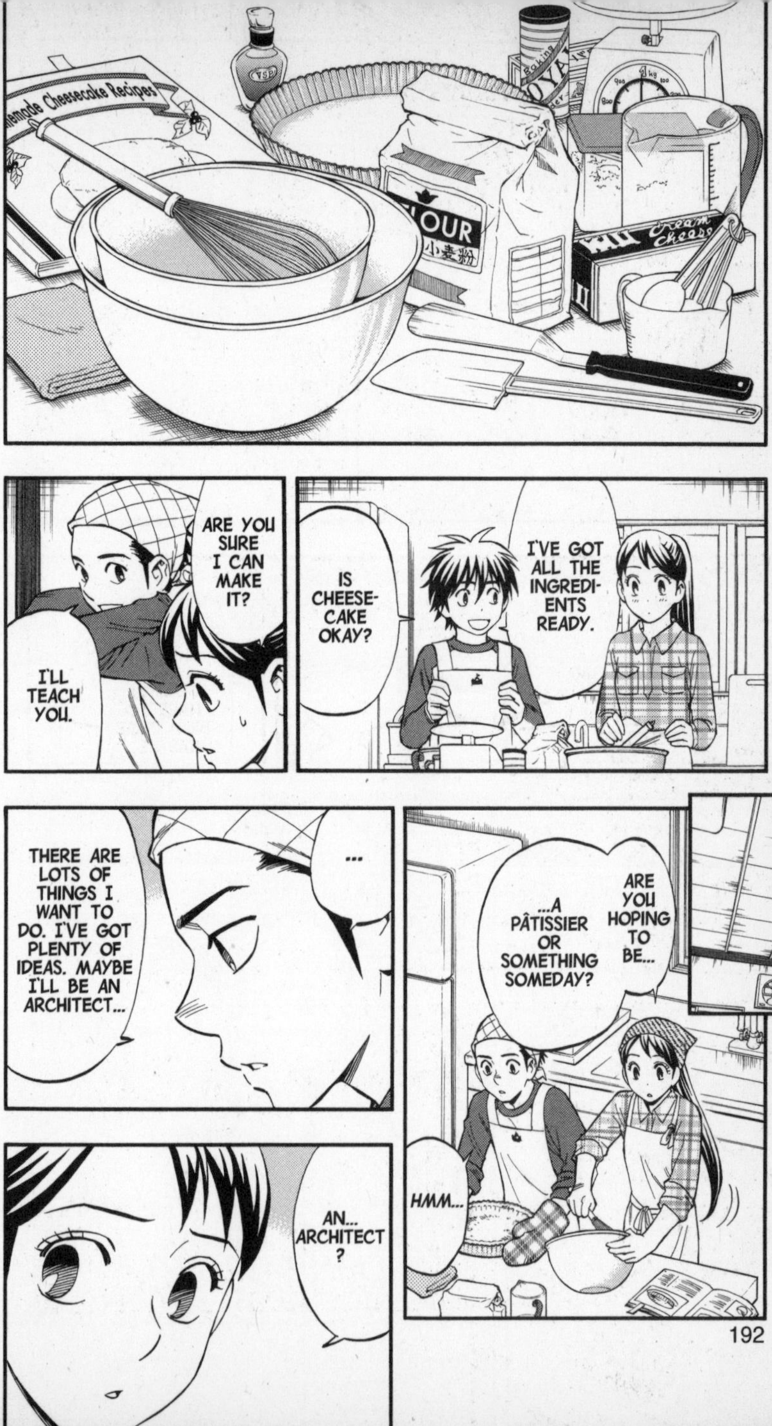

Cream Cheese
小麦粉
I'VE GOT ALL THE INGREDI-ENTS READY.
IS CHEESE-CAKE OKAY?
ARE YOU SURE I CAN MAKE IT?
I'LL TEACH YOU.
ARE YOU HOPING TO BE...
...A PÂTISSIER OR SOMETHING SOMEDAY?
HMM...
...
THERE ARE LOTS OF THINGS I WANT TO DO. I'VE GOT PLENTY OF IDEAS. MAYBE I'LL BE AN ARCHITECT...
AN... ARCHITECT?

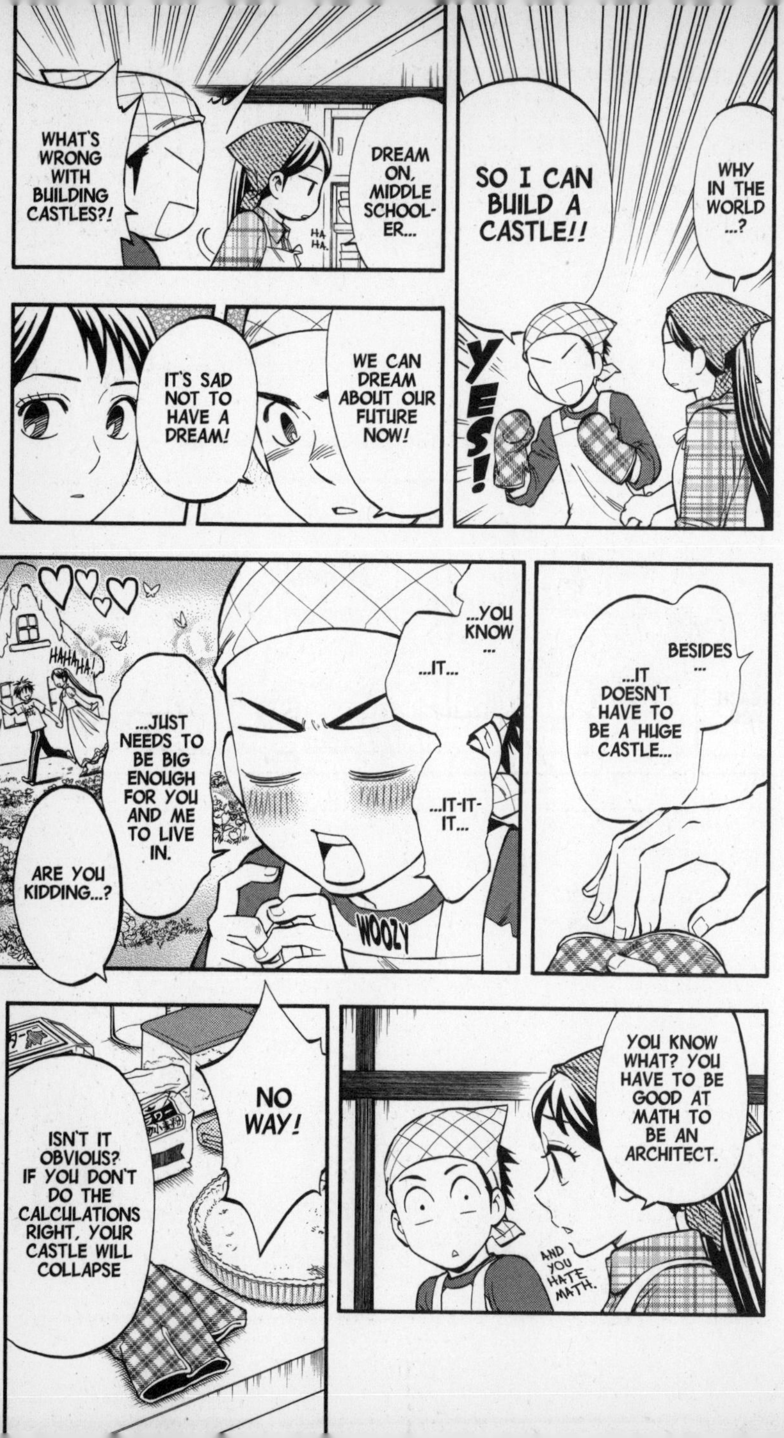
WHY IN THE WORLD ...?
SO I CAN BUILD A CASTLE!!
YES!
DREAM ON, MIDDLE SCHOOL- ER...
HA HA.
WHAT'S WRONG WITH BUILDING CASTLES?!
WE CAN DREAM ABOUT OUR FUTURE NOW!
IT'S SAD NOT TO HAVE A DREAM!
BESIDES ...
...IT DOESN'T HAVE TO BE A HUGE CASTLE...
...YOU KNOW ...
...IT...
...IT-IT-IT...
...JUST NEEDS TO BE BIG ENOUGH FOR YOU AND ME TO LIVE IN.
WOOZY
HAHAHA!
HA HA HA HA!
ARE YOU KIDDING...?
YOU KNOW WHAT? YOU HAVE TO BE GOOD AT MATH TO BE AN ARCHITECT.
AND YOU HATE MATH.
NO WAY!
ISN'T IT OBVIOUS? IF YOU DON'T DO THE CALCULATIONS RIGHT, YOUR CASTLE WILL COLLAPSE

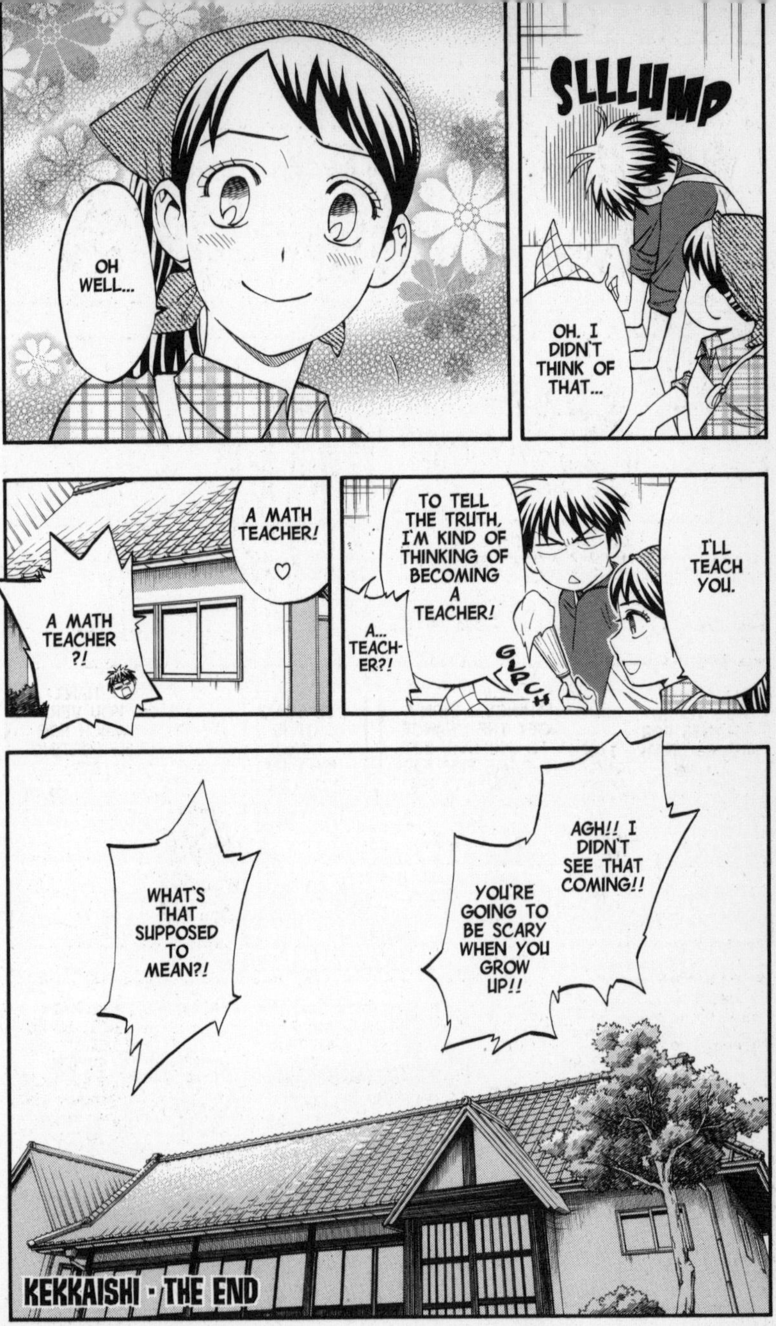
SLLLUMP
OH. I DIDN'T THINK OF THAT...
OH WELL...
I'LL TEACH YOU.
TO TELL THE TRUTH, I'M KIND OF THINKING OF BECOMING A TEACHER!
A... TEACHER?!
GLPCH
A MATH TEACHER! ♡
A MATH TEACHER ?!
AGH!! I DIDN'T SEE THAT COMING!!
YOU'RE GOING TO BE SCARY WHEN YOU GROW UP!!
WHAT'S THAT SUPPOSED TO MEAN?!
KEKKAISHI · THE END

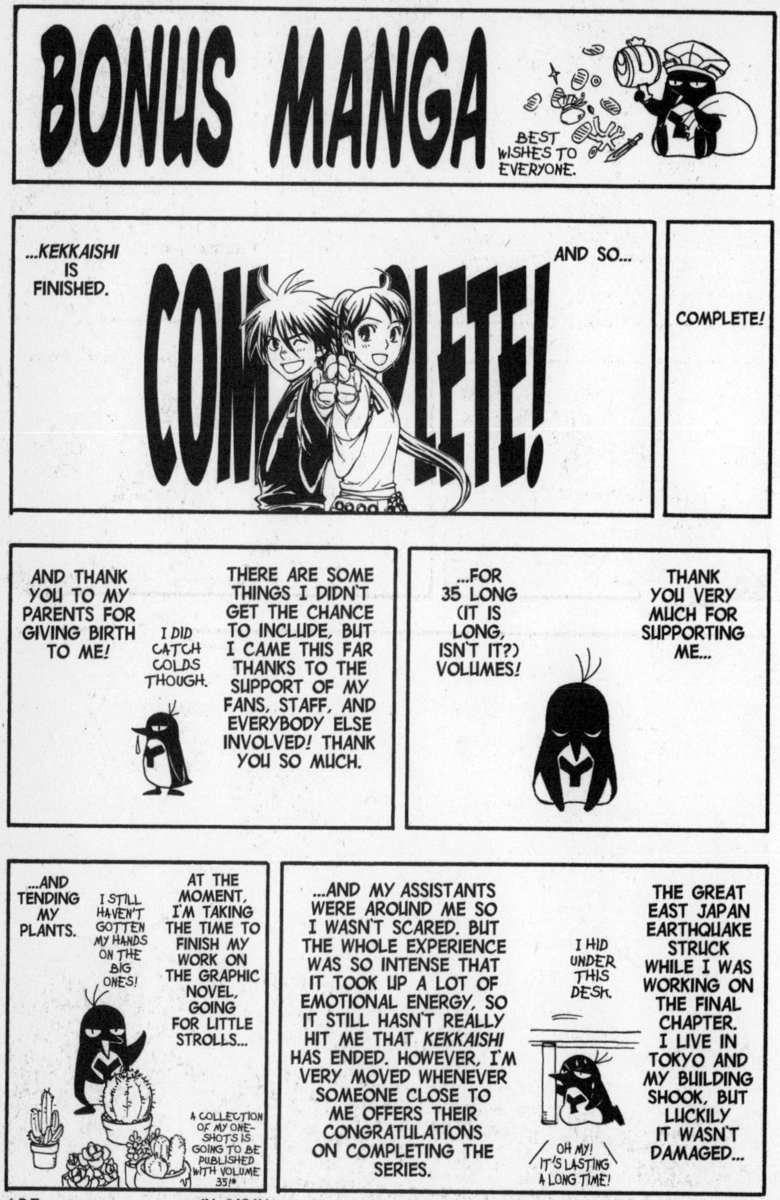
BONUS MANGA
BEST WISHES TO EVERYONE.
COMPLETE!
AND SO...
COM PLETE!
...KEKKAISHI IS FINISHED.
THANK YOU VERY MUCH FOR SUPPORTING ME...
...FOR 35 LONG (IT IS LONG, ISN'T IT?) VOLUMES!
THERE ARE SOME THINGS I DIDN'T GET THE CHANCE TO INCLUDE, BUT I CAME THIS FAR THANKS TO THE SUPPORT OF MY FANS, STAFF, AND EVERYBODY ELSE INVOLVED! THANK YOU SO MUCH.
I DID CATCH COLDS THOUGH.
AND THANK YOU TO MY PARENTS FOR GIVING BIRTH TO ME!
THE GREAT EAST JAPAN EARTHQUAKE STRUCK WHILE I WAS WORKING ON THE FINAL CHAPTER. I LIVE IN TOKYO AND MY BUILDING SHOOK, BUT LUCKILY IT WASN'T DAMAGED...
I HID UNDER THIS DESK.
...AND MY ASSISTANTS WERE AROUND ME SO I WASN'T SCARED. BUT THE WHOLE EXPERIENCE WAS SO INTENSE THAT IT TOOK UP A LOT OF EMOTIONAL ENERGY, SO IT STILL HASN'T REALLY HIT ME THAT KEKKAISHI HAS ENDED. HOWEVER, I'M VERY MOVED WHENEVER SOMEONE CLOSE TO ME OFFERS THEIR CONGRATULATIONS ON COMPLETING THE SERIES.
OH MY! IT'S LASTING A LONG TIME!
AT THE MOMENT, I'M TAKING THE TIME TO FINISH MY WORK ON THE GRAPHIC NOVEL, GOING FOR LITTLE STROLLS...
I STILL HAVEN'T GOTTEN MY HANDS ON THE BIG ONES!
...AND TENDING MY PLANTS.
A COLLECTION OF MY ONE-SHOTS IS GOING TO BE PUBLISHED WITH VOLUME 35!*

*IN JAPAN

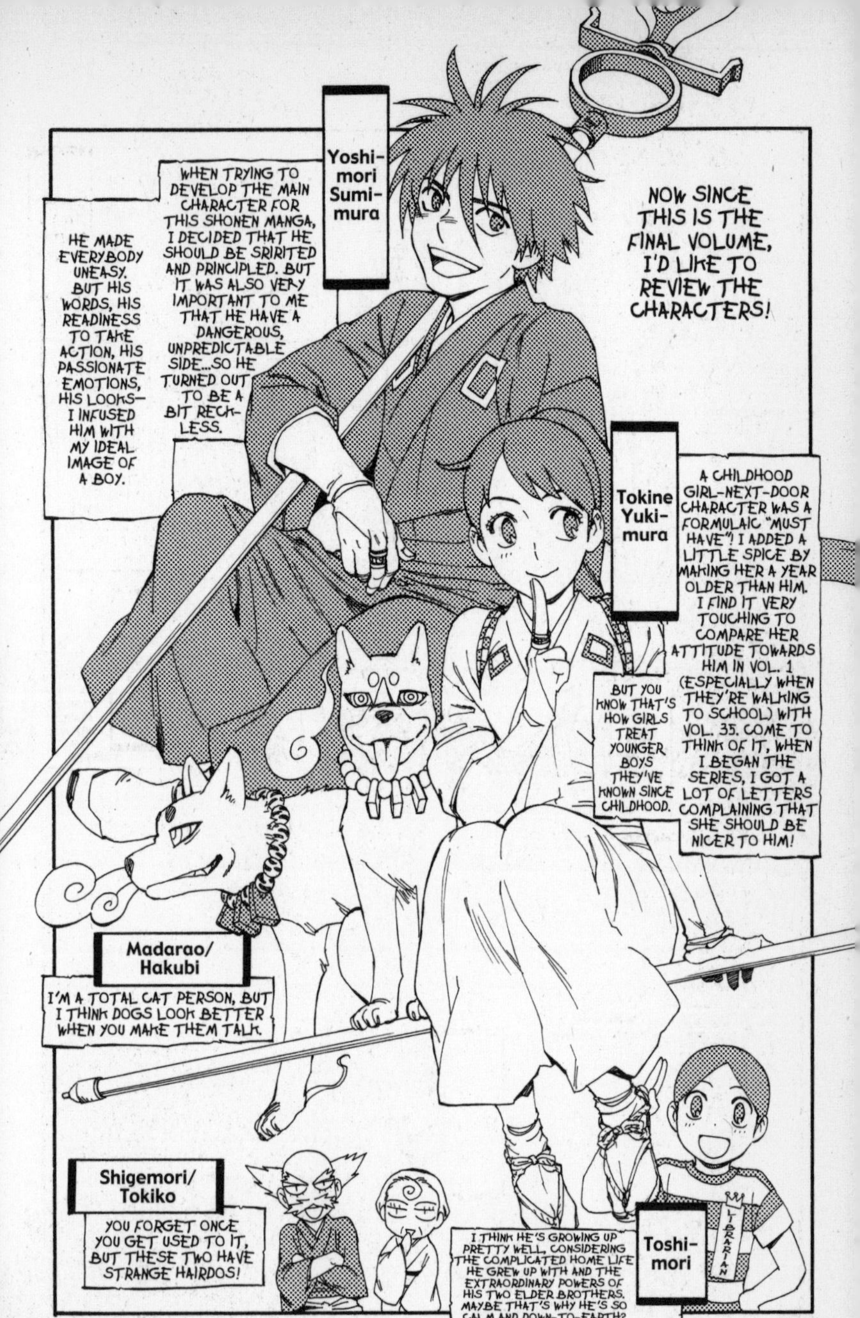
NOW SINCE THIS IS THE FINAL VOLUME, I'D LIKE TO REVIEW THE CHARACTERS!
Yoshimori Sumimura
WHEN TRYING TO DEVELOP THE MAIN CHARACTER FOR THIS SHONEN MANGA, I DECIDED THAT HE SHOULD BE SRIRITED AND PRINCIPLED. BUT IT WAS ALSO VERY IMPORTANT TO ME THAT HE HAVE A DANGEROUS, UNPREDICTABLE SIDE...SO HE TURNED OUT TO BE A BIT RECK-LESS.
HE MADE EVERYBODY UNEASY. BUT HIS WORDS, HIS READINESS TO TAKE ACTION, HIS PASSIONATE EMOTIONS, HIS LOOKS— I INFUSED HIM WITH MY IDEAL IMAGE OF A BOY.
Tokine Yukimura
A CHILDHOOD GIRL-NEXT-DOOR CHARACTER WAS A FORMULAIC "MUST HAVE"! I ADDED A LITTLE SPICE BY MAKING HER A YEAR OLDER THAN HIM. I FIND IT VERY TOUCHING TO COMPARE HER ATTITUDE TOWARDS HIM IN VOL. 1 (ESPECIALLY WHEN THEY'RE WALKING TO SCHOOL) WITH VOL. 35. COME TO THINK OF IT, WHEN I BEGAN THE SERIES, I GOT A LOT OF LETTERS COMPLAINING THAT SHE SHOULD BE NICER TO HIM!
BUT YOU KNOW THAT'S HOW GIRLS TREAT YOUNGER BOYS THEY'VE KNOWN SINCE CHILDHOOD.
Madarao/ Hakubi
I'M A TOTAL CAT PERSON, BUT I THINK DOGS LOOK BETTER WHEN YOU MAKE THEM TALK.
Toshi-mori
LIBRARIAN
I THINK HE'S GROWING UP PRETTY WELL, CONSIDERING THE COMPLICATED HOME LIFE HE GREW UP WITH AND THE EXTRAORDINARY POWERS OF HIS TWO ELDER BROTHERS. MAYBE THAT'S WHY HE'S SO CALM AND DOWN-TO-EARTH?
Shigemori/ Tokiko
YOU FORGET ONCE YOU GET USED TO IT, BUT THESE TWO HAVE STRANGE HAIRDOS!

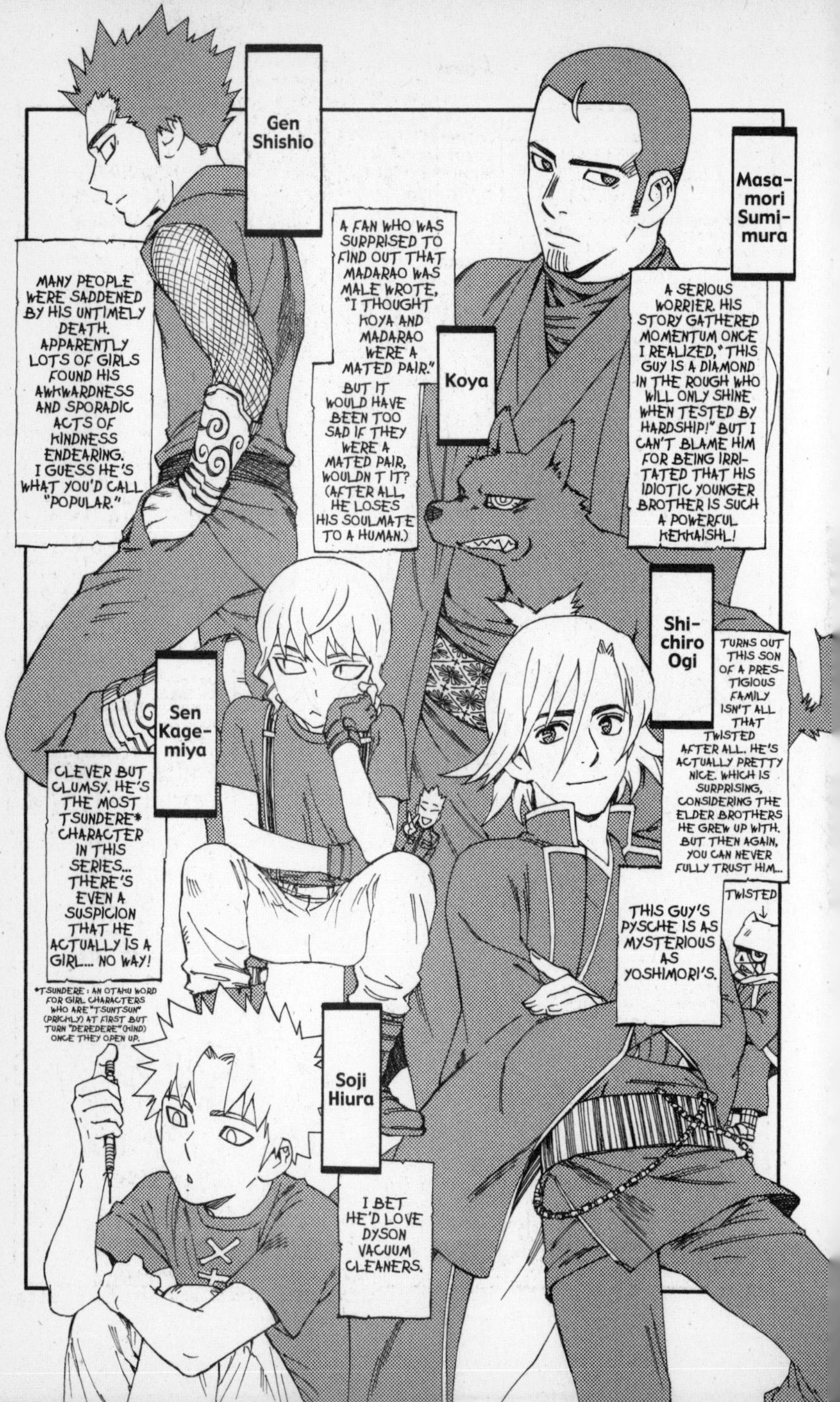
Masa-mori Sumi-mura
A SERIOUS WORRIER. HIS STORY GATHERED MOMENTUM ONCE I REALIZED, "THIS GUY IS A DIAMOND IN THE ROUGH WHO WILL ONLY SHINE WHEN TESTED BY HARDSHIP!" BUT I CAN'T BLAME HIM FOR BEING IRRI-TATED THAT HIS IDIOTIC YOUNGER BROTHER IS SUCH A POWERFUL KEKKAISHI!
Koya
A FAN WHO WAS SURPRISED TO FIND OUT THAT MADARAO WAS MALE WROTE, "I THOUGHT KOYA AND MADARAO WERE A MATED PAIR."
BUT IT WOULD HAVE BEEN TOO SAD IF THEY WERE A MATED PAIR, WOULDN'T IT? (AFTER ALL, HE LOSES HIS SOULMATE TO A HUMAN.)
Gen Shishio
MANY PEOPLE WERE SADDENED BY HIS UNTIMELY DEATH. APPARENTLY LOTS OF GIRLS FOUND HIS AWKWARDNESS AND SPORADIC ACTS OF KINDNESS ENDEARING. I GUESS HE'S WHAT YOU'D CALL "POPULAR."
Shi-chiro Ogi
TURNS OUT THIS SON OF A PRES-TIGIOUS FAMILY ISN'T ALL THAT TWISTED AFTER ALL. HE'S ACTUALLY PRETTY NICE, WHICH IS SURPRISING, CONSIDERING THE ELDER BROTHERS HE GREW UP WITH. BUT THEN AGAIN, YOU CAN NEVER FULLY TRUST HIM...
TWISTED
Sen Kage-miya
CLEVER BUT CLUMSY. HE'S THE MOST TSUNDERE* CHARACTER IN THIS SERIES... THERE'S EVEN A SUSPICION THAT HE ACTUALLY IS A GIRL... NO WAY!
*TSUNDERE: AN OTAKU WORD FOR GIRL CHARACTERS WHO ARE "TSUNTSUN" (PRICKLY) AT FIRST BUT TURN "DEREDERE" (KIND) ONCE THEY OPEN UP.
THIS GUY'S PYSCHE IS AS MYSTERIOUS AS YOSHIMORI'S.
Soji Hiura
I BET HE'D LOVE DYSON VACUUM CLEANERS.

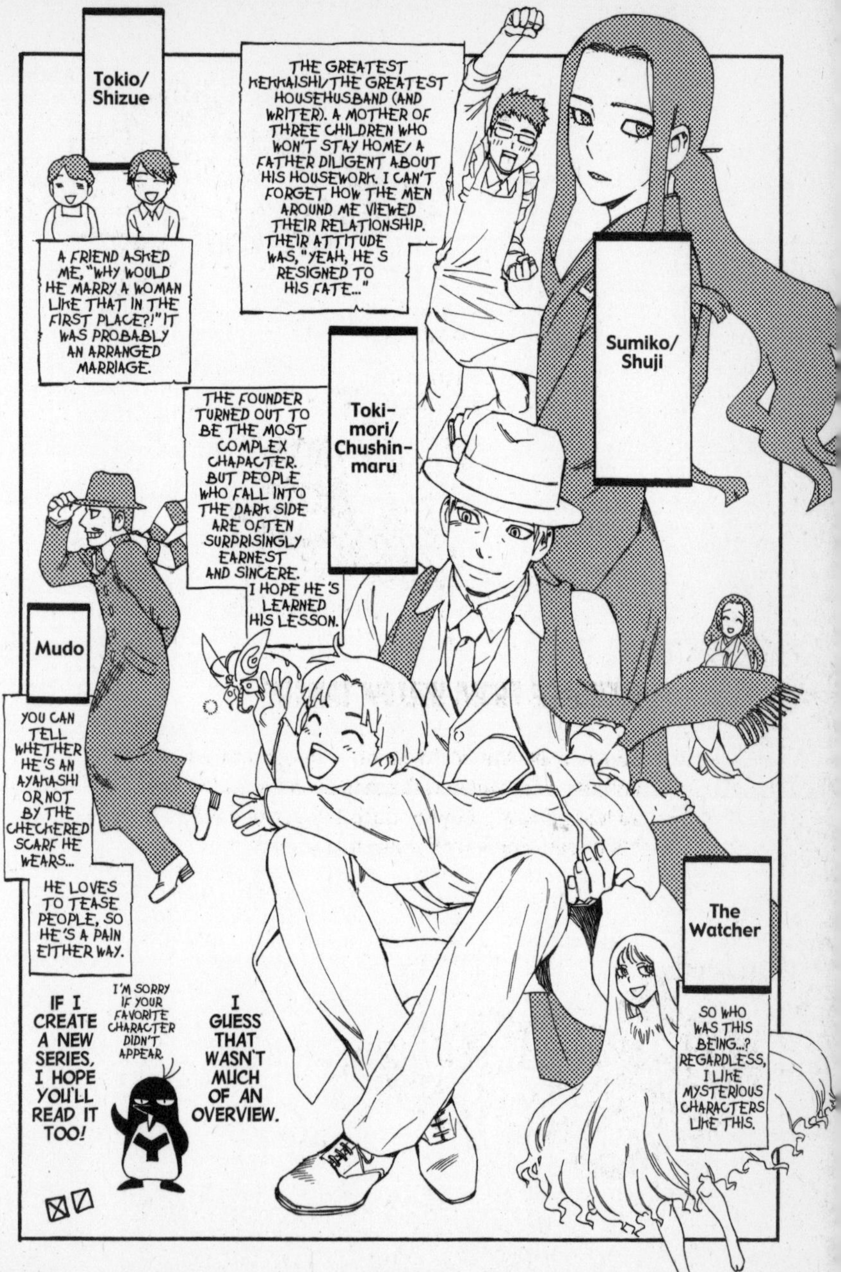
Sumiko/ Shuji
THE GREATEST KEKKAISHI/THE GREATEST HOUSEHUSBAND (AND WRITER). A MOTHER OF THREE CHILDREN WHO WON'T STAY HOME/ A FATHER DILIGENT ABOUT HIS HOUSEWORK. I CAN'T FORGET HOW THE MEN AROUND ME VIEWED THEIR RELATIONSHIP. THEIR ATTITUDE WAS, "YEAH, HE S RESIGNED TO HIS FATE..."
Tokio/ Shizue
A FRIEND ASKED ME, "WHY WOULD HE MARRY A WOMAN LIKE THAT IN THE FIRST PLACE?!" IT WAS PROBABLY AN ARRANGED MARRIAGE.
Toki-mori/ Chushin-maru
THE FOUNDER TURNED OUT TO BE THE MOST COMPLEX CHAPACTER. BUT PEOPLE WHO FALL INTO THE DARK SIDE ARE OFTEN SURPRISINGLY EARNEST AND SINCERE. I HOPE HE'S LEARNED HIS LESSON.
Mudo
YOU CAN TELL WHETHER HE'S AN AYAKASHI OR NOT BY THE CHECKERED SCARF HE WEARS...
HE LOVES TO TEASE PEOPLE, SO HE'S A PAIN EITHER WAY.
The Watcher
SO WHO WAS THIS BEING...? REGARDLESS, I LIKE MYSTERIOUS CHARACTERS LIKE THIS.
I GUESS THAT WASN'T MUCH OF AN OVERVIEW.
I'M SORRY IF YOUR FAVORITE CHARACTER DIDN'T APPEAR.
IF I CREATE A NEW SERIES, I HOPE YOU'LL READ IT TOO!

THE
HAWORTHIA
IS MY
FAVORITE
SUCCULENT
PLANT AT THE
MOMENT. IT'S
AWESOME!
↓

MESSAGE FROM YELLOW TANABE

So it's finally the final volume. I thought it was
important to continue the series. And it ended up
so long. Thank you very much to everyone who's
been following it over these many years.

KEKKAISHI

VOLUME 35
SHONEN SUNDAY EDITION

STORY AND ART BY YELLOW TANABE

© 2004 Yellow TANABE/Shogakukan
All rights reserved.
Original Japanese edition "KEKKAISHI" published by SHOGAKUKAN Inc.

Translation/Tetsuichiro Miyaki
English Adaptation/Annette Roman
Touch-up Art & Lettering/Stephen Dutro
Cover Design & Graphic Layout/Ronnie Casson
Editor/Annette Roman

Printed in Canada

Published by VIZ Media, LLC
P.O. Box 77010
San Francisco, CA 94107

10 9 8 7 6 5 4 3 2 1
First printing, December 2012

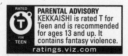

PARENTAL ADVISORY
KEKKAISHI is rated T for
Teen and is recommended
for ages 13 and up. It
contains fantasy violence.
ratings.viz.com

www.viz.com

WWW.SHONENSUNDAY.COM

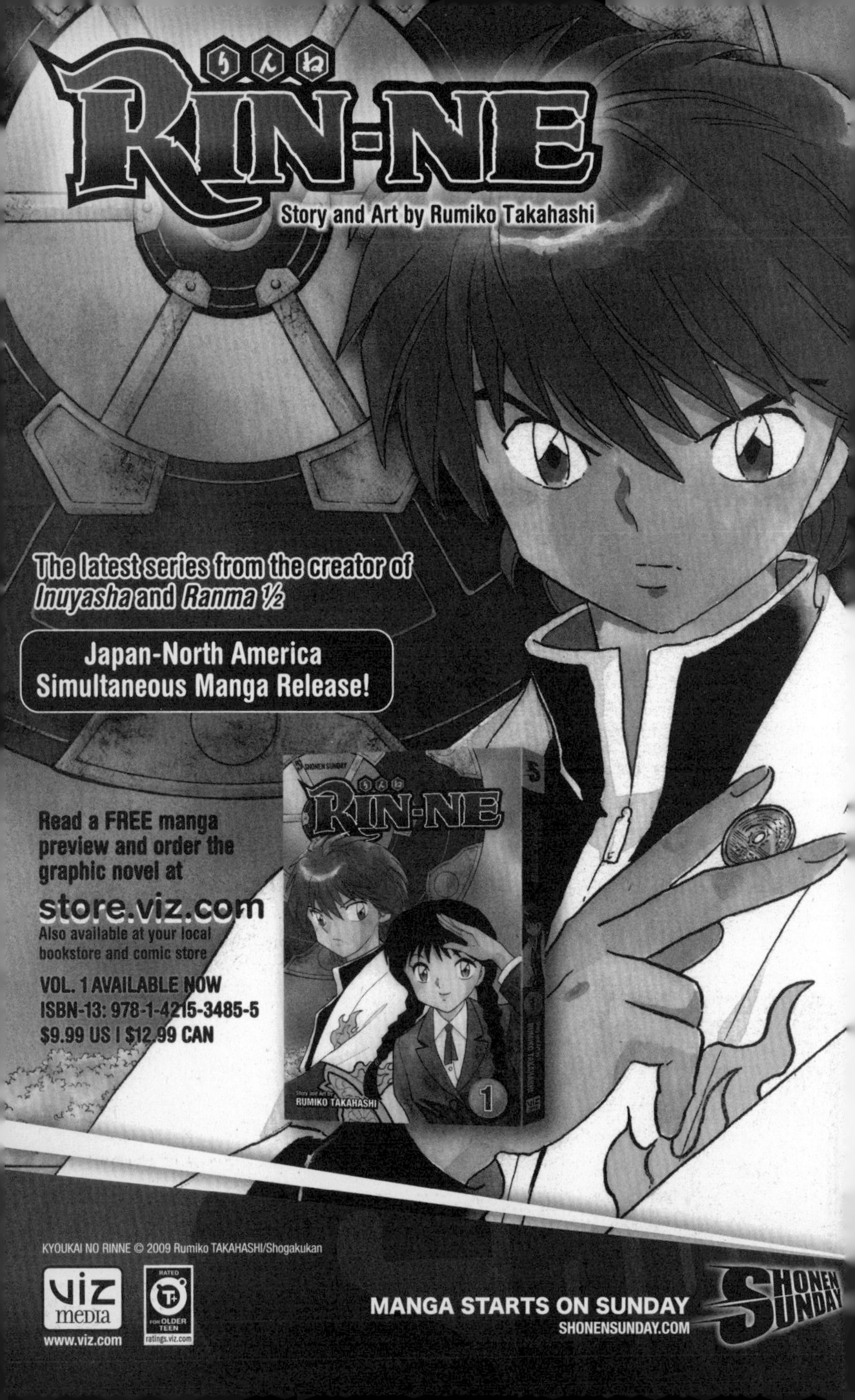

RIN-NE
Story and Art by Rumiko Takahashi
The latest series from the creator of *Inuyasha* and *Ranma ½*
Japan-North America Simultaneous Manga Release!
Read a FREE manga preview and order the graphic novel at
store.viz.com
Also available at your local bookstore and comic store
VOL. 1 AVAILABLE NOW
ISBN-13: 978-1-4215-3485-5
$9.99 US | $12.99 CAN
KYOUKAI NO RINNE © 2009 Rumiko TAKAHASHI/Shogakukan
viz media
www.viz.com
RATED T+ FOR OLDER TEEN
ratings.viz.com
MANGA STARTS ON SUNDAY
SHONENSUNDAY.COM
SHONEN SUNDAY

Five Leaves

Complete Series Premium Edition

This beautiful box set features the complete two-volume, twelve-episode DVD set of the acclaimed anime series and features the original Japanese audio with English subtitles, as well as a sturdy slipcase and full-color hardcover art book.

House of Five Leaves Complete Series Premium Edition comes with a hardcover art book (full-color, 30+ pages), featuring character information, episode guides, artwork, behind-the-scenes storyboards, draft designs, concept art, and even a glossary of terms for insight on the culture of feudal Japan.

House of Five Leaves
Complete Series Premium Edition
12 episodes • approx. 274 minutes • color
Bonus Content:
Clean Opening and Ending, Japanese Trailer

T 13+ Teen | **DVD** VIDEO | **1** NTSC

For more information, visit
NISAmerica.com

House of

from groundbreaking
manga creator
Natsume Ono!

The ronin Akitsu Masanosuke was working as a bodyguard in Edo, but due to his shy personality, he kept being let go from his bodyguard jobs despite his magnificent sword skills. Unable to find new work, he wanders around town and meets a man, the playboy who calls himself Yaichi. Even though Yaichi and Masanosuke had just met for the first time, Yaichi treats Masanosuke to a meal and offers to hire him as a bodyguard. Despite the mysteries that surround Yaichi, Masanosuke takes the job. He soon finds out that Yaichi is the leader of a group of kidnappers who call themselves the "Five Leaves." Now Masanosuke is faced with the dilemma of whether to join the Five Leaves and share in the profits of kidnapping, or to resist becoming a criminal.